THE BROADVIEW BOOK OF

Medieval Anecdotes

THE BROADVIEW BOOK OF

Medieval Anecdotes

Compiled by Richard Kay

broadview press

Canadian Cataloguing in Publication Data

Main entry under title:
The Broadview Book of Medieval Anecdotes
ISBN 0–921149–25–5
1. Biography — Middle Ages, 500–1500 — Anecdotes.
I. Kay, Richard, 1931– . II. Title: Medieval anecdotes
D115.B76 1988   940.1'092'2   C88–94567–2

broadview press   in the U.S.: broadview press
P.O. Box 1243   421 Center Street
Peterborough, Canada, K9J 7H5   Lewiston, N.Y. 14092

Printed and bound in Canada by
Gangné Ltd.

John F. McGovern
in memoriam

Contents

Introduction

Above all, this is a book for browsing and enjoyment. As such, it may need no introduction, but for those who wish to know why and how this collection grew, I prefix these explanatory pages.

The term "anecdote" puzzles many people, and rightly so, for it is a slippery word with many shifting senses. For the Greeks an *anekdotos* was something "secret," and hence "unpublished"; in this sense Martène, for example, entitled his collection of unpublished historical documents *Thesaurus novus anecdotorum* (1717). In the meantime, the term also came to be applied to stories that circulated privately, for example the collection of "Merry Passages and Jests" apparently made in the 1640's by Sir Nicholas L'Estrange (British Library, MS. Harley 6395), three-quarters of which were deemed too obscene for publication (ed. William John Thoms for the Camden Society, 1839). In eighteenth-century English, items of gossip, whether printable or not, were dignified by calling them "anecdotes" in the French fashion; soon the scope of the term was enlarged to cover "the narrative of a detached incident or of a single event told as being in itself interesting or striking" (*Oxford English Dictionary*), in which sense the word is still usually used in English, as in this collection.

Although the collection of anecdotes is a well-established *genre*, its history remains to be written. Classical biographers illustrated famous lives with a wealth of anecdote, and medieval chroniclers with rhetorical pretensions often imitated them. Medieval preachers, moreover, amassed suitable stories to point up a moral, such as Guibert of Nogent appended to each book of his *Memoirs* (1115). The impulse to anthologize such stories separately, however, probably stems from Petrus Alfonsi's early twelfth-century collection of moralistic tales entitled *The Scholar's Guide*, which was based on oriental, especially Arabic, models. Transplanted as they were from one culture to another, Alfonsi's tales were generalized rather than historical anecdotes. Perhaps the first collection of anecdotes for their own sake—though not wholly detached from their historical context—was Walter Map's book of *Courtiers' Trifles*, written towards the end of the twelfth century; a case could be made, however, for Gerald of Wales' *Mirror of the Church*, the material for which was being collected at the same time, although it was published somewhat later. These forerunners were followed in the thirteenth century by many anecdotal collections. Caesarius of Heister-bach, Jacques de Vitry, Etienne de Borbone, and the *Gesta Romanorum* collected edifying tales, or *exempla*, in the generalized, moralistic tradition of Petrus Alfonsi, which only occasionally incorporated recognizably historical materials. Towards the end of the thirteenth century, however, a vernacular counterpart appeared in Italy that established a distinct *genre* of anecdotal collections. *The Hundred Old Tales* (*Il Novellino*), written in the Florentine dialect of Italian, had its share of *exempla* but also included many anecdotes, called *novelle*, about particular persons, communities, or events. Such stories were primarily intended to please and secured immediate and enduring popularity, as is evident from subsequent collections made, for example, by Sacchetti, Domenichi, Poggio Bracciolini, and Boccaccio. The Italian *novella* spread to France, where it has flourished since the fifteenth century in collections of *nouvelles* or *contes* and, at least since the eighteenth century, of *anecdotes* as well. The last and greatest of these French collections was Guérard's two-volume encyclopedic dictionary of anecdotes, which appeared in 1872 as an epitome of its predecessors [p. 9]. More recently, the English-speaking world has enjoyed the Oxford books of literary, legal, and theatrical anecdotes.

Although the present anthology stands in this tradition, it differs somewhat from the more conventional collections in several respects. From the foregoing sketch of the development of anecdotal anthologies, one might expect that this is simply a collection of such stories culled from its medieval counterparts. Some are, to be sure, but more come from chronicles, and a quite a few are not stories or tales in the strict sense, but rather are narratives of medieval events, such as a battle or a miracle, that should be interesting or striking to a modern reader. Whereas the medieval *novella* was, from the start, an occasion for the collector to exhibit his rhetorical skill in the re-telling of a story, my procedure has been to seek out an early version of the anecdote and let the source speak for itself—in English translation. This attention to authenticity adds, I believe, another historical dimension to the reader's entertainment, since voices from the past can recall and illustrate it no less vividly than material artifacts.

This collection acquired a distinctive character as it grew, and this can perhaps be conveyed most readily by telling how it developed. When I began teaching medieval history over twenty-five years ago, I modelled my lectures on those I had heard as a student. Although I knew that some colleagues kept files of jokes and stories to enliven their lectures, my approach was less systematic and more typical: I repeated what I had enjoyed as a student and added new material gleaned from my reading. Unconsciously, like most lecturers, I was accumulating a repertory of anecdotes haphazardly, with little attention to accuracy or authenticity. My anecdotal consciousness was raised, however, as I heard "anecdotal evidence" being derided by devotees of statistical, supposedly scientific history. Their goal, of course, was to eliminate not simply amusing stories from history, but narrative of any kind. To my mind, such enthusiasts fail to appreciate the difference between science and history, which Dionysius of Halicarnassus aptly expressed: "History is philosophy teaching by examples" (*Art of Rhetoric* 11.2); but theoretical disputes over the nature of history aside, the exclusion of "anecdotal evidence" would doom any history lecture to inevitable boredom. Arguing thus, I was drawn to consider more closely the role of narrative, example, and anecdote in history, especially as communicated in the classroom.

The seed from which this collection grew was the realization that many of the anecdotes I tell in class have been received in an oral tradition through lectures I heard as a student. It occurred to me that I and my fellow medieval historians would benefit from a collection of these anecdotes in their original form. A little exploration confirmed my suspicions: often the story had been distorted by oral transmission, and occasionally no source for it could be found at all. Thus assured that the project would indeed be useful, about ten years ago I began to collect medieval anecdotes in earnest. I began, of course, by listing the ones I already used in class, to which I added those I remembered from childhood; then I began asking friends and acquaintances which ones they used in class. About half of the collection came through these channels; the other half was assembled by conventional research in the library. The collections mentioned above and other anthologies, such as those made by G. G. Coulton, brought many prospects to my attention; moreover, the more anecdotal chroniclers, such as William of Malmesbury and Ordericus Vitalis, offered more than enough for their periods.

As the collection grew, its scope was gradually defined. From the first, the chronological limits were the same as those of the usual college-level survey of medieval history, which conventionally runs from Diocletian to Luther (285-1517). Such a course also suggested not only geographical limits but also the relative stress to be laid on the several parts: the focus was to be on western Europe, with Byzantium and Islam on the periphery. Given these limits, I attempted to achieve some balance in the collection by securing at least a dozen items from each century, while allowing considerably more from the better documented centuries after 1000. (It was difficult to find as many as 15 items for the obscure seventh century; it was not easy to restrict the thirteenth century, which I know best, to 54.) Similarly, by seeking out anecdotes from each of the principal countries on the Continent, I tried to resist a natural Anglocentric tendency.

At first I looked only for brief, witty stories with a punchline—anecdotes of the type familiar to Americans as fillers in *The Reader's Digest*—but, because I wanted to include material that would illustrate the events and topics commonly touched on in any survey of medieval history, my criteria eventually expanded to include narratives of events or incidents that were striking or interesting in themselves without being overtly, or even necessarily humorous. This broader definition of my *genre* accorded well with the definition quoted above from the *Oxford English Dictionary*; but it implied a further definition of my intended audience, for the student of medieval history will find an account of Charlemagne's coronation more interesting and striking than would the less informed reader. Accordingly, the latter will find here much to entertain him, but the former will inevitably find more.

A few items are not narratives at all but are no less entertaining and should enliven any lecture, for example with a practical demonstration of the sign language used at Syon Abbey [p. 299]. By the same token, a modern anecdote *about* the Middle Ages finds a place here as it has done in countless lectures [p. 274].

For the most part, my selections appeal to modern tastes, though an occasional odd sample of medieval humor has slipped in [e.g. p. 190]. The medieval predilection for tales of sex and violence, which Victorians deplored and smoothed over, is now too close to our own to be ignored, though it still may astonish those who idealize the Middle Ages. I have endeavored to counterbalance the great world of kings and popes, which occupies the foreground in most medieval sources, with anecdotes illustrating everyday life, which some readers may relate to more readily. While I have tried to steer a middle course between the interests of the general reader and the medievalist, the ultimate criterion has been whether I myself enjoyed an anecdote; I hope not a few readers will share this pleasure.

The anecdotes might have been arranged topically—perhaps in the categories listed below—or even geographically, but from the first a chronological presentation seemed best, if only for its apparent simplicity. (I say "apparent" because the determination of dates was one of the harder tasks of the compiler.) Moreover, this system constrained me to discard materials that could not be dated to within a century. The result, I think, has been worth the trouble, because the chronological dimension provides the cover-to-cover reader with a peculiar, historical pleasure as he perceives the concerns of one period slowly replacing those of the next. Like a photograph album, this collection can be enjoyed as a succession of images that illustrate their changing times.

Once the anecdotes had been identified, it remained to authenticate them, because from the outset I was concerned to locate the original source, or at least the earliest presentable one. The task provided a challenging series of practical exercises for graduate students who were learning to use the bibliographic tools of the medieval historian in my seminars during the spring semesters of 1982 and 1985. Altogether they skillfully identified the sources of perhaps half the anecdotes in this collection, as well as of some others that were not included; their efforts, like those of other contributors, are duly acknowledged in the notes. For a few good stories no source could be found, so this too constituted a criterion that eliminated some prospects.

* * * *

How did these criteria work out in practice? The character of the collection can perhaps best be shown by dividing the anecdotes into ten broad categories, which sometimes overlap.

1. Kings, princes and other secular rulers. Several reasons converge to make this the largest category (117 items—about a third). Medieval narrative sources chiefly concern the doings of the great, and moreover when a ruler was as popular as Charlemagne or as unpopular as John of England, the chronicler had a rich oral tradition to draw upon. These

tendencies are reinforced by the ordinary present day survey course in medieval history, which is primarily political and—if it is not painfully dull—highlights the personality of political leaders, so that anecdotes about them are more generally known today. Thus, for better or for worse, both the supply and demand for such anecdotes is greater than for any other kind.

2. Famous events (68) also have often been made memorable, or at least vivid, by an anecdote: e.g. the conversion of Northumbria [p. 66]. The good stories need no apology, but in some cases I have included a chronicler's rather colorless account that has subsequently been improved in the re-telling: e.g. the call to the first crusade [p. 168], as a reminder to teachers and students that lecturers often improve on a pallid original. For similar reasons I have included a very few "landmark" events that are turning points better perceived in retrospect: e.g. the years 476 and 1000. Among famous events I count about a dozen war stories and accounts of battles, some included for their obvious interest and others because they are epochal events: e.g. the ruination of Byzantium at Manzikert in 1071 [p. 155] or the end of the Hundred Years War at Châtillon in 1453 [p. 309]. Just as a photograph of the battle of San Juan Hill would be of more interest today than any other episode in the Spanish-American War, so many of these medieval events have been included to gratify the curiosity of those already familiar with them.

3. Saints' lives are a rich vein for medieval anecdote; I have included some 42 specimens that are more to modern than medieval taste, as I have generally avoided the miraculous in favor of human interest.

4. Popes and church history in its unsanctified aspects counterbalance the saints with over three dozen tales.

5. Women are less prominent in monastic chronicles than here, where they play the leading part in at least 33 stories. The surprising variety of female roles presented should help the reader to see beyond familiar sterotypes.

6. Education and Latin clerical culture supply several dozen stories, which show the precarious state of Latin learning during the Dark Ages

[p. 71] and afford some glimpses of scholastic and university culture [p. 261] or the lack of it [p. 274], though hardly any of Renaissance Humanism [pp. 318, 322].

7. Social history, or the way people lived, is illustrated by another two dozen anecdotes that do not quite fit into the categories described above, including some of my favorites, such as Richer's difficult journey [p. 135] and Christmas at Saint Gall [p. 113].

8. Legends are sparingly represented (15); my choices are by and large limited to stories that were taken for fact rather than fiction in the Middle Ages and that are so well known today as to be missed in an anthology of medieval anecdote: e.g. Arthur of Britain [p. 30], Popess Joan [p. 105], Robin Hood [p. 218], and William Tell [p. 269].

9. Literature and art (10), like the Italian Renaissance, is a category that doubtless could have been greatly enlarged by another compiler and perhaps deserves a separate collection.

10. Miscellaneous best categorizes four oddities: stranger than science fiction [p. 54], Charlemagne's clock [p. 97], a parcel of prodigies [p. 100], and two good years [p. 314].

*　　　*　　　*　　　*

The reader is warned that a great many of these anecdotes are medieval fictions, not facts. For example, the story of Edward III's ominous landing in France [p. 278] was also told of William the Conqueror and probably never happened to either of them, though it is also possible that both encouraged their men with a jest that was already well worn in 1066. To inquire whether each story was true or not would have required tedious and often inconclusive discussion from which the reader would gain little if anything. For the critical user, however, the source cited should permit a shrewd guess about the reliability of the witness; in particular, the *date* given for each source will suggest whether the writer was likely to be reliably informed about the event, which is also dated (after the caption).

The English translations gathered together here have been made by many hands, a few as long as five hundred years ago, and hence the style is necessarily uneven. I have not hesitated to modernize the style to make it more accessible to my readers, however, and such alterations are regularly signaled by the annotation, "rev. R. Kay." At least the reader has been spared countless occurrences of "hast thou" and similar archaisms beloved of nineteenth-century translators.

Finally, a few words about the presentation. Prefatory remarks have been limited to a caption, which is sometimes simply descriptive but at other times comments laconically on the text. The date that follows the caption indicates when the event supposedly took place. The text of the anecdote is always quoted (in translation) from the source. Occasionally a word or phrase will also be given in the original language, in which case it has been enclosed in (parentheses). More often, in lieu of explanatory footnotes, I have eased the reader's way by inserting a comment in the text; these editorial interpolations are indicated by [square brackets]. After the text, the source is cited, usually in translation and often in abbreviated form, followed by the date at which it was composed and by a superscript number that refers to the endnotes. The endnotes themselves begin with a full citation of the source by author, title, and subdivision(s); next, the edition of the original text is cited, and finally the source of the translation is identified. The help of collaborators is acknowledged by placing their names in «guillmets»; they of course are not responsible for any errors that have slipped past me. Now and again I have also added a comment on some technicality, for instance, to justify a dating or to identify an allusion.

Such a collection will never be complete, and no doubt many excellent anecdotes could be added to this one. Since it is not impossible that I may some day have an opportunity to enlarge this work, I would be grateful for suggestions from my readers.

Lawrence, Kansas
28 July 1988

The only part of history I like is the anecdotes.

Prosper Mérimée[1]

A Compiler's Prologue

I have observed that the temperament of man is delicate; it must be instructed by being led, as it were, little by little, so that it will not become bored. I am mindful also of its hardness, which must to some extent be softened and sweetened, so that it may retain what it learns with greater facility, remembering that, as it is forgetful, it needs many things to help it remember what it tends to forget. For this reason I have compiled this small volume ... knowing that if I should write more than is necessary, it might be a burden rather than an aid. The knowledgeable will remember what they have forgotten by means of the things which are contained here.

Petrus Alfonsi (fl. 1106), *The Scholar's Guide*[2]

The Sins of an Anthologist

S. Augustine: ... You keep toiling and toiling to satisfy the public, wearying yourself to please the very people who, to you, are the most displeasing; gathering now a flower of poesy, now of history—in a word, employing all your genius of words to tickle the ears of the listening throng.

Petrarch: I beg your pardon, but I cannot let that pass without saying a word. Never since I was a boy have I pleased myself with elegant extracts and flowerets of literature. For often have I noted what neat and excellent things Cicero has uttered against butchers of books, and especially, also, the phrase of Seneca in which he declares, "It is a disgrace for a man to keep hunting for flowers and prop himself up on familiar quotations, and only stand on what he knows by heart."

S. Augustine: In saying what I did, I neither accuse you of idleness nor scant memory. What I blame you for is that in your reading you have picked out the more flowery passages for the amusement of your cronies, and, as it were, packed up boxes of pretty things out of a great heap, for the benefit of your friends—which is nothing but pandering to a desire of vainglory.

Francis Petrarch, *My Secret* (1342)[3]

9

The Fourth Century

Diocletian's Vegetables (305)

But Diocletian, voluntarily resigning the imperial emblems at Nicomedia, retired on his own land [at Salona in Illyria]. When he was asked by Herculius and Galerius to take up the rule again, rejecting it like some plague, he answered: "I wish you would take a look at the vegetables planted with my own hands at Salona. You'd certainly think you never ought to try that suggestion of yours on me."

Epitome de Caesaribus (4th century)[1]

The Conversion of Constantine (312)

[The Emperor Constantine] being convinced, however, that he needed some more powerful aid than his military forces could afford him, on account of the wicked and magical enchantments which were so diligently practiced by the tyrant [his rival, the Emperor Maxentius], he sought Divine assistance, deeming the possession of arms and numerous soldiery of secondary importance, but believing the cooperating power of Deity invincible and not to be shaken. He considered, therefore, on what God he might rely for protection and assistance.... He judged it to be folly indeed to join in the idle worship of those who were no gods, and ... therefore felt it incumbent on him to honour his father's God alone.

Accordingly he called on Him with earnest prayer and supplications that He would reveal to him who He was, and stretch forth His right hand to help him in his present difficulties. And while he was thus praying with fervent entreaty, a most marvelous sign appeared to him from heaven, the account of which it might have been hard to believe had it been related by any other person. But since the victorious emperor himself long afterwards declared it to the writer of this history, when he was honoured with his acquaintance and society, and confirmed his statement by an oath, who could hesitate to accredit the relation, especially since the testimony of after-time has established its truth? He said that about noon, when the day was already beginning to decline, he saw with his own eyes the trophy of a cross of light in the heavens, above the sun, and bearing the inscription, "Conquer by this" (*In hoc signo vinces*). At this sight he himself was struck with amazement, and his whole army also, which followed him on this expedition, and witnessed the miracle.

He said, moreover, that he doubted within himself what the import of this apparition could be. And while he continued to ponder and reason on its meaning, night suddenly came on; then in his sleep the Anointed of God appeared to him with the same sign which he had seen in the heavens, and told him to use it as a safeguard in all engagements with his enemies.

At the dawn of day he arose, and communicated the marvel to his friends: and then, calling together the workers in gold and precious stones, he sat in the midst of them, and described to them the figure of the sign he had seen, bidding them represent it in gold and precious stones. And this representation I myself have had an opportunity of seeing.

Now it was made in the following manner. A long spear, overlaid with gold, formed the figure of the cross by means of a transverse bar laid over it. On the top of the whole was fixed a wreath of gold and precious stones; and within this, the symbol of the Saviour's name, two letters indicating the name of Christ (ΧΡΙΣΤΟΣ) by means of its initial characters [in Greek], the letter P [rho] being intersected by X [chi] in its centre: and these letters the emperor was in the habit of wearing on his helmet at a later period. From the cross-bar of the spear was suspended a cloth, a royal piece, covered with a profuse embroidery of most precious stones; and which, being also richly interlaced with gold, presented an indescribable degree of beauty to the beholder.... The emperor constantly made use of this sign of salvation as a safeguard against every adverse and hostile power, and commanded that others similar to it should be carried at the head of all his armies.

These things were done shortly afterwards. But at the time above specified, being struck with amazement at the extraordinary vision, and resolving to worship no other God save Him who had appeared to him, he sent for those who were acquainted with the mysteries of His doctrines, and inquired who that God was, and what was intended by the sign of the vision he had seen.

They affirmed that He was God, the only begotten Son of the one and only God: that the sign which had appeared was the symbol of immortality, and the trophy of that victory over death which He had gained in time past when sojourning on earth. They taught him also the causes of His advent, and explained to him the true account of His incarnation. Thus he was instructed in these matters, and was impressed with wonder at the divine manifestation which had been presented to his sight. Comparing, therefore, the heavenly vision with the interpretation given, he found his judgment confirmed; and, in the persuasion that the knowledge of these things had been imparted to him by Divine teaching, he determined thenceforth to devote himself to the reading of the inspired writings.

Moreover, he made the priests of God his counselors, and deemed it incumbent on him to honour the God who had appeared to him with all devotion. And after this, being fortified by well-grounded hopes in Him, he hastened to quench the threatening fire of tyranny.

Eusebius (d. 340), *Life of Constantine*[2]

A Famous Forgery:
The Donation of Constantine (324?)

[The Emperor Constantine explains why he owes Pope Sylvester a debt of gratitude:] At a time when a mighty and filthy leprosy had invaded all the flesh of my body, after many physicians had come together to attend me and none of them had cured me, the [pagan] priests of the Capitol came here, saying to me that a font should be made on the Capitol, and that I should fill this with the blood of innocent infants; and that, if I bathed in it while it was warm, I might be cleansed. And very many innocent infants having been brought together according to their words, when the sacrilegious priests of the pagans wished them to be slaughtered and the font to be filled with their blood: our serenity perceived the tears of their mothers, and I straightway abhorred the deed. And pitying them, I ordered their own sons to be restored to them; and, giving them transportation and gifts, sent them off rejoicing to their own homes.

That day having passed therefore—the silence of night having come upon us—when the time of sleep had arrived, Saints Peter and Paul the apostles appeared, saying to me: "Since you have put an end to your crimes, and have abhorred the pouring forth of innocent blood, we are sent by Christ our Lord God, to advise you how to recover your health.

Hear our commands, therefore, and do what we indicate to you. Sylvester—the bishop of the city of Rome—is on Mount Soracte [25 miles north of Rome], where he fled from your persecutions and cherishes the darkness with his clergy in the rocky caverns. When you have this man brought to you, he will show you a sacred pool, in which he will dip you three times until all the strength of the leprosy will leave you. And, when this has been done, do this in return to your Saviour: order that the churches throughout the whole world may be restored. Moreover, purify yourself by renouncing all the superstition of idols, and instead adore and cherish the one, true, and living God, and seek to do his will....

[Sylvester cured and baptised Constantine, who out of gratitude makes the following donation:] We give over to the most blessed pontiff, our father Sylvester the universal pope, not only our [Lateran] palace, but also the city of Rome and all the provinces, districts, and cities of Italy and the Western regions [of the empire]; and we relinquish them, by our inviolable gift, to the power and sway of himself and the pontiffs who are his successors....

Having done this, it seems fitting that our empire and the power of our kingdom should be transferred and translated to the regions of the East; and that, in the province of Byzantium, in a most fitting place, a city should be built in our name [Constantinople]; and that our empire should be established there. For it is not just that an earthly ruler should have jurisdiction where the supremacy of priests and the head of the Christian religion has been established by a heavenly ruler.

The Donation of Constantine (ca. 756)[3]

The End of an Heresiarch (ca. 336)

The emperor Constantine was induced by the party of Eusebius to send for Arius [who had been banished after the council of Nicaea]. Upon his arrival, the emperor asked him whether he hald the faith of the catholic church. Arius replied with oaths that his faith was orthodox, and presented a written summary of his belief; concealing, however, the reasons of his ejection from the church by the bishop Alexander, and deceitfully endeavouring to imitate the language of the Holy Scriptures. When, therefore, he had declared upon oath that he did not hold the errors for which he had been expelled from the church by Alexander [i.e. the Arian heresy], Constantine dismissed him, saying, "If your faith be orthodox, your oaths are honourable; but if you do not really hold that belief which you have professed upon oath, God will judge you from heaven...."

A horrible and unexpected catastrophe ensued. The partisans of Eusebius had launched out into threats, while the bishop [of Constantinople] had recourse to prayer. Arius, emboldened by the protection of his party, delivered many trifling and foolish speeches, when he was suddenly compelled by the call of nature to retire, and immediately, as it is written [Acts 1:18], "he burst asunder [in the middle and all his bowels gushed out]," and he fell down and expired, being deprived at once both of communion and of life. This, then, was the end of Arius. The partisans of Eusebius were covered with shame; yet, as he had held the same sentiments as themselves, they buried him.

Athanasius (ca. 296–373) *Letter to Apian*[4]

Edifying Death of the Last Pagan Emperor (363)

[Julian the Apostate] led his troops far away from all inhabited places, and made them march through a desert [in Mesopotamia]. Oppressed by hunger and by thirst, and without any efficient guide, the soldiers were compelled to wander about in the desert through the imprudence of this wisest of emperors.

In the very midst of their consequent complaints and lamentations, they beheld him who was madly contending with his Creator fall down wounded: he was unaided by the warlike Mars who had promised his support; unassisted by Apollo who had given so false and perplexing an oracle; and even Jove the Thunderer did not hurl one of his thunderbolts against him by whom he was slain. Thus were his threats overthrown and shown to be vain. No one knows even to this day by whom this mortal blow, which he had so justly deserved, was inflicted. Some say that it was by one of the invisible order of beings, others that it was by the hand of an individual belonging to one of the nomadic tribes generally called Ishmaelites; others say that he was killed by a soldier reduced to despair by hunger and by wandering in the desert. But whether the sword were that of an angel or of a man, certain it is that whoever committed the deed was but the instrument of the divine will.

It is said that directly after he had received the wound, Julian took some of the blood in his hand, and threw it up towards heaven, saying,

15

"Galilean! you have conquered!" So great was his stupidity that thus, at one and the same instant, he acknowledged his defeat and gave utterance to blasphemy.

Theodoret, *Ecclesiastical History* (after 427)[5]

Saint Augustine Tastes Forbidden Fruit (ca. 370)

I had a desire to commit theft and did it, compelled not by hunger or poverty but by a lack of appetite for righteousness and by a diet of iniquity. For I stole something that I had enough of my own, and much better. And when I had done the deed, I did not even care to enjoy what I had stolen, but rejoiced instead in the theft and in sin itself.

Near our vineyard there was a pear tree laden with fruit that was not attractive in either flavour or form. One night, when I [age 16] had played until dark on the sandlot with some other juvenile delinquents, we went to shake that tree and carry off its fruit. From it we carried off huge loads, not to feast on, but to throw to the pigs, although we did eat a few ourselves. We did it just because it was forbidden.

Augustine of Hippo, *Confessions* (ca. 397)[6]

Christian or Ciceronian? (ca. 374)

Many years ago [ca. 374], when for the kingdom of heaven's sake I had cut myself off from home, parents, sisters, relations, and—harder still—from the dainty food to which I had been accustomed; and when I was on my way to Jerusalem to wage my warfare, I still could not bring myself to forego the library which I had formed for myself at Rome with great care and toil. And so, miserable man that I was, I would fast only that I might afterwards read Cicero. After many nights spent in vigil, after floods of tears called from my inmost heart, after the recollection of my past sins, I would once more take up Plautus. And when at times I returned to my right mind, and began to read the prophets, their style seemed rude and repellent. I failed to see the light with my blinded eyes; but I attributed the fault not to them, but to the sun. While the old serpent was thus making me his plaything, about the middle of Lent a deep-seated fever fell upon my weakened body, and while it destroyed my rest completely—the story seems hardly credible—it so wasted my unhappy frame that scarcely anything was left of me but skin and bone. Meantime preparations for my funeral went on; my body grew gradually colder, and the warmth of life lingered only in my throbbing breast. Suddenly I was caught up in the spirit and dragged before the judgment seat of the Judge; and here the light was so bright, and those who stood around were so radiant, that I cast myself upon the ground and did not dare to look up. Asked who and what I was I replied: "I am a Christian." But he who presided said: "You are lying; you are a follower of Cicero and not of Christ (*Ciceronianus es, non Christianus*). For 'where thy treasure is, there will thy heart be also' [Matt. 6:21]." Instantly I became dumb, and amid the strokes of the lash—for He had ordered me to be scourged—I was tortured more severely still by the fire of conscience, considering with myself that verse, "In the grave who shall give you thanks?" [Ps. 6:5]. Yet for all that, I began to cry and to bewail myself, saying: "Have mercy upon me, O Lord: have mercy upon me."

Jerome (d. 420), *Letters*[7]

How Ambrose was Elected Bishop of Milan (374)

[Saint Ambrose] studied letters at Rome, and pleaded cases at law in the Praetorium with such effect that the Emperor Valentinian appointed him to govern the provinces of Liguria and Emilia. He went therefore to Milan, where the populace was gathered together to choose a bishop. And as the Arians and the Catholics were locked in dispute over the election, Ambrose intervened to put an end to their quarrel. And suddenly a child's voice was heard to say that Ambrose himself should be elected bishop; and to this all the people gave their assent, so that he was elected by acclamation. But as soon as he saw what had happened, he sought to dissuade them from their choice. From the church he went straight to his tribunal, and, departing from his custom sentenced several prisoners to bodily punishments. Nevertheless the populace persisted in its choice, and cried out: "May the guilt of your sin fall upon us!" Then, much distraught, Ambrose returned to his house and pretended to be a pagan philosopher, but he was persuaded to desist from this deception. Then he caused women of pleasure to be brought in to him, in the sight of all, hoping that the spectacle of this scandal would turn the people against making him their bishop. But even this was of no avail, for the multitude continued to clamour: "May your guilt be upon us!" At this Ambrose, in desperation, resolved to flee in the middle of the night, and set out for the Tessino. But after travelling throughout the night, he found himself, in the morning, before one of the gates of Milan, called the Roman Gate. There the folk knew him at sight, and held him. Meanwhile the whole affair was reported to the Emperor Valentinian, who was much pleased to learn that one of his officials had been chosen to be bishop. And the good prefect [Ambrose's father] also rejoiced that his prophecy had been fulfilled, for he had said to him once at parting: "Depart, but do not conduct yourself like a judge but like a bishop." In the meantime Ambrose, in Milan, had again gone into hiding, and once more had been found out. He was baptised (for as yet he was but a catechumen), and eight days later mounted the episcopal throne.

Jacobus de Voragine (d. ca. 1298), *Golden Legend*[8]

The Diabolical Origin of the Huns (375)

The race of the Huns, fiercer than ferocity itself, flamed forth against the Goths. We learn from old traditions that their origin was as follows: Filimer, king of the Goths ... found among his people certain witches, whom he called in his native tongue *Haliurunnae*. Suspecting these women, he expelled them from the midst of his race [which was then living on the northern shores of the Black Sea] and compelled them to wander in solitary exile far from his army. There unclean spirits, who beheld them as they wandered through the wilderness, bestowed their embraces upon them and begat this savage race, which dwelt at first in the swamps, a stunted, foul, and puny tribe, scarcely human and having no language save one which bore but slight resemblance to human speech. Such was the descent of the Huns who came to the country of the Goths.

Jordanes, *The Gothic History* (551)[9]

Saint Ambrose Excommunicates the Emperor (390)

At the same time on account of the city of Thessalonica no little distress came upon the bishop [Ambrose], when he learned that that city had been almost wiped out. For the emperor [Theodosius I] had promised him that he would grant pardon to the citizens of the above mentioned city [who had defied and dishonoured his officials], but when the counts had consulted secretly with the emperor without the knowledge of the bishop the city was given to the sword for almost three hours and many innocent were slain. When the bishop learned of this deed he refused the emperor any opportunity of entering the church, nor did he judge him worthy of union with the church or of the participation in the sacraments, before he should do public penance. On the other hand, the emperor declared to him that David had committed adultery and also homicide. But straightway the reply was given: "You who have followed him as he sinned, follow him as he corrected himself." When the most merciful emperor heard this he so took it to heart that he did not scorn public penance, and the progress of this correction prepared for him a favourable victory.

Paul of Milan (d. 422), *Life of Saint Ambrose*[10]

The Fifth Century

Britain Stripped of Roman Troops (407)

In the year 407 ... when the nations of the Alans, Sueves, Vandals, and many others with them, having defeated the Franks and passed the Rhine, ravaged all Gaul, a citizen named Gratian was set up as tyrant in Britain and killed. In his place, Constantine, one of the least worthy soldiers, was chosen as emperor with nothing to recommend him but his name. As soon as he had assumed command, he crossed over into France, where he injured the interests of the state by often making dubious treaties with the barbarians. It was not long before Count Constantius, by command of the emperor Honorius, marched into Gaul with an army, besieged Constantine in the city of Arles, and put him to death.... From that time, the south part of Britian was wholly exposed to plundering because it lacked armed soldiers, military equipment, and all the youth of military age, who by the rashness of the usurpers had been led away, never to return. Britain was all the more vulnerable because its people were totally ignorant of the use of weapons.

Bede (d. 735), *Ecclesiastical History*[1]

The Sack of Rome by Alaric the Visigoth (410)

[The Germanic tribe of Visigoths, under its chieftain Alaric, besieged Rome until starvation forced the Romans to seek terms.] They decided to send an embassy to the enemy announcing that they were prepared for peace provided the terms were moderate, yet were even more prepared for war since they had taken their weapons in hand and as a result of their continuous handling of them would no longer scruple about fighting....

When the envoys reached Alaric ... they announced the Senate's business. Alaric listened, above all to the statement that the people were under arms and prepared for battle, and replied, "Thick grass is more easily cut than thin." At this utterance he let loose upon the envoys a big belly-laugh. When they turned to discussions about a peace he employed language that surpassed even a barbarian's insolence, for he said that he would under no circumstances put an end to the siege unless he received all the gold that the city possessed and all the silver, plus all the movables he might find throughout the city and all the barbarian slaves as well. When one of the envoys asked, "If you should take all these things, what would be left over for those who are inside the city?" Alaric answered, "Their lives."

Upon receipt of this answer the envoys sought permission to consult with those inside the city as to what should be done. Permission granted, they reported back what words had been exchanged in their mission.... Then the Romans ... despairing of all things that pertain to human strength, recalled the resources which the city had formerly known in times of crisis and of which they were now bereft because they had violated the ancestral rites [by deserting paganism].

Zosimus, *Recent History* (ca. 510)[2]

The Death of Alaric the Visigoth (410)

Alaric ... while deliberating what he should do [in southern Italy after the sack of Rome] was suddenly overtaken by an untimely death and departed from human cares. His people mourned for him with the utmost affection. Then turning from its course the river Busentus near the city of Cosenza—for this stream flows with its wholesome waters from the foot of a mountain near that city—they led a band of captives into the midst of its bed to dig out a place for his grave. In the depths of this pit they buried Alaric, together with many treasures, and then turned the waters back into their channel. And that none might ever know the place, they put to death all the diggers.

Jordanes (fl. 550), *Getica*[3]

Galla Placidia and the Visigoths (411)

When Athavulf became king [of the Visigoths after the death of Alaric in 410], he returned again to Rome, and whatever had escaped the first sack his Goths stripped bare like locusts, not merely despoiling Italy of its private wealth, but even of its public resources. The Emperor Honorius was powerless to resist even when his sister Placidia, the daughter of the Emperor Theodosius by his second wife, was led away captive from the city. But Athavulf was attracted by her nobility, beauty, and chaste purity, and so he took her to wife in lawful marriage at Forum

Julii, a city of Aemilia. When the barbarians learned of this alliance, they were the more effectually terrified, since the empire and the Goths now seemed to be made one. Then Athavulf set out for Gaul, leaving Honorius Augustus stripped of his wealth, to be sure, yet pleased at heart because he was now a sort of kinsman of his....

[After Athavulf died in 415], Honorius was eager to free his sister Placidia from the disgrace of servitude, and made an agreement with [his general] Constantius that if by peace or war or any means soever he could bring her back to the kingdom, he should have her in marriage. Pleased with this promise, Constantius set out for Spain with an armed force and in almost royal splendor. Valia, [the new] king of the Goths, met him at a pass in the Pyrenees with as great a force. Hereupon embassies were sent by both sides and it was decided to make peace on the following terms, namely that Valia should give up Placidia, the emperor's sister, and should not refuse to aid the Roman Empire when occasion demanded.

Jordanes (fl. 550), Getica[4]

The Angles and Saxons Come to Britain (449)

In the year of our Lord 449 ... the nation of the Angles, or Saxons, being invited by the aforesaid king [Vortigern], arrived in Britain with three long ships, and had a place assigned them to reside in by the same king, in the eastern part of the island, that they might thus appear to be fighting for their country, whilst their real intentions were to enslave it. Accordingly they engaged with the enemy, who were come from the north to give battle, and obtained the victory; which, being known at home in their own country, as also the fertility of the country, and the cowardice of the Britons, a more considerable fleet was quickly sent over, bringing a still greater number of men, which, being added to the former, made up an invincible army. The newcomers received of the Britons a place to inhabit, upon condition that they should wage war against their enemies for the peace and security of the country, whilst the Britons agreed to furnish them with pay.... In a short time, swarms of the aforesaid nations [Saxons, Angles, and Jutes] came over into the island, and they began to increase so much that they became terrible to the natives themselves who had invited them.

Bede (d. 735), Ecclesiastical History[5]

Honoria Incites Attila to Invade the West (450)

[In June 450 a messenger from the West arrived at Constantinople] announcing that Attila [the Hun] was involved with the royal family at Rome, since Honoria [the daughter of Galla Placidia and sister of Valentinian III, the ruler of the Western Roman Empire] had summoned Attila to her help. Honoria, though of the royal line and herself possessing the symbols of authority, was caught going secretly to bed with a certain Eugenius, who had the management of her affairs. He was put to death for this crime, and she was deprived of her royal position and betrothed to Herculanus, a man of consular rank and of such good character that it was not expected that he would aspire to royalty or revolution.

She brought her affairs to disastrous and terrible trouble by sending Hyacinthus, a eunuch, to Attila so that for money he might avenge her marriage. In addition to this she also sent a ring pledging herself to the barbarian, who made ready to go against the Western Empire....

When Theodosius [II, the Eastern Roman emperor] learned of these things, he sent to Valentinian to surrender Honoria to Attila. Valentinian arrested Hyacinthus and examined the whole matter thoroughly; after inflicting many bodily tortures on him, he ordered that he be beheaded. Valentinian granted his sister Honoria to his mother as a boon, since she persistently asked for her. And so Honoria was freed from her danger at this time....

Attila sent men to the ruler of the Western Romans to argue that Honoria, whom he had pledged to himself in marriage, should in no way be ill-treated, for he would avenge her if she did not receive the scepter of sovereignty.... The Romans of the West answered that Honoria could not come to him in marriage having been given to another man and that the royal power did not belong to her, since the control of the Roman Empire belonged to males not to females....

Attila again sent certain men of his court to Italy to persuade the Romans to surrender Honoria. He said that she had been joined to him in marriage, and as proof he dispatched the ring sent by her in order that it might be shown. He also said that Valentinian should withdraw from half of the empire in his favour, since Honoria had received its control from her father and had been deprived of it by the greed of her brother. When the Western Romans held to their former opinion and paid no attention to his proposal, he devoted himself eagerly to preparation for war and collected the whole force of his fighting men.

Priscus (fl. 448–474) and John of Antioch (7th century)[6]

Aëtius Defeats Attila the Hun (451)

The Huns, therefore, issuing from Pannonia [Hungary], reached the town of Metz ... devastating all the country. They gave the city to the flames, and slew the people.... But Attila, king of the Huns, going forth from Metz, subdued many cities of Gaul; and he came to Orleans, and battered it with rams, striving so to take the city.... And now the walls were already shaking under the shock of the rams, and on the point of falling, when behold Aëtius [commander of the Roman army] came; and Theodoric, king of the [Visi]goths, and Thorismund, his son, with their armies swiftly advanced upon the town, and cast forth and flung back the enemy. The city thus freed ... they put Attila to flight, who withdrew to the plain of Méry [or Moirey, the "Mauriac" or "Catalaunian" plain near Troyes], and disposed his forces for battle. Which when they heard, they manfully made them ready against him.... Now Aëtius, in alliance with the Goths and Franks, fought with Attila, who seeing his army being worn down even to destruction, left the field in flight. Theodoric, king of the Goths, succumbed in this battle.... But the patrician Aëtius won the victory with Thorismund, and utterly destroyed the enemy. And when the war was ended, Aëtius said to Thorismund: "Make haste to return with all speed to your country [Spain and southern Gaul], lest by the action of your brother you be despoiled of your father's kingdom." At these words Thorismund departed in haste to forestall his brother and take first possession of his father's throne. With like craft he sent off the king of the Franks. And as soon as they were gone he collected the spoil from the field and returned home with great booty. But Attila retired with a small number of men.

Gregory of Tours (538–594), *History of the Franks*[7]

The Emperor Assassinates Aetius (454)

The affairs of the Western Romans were in confusion, and Maximus, a well-born man, powerful and twice consul [in 433 and 443], was hostile to Aëtius, the general of the forces in Italy. Since he knew that Heraclius, a eunuch who had the greatest influence with the ruler [Valentinian III], was also hostile to Aëtius, he made an agreement with him with the same end in view (for both were striving to substitute their power for his). They persuaded the emperor that unless he quickly slew Aëtius, he would be slain by him.

Since Valentinian was fated to come to grief by losing the defense of his office [i.e. Aëtius], he approved of the words of Maximus and Heraclius and contrived the death of the man when Aëtius was about to consult the emperor in the palace on his resolutions and was examining proposals to bring in money. While Aëtius was laying the matter of the revenues before him and was making a calculation of the total money collected from the taxes, Valentinian jumped up with a cry from his seat and said he would no longer stand being abused by such treacheries. He charged Aëtius with being to blame for his troubles and indicated that Aëtius desired the power of the Western as well as of the Eastern Empire. As Aëtius stood amazed at the unexpectedness of his anger and tried to appease his unreasoning wrath, the emperor drew his sword from its scabbard. He attacked together with Heraclius, for this fellow was carrying a cleaver under his cloak (for he was a chamberlain). Both of them together directed their blows against the head of Aëtius and killed him—a man who had performed many brave deeds against both internal and foreign enemies.

When he had been put to death the emperor said to a person able to surmise the truth, "Was the death of Aëtius not well accomplished?" He answered, "Whether well or not I do not know, but I do know that you have cut off your right hand with your left."

John of Antioch, *History* (7th century)[8]

"He Fell Amid his Pleasures":
The Death of Attila the Hun (454)

Shortly before Attila died, he took in marriage a very beautiful girl named Ildico, after countless other wives, as was the custom of his race. He had given himself up to excessive joy at his wedding, and as he lay on his back, heavy with wine and sleep, a rush of superfluous blood, which would ordinarily have flowed from his nose, streamed in deadly course down his throat and killed him, since it was hindered in the usual passages. Thus did drunkenness put a disgraceful end to a king renowned in war. On the following day, when a great part of the morning was spent, the royal attendants suspected some ill and, after a great uproar, broke in the doors. There they found the death of Attila accomplished by bloodshed without any wound, and the girl with downcast face weeping beneath her veil.

Jordanes, *The Gothic History* (551)[9]

From Rags to Riches:
Odoacer Goes to Italy (ca. 470)

The whole nation of the Rugii resorted to the man of God [Saint Severinus, in his monastic cell near Vienna] and began to render grateful obedience, and to ask help for their diseases.... With the same reverence ... some barbarians turned aside on their way to Italy in order to get his blessing. Among such visitors was Odoacer [or Odovacer], who afterwards ruled Italy [476–493]. He was then a young man, dressed in the poorest kind of clothes, and notable for his height. When he entered the saint's cell, the roof was so low that Odoacer had to bend down to avoid striking his head. As he was bowing thus, he learned from the man of God that glory was in store for him in the future. In fact, as Odoacer was saying goodbye, the saint said: "Go to Italy, go! Now you are dressed humbly in cheap skins, but soon you will generously bestow much wealth on many people...."

[Later, when Odoacer became king] he addressed a friendly letter to Saint Severinus, and remembering that prophecy by which the saint had once foretold that Odoacer should become king, he begged him to choose whatever he might desire as a gift. In response to this royal invitation, the saint asked that one Ambrose, who was living in exile, might be pardoned. Odoacer joyfully obeyed his command.

Eugippus (fl. 511), *Life of Saint Severinus*[10]

The Last Roman Emperor in the West (476)

When the Emperor Nepos heard of this [failure of his general Ecdicius to control the Visigoths in Gaul], he ordered Ecdicius to leave Gaul and come to him, appointing Orestes in his stead as Master of the Soldiery.

This Orestes thereupon received the army, set out from Rome against the enemy and came to Ravenna. Here he tarried while he made his son Romulus Augustulus emperor. When Nepos learned of this, he fled to Dalmatia and died there [in Salona], deprived of his throne....

Now when Augustulus had been appointed emperor by his father Orestes in Ravenna, it was not long before Odoacer, king of the Torcilingi, invaded Italy, as leader of the Sciri, the Heruli, and allies of various races. He put Orestes to death, drove his son Augustulus from the throne, and condemned him to the punishment of exile in the castle of Lucullus in Campania.

Thus the Western Empire of the Roman race, which Octavianus Augustus, the first of the Augusti, began to govern in the seven hundred and ninth year from the founding of the city [44 B.C.], perished with this Augustulus in the five hundred and twenty-second year [A.D. 476] from the beginning of the rule of his predecessors and those before them, and from this time onward kings of the Goths held Rome and Italy. Meanwhile Odoacer, king of nations, subdued all Italy and then at the very outset of his reign slew Count Bracila at Ravenna that he might inspire a fear of himself among the Romans.

Jordanes, *The Gothic History* (551)[11]

Clovis and the Vase at Soissons (486)

At that time [when Clovis, king of the Franks, defeated Syagrius, "king of the Romans"] many churches were despoiled by Clovis's army, since he was as yet involved in heathen error. Now the army had taken from a certain church a vase of wonderful size and beauty, along with the remainder of the utensils for the service of the church. And the bishop of the church sent messengers to the king asking that the vase at least be returned, if he could not get back any more of the sacred dishes. On hearing this the king said to the messenger: "Follow us as far as Soissons, because all that has been taken is to be divided there and when the lot assigns me that dish I will do what the father asks." Then when he came to Soissons and all the booty was set in their midst, the king said: "I ask of you, brave warriors, not to refuse to grant me in addition to my share, yonder dish," that is, he was speaking of the vase just mentioned. In answer to the speech of the king, those of more sense replied: "Glorious king, all that we see is yours, and we ourselves are subject to your rule. Now do what seems well-pleasing to you; for no one is able to resist your power." When they said this a foolish, envious, and excitable fellow lifted his battle-axe and struck the vase, and cried in a loud voice: "You shall get nothing here except what the lot fairly bestows on you." At this all were stupefied, but the king endured the insult with the gentleness of patience, and taking the vase he handed it over to the messenger of the church, nursing the wound deep in his heart.

And at the end of the year he ordered the whole army to come with their equipment of armour, to show the brightness of their arms on the field of March. And when he was reviewing them all carefully, he came to the man who struck the vase, and said to him: "No one has brought armour so carelessly kept as you; for neither your spear nor sword nor axe is in serviceable condition." And seizing his axe he cast it to the earth, and when the other had bent over somewhat to pick it up, the king raised his hands and drove his own axe into the man's head. "This," said he, "is what you did at Soissons to the vase." Upon the death of this man, he ordered the rest to depart, raising great dread of himself by this action.

Gregory of Tours (538–594), *History of the Franks*[12]

"Go West, Young Ostrogoth, Go West!" (488)

Now while Theodoric [the Ostrogoth] was in alliance by treaty with the [East Roman] Empire of Zeno and was himself enjoying every comfort in the city [of Constantinople, where he was a hostage], he heard that his tribe, dwelling as we have said in Illyricum [Yugoslavia], was not altogether satisfied or content. So he chose rather to seek a living by his own exertions, after the manner customary to his race, rather than to enjoy the advantages of the Roman Empire in luxurious ease while his tribe lived apart.

After pondering these matters, he said to the emperor [Zeno]: "Though I lack nothing in serving your empire, yet if Your Piety deem it worthy, be pleased to hear the desire of my heart." And when as usual he had been granted permission to speak freely, he said: "The western country [Italy], long ago governed by the rule of your ancestors and predecessors, and that city [Rome] which was the head and mistress of the world—wherefore is it now shaken by the tyranny of the Torcilingi and the Rugi [under Odoacer]? Send me there with my race. Thus if you but say the word, you may be freed from the burden of expense here, and, if by the Lord's help I shall conquer, the fame of Your Piety shall be glorious there. For it is better that I, your servant and your son, should rule that kingdom, receiving it as a gift from you if I conquer, than that one whom you do not recognize should oppress your Senate with his tyrannical yoke and a part of the republic with slavery. For if I prevail, I shall retain it as your grant and gift; if I am conquered, Your Piety will lose nothing—nay, as I have said, it will save the expense I now entail."

Although the emperor was grieved that he should go, yet when he heard this he granted what Theodoric asked, for he was unwilling to cause him sorrow. He sent him forth enriched by great gifts and commended to his charge the Senate and the Roman People. Therefore Theodoric departed from the royal city and returned to his own people. In company with the whole tribe of the [Ostro]goths, who gave him their unanimous consent, he set out for Hesperia [i.e. the West].

Jordanes, *The Gothic History* (551)[13]

How Clovis United the Franks (ca. 490)

There was at that time in Cambrai a king named Ragnachar [whom Clovis wanted to remove].... Clovis presented armlets and baldrics of false gold to the *leudes* [sworn friends] of Ragnachar [who were already dissatisfied with him] in order that they might call Clovis in against their lord. The supposed gold was only copper, cunningly gilded.... Clovis came, and drew up his battle array. And when Ragnachar saw his army vanquished, he made ready to escape in flight, but he was caught by his own men and brought before Clovis with his arms bound behind his back; so likewise was Ricchar his brother. Clovis said to him: "Why have you disgraced our family by permitting yourself to be bound? It would have been better for you to die"; he then raised his axe and buried it in his head. Afterwards he turned to the brother, and said: "If you had stood by your brother, he would not have been bound thus," and slew him in the same way with a blow of his axe. After their death, their betrayers for the first time discovered that the gold which Clovis had given them was false. But when they remonstrated with the king, men say that he replied: "This is the kind of gold that a man deserves when

29

he lures his lord to his death," adding that they ought to be content to have escaped with their lives, not expiating the betrayal of their lords by a death amid torments. When they heard this, they chose to beg for mercy, declaring that it was enough for them if they were judged worthy to live.

The two kings of whom I have spoken [Ragnachar and Chararic] were kinsmen of Clovis. Their brother, Rignomer, was slain at Le Mans by his command, and the kingdom and treasures of all three passed into his possession. He caused many other kings to be slain and also his near relatives whom he suspected of usurping his kingdom; in this way he extended his dominion over all Gaul.

One day when he had assembled his own people, he is said to have spoken as follows of the kinsmen whom he had destroyed: "Woe unto me who remain as a traveller among strangers, and have none of my kin to help me in the evil day." But he did not thus allude to their death out of grief, but craftily, to see if he could bring to light some new relative to kill.

Gregory of Tours (538–594), *History of the Franks*[14]

Arthur Defends Britain from the Saxons (ca. 493)

At that time the Saxons increased in number and grew powerful in Britain. After Hengist's death, his son Octha migrated from the left side of Britain to the kingdom of Kent, and the kings of Kent are his descendants. Then in those days Arthur fought against these Saxons. The kings of the Britons fought on his side, but he was the leader of battles (*dux bellorum*). The first battle was at the mouth of the river called Glein. The second, third, fourth, and fifth battles were fought on another river that is called Dubglas, which is in the area of Linnuis. The sixth battle was on the river called Bassas. The seventh battle was in the forest of Celidon, i.e. Cat Coit Celidon. The eighth battle was at Guinnion castle; in this engagement Arthur carried the image of Saint Mary, the perpetual virgin, on his shoulders, and on that day the pagans were put to flight, and through the power of our Lord Jesus Christ and through the power of his mother the Blessed Virgin Mary there was great slaughter. The ninth battle took place at the Legion's city. The tenth battle he waged on the shore of the river called Tribruit. The eleventh battle happened on the mountain called Agned. The twelfth battle was on the mountain of Badon; in this engagement 960 men were overthrown in one day by one charge, and Arthur and no one else was the cause of their downfall; and in all the battles he was the victor.

Nennius, *History of the Britons* (ca. 825)[15]

Theodoric and Odoacer (493)

Theodoric [the Ostrogoth] and Odoacer agreed in a treaty with each other that both should rule the [Western] Roman Empire, and thereafter they talked together and frequently went to see each other. But ten days had not passed when Odoacer was at Theodoric's headquarters and two of the latter's henchmen came forward as though suppliants and grasped Odoacer's hands. Therewith those hidden in ambush in the rooms on either side rushed out with their swords. They were panic-stricken at the sight of their victim, and when they did not attack Odoacer, Theodoric himself rushed forward and struck him with a sword on the collarbone. When he asked "Where is God?" Theodoric answered, "This is what you did to my friends." The fatal blow pierced Odoacer's body as far as the hip, and they say Theodoric exclaimed, "There certainly wasn't a bone in this wretched fellow." Sending the corpse outside to the meeting places of the Hebrews, he buried it in a stone coffin. Odoacer had lived sixty years and ruled fourteen.

John of Antioch, *History* (7th century)[16]

Saint Benedict: A Teenage Dropout (ca. 495)

Benedict was a man of venerable life, blessed in grace as in name, and with the wisdom of an elder from the very time of his boyhood. He was mature beyond his years, and did not yield to pleasure. While still on earth, when he could have enjoyed himself freely for the time, he already considered the world with its flower a barren thing.

He was born in the province of Nursia [about 75 miles northwest of Rome] into a family of high station, and had been sent to Rome to study the liberal arts. But since he observed the spiritual fall of many students, he drew back the foot which he had set upon the threshold of the world; for he was afraid that he too, after gaining some of its knowledge, would drop fatally into the huge abyss. He therefore rejected the study of literature and left his home and his father's affairs. His sole desire was to find favour with God, and so he made the religious life his goal. He withdrew then, knowingly ignorant and wisely unlearned (*scienter nescius et sapienter indoctus*).

Pope Gregory the Great (ca. 540–604), *Dialogues*[17]

Saint Benedict
Discovers Negative Reinforcement (ca. 496)

One day while he was alone [living the life of a hermit] ... a greater temptation of the flesh than he had ever experienced overtook the holy man. For the evil spirit brought back before his mind's eye a certain woman whom he had once seen. So intensely did the Tempter inflame his mind by the sight of that woman that he could hardly control his passion. He was overcome by sensuality, and almost considered abandoning his solitary retreat. Then suddenly God graciously looked upon him and he returned to himself. Since he saw that thickets of nettles and thorn bushes were growing nearby, he stripped off his garments and flung himself naked upon those stinging thorns and the burning nettles. He rolled about there for a long time, and came out with his whole body wounded by them. So through the wounds of the skin he drew out from his body the wound of the mind by changing his lust to pain. Although he burned painfully on the outside, he had put out the forbidden flame within. He conquered sin, then, by transforming the fire. From that time on, as he later used to tell his disciples, he had such control over temptation of the flesh that he never again experienced a sensation like that.

Pope Gregory the Great (ca. 540–604), *Dialogues*[18]

The Conversion and Baptism of Clovis (496)

Now [Clotild, Clovis's] queen, without ceasing urged the king to confess the true God, and forsake his idols; but in no wise could she move him to this belief, until at length he had occasion to make war against the Alamanni, when he was driven of necessity to confess what of his free will he had denied. It befell that when the two hosts joined battl⌐ there was grievous slaughter, and the army of Clovis was being swept to utter ruin. When the king saw this he lifted up his eyes to heaven and ... cried aloud: "Jesus Christ, you whom Clotild calls the son of the living God....

If you grant me victory over these enemies ... then will I also believe on you and be baptized in your name. I have called upon my own gods, but here is proof that they have withdrawn themselves from helping me; wherefore I believe that they have no power, since they come not to the succour of their servants...." And as he said this, lo, the Alamanni turned their backs, and began to flee. And when they saw that their king was slain, they yielded themselves to Clovis.... Then the king ... returned in peace, relating to the queen how he had called upon the name of Christ and had been found worthy to obtain the victory....

Then the queen commanded the holy Remigius, bishop of Rheims, to be summoned secretly, entreating him to impart the word of salvation to the king. The bishop, calling the king to him privately, began to instil into him faith in the true God ... and urged him to forsake his idols, which were unable to help either himself or others.

But Clovis replied: "I myself, most holy father, will listen to you gladly; but one thing yet remains. The people that follow me will not let me forsake their gods; yet will I go and reason with them according to your word." But when he came before the assembled people, even before he opened his mouth, the divine power had gone forth before him, and all the people cried with one voice: "O gracious king, we drive forth our gods that perish, and we are ready to follow that immortal God whom Remigius preaches."

News of this was brought to the bishop, who was filled with great joy and commanded the font to be prepared.... Like a new Constantine, [Clovis] moved forward to the water.... As he entered to be baptized, the saint of God [Remigius] spoke these words with eloquent lips: "Meekly bow your proud head, Sicamber [i.e. Frank]; adore that which you have burned, burn that which you have adored." ... The king therefore ... was baptized ... and anointed with holy chrism.... Of his army were baptized more than three thousand....

Gregory of Tours (ca. 540–594), *History of the Franks*[19]

The Sixth Century

Clovis Defeats the Visigoths (507)

Now King Clovis said to his men: "I can't stand to see these Arians holding a part of Gaul. Let us go forth, then, and with God's aid bring the land under our own sway." This speech finding favour with all, he assembled his army, and marched on Poitiers, where King Alaric then happened to be. Part of the troops had to traverse the territory of Tours, and out of reverence for the blessed Martin [the local saint] the king issued an edict that none should take anything from that region but water and grass. Now a certain soldier, finding some hay belonging to a poor man, said: "Was it not the king's order that we should take grass and nothing besides? Well, this is grass, and if we take it we shall not transgress his bidding." So he took the hay from the poor man by force, taking advantage of his own strength. The matter came to the ears of the king, who straightway cut the man down with his own sword, saying: "Where shall be our hope of victory, if we offend the blessed Martin?" And the army was content to take nothing more from this region....

In the meantime King Clovis encountered Alaric, king of the [Visi]goths, on the field of Vouillé at the tenth milestone out of Poitiers. Part of the combatants fought with missiles from a distance, another part hand to hand. But when, as their habit is, the Goths turned to fly, King Clovis by God's aid obtained the victory.... When the Goths were put to flight, and the king had slain Alaric, two of the enemy suddenly came up and struck at [Clovis] with their spears on each side; the cuirass which he wore and the speed of his horse preserved him from death.... From this battle Amalaric, son of Alaric, fled into Spain and ruled with prudence his father's kingdom.

Gregory of Tours (ca. 540-594), *History of the Franks*[1]

Saint Benedict's Power of Telekinesis (ca. 510)

On another occasion, a humble Goth came to adopt the religious life and Benedict willingly received him [into his monastery]. One day he ordered an iron brush hook to be given to him for cutting the bramble bushes where a garden was to be planted. Now it happened that the spot assigned to the Goth for clearing lay above the shore of a lake. While he was cutting the thick bramble bushes with all his might, the iron slipped from the handle and fell into the lake. Since the water at that spot was deep, there was no hope of finding the iron tool; and so the Goth ran in agitation to the monk Maurus [Benedict's lieutenant]. He reported his loss and expressed sorrow for what he had done. When Maurus told Benedict what had happened, the man of God went to the lake, took the handle from the Goth's hand, and thrust it into the water. In an instant the iron came up from the bottom and inserted itself into the handle. Then Benedict gave the tool right back to the Goth and said to him, "Here you are. Do your work and do not be sad."

Pope Gregory the Great (ca. 540-604), *Dialogues*[2]

Saint Benedict Receives Unhesitating Obedience (ca. 510)

One day when the venerable Benedict was staying in his cell, young Placidus went out to draw water from the lake. As he was carelessly lowering his vessel, he toppled after it into the water. Soon the current caught hold of him and carried him away about the distance of an arrow's flight. The man of God in his cell became aware of this at once and quickly called to [his disciple] Maurus, "Run, Brother Maurus! The boy who went to draw water has fallen into the lake, and now the current is carrying him far away." A miracle which had not happened since the time of Peter the Apostle! [Matt. 14.28–29]: Maurus first asked his abbot for a blessing and received it. Then he was so spurred on by Benedict's command that he continued running over the water, thinking he was still on land. When he had reached the spot where Placidus was being drawn away by the current, he grasped the boy by the hair and ran back to shore as fast as he had come.

As soon as he touched land, he came to himself. When he had looked back and realized that he had run on the water, he trembled in amazement, since he could not imagine how it had happened. And so he returned to the abbot and told him about the incident. Then Benedict began to assign the credit to Maurus's obedience and not to his own merits. Maurus, on the other hand, said that he had merely carried out Benedict's order, and that he did not deserve a share of the credit for what he had done unconsciously. But while they were having this friendly contest in humility, the rescued boy acted as arbiter by saying: "While I was being drawn from the water, I saw the abbot's cowl above my head, and thought that he was taking me out of the water."

Pope Gregory the Great (ca. 540-604), *Dialogues*[3]

Theodora's Progress From Actress to Empress (527)

As soon as she arrived at the age of youth, and was now ready for the world, her mother put her on the stage. Forthwith, she became a courtesan, and such as the ancient Greeks used to call a common one, at that: for she was not a flute or harp player, nor was she even trained to dance, but only gave her youth to anyone she met, in utter abandonment. Her general favours included, of course, the actors in the theater; and in their productions she took part in the low comedy scenes. For she was very funny and a good mimic, and immediately became popular in this art. There was no shame in the girl, and no one ever saw her dismayed: no role was too scandalous for her to accept without a blush.

She was the kind of comedienne who delights the audience by letting herself be cuffed and slapped on the cheeks, and makes them guffaw by raising her skirts to reveal to the spectators those feminine secrets here and there which custom veils from the eyes of the opposite sex. With pretended laziness she mocked her lovers, and coquettishly adopting ever new ways of embracing, was able to keep in a constant turmoil the hearts of the sophisticated.... And though she flung wide three gates to the ambassadors of Cupid, she lamented that nature had not similarly unlocked the straits of her bosom, that she might there have contrived a further welcome to his emissaries....

Often, even in the theatre, in the sight of all the people, she removed her costume and stood nude in their midst, except for a girdle about the groin: not that she was abashed at revealing that, too, to the audience, but because there was a law against appearing altogether naked on the stage, without at least this much of a fig-leaf. Covered thus with a ribbon, she would sink down to the stage floor and recline on her back. Slaves to whom the duty was entrusted would then scatter grains of barley from above into the calyx of this passion flower, whence geese, trained for the purpose, would next pick the grains one by one with their bills and eat. When she rose, it was not with a blush, but she seemed rather to glory in the performance....

Later, she followed Hecebolus, a Tyrian who had been made governor of Pentapolis, serving him in the basest of ways; but finally she quarreled with him and was sent summarily away. Consequently, she found herself destitute of the means of life, which she proceeded to earn by prostitution, as she had done before this adventure. She came thus to Alexandria, and then traversing all the East, worked her way to Constantinople; in every city plying a trade (which it is safer, I fancy, in the sight of God not to name too clearly) as if the Devil were determined there be no land on earth that should not know the sins of Theodora.... But when she came back to Constantinople, Justinian fell violently in love with her. At first he kept her only as a mistress, though he raised her to patrician rank....

It was then [after the death of the Empress Euphemia, his prudish aunt] that he undertook to complete his marriage with Theodora. But as it was impossible for a man of senatorial rank to make a courtesan his wife, this being forbidden by ancient law, he made the emperor [Justin, his uncle] nullify this ordinance by creating a new one, permitting him to wed Theodora, and consequently making it possible for anyone else to marry a courtesan.

Procopius, Secret History (ca. 550)[4]

"Royalty is a Good Burial Shroud" (532)

[In 532 the Nika Riots of the circus factions in Constantinople threatened to overthrow the government.] Now the emperor [Justinian] and his court were deliberating as to whether it would be better for them if they remained or if they took to flight in the ships. And many opinions were expressed favouring either course. And the Empress Theodora also spoke to the following effect: "As to the belief that a woman ought not to be daring among men or to assert herself boldly among those who are holding back from fear, I consider that the present crisis most certainly does not permit us to discuss whether the matter should be regarded in this or in some other way. For in the case of those whose interests have come into the greatest danger nothing else seems best except to settle the issue immediately before them in the best possible way. My opinion then is that the present time, above all others, is inopportune for flight, even though it bring safety. For while it is impossible for a man who has seen the light not also to die, for one who has been an emperor it is unendurable to be a fugitive. May I never be separated from this purple; and may I not live that day on which those who meet me shall not address me as mistress. If, now, it is your wish to save yourself, O emperor, there is no difficulty. For we have much money, and there is the sea, here the boats. However consider whether it will not come about after you have been saved that you would gladly exchange that safety for death. For as for myself, I approve a certain ancient saying that royalty is a good burial-shroud." When the queen had spoken thus, all were filled with boldness, and, turning their thoughts towards resistance, they began to consider how they might be able to defend themselves if any hostile force should come against them.

Procopius (fl. 500-562), History of the Wars[5]

Saint Benedict and King Totila (546)

In the time of the [Ostro]goths, King Totila [541-552] heard that the saint possessed the spirit of prophecy. As he traveled toward Benedict's monastery [at Montecassino], he stopped some distance away and sent a message that he would come to the monastery. He was immediately invited to do so. But since he was treacherous, he tried to test whether Benedict really had the spirit of prophecy. He therefore gave his sword-bearer, Riggo, his own shoes, dressed him in the royal robes, and ordered him to go to Benedict disguised as the king. As Riggo's escort, Totila sent three attendants who had been particularly close to him, namely Vul, Ruderic, and Blidin. In Benedict's presence, they were to pretend that Riggo was King Totila and to walk beside him. He furnished other escorts and swordbearers also to increase the appearance of royalty created by the purple robes.

As Riggo entered the monastery decked out in the robes and accompanied by many attendants, the man of God was seated at a distance. He caught sight of Riggo, and when he was close enough to be heard, he called out, "O my son, put aside what you are wearing. It is not yours." Riggo fell to the ground at once, terrified at his presumption in making sport of so great a man. All his attendants, too, prostrated themselves on the ground. When they stood up, they did not presume to approach Benedict, but returned to their king. They were still trembling as they reported how quickly they had been detected.

Then Totila himself went to Benedict. As he saw Benedict sitting at a distance, he did not dare to approach, but prostrated himself. Two or three times the man of God said to him, "Stand up," but the king did not dare to stand upright before him. Therefore Benedict, the servant of Jesus Christ, graciously approached the prostrate king, raised him from the ground, reproached him for his actions, and in a few words foretold everything that would happen to him.

"Your evil deeds, past and present, are many. It is time at last to refrain from sin. You are about to enter Rome and to cross the sea. For nine years you will rule, and in the tenth you will die." The king was terror-stricken by these words. After asking a blessing, he withdrew and was less cruel from that time on. Not long after, he went to Rome, proceeded to Sicily, and died in the tenth year of his reign [552]. He lost his kingdom and his life according to the judgment of almighty God.

Now it happened that Benedict received frequent visits from a priest of the church of Canosa, a man dearly beloved by the saint because of his virtuous life. In discussing King Totila's entry and the destruction of Rome, he said, "Rome will be destroyed by this king so that it will no longer be inhabited." But Benedict answered, "Rome will not come to an end through barbarians, but will be exhausted by flashing storms, whirlwinds, and earthquakes. Then it will crumble upon its foundations." The secret meaning of this prophecy has become clearer than light to us, who [a generation later, ca. 593] observe the walls broken to bits, houses overturned, and churches destroyed by the whirlwind. More often all the time we see Roman buildings, wearied with old age, collapsing into ruins.

Pope Gregory the Great (ca. 540-604), *Dialogues*[6]

The Emperor Justinian Vilified by Procopius (ca. 550)

I think this is as good a time as any to describe the personal appearance of the man. Now in physique he was neither tall nor short, but of average height; not thin, but moderately plump; his face was round, and not bad looking, for he had good colour, even when he fasted for two days....

Now such was Justinian in appearance; but his character was something I could not fully describe. For he was at once villainous and amenable; as people say colloquially, a moron. He was never truthful with anyone, but always guileful in what he said and did, yet easily hoodwinked by anywho wanted to deceive him. His nature was an unnatural mixture of folly and wickedness. What in olden times a peripatetic philosopher said was also true of him, that opposite qualities combine in a man as in the mixing of colours. I will try to portray him, however, insofar as I can fathom his complexity.

This emperor, then was deceitful, devious, false, hypocritical, two-faced, cruel, skilled in dissembling his thought, never moved to tears by either joy or pain, though he could summon them artfully at will when the occasion demanded, a liar always, not only offhand but also in writing and when he swore sacred oaths to his subjects in their very hearing. Then he would immediately break his agreements and pledges, like the vilest of slaves whom indeed only the fear of torture drives to confess their perjury. A faithless friend, he was a treacherous enemy, insane for murder and plunder, quarrelsome and revolutionary, easily led to anything evil, but never willing to listen to good counsel, quick to plan mischief and carry it out, but finding even the hearing of anything good distasteful to his ears.

How could anyone put Justinian's ways into words? These and many even worse vices were disclosed in him as in no other mortal: nature seemed to have taken the wickedness of all other men combined and planted it in this man's soul. And besides this, he was too prone to listen to accusations; and too quick to punish. For he decided such cases without full examination, naming the punishment when he had heard only the accuser's side of the matter. Without hesitation he wrote decrees for the plundering of countries, sacking of cities, and slavery of whole nations, for no cause whatever. So that if one wished to take all the calamities which had befallen the Romans before this time and weigh them against his crimes, I think it would be found that more men had been murdered by this single man than in all previous history.

He had no scruples about appropriating other people's property and did not even think any excuse necessary, legal or illegal, for confiscating what did not belong to him. And when it was his, he was more than ready to squander it in insane display or give it as an unnecessary bribe to the barbarians. In short, he neither held on to any money himself nor let anyone else keep any: as if his reason were not avarice, but jealousy of those who had riches. Driving all wealth from the country of the Romans in this manner, he became the cause of universal poverty.

Now this was the character of Justinian, so far as I can portray it. [As to his habits:] he was untiring; and hardly slept at all, generally speaking; he had no appetite for food or drink, but picking up a morsel with the tips of his fingers, tasted it and left the table, as if eating were a duty imposed upon him by nature and of no more interest than a courier takes in delivering a letter. Indeed, he would often go without food for two days and nights, especially when the time [Lent] before the festival called Easter enjoins such fasting. Then, as I have said, he often went without food for two days, living only on a little water and a few wild herbs, sleeping perhaps a single hour, and then spending the rest of the time walking up and down.... His constant wakefulness, his privations and his labours were undergone for no other reason than to contrive each day ever more exaggerated calamities for his people.

Procopius of Caesarea, *Secret History*(ca. 550)[7]

God Punishes Two Merovingians: Chramm and Lothar (560-561)

Now King Lothar [the last surviving son of Clovis] was raging against [his own son] Chramm and marched with his army into Brittany against him. Nor was Chramm afraid to come out against his father. And when both armies were gathered and encamped on the same plain and Chramm with the Bretons had marshaled his line against his father, night fell and they refrained from fighting. During the night Chanao, count of the Bretons, said to Chramm: "I think it wrong for you to fight against your father; allow me tonight to rush upon him and destroy him with all his army." But Chramm would not allow this to be done, being held back I think by the power of God. When morning came they set their armies in motion and hastened to the conflict. And King Lothar was marching like a new David to fight against Absalom his son [2 Samuel 18], crying aloud and saying: "Look down, Lord, from heaven and judge my cause since I suffer wicked outrage from my son; look down, Lord, and judge justly, and give that judgment that you once gave between Absalom and his father." When they were fighting on equal terms the count of the Bretons fled and was slain. Then Chramm started to flee to ships he had ready by the shore, but he lost time trying to save his wife and daughters and was overtaken by his father's soldiers, who captured him and put him in bonds. This news was taken to King Lothar and he gave orders to burn Chramm together with his wife and daughters. They were shut up in a hut belonging to a poor man and Chramm was stretched on a bench and strangled with a towel; then the hut was burned over them, so his wife and daughters perished with him.

[A year later, in 561, Lothar] ... was seized with a fever while hunting in the forest of Cuise and returned thence to a villa in Compiègne. There he was painfully harassed by the fever and said: "Alas! What do you think the king of heaven is like when he kills such great kings in this way?" Labouring under this pain he breathed his last.... He died on the first anniversary of the day on which Chramm had been slain.

Gregory of Tours (ca. 540-594), *History of the Franks*[8]

Finnian vs. Columba:
The First Copyright Violation (561)

Once upon a time [in Ireland] Colum Cille [Saint Columba] visited [Saint] Finnian of Druim Finn [his former teacher]. He asked the latter for the loan of a book [that Finnian had brought back from Rome], which he obtained. And the office and mass being over, he used to remain after the rest of the [monastic] community in the church of that place, engaged in transcribing that book unknown to Finnian. At night time, while engaged at that transcription, the fingers of his right hand were as candles, which shone like five very bright lamps, whose light and brightness filled the entire church. On the last night, when Collum Cille was completing the transcription of that book, Finnian sent for it. When the messenger arrived at the door of the church wherein was Colum Cille, he was astonished at the great light he saw within, and great fear seized him. Timorously he glanced through a hole which was in the door at the entry of the church, and when he beheld Colum Cille as we have described him, he dared not address him or demand the book of him. It was revealed to Colum Cille, however, that the youth was thus watching him, whereat he became very angry, and, addressing a pet crane of his, said: "If God permits it, you have my permission to pluck out that youth's eyes, who came to observe me without my knowledge." With that the crane immediately went and drove its beak through the hole of the door towards the youth's eye, plucked it out, and left it resting on his cheek. The youth then returned to Finnian, and related to him the whole of his adventure. Thereupon Finnian was displeased, and he blessed and healed the youth's eye, and restored it to its place, so that it was as well as ever, without being injured or affected in any way.

When Finnian discovered that his book had been copied without his permission, he went to reprove Colum Cille, and said he had acted wrongly in transcribing his book without permission. "I shall appeal to the king of Ireland, namely Diarmaid MacCerbuill [544-565], for judgment," says Colum Cille. "I shall agree to that," says Finnian. They then proceeded together to Tara of the Kings, where Diarmaid MacCerbuill resided.

Finnian pleaded his case first to the king as follows: "Colum Cille transcribed my book without my knowledge," says he, "and I maintain that the transcript belongs to me." "I hold," says Colum Cille, "that Finnian's book has not decreased in value because of the transcript I have made from it, and that it is not right to extinguish the divine things it contained [psalms], or to prevent me or anybody else from copying it, or reading it, or from circulating it throughout the provinces. I further maintain that if I benefited by its transcription, which I desired to be for the general good, provided no injury accrues to Finnian or his book thereby, it was quite permissible for me to copy it."

Then Diarmaid declared the famous judgment, which was: "to every cow her offspring"—that is, her calf—"and to every book its transcript (*le gach lebhur a leabràn*). And therefore," says Diarmaid, "the transcript you have made, O Colum Cille, belongs to Finnian." "It is a wrong judgment," says Colum Cille, "and you shall be punished for it." [Therefore he fomented a rebellion against the high king and subsequently went into exile in Scotland, where he built a monastery at Iona as a missionary center for the conversion of the Scots.]

Manus O'Donnell, *Life of Saint Columba* (1532)[9]

Narses' Revenge (568)

[The Byzantine general Narses had reconquered Italy from the Ostrogoths and then served as its governor.] Then the Romans, influenced by envy, complained to [the Byzantine emperor] Justin [II] and [the empress] Sophia that they had been better off under the Goths than they were now under the Greeks. "Where Narses the Eunuch rules," they said, "we are no better than slaves. And the most devout emperor is ignorant of this. Therefore either free us and the city of Rome from his hand, or else we will assuredly become servants of the barbarians." When Narses heard this, he said: "If I was bad to the Romans, it will be bad for me.

Liber Pontificalis: Life of Pope John III (579-590)[10]

Then the august emperor was so greatly moved with anger against Narses that he immediately sent the prefect Longinus into Italy to take Narses' place. But when Narses learned of these things, he was much afraid, and he was so terrified by that empress Sophia that he did not dare to return to Constantinople. For she is said to have sent him a message saying, among other insults, that since he was a eunuch, she would employ him in the women's quarters to give the girls their daily allotment of wool for weaving. To these words Narses is said to have given this answer, that he would give her something to weave on her loom that would keep her busy for the rest of her life. Therefore, being racked by fear and hatred, he departed to Naples, and soon sent agents to the nation of the Lombards, telling them to leave the poverty-stricken fields of Pannonia [Hungary] and come to possess Italy, teeming as it was with all sorts of wealth. At the same time he sent many kinds of fruit and samples of other produce in which Italy abounds, so they would be tempted into coming. The Lombards received with satisfaction the glad tidings, which fitted their own previous desires, and they lifted up their hearts at the thought of their future posperity.

Paul the Deacon, *History of the Lombards* (ca. 799)[11]

An Apology for Bad Latin (ca. 574)

I will relate for posterity as many current miracles as I can recall. I would not presume to do this, had I not been warned twice and thrice in a vision. Nevertheless I call Almighty God to witness that by chance I saw in a dream at noon in the basilica of Saint Martin [of Tours] many sick and oppressed by different diseases cured, and I saw these things while my mother [Armentaria] was watching, who said to me: "Why are you slow in writing that which you see?" I answered: "You know that I am not learned in literature and being simple and unskilled would not dare describe such awe-inspiring miracles.... Since I am incompetent, I would incur shame if I tried to do this." And she said to me: "Do you not know that on account of the ignorance of our people the way you can speak is considered more intelligible? So do not hesitate and do not delay doing this since it will be a charge against you if you pass over these deeds in silence." So I wish to do this but am afflicted by ... fear of approaching so excellent a work, since I am a rustic.... [But God] is able, I believe, to display these things through me though I lack eloquence. It will certainly be evident that He has again opened the mouth of an ass if opening my unlearned lips He deems it worthy to expound these deeds. But why do I fear my rusticity when the Lord ... chose for the destruction of the vanity of worldly wisdom not orators but fishermen, not philosophers but rustics? And so I am confident ... that even if my rude speech cannot decorate the page, the glorious priest [Saint Martin] will make it gleam with his famous miracles.

Gregory of Tours (ca. 540-594) *Miracles of St. Martin*[12]

The Bonds of Serfdom and Matrimony Abused (ca. 575)

Rauching [a Frankish duke] treated those under him in such a way that one could not perceive that he had any human feeling in him, and he vented his rage on his own people beyond the limits of human wickedness and folly and committed unspeakable wrongs.... Certain ones tell the story that two of his serfs at that time loved one another, namely, a man and a girl—a thing that often happens. And when this love had lasted a space of two years or more, they were united together and took refuge in the church. When Rauching found it out he went to the priest of the place and demanded that his serfs be returned to him at once, and said they would not be punished. Then the priest said to him: "You know what respect should be paid to the churches of God; you cannot take them unless you give a pledge of their permanent union, and likewise proclaim that they shall remain free from every bodily punishment." When he had continued silent for a long time in doubtful thought, he finally turned to the priest and placed his hands on the altar and swore, saying: "They shall never be parted by me but I will rather cause them to continue in this union permanently, because although it is annoying to me that this was done without my consent, still I welcome this feature of it, that he has not married a girl belonging to another nor she another's serf." The priest in a simple-hearted way believed the crafty fellow's promise and restored the slaves under the promise that they would not be punished. Rauching took them and thanking the priest went home. He at once directed a tree to be cut down and the trunk cut off close to the branches and split with wedges and hollowed out. He ordered the earth to be dug to a depth of three or four feet and half the trunk put in the trench. Then he placed the girl there as if she were dead and ordered them to throw the man in on top. And he put the covering on and filled the trench and buried them alive, saying: "I have not broken my oath that they should never be separated." When this was reported to the priest he ran swiftly, and fiercely rebuking the man he finally succeeded in having them uncovered. However it was only the man who was alive when dragged out; he found the girl suffocated.

Gregory of Tours (ca. 540-594), *History of the Franks*[13]

The Perfect Squelch (576)

[Bishop Gregory of Tours recalled that] at this time Felix, bishop of Nantes [in Brittany] wrote me letters full of abuse.... The reason for writing in this sort was that he coveted a domain belonging to the church; because I would not agree that he should have it, he was filled with rage and poured forth a thousand invectives against me. In the end I made answer to him in these words: ... "O that Marseilles had received you for her bishop! For the ships would never have brought you oil or other wares, but only papyrus [from Egypt], that you might have greater opportunity to write calumnies against good men. Now scarcity of papyrus cuts short your wordiness." For his greed and arrogance knew no bounds. But lest I seem as one like to him, I leave all this on one side....

Gregory of Tours (ca. 540-594), *History of the Franks*[14]

"Not Angles but Angels" (ca. 577)

In the time of King Alla [or Aelli, 560-590], youths from Northumbria were exposed for sale, after the common and almost native custom of this people.... Some of these youths then, carried from England for sale to Rome, became the means of salvation to all their countrymen. For exciting the attention of that city, by the beauty of their countenances and the elegance of their features, it happened that, among others, the blessed Gregory [the Great], at that time archdeacon of the apostolical see, was present. Admiring such an assemblage of grace in mortals, and, at the same time, pitying their abject condition, as captives, he asked the bystanders, "Of what race are these? whence come they?" They reply, "By birth they are Angles; by country are Deiri (Deira being a province of Northumbria), subjects of King Alla, and pagans." Their concluding characteristic he accompanied with heartfelt sighs: to the others he elegantly alluded, saying "that these Angles, *angel*-like, should be delivered from wrath (*de ira*), and taught to sing *Alle-luia.*"

Obtaining permission without delay from Pope Benedict [575-579], the industry of this excellent man was all alive to enter on the journey to convert them; and certainly his zeal would have completed this intended labour, had not the mutinous love of his fellow citizens recalled him, already on his progress.... His good intention, though frustrated at this time, received afterwards, during his pontificate [590-604], an honourable termination....

William of Malmesbury (d. 1143?), *The Kings of England*[15]

R. S. V. P. (577)

[In 575 Duke Gunthram Boso had taken sanctuary in the church of Saint Martin of Tours.] And [in 577] because Gunthram was accused ... of the death of Theudebert [his father], King Chilperic sent messengers with a letter for the tomb of the holy Martin, in which he wrote a request that the blessed Martin should write back to him, whether it might be lawful for Gunthram to be dragged out of the saint's church or not. The deacon Baudegil, who brought this letter, put on the holy tomb, as well as the written sheet, a piece of blank paper. But after waiting three days and getting no answer, he went back to Chilperic.

Gregory of Tours (ca. 540-594), *History of the Franks*[16]

Brunhilda as Regent Keeps Peace in Austrasia (581)

Now Lupus, duke of Champagne, had long been continually harried and despoiled by his enemies, and above all by Ursio and Bertefried, who finally agreed together to take his life, and marched against him with an army. At sight whereof, Queen Brunhilda, sore at heart for her loyal servant thus unjustly persecuted, armed herself with a man's courage and threw herself between the hostile armies, crying: "Desist, O warriors, from this wickedness; cease to persecute the innocent; join not battle on account of one man, nor destroy the strength of our country." But in answer to these words Ursio said: "Stand back from us, O woman; let it suffice you to have ruled under your husband [King Sigibert, d. 575]. But now the kingdom belongs to your son [Childebert II, still underage], and it is upheld not by your protection but by ours. Therefore stand back from us, lest our horses' hoofs trample you." For a great while did they thus dispute together, till the queen by her perseverance succeeded in preventing a conflict.

Gregory of Tours (ca. 540-594), *History of the Franks*[17]

The Dowry of a Frankish Princess (584)

[In 584 Princess Rigunth, daughter of King Chilperic, set out for Spain to marry the Visigothic prince Recared.] Chilperic ... ordered many households of serfs to be taken from various royal estates and carried off in wagons. Many of them wept and were loath to go; these he had imprisoned, that he might the more easily send them with his daughter.... King Chilperic ... invited the chief among the Franks and other of his loyal subjects to celebrate the betrothal of his daughter. He then gave her great treasures, and entrusted her to the [Visigothic] envoys. Her mother [Fredegund] also brought out an immense weight of gold and silver, with fine raiment; so much, that at sight of it the king thought nothing was left to him. The queen, seeing him vexed, turned to the Franks and said: "Think not that anything here is taken from the treasures of former kings; everything before your eyes I am presenting from my own possessions. For the most glorious king has given to me generously; but somewhat I have amassed from my own resources, and much I have acquired from the estates granted to me [as a bridal portion], derived both from the revenues and from the taxes. And you, too, have yourselves ofttimes given me a wealth of gifts; from these sources come the things that now lie before you; nothing here is taken from the public treasure." By these words was the king hoodwinked. Such was the multitude of things that the gold, silver, and other ornaments filled fifty wagons. Moreover, the Franks themselves brought many presents, some gold, some silver, some horses; many offered raiment; each gave according to his means.

Gregory of Tours (ca. 540-594), *History of the Franks*[18]

An Enlightened Despot: Chilperic, King of the Franks (561-584)

Chilperic [grandson of Clovis] ... had amphitheatres built at Soissons and at Paris, and began presenting shows to the people.... About the same time [575] King Chilperic wrote an ordinance enjoining that in the Holy Trinity we should make no distinction of Persons, but call it only God, declaring it unseemly that in the case of God we should speak of a Person, as if He were man in the flesh; moreover, he affirmed that the Father is the same as the Son, and the Holy Ghost is the same as the Father and the Son. [His bishops finally dissuaded him.] ...

He also added certain letters to our alphabet, the long *o* of the Greeks, and the *ae, the,* and *wi,* to be represented by the Greek letters omega, psi, zeta, and delta. And he sent letters to all the cities in his kingdom, ordering that they should so be taught to boys, and that old books should be erased with pumice-stone and rewritten with the new characters.

[In 584] Chilperic, the Nero and Herod of our time ... breathed out his wicked soul.... Many a region did he lay waste and burn again and again; whereat he felt no grief, but rather pleasure, like Nero, who of old sang play-verses amid the flames of his palace. Many a time did he unjustly punish men, to confiscate their goods. In his days few priests were raised to bishoprics. He gave himself to gluttony, and his god was his belly. No man, he would declare, was cleverer than he. He wrote two books in verse, taking Sedulius as his model; but as, in his ignorance, he put short syllables for long and long for short, his feeble lines had no feet to stand on. He wrote other short pieces, hymns and chants for the Mass; but by no possibility could they have been used. He hated the cause of the poor. Ever he spoke evil of the priests of the Lord; and in his private hours no men were more often the butt of his ridicule and his jests than the bishops. To one he imputed levity, to a second arrogance, to a third excess, to a fourth loose living; one bishop he would call a vain fool, another pompous. He hated nothing so much as the churches. He would often say: "See how poor our treasury always is! Look how the churches have drained our riches away! Truly, no one at all rules except bishops. Our royal office is lost and gone; it has passed to the bishops in their cities." ... The mind can conceive no lust or debauchery that this man did not practice.

Gregory of Tours (ca. 540-594), History of the Franks[19]

Saint Vulfolaic the Stylite Gets Tit for Tat
(before 585)

[While travelling up the Moselle in 585, Bishop Gregory met Saint Vulfolaic (or Walfroy, in French), a Lombard who told him the story of his life. When young he spent some time in a monastery at Limoges.] "Then I came to the territory of Trèves and on the mountain where you are now built with my own hands the dwelling you see. [It was a monastery with 'a great church.'] I found here an image of Diana which the unbelieving people worshiped as a god. I also built a column on which I stood in my bare feet with great pain. And when the winter had come as usual I was so nipped by the icy cold that the power of the cold often caused my toe-nails to fall off and frozen moisture hung from my beard like candle-wax. For this country is known for its very cold winters."

And when I asked him urgently what food or drink he had and how he destroyed the images on the mountain, he said: "My food and drink were a little bread and vegetables and a small quantity of water. And when a multitude began to flock to me from the neighbouring villages, I preached always that Diana was nothing, that her images and the worship which they thought it well to observe were nothing; and that the songs which they sang at their cups and wild debauches were disgraceful.... And the Lord's mercy turned the rustic mind to listen to my words and to follow the Lord, abandoning their idols.

"Then I gathered some of them together so that by their help I could hurl down the huge image which I could not budge with my own strength, for I had already broken the rest of the small images, which was an easier task. When many had gathered at this statue of Diana, ropes were fastened and they began to pull but their toil could accomplish nothing. Then I hastened to the church and threw myself on the ground and weeping begged the divine mercy that the power of God should destroy that which human energy could not overturn. After praying I went out to the workmen and took hold of the rope, and as soon as I began to pull at once the image fell to the ground where I broke it with iron hammers and reduced it to dust.

"[But the devil returned him tit for tat:] ... and inasmuch as he enviously seeks to injure those who seek God, the bishops, who should have urged me the more to continue wisely the work I had begun, came and said: 'This way which you follow is not the right one, and a baseborn man like you cannot be compared with Simon of Antioch who lived on a column. Moreover the situation of the place does not allow you to endure the hardship. Come down rather and dwell with the brethren you have gathered.' At their words I came down, since not to obey the bishops is called a crime. And I walked and ate with them. And one day the bishop summoned me to a village at a distance and sent workmen with crowbars and hammers and axes and destroyed the column I was accustomed to stand on. I returned the next day and found it all gone. I wept bitterly but could not build again what they had torn down for fear of being called disobedient to the bishop's orders. And since then I am content to dwell with the brothers just as I do now."

Gregory of Tours (ca. 540-594), *History of the Franks*[20]

Saint Columba as a Marriage Counsellor (ca. 585)

When the holy man was a guest in the island of Rechru [Rathlin, off the northern coast of Ireland], a certain layman came to him and complained regarding his wife, who, as he said, had an aversion to him, and would not allow him to sleep with her. Hearing this, the saint bade the wife approach, and began to chide her as well as he could on that account, saying: "Why, woman, do you attempt to put from you your own flesh? The Lord says, 'Two shall be in one flesh.' Therefore the flesh of your husband is your flesh." She replied: "I am ready to perform all things whatsoever that you may enjoin on me, however burdensome: save one thing, that you do not constrain me to sleep in one bed with

Lugne. I do not refuse to carry on the whole management of the house; or, if you command it, even to cross the seas and remain in some monastery of nuns." Then the saint said: "What you suggest cannot rightly be done. Since your husband is still alive, you are bound by the law of the husband; for it is forbidden that that should be separated that God has lawfully joined." After saying this, he continued: "On this day let us three—myself, and the husband with his wife—pray to the Lord, fasting." Then she said: "I know it will not be impossible that things appearing difficult or even impossible may be granted by God to you, when you ask for them."

In short, the wife agreed to fast on the same day, and the husband also, with the saint. And on the night following, in sleep, the saint prayed for them. On the next day the saint thus addressed the wife, in the presence of her husband: "Woman, are you today, as you said yesterday, ready to depart to a monastery of nuns?" She said: "I know now that your prayer concerning me has been heard by God. For him whom I loathed yesterday I love today. In this past night (how, I do not know) my heart has been changed in me from hate to love."

Why prolong the story? From that day until the day of her death, that wife's affections were indissolubly set in love of her husband; so that the dues of the marriage bed, which she had formerly refused to grant, she never again denied.

Adamnan, Life of Columba (ca. 690)[21]

The Bishops of Gaul Insist that Women are Human (585)

At this council [held in Mâcon] there was a certain bishop who defended the opinion that women could not be included under the general description "man" (*homo*); but he accepted the reasoning of his brethren and said no more. Their arguments were as follows: the holy book of the Old Testament teaches that in the beginning, when God created man, "He created them male and female, and called their name Adam" [Gen. 5:2], which name being interpreted means "earthly man"; even so He called the woman Eve; of both He used the word "man" (*homo*). And the Lord Jesus Christ is therefore called Son of man, because he was the Virgin's son, which is to say, the son of a woman.... They brought other convincing testimony, and there this matter rested.

Gregory of Tours (ca. 540-594), *History of the Franks.*[22]

Wine and Winnoch the Breton (577-585)

At this time [587] Winnoch the Breton, one most austere in fasting, came to Tours, desiring to visit Jerusalem; his only garments were of sheepskin shorn of the wool. In order to induce him to abide with us, as he seemed to us of great holiness, we conferred on him the dignity of the priesthood. Ingitrude, the religious, was in the habit of collecting water from the tomb of the holy Martin [because, in being used to wash the tomb, the water acquired miraculous healing powers]. Water one day failing, she asked leave to bring a vessel of wine to the saint's tomb. After it had remained there a whole night, she ordered it to be taken up in the presence of this priest, and when it was brought to her she said to him: "Draw off some wine, and pour in a single drop of the blessed water, of which I have but a little left." He did so; and, wondrous to relate, the vessel, which had been half empty, was filled to the brim on the falling into of it of the single drop. Likewise, when it had been emptied two or three times again, each time one drop filled it. Without doubt the power of the blessed Martin was seen in this....

Since the prince of darkness has a thousand harmful arts, I will relate what recently befell certain hermits and persons dedicated to God [about the year 585]. After Winnoch the Breton was ordained priest, he vowed himself to such abstinence that he used only skins for clothing, and, for food, uncooked herbs of the field; while he would do no more than set the winecup to his mouth, seeming rather to touch it with his lips than to drink. But the pious were free-handed; he was too often given brimming cups of wine, and learned, alas! to drink beyond measure, being so overcome by his potations that he was often seen drunken. The end whereof was that, his intemperance growing upon him as time passed, he was possessed by a demon and driven to such madness that he would take a knife or any other weapon, whether a stone or a club, upon which he could lay hands, and rush after people in an insane fury, till at last he had to be bound with chains and imprisoned in a cell. Two years he passed raging in this punishment, and then gave up the ghost.

Gregory of Tours (ca. 540-594) *History of the Franks*[23]

The Conversion of King Recared (587)

In Spain at this time [587, the Visigothic] King Recared, touched by God's mercy, convoked the bishops of his own [heretical Arian] church and said: "Between you and those bishops who proclaim themselves Catholics, wherefore are causes of offence spread without ceasing? Why is it that these by their faith perform many miracles, while you are unable to do as they? Meet together, therefore, I beg you; discuss the doctrines of both parties, and let us discover which are true. Then either must they accept our arguments and believe what you profess, or you in your turn must recognize the truth of their creed and believe that which they preach."

It was done; and in an assembly of bishops of the two parties the [Arian] heretics made the profession of [their] faith.... In like manner the Catholic bishops replied with [their] arguments.... The king maintained that the heretic bishops wrought no miracles for the healing of the sick.... He then called aside the bishops of the Lord and questioned them about their doctrines.... Having understood the truth, Recared put an end to all dispute, submitted to the Catholic law, and received the sign of the blessed Cross with unction of holy chrism.... He then sent messengers to the [Visigothic] province of Narbonne to relate what he had done, so the people in those parts might join with him in the same faith.

Gregory of Tours (ca. 540-594), *History of the Franks*[24]

Stranger than Science Fiction (587)

Many prodigies were now seen [in the year 587]. In the houses of various persons, vessels were found inscribed with unknown characters which could in no wise be either scraped or rubbed away. This wonder began in the territory of Chartres, and passing by way of Orleans, reached that of Bordeaux, leaving out no single intermediate city.

Gregory of Tours (ca. 540-594), *History of the Franks*[25]

A Frankish Nun
Between her Husband and Mother-Superior (589)

At this time [589] Ingitrude, who had founded a nunnery in the fore-court of Saint Martin's church at Tours, went to the king to complain of her daughter.... The matter between Ingitrude and her daughter I think it well to relate from its beginning. When, some years before, Ingitrude founded the convent, as I have said, within the forecourt of Martin, she sent a message to her daughter, to the following effect: "Leave your husband and come to me so I may make you abbess of this flock which I have assembled." Her daughter, on receiving this foolish advice, came with her husband to Tours, where she entered her mother's nunnery, saying to him: "Return hence and look after our property and our children; I shall not go back with you. For none that is joined in wedlock shall behold the kingdom of God." But the husband sought me and told me all that his wife had said. Thereupon I [Bishop Gregory of Tours] went to the nunnery and there read aloud those canons of the Nicene Council in which it is said: "If a woman abandon her husband and spurn the nuptial state in which she has lived with honour, on the plea that she who has been joined in wedlock shall have no part in the glory of the celestial kingdom, let her be accursed" [actually c.14 of the Council of Gangres, ca. A.D. 340]. When she heard this, Berthegund was afraid of excommunication at the hands of the bishops of God; she therefore quitted the convent and returned home with her husband.

But after three or four years the mother again sent her a message entreating her to come to her. Thereupon she loaded vessels with her own goods and those of her husband, who was away from home, took one of her sons with her, and came to Tours. But her mother could not keep her there on account of the husband's obstinate pursuit; she also feared to become involved in the charge [of theft] to which her daughter had exposed them both by her dishonesty. She therefore sent her to Bertram, bishop of Bordeaux, her own son and brother of Berthegund. The husband following her, the bishop said to him: "She shall no longer be your wife because you married her without the assent of her parents." At this time, be it said, they had been married nearly thirty years. The husband came several times to Bordeaux, but the bishop always refused to give her up.... [Finally, under pressure from the king, the bishop could no longer protect his sister, so he advised her] to put off her secular garb, do penance, and withdraw to the church of the holy Martin; which things she straightway did. Her husband then came with a following of many men to remove her from the sacred place. She was in the habit of a nun and declared that she was vowed to penitence; she therefore refused to go with him.

Meanwhile [her brother] Bishop Bertram died at Bordeaux. She now came to her senses and said: "Woe is me, that ever I listened to the advice of a wicked mother. My brother is dead; I am forsaken by my husband and separated from my children. Where shall I go in my misery? what shall I do now?" After reflecting for awhile, she decided to go to Poitiers; and though her mother wanted to keep her with her, she did not have her way. In consequence enmity arose between them and they were always coming before the king in a dispute about property....

Gregory of Tours, (ca. 540-594), *History of the Franks*[26]

Another Merovingian Mother-Daughter Quarrel (ca. 589)

Rigunth, daughter of [the late King] Chilperic, was always attacking her mother [Queen Fredegund], declaring that she was the real mistress [because she had been born a lady] and that her mother owed her service [because she had been born a serf]. The daughter would often assail her mother with abuse, and sometimes they even came to blows and slapped one another. Once day her mother said to her: "Why do you keep nagging me, daughter? Here are your father's possessions which I have under my control; take them and do what you want to with them." She then went into her treasure chamber and opened a chest full of necklets and precious ornaments, for a long time taking out one thing after another and handing them to her daughter, who stood by. At last Fredegund said: "I am tired. Put your hand in and take out whatever you may find." Rigunth put her arm into the chest to take out more things, when her mother seized the lid and forced it down upon the girl's neck. She pressed down upon it with all her strength until the edge of the chest beneath pressed the girl's throat so hard that her eyes seemed about to pop from her head. Then one of the maids who was there cried out as loud as she could: "Help, help! my mistress is being choked to death by her mother!" The attendants outside, who were waiting for them to come out, broke into the small chamber and brought out the girl whom they thus saved from the threat of death. Afterwards the hatred of mother and daughter flared up ever more fiercely, for the most part ending in brawls and blows. The chief cause lay in the sexual misconduct of Rigunth.

Gregory of Tours (ca. 540-594), *History of the Franks*[27]

Scenes from the Scriptorium of Saint Columba (died 597)

One day [at Columba's monastery on the island of Iona off the eastern coast of Scotland, his assistant] Baithene went to the saint and said: "I have need of one of the brothers, to run through and emend with me the psalter that I have written." Hearing this, the saint spoke thus: "Why do you impose this trouble upon us, without cause? Since in this psalter of yours, of which you speak, neither will one letter be found to be superfluous, nor another to have been left out; except a vowel *I*, which alone is missing." And so, when the whole psalter had been read through, exactly what the saint had foretold was found to be confirmed....

[On the day that Columba died, 7/8 June 597] he returned to the monastery, and sat in the hut, writing a psalter. And when he came to that verse of the thirty-third Psalm where it is written, "But they that seek the Lord shall not want for anything that is good," he said: "Here, at the end of the page, I must stop. Let Baithene write what follows."

The last verse that he wrote aptly befits the holy predecessor, who will never lack eternal good things. And the verse that follows, "Come, my sons, hear me; I will teach you the fear of the Lord," is fittingly adapted to the successor, the father of spiritual sons, a teacher, who, as his predecessor enjoined, succeeded him not in teaching only, but in writing also.

After he had written the former verse, at the end of the page, the saint entered the church for the vesper office of the Lord's night. As soon as that was finished, he returned to his lodging, [slept until the midnight bell, then ran to the church and died there as his monks assembled for matins].

Adamnan, *Life of Columba* (ca. 690)[28]

Queen Brunhilda's Exile (599)

In this year [599] Brunechildis [Brunhilda] was hunted out of Austrasia. A poor man found her wandering alone near Arcis in Champagne and took her, at her request, to Theuderic [king of Burgundy] who made his grandmother welcome and treated her with ceremony. Brunechildis had the poor man made bishop of Auxerre in return for the service he had done her.

The Chronical of Fredegar (written ca. 614)[29]

The Seventh Century

Who Knows Everything? (ca. 600)

You only become wise when you realise your own unwisdom, as may be seen in this story which I have heard. In the time of Khusraw Parwîz [Chosroës II of Persia], when the vizier was Buzurjmihr [or Burzûya, who brought the game of chess from India], an envoy arrived from Rome [i.e. Byzantium]. As was the custom of the Persian kings, Khusraw seated himself upon the throne and, while giving audience to the envoy, was desirous of displaying his pride in having so wise a vizier in his service. But the envoy, addressing the vizier, demanded, "Oh, Thus-and-thus, do you know everything in the world?" Buzurjmihr replied, "I do not, O lord of the world." Enraged at the reply and abashed before the envoy, Khusraw inquired, "Who is it then that knows all?" Buzurjmihr answered, "It is the whole of mankind that knows everything, and the whole of mankind has not yet been born."

There is a story of how during Chosroës' [or Khusraw] reign a woman presented herself before Buzurjmihr and asked him a question. His thoughts being elsewhere at the moment, he replied that he did not know, whereat the woman remarked, "If you do not know, why do you enjoy your master's bounty?" "It is for what I know," he replied. "The king gives me nothing for what I do not know, and if you do not understand that, come and inquire of the king."

Kai Kâ'ûs ibn Iskandar, *A Mirror for Princes* (1082)[1]

The Pope Scolds a Clergyman
for Teaching Latin Literature (601)

Gregory to Desiderius, bishop of [Vienne in] Gaul. Many good things having been reported to us with regard to your pursuits, such joy arose in our heart that we could not bear to refuse your request. But it afterwards came to our ears, what we cannot mention without shame, that you are in the habit of expounding grammar to certain persons. This thing we took so much amiss, and so strongly disapproved it, that we changed what had been said before into groaning and sadness, since the praises of Christ cannot find room in one mouth with the praises of Jupiter. And consider yourself what a grave and heinous offence it is for bishops to sing what is not becoming even for a religious layman. And, though our most beloved son Candidus the priest, having been, when he came to us, strictly examined on this matter, denied it, and endeavoured to excuse you, yet still the thought has not departed from our mind that in proportion as it is execrable for such a thing to be related of a clergyman, it ought to be ascertained by strict and veracious evidence whether or not it be so. Whence, if hereafter what has been reported to us should prove evidently to be false, and it should be clear that you do not apply yourself to trifles and secular literature, we shall give thanks to our God, who has not permitted your heart to be stained with the blasphemous praises of the abominable; and without misgiving or hesitation we will reconsider your request....

Pope Gregory I the Great (590-604), *Letters.*2

How the English Got Tails (604)

After this, Saint Augustine [of Canturbury] entered into Dorsetshire and came into a town where there were wicked people who utterly rejected his teaching and preaching. They threw at him the tails of thornbacks and similar fishes; so he prayed God to show his judgment on them, and God sent them a shameful token: for the children that were born afterwards in that place had tails, it is said, as long as this folk was unrepentant. It is commonly said that this happened at Strood in Kent, but blessed be God, no such deformity occurs there in our time.

William Caxton's *Golden Legend* (1483)[3]

Protadius: A Merovingian Mayor of the Palace (605)

In the tenth year of his reign [605] and at the wish of Brunechildis [or Brunhilda, his grandmother, King] Theuderic made Protadius mayor of the palace [i.e. prime minister for the kingdom of Burgundy]. In every way Protadius was as clever and as capable as a man could be, but in certain cases he was monstrously cruel, extorting the last penny for the fisc [treasury] and with ingenuity both filling the fisc and enriching himself at the expense of others. He set himself to undermine all those of noble birth, so that nobody could deprive him of the position he had acquired. In these and other ways his excessive cunning harassed everyone, and not least the Burgundians, every man of whom he made his enemy.

Brunechildis was persistent in urging her grandson Theuderic to attack [his brother] Theudebert [king of Austrasia]; he was a gardener's son, she declared, not [her son] Childebert's. Protadius concurring with this advice, Theuderic at length gave orders to raise a force. While they were encamped at a place called Quierzy, Theuderic's warriors begged him to come to terms with Theudebert, Protadius alone urging battle; for Theudebert and his men were not far away. Thereupon all the warriors took their chance to set upon Protadius—a single death, in their view, being a great deal preferable to the endangering of a whole army.

Protadius was sitting in King Theuderic's tent playing dice with Peter, the court physician. The warriors surrounded the tent and his men-at-arms detained Theuderic in case he should enter. However, the king sent Uncelen with orders that they should stop molesting Protadius. Uncelen, on the contrary, forthwith declared to the warriors: "The Lord Theuderic orders Protadius' execution!" Accordingly they cut the royal tent to ribbons and hurled themselves on Protadius and killed him. Theuderic, now not knowing what he was doing, was made to agree to terms with his brother Theudebert. The two forces went home without a fight.

The Chronicle of Fredegar (written ca. 614).[4]

Not-So-Romantic Adventures Among the Avars (611)

The king of the Avars, whom they call Kagan in their language, came with a countless multitude and invaded the territories around Venice. Gisulf, the duke of Friuli, boldly came to meet him with all the Lombards he could get, but although he waged war with a few against an immense multitude with indomitable courage, nevertheless he was surrounded on every side and killed with nearly all his followers.

The wife of this Gisulf, Romilda by name, together with the Lombards who had escaped and with the wives and children of those who had perished in war, fortified herself within the walls of the fortress of Cividale [the town of Friuli]. She had two sons, Tasso and Cacco, who were already growing youths, and [two others] Raduald and Grimoald, who were still in the age of boyhood. And she also had four daughters, of whom one was called Appa and another Gaila, but of two we do not preserve the names.

The Avars, roaming through all the territories of Friuli, devastating everything with burnings and plunderings, shut up the town of Friuli by siege and strove with all their might to capture it. While their king, i.e. the kagan, was ranging around the walls in full armour with a great company of horsemen to find out from what side he might more easily capture the city, Romilda gazed upon him from the walls, and when she beheld him in the bloom of his youth, the abominable harlot was seized with desire for him and straightway sent word to him by a messenger that if he would take her in marriage she would deliver to him the city with all who were in it. Tha barbarian king, hearing this, promised her with wicked cunning that he would do what she had stipulated, and he vowed that he would take her in marriage. Without delay she then opened the gates of the fortress of Friuli and let the enemy in—to her own ruin and that of all who were there.

The Avars indeed with their king, having entered Friuli, laid waste with their plunderings everything they could discover, consumed in flames the city itself, and carried away as captives everybody they found, falsely promising them, however, to settle them in the territories of Pannonia [western Hungary], from which they had come. When on their return to their country they had come to the plain they called Sacred, they decreed that all the Lombards who had attained full age should perish by the sword, and that slavery was to be the lot of the women and children.

But Tasso and Cacco and Raduald, the sons of Gisulf and Romilda, when they knew the evil intention of the Avars, straightway mounted their horses and took flight. One of them, when he thought that his brother Grimoald, a little boy, could not keep himself upon a running horse, since he was so small, considered it better that he should perish by the sword than bear the yoke of captivity, and wanted to kill him. When therefore, he lifted his lance to pierce him through, the boy wept and cried out, saying: "Do not strike me for I can keep on a horse." And his brother, seizing him by the arm, put him upon the bare back of a horse and urged him to stay there if he could; and the boy, taking the rein of the horse in his hand, followed his fleeing brothers.

The Avars, when they learned this, mounted their horses and followed them, but although the others escaped by swift flight, the little boy Grimoald was taken by one of those who had run up most swiftly. His captor, however, did not condescend to strike him with the sword on account of his slender age, but rather kept him to be his servant. So the Avar took hold of the bridle of the horse and led the boy away, back towards the Avar camp, and he exulted over so noble a booty—for the little fellow was of elegant form with gleaming eyes and a full head of long blonde hair.... But Grimoald had a small sword, such as he was able to carry at that age; he took it out of the scabbard and struck the Avar who was leading him, with what little strength he could, on the top of the head. The blow passed right through to the skull and the enemy was thrown from his horse. And the boy turned his own horse around and took flight, greatly rejoicing, and at last joined his brothers and gave them incalculable joy by his escape and by announcing, moreover, the destruction of his enemy. [Grimoald grew up to be king of the Lombards, 662-671.]

The Avars now killed by the sword all the Lombards who were already of the age of manhood, but they made slaves of the women and children. Romilda indeed, who had been the cause of all this evil-doing, was kept for one night, as if in marriage, by the king of the Avars, who thus fulfilled his promise to her. But the next night he turned her over to twelve Avars, who abused her through the whole night with their lust, succeeding each other by turns. Afterwards too, ordering a stake to be fixed in the midst of a field, he commanded her to be impaled upon the point of it, uttering these words, moreover, in reproach: "It is fit you should have such a husband." Therefore the detestable betrayer of her country, who looked out for her own lust more than for the preservation of her fellow citizens and kindred, perished by such a death.

Her daughters, indeed, did not follow the sensual inclination of their mother, but striving from love of chastity not to be contaminated by the barbarians, they put the flesh of raw chickens between their breasts, under the band that covered them, and the flesh, when putrified by the heat, gave out an evil smell. And the Avars, when they wanted to touch them, could not endure the stench that they thought was natural to them, but moved far away from them with cursing, saying that all the Lombard women had a bad smell. By this trick then the noble girls, escaping from the lust of the Avars, not only kept themselves chaste but handed down a useful example for preserving chastity if any such thing should happen to women hereafter.

Paul the Deacon, *History of the Lombards* (ca. 799)[5]

The Execution of Brunhilda (613)

[In 613 Queen Brunhilda, or Brunechildis, was deserted by her troops, who refused to fight against the Franks of King Lothar, or Chlotar, II of Neustria.]   Brunechildis was arrested at the villa of Orbe, in Transjuran territory, by the constable Herpo and taken to Chlotar.... Brunechildis was brought before Chlotar, who was boiling with fury against her. He charged her with the deaths of ten Frankish kings—namely [her first husband] Sigebert, [her second husband] Merovech, [Lothar's father] Chilperic, [her grandson] Theudebert and his son Chlotar, Chlotar's son the other Merovech, [her other grandson] Theuderic and Theuderic's three sons who had just perished [by order of Lothar himself]. She was tormented for three days with a diversity of tortures, and then on his orders was led through the ranks on a camel. Finally she was tied by her hair, one arm, and one leg to the tail of an unbroken horse, and she was cut to shreds by its hoofs at the pace it went.

The Chronicle of Fredegar (written ca. 614).[6]

How Samo Acquired His Kingdom (623)

In the fortieth year of Chlotar's reign [623], a certain Frank named Samo, from the district of Soignies, joined with other merchants in order to go and do business with those Slavs who are known as Wends. The Slavs had already started to rise against the Avars (called Huns) and against their ruler, the khagan. The Wends had long since been subjected to the Huns.... Whenever the Huns took the field against another people, they stayed encamped in battle array while the Wends did the fighting. If the Wends won, the Huns advanced to pillage, but if they lost the Huns backed them up and they resumed the fight.... Every year the Huns wintered with the Slavs, sleeping with their wives and daughters, and in addition the Slavs paid tribute and endured many other burdens. The sons born to the Huns by the Slavs' wives and daughters eventually found this shameful oppression intolerable; and so, as I said, they refused to obey their lords and started to rise in rebellion. When they took the field against the Huns, Samo, the merchant of whom I have spoken, went with them and his bravery won their admiration: an astonishing number of Huns were put to the sword by the Wends. Recognising his parts, the Wends made Samo their king; and he ruled them well for thirty-five years. Several times they fought under his leadership against the Huns and his prudence and courage always brought the Wends victory. Samo had twelve Wendish wives, who bore him twenty-two sons and fifteen daughters.

Addition to *The Chronicle of Fredegar* (before 660)[7]

A Lombard Queen's Trial by Combat (623)

The lovely Queen Gundeberga was in all things good-natured and full of Christian piety. She was generous in almsgiving and universally loved for her bounty. A certain Lombard named Adalulf, who was constantly at court in the king's service, one day found himself in her presence. The queen was as well disposed to him as she was to all others and accordingly remarked what a fine upstanding man he was. Hearing this, he said quietly to the queen, "You deign to like my looks; pray, then, bid me sleep with you." But she violently refused and spat in his face to show her contempt for him.

Adalulf saw that he had endangered his life and thereupon made haste to [her husband] King Charoald, for whom he said he had secret information. An audience being granted, he said to the king: "My lady Queen Gundeberga has for three days been scheming with [the rebel] Duke Taso [of Tuscany]. She wants to poison you and then marry him and place him on the throne." King Charoald took these lies seriously. He sent the queen into exile to the fortress of Lomello, where she was shut up in a tower.

Chlotar [II, king of the Franks] sent a deputation to Charoald to enquire why he had humiliated his kinswoman Queen Gundeberga, and sent her into exile. Charoald replied by reporting the above-mentioned lies as if they had been the truth, whereat Ansoald, one of the deputation, remarked to Charoald as if on his own account, without any authority: "You could get out of this difficulty without loss of face by ordering your informer to arm himself and do single combat with a representative of the queen. By such combat the judgment of God would determine Gundeberga's innocence or—who can tell?—guilt."

King Charoald and all his magnates liked this advice. Adalulf was ordered to arm himself for the fight; while Gundeberga and her cousin Aripert arranged that a certain Pitto should be Adalulf's opponent in arms. They fought, and Pitto killed Adalulf. So Gundeberga was forthwith reestablished as queen, after three years in exile.

Addition to *The Chronicle of Fredegar* (before 660)[8]

The Conversion of Northumbria (627)

King Edwin hesitated to receive the word of God from the preaching of Paulinus.... He would sit alone for hours on end considering what he was to do and what religion he was to follow.... [Finally] he answered that he was both willing and bound to receive the [Christian] faith which Paulinus taught, but he wanted to confer first with his principal friends and counsellors so that, if they shared his opinion, they might all be cleansed together in the fountain of life. When Paulinus agreed, the king carried out his plan. He called a council of his wise men and asked each one in turn what he thought of the new doctrine and the new worship that were being preached.

Coifi, the chief priest, immediately replied: "O king, you should pay good attention to the doctrine that is now being preached to us, because I indeed admit that as far as I can tell the religion which we have followed up to now lacks power. For none of your people has devoted himself more diligently to the worship of our gods than I have, and yet there are many men who receive greater favours from you, and are honoured more, and are more successful in all their affairs. Now if the gods were good for anything, they would have favoured me instead, because I have been more zealous in serving them. Consequently, if after examining these new doctrines which have been preached to us, you decide they are better and more potent, let us receive them immediately and without any delay."

Another of the king's chief men expressed his agreement with Coifi's arguments and conclusion, to which he added: "O king, let me compare the present life of man with that time which is unknown to us. This life is like the swift flight of a sparrow through the hall where you sit in winter feasting with your ealdormen and thegns, warmed by a good fire while some storm of rain or snow rages outside. The sparrow who flies quickly in one door and out the other is safe from the winter storm while he is inside, but after this moment of calm he disappears into the dark storm from which he came. Just so this life of man lasts for a brief moment, but of what went before, or what is to follow, we are utterly ignorant. If this new doctrine brings us more certainty, then it seems right that we follow it.

Other elders and royal counsellors, being inspired by God, gave the same advice. Coifi added that he wished to hear Paulinus tell more about his God, which he did at the king's command. After hearing him, Coifi cried out: "I have known for a long time that our cult is worthless, because the harder I looked for truth in our religion, the less I found it. But now I freely confess that the truth appears plainly in this doctrine, which can confer on us the gifts of life, salvation, and eternal happiness. Therefore it is my advice, O king, that we immediately desert and set fire to those temples and altars that we have held sacred without reaping any benefit from them."

In short, the king publicly gave his approval to Paulinus's mission and himself renounced idolatry and confessed his faith in Christ. When he asked the pagan high priest who should be the first to profane the altars and shrines of their idols, together with the temple precincts, Coifi answered: "I will. For who can set a better example than I can? Those things that I worshipped through ignorance I will destroy though the wisdom given me by the true God!" He then asked the king to supply him with arms and a stallion, which he did in contempt of his former superstitions, for the high priest was forbidden to bear arms or to ride except on a mare. But Coifi girded himself with a sword, took a spear in his hand, mounted the king's stallion, and rode off to destroy the idols. Most people who saw him thought he was crazy, but he paid no attention; as soon as he got to the shrine, he profaned it by casting therein the spear he was holding. Then, rejoicing in the knowledge of the worship of the true God, he commanded his companions to destroy the shrine and all its precincts by setting them afire. This place where idols once stood is still shown, not far from York....

Bede (d. 735), *Ecclesiastical History*[9]

"Good King Dagobert"
Weighed in a Monk's Balance (629)

In the eighth year of his reign, while he was making a royal progress through Austrasia, Dagobert admitted to his bed a girl named Ragnetrudis; and by her he had, in the course of the year, a son named Sigebert. Then he returned to Neustria and, finding that he liked his father Chlotar's residence, decided to make it his home. But he forgot the justice that he had once loved. He longed for ecclesiastical property and for the goods of his subjects and greedily sought by every means to amass fresh treasure. He surrendered himself to limitless debauchery, having three queens and mistresses beyond number. The queens were Nantechildis, Wulfegundis, and Berchildis; the names of his mistresses it would be wearisome to insert in this chronicle—there were too many of them. And so his heart was corrupted, as we noted earlier, and his thoughts turned away from God; but—and would that this might have profited him to the obtaining of his true reward!—he had once been prodigal in his almsgiving; and had this earlier wise almsgiving not foundered through the promptings of cupidity, he would indeed in the end have merited the eternal kingdom.

Addition to *The Chronicle of Fredegar* (before 660)[10]

Cadwallon: The Wrong Kind of Christian (633)

Edwin reigned most gloriously for seventeen years over English and British peoples ... when Caedwalla [or Cadwallon in Welsh], king of the Britons, rebelled against him. He was supported by Penda, a most warlike [English] man of the royal family of Mercia.... A great battle was fought on the plain that is called Haethfelth [Hatfield Chase] and Edwin was killed.... At this time [633] there was a great slaughter of the clergy and people in Northumbria, which was worse because of the two kings who were responsible for the massacre, since one was a heathen and the other a barbarian who was even more cruel than a heathen. For Penda and the whole Mercian people worshipped idols and cared nothing for the name of Christ, but Cadwallon, although nominally a professed Christian, was so barbarous in his behaviour and feelings that he spared neither women nor innocent children. With savage cruelty he had them tortured to death and ravaged their country for a long time, because he wanted to exterminate all Englishmen living in territory that he considered British. Nor did he have any respect for the Christian religion, which the English had recently accepted. Indeed, even today [a century later] the Britons habitually do not consider the English to be true Christians but treat them instead like pagans.

Bede (d. 735), *Ecclesiastical History*[11]

A Punny Scientist:
Isidore of Seville on Bees (before 636)

Bees (*apes*) are so called because they interlock with one another with their feet (*pedibus*, from *pes*), or for the reason that they are born without feet [*a* + *pes*]. For they get their feet and wings later on. Being assiduous in the task of manufacturing honey, they live in the places assigned to them, put together hives with indescribable skill, establish the honeycomb from various flowers, fill their encampment in structured wax with numberless offspring, have armies and kings, start battles, avoid smoke, and are upset by disorder. Many people have found that bees are born from the corpses of cattle, for in order to produce them, the flesh of slain calves is pounded so that worms are created from the putrified blood which afterwards become bees. Those creatures which arise from cattle are properly called bees, just as beetles come from horses, drones from mules, and wasps from donkeys. The Greeks call those creatures "costri" [*oistroi!*] which are born of larger size in the farthest part of the hives. Others call them "kings." They are so called because they lead the swarm. A drone is bigger than a bee, smaller than a beetle. It is called a drone (*fugus*) because it eats the produce of others [*fagus*, "eater"] like a parasite, for it feeds where it has not laboured. Concerning it, Virgil says: "They ward off the lazy race of drones from the nursery" [*Georgics* 4.168].

Isidore of Seville (d. 636), *Etymologies.*[12]

Saint Oswald's Miraculous Dirt (after 641)

[In 641] Oswald, the most Christian king of Northumbria ... was killed in a great battle by [Penda] ... the same heathen king of Mercia who had killed his predecessor Edwin, in a place which in the English tongue is called *Maserfelth* [Maserfield].... In that place where he was killed by the heathen while fighting for his country, sick men and cattle are healed to this day [731]. People have frequently taken soil from the place where his body fell and, after putting it in water, have done much good with it for their sick friends. This custom became so popular that the gradual removal of earth has left a hole as deep as a man's height....

The story is told that [not long after Oswald's death] a Briton was travelling near the place where the battle had been fought, when he noticed that one particular patch of ground was greener and more beautiful than any other part of the field. He wisely guessed that the cause of this unusual greenness could only be that some man more holy than any other in the army had been killed there. Therefore he wrapped some of the soil up in a cloth and took it along with him because he thought that sooner or later it might prove useful for curing the sick.

Continuing on his way, at nightfall the traveller came to a certain village and entered a house where the villagers were feasting together. The owners of the house invited him to join them, so he sat down to enjoy the feast with them, but first he hung up the cloth containing the dirt on a post by the wall. They sat long at supper and drank hard, while a great fire burned in the middle of the room. A few sparks happened to fly up to the roof, which was made of wattles thatched with hay, and suddenly it burst into flames. The guests were terrified; as they were in no state to fight the fire, they fled outside. Consequently the house burned down, except for the post on which the bag with the dirt was hanging; this alone remained intact and untouched. All who saw this miracle were amazed and sought an explanation. Eventually they discovered that the soil had been taken from the place where King Oswald had shed his lifeblood.

Bede (d. 735), *Ecclesiastical History*[13]

The Destruction of the Alexandrian Library (642)

Yahyâ [John the Grammarian, a Greek philosopher] lived until 'Amr ibn al-'As conquered Egypt and Alexandria. He went to see 'Amr, who was well informed about his vast knowledge, his creed, and what happened between him and the Christians. 'Amr respected him highly and saw that he was really worthy of great honour.... One day Yahyâ said to him: "You have already put all the depots of Alexandria under your control and sealed everything in it. I have no objection as to the things which may be of any use to you, but as for those other things of which you and your people can make no use, we should rather have them. Please give orders to set them free." "What are the things that you need?" He answered: "The books of wisdom which are in the royal treasuries...." 'Amr felt that what Yahyâ said was important and kept wondering about it and said: "I cannot dispose of these books without the permission of 'Umar ibn al-Khittab [the caliph]." He then wrote to 'Umar [in Damascus] telling him all that Yahyâ said and asked him to instruct him as to what he should do with them. 'Umar in his answer said: "... and as for the books you mentioned: if their contents agree with the Book of Allah [the Koran], we can dispense with them, as the Book of Allah is—in this case—more than enough. If they contain anything against what is in the Book of Allah, there is no need to keep them. Go on and destroy them." 'Amr began, upon receiving these instructions, to distribute them among the baths of Alexandria to be burnt in their stoves.... It is related that the baths took six months to burn them.

Ali ibn al-Kifti (1172-1248), Ta'rikh al-Hukama[14]

O Most Trivial Art! (ca. 650)

Galbungus and Terence [two grammarians in southern Gaul] are actually reported to have spent fourteen whole days and nights debating to determine whether, according to all the works of the ancient grammarians that were available to them, the pronoun *ego* ["I"] did or did not have a vocative case. Terence denied that *ego* has a vocative case because the vocative case must always be joined to the second person, whereas *ego* is always in the first person. Galbungus, however, maintained that this pronoun could be in the vocative case, especially in a question when the verb is in the first person: e.g. *"O egone recte feci vel* *dixi?* (*O ego*, have I acted and spoken rightly?),*" even though this voca-tive (i.e. *ego*) could not exist out of context but needed the support of *O* and *ne* surrounding it.

Virgil the Grammarian, *Letters to Julian* (ca. 650)[15]

Bede's Obituary of Saint Aidan (died 651)

I have written much in my history about the character and work of Aidan [bishop of Lindesfarne], but this does not mean that I endorse or praise his misunderstanding about the correct time to observe Easter. On the contrary, I detest his view of the matter, as I have clearly shown in the book I have written *De temporibus*. Nonetheless, as an impartial his-torian I have related what was done by him or through him, praising what was praiseworthy and preserving the memory of such deeds for my readers.

Praiseworthy in him were: his love of peace and charity; his conti-nence and humility; his mind that rose above anger and avarice while despising pride and vainglory; his industry in keeping and teaching the divine commandments; his diligence in reading and in keeping vigil; his exemplary conduct as a priest, not only in rebuking the proud and the powerful but also in tenderly comforting the weak and relieving or pro-tecting the poor. In sum, as far as I can learn from those who knew him, Aidan was careful not to omit any of the commands of the gospels, the apostles, and the prophets; instead, he tried to obey them all as far as he was able.

I greatly admire and love these things in that bishop because I have no doubt that they were pleasing to God. But I cannot praise or ap-prove of his failure to observe Easter at the proper time, either because he was ignorant of the law of the Church or because he knew it but was forced by public opinion to ignore it.

Bede (d. 735), *Ecclesiastical History*[16]

A Royal English Monk Dies in Battle (652?)

At this time Sigeberht ruled the kingdom of the East Angles.... He was a good and religious man who had lived in exile for a long time in France, where he had been baptized.... When he returned home and became king, he wanted to imitate some of the good institutions that he had seen in France, so he set up a school where boys could learn Latin. The plan was implemented by Bishop Felix [of East Anglia], who had come to him from Kent and who supplied him with masters and teachers, as was the custom in France.

Sigeberht loved the kingdom of heaven so much that he finally abdicated the crown in favour of his brother Ecgric, who previously had ruled part of the kingdom, and entered a monastery that he had built. There he received the tonsure [of a monk] and so became a warrior only for the heavenly kingdom.

After Sigeberht had been in the monastery for some time, King Penda and his Mercians attacked the East Angles. The East Angles realized that they were no match for their enemies, so they begged Sigeberht to accompany them into battle in order to inspire the soldiers with confidence. When he refused, they dragged him from the monastery against his will and brought him to the army in the hope that the soldiers would be less apt to flee when accompanied by one who had been a famous and brave commander. But Sigeberht did not forget his monastic vows; although he was placed at the head of the royal army, he refused to carry anything but a staff in his hand. He was killed along with King Ecgric, and then their whole army was either slaughtered or scattered by the heathen.

Bede (d. 735), *Ecclesiastical History*[17]

The Rise of Islam as Seen from Frankland (ca. 660)

In the reign of Constans [Byzantine emperor, 641-668], the empire suffered very great devastation at the hands of the Saracens. Having taken Jerusalem [637] and razed other cities, they attacked upper and lower Egypt, took and plundered Alexandria [643], devastated and quickly occupied the whole of Roman Africa, and killed there the patrician Gregory [647]. Only Constantinople, the province of Thrace, a few islands, and the duchy of Rome remained in imperial control, for the greater part of the empire had been overrun by Saracens. So reduced, Constans became in the last resort their tributary, merely controlling Constantinople and a handful of provinces and islands [654]. It is said that for three years and more Constans paid one thousand gold solidi a day to the Saracens; but then he somewhat recovered his strength, little by little won back his empire, and refused to pay tribute [658].

Addition to *The Chronicle of Fredegar* (written before 660)[18]

Columba vs. Peter: The Council of Whitby (664)

In those days there arose a great and recurrent controversy about the observance of Easter. Those who had come [to Northumbria] from Kent or France claimed that the Irish [missionaries based at Lindisfarne] kept Easter Sunday contrary to the custom of the universal church.... [The dispute became worse when the Irish monk Colman was made bishop of Lindisfarne.] All this reached the ears of King Oswy [of Northumbria] and his son Alfrid. Oswy had been educated and baptized by the Irish and was fluent in their language, so he thought that nothing was better than what they had taught him. But Alfrid had been instructed in the Christian faith by Wilfrid, a most learned man, who had once gone to Rome to learn church doctrine ... so Alfrid naturally thought this man's views were preferable to any customs of the Irish....

When this question of Easter ... was raised, it was decided to hold a council to settle the dispute at the monastery called Streanaeshealh [later called Whitby].... There came to the council the two kings, both father and son, as well as Bishop Colman and his Irish clergy, and ... Wilfrid.

King Oswy began by declaring that it was fitting that those who served one God should observe the one rule of life and not differ in the celebration of the sacraments, since they all expected to dwell together in the same kingdom of heaven. Therefore they ought to inquire which was the truest tradition so they all might follow it together. He then directed his bishop, Colman, to declare first what customs he followed and then how they originated.

Then Colman said: "The method of keeping Easter that I follow is the one I received from my seniors who sent me here [from Ireland] as bishop. All our forefathers, men beloved of God, are known to have kept it in the same way we do.... I cannot believe that our most reverend father Columba and his successors, men beloved by God, who all celebrated Easter when we do, ever thought or acted contrary to the holy scriptures. I do not doubt that many of them are saints, since their holiness is attested by signs and miracles, and therefore I shall never cease to follow their way of life, their customs, and their teaching."

Wilfrid replied: "... As to your father Columba and his followers, whose holiness you say you imitate, and whose rules and precepts you observe because they have been confirmed by signs from heaven, I might answer that on the day of Judgment, when many shall say to our Lord 'that in his name they prophesied, and cast out devils, and wrought many wonders,' our Lord will reply 'that he never knew them' [Matt. 7:22-23]. But far be it from me to say this about your fathers, because it is much more just to believe good rather than evil about people one does not know. Therefore I do not deny that those who loved God with pious intent, however simple and unlearned they might be, were God's servants and beloved by him. Nor do I think that they were harmed by keeping Easter at the wrong time as long as they had no way of knowing better. Indeed, I am certain that if anyone had come and taught them the catholic rule, they would have followed it, just as they certainly kept all those commandments of God with which they were familiar.

"But as for you, you certainly do sin if you refuse to follow the decrees of the papacy, or rather of the universal Church, once you have heard them, since they are confirmed by holy scripture. Though your fathers were holy men, do you think that a few people in a corner of the remotest island are to be preferred to the universal church of Christ that extends throughout the world? And even if that Columba of yours— yes, and ours too, if he served Christ—was a holy man who performed great miracles, still is he to be preferred to the most blessed prince of the apostles, to whom our Lord said, 'you are Peter, and upon this rock I will build my church; and the gates of hell shall not prevail against it. And I will give unto you the keys of the kingdom of heaven' [Matt. 16:18-19]?"

When Wilfrid had finished, the king said, "Is it true, Colman, that these words were spoken to Peter by our Lord?" He answered, "It is true, O king!" Next the king asked, "Can you show any such power given to your Columba?" Colman answered, "No." Then the king said, "Do you both agree that these words were primarily addressed to Peter, and that the keys of heaven were given to him by our Lord?" They both answered, "Yes." To this the king responded, "And I tell you that I will not contradict Peter because he is the doorkeeper. Instead, I mean to obey his commands to the best of my knowledge and ability; otherwise, when I come to the gates of the kingdom of heaven there may be no one to open them because I have displeased the one you agree has the keys." When the king had spoken, all the counsellors and spectators, both the mighty and the humble, signified their assent and agreed to accept those customs that they acknowledged were better and to discard those that were less perfect.

Bede (d. 735), *Ecclesiastical History*[19]

The Virgin Queen of Northumbria (659-671)

King Egfrid [of Northumbria] married Etheldrida.... She had previously been married to an ealdorman ... but he died soon after the marriage, and she was given to the king instead. Though she lived with him for twelve years, she still preserved the glory of perfect virginity. I know this is true because, when some people doubted it, I asked Bishop Wilfrid of blessed memory, and he told me how he knew for certain that she was a virgin. Her husband, Egfrid, had promised to give the bishop many lands and much money if he could persuade the queen to consummate their marriage, because the king knew that his queen esteemed Wilfrid more than anyone else.... Moreover, after she was buried, her flesh did not decay, and this miracle is a token and proof that she had never been defiled by familiarity with any man. [She finally left her husband, became a nun, and was an abbess when she died in 679.]

Bede (d. 735), *Ecclesiastical History*[20]

Even the King Must Obey the Law (675)

The [Frankish Merovingian] King Childeric [II] was altogether too light and frivolous. [He was thirteen years old.] The scandal and contempt that he aroused stirred up sedition among the Frankish people, until bitter hatred sprang up and he became a rock of offence to his own ruin. To make matters worse, he ordered, illegally, that a noble Frank named Bodilo, should be bound to a stake and thrashed [contrary to the *Salic Law*, chapter 51]; and this infuriated the Franks who saw it. Ingobert, Amalbert, and other Frankish notables stirred up insurrection against

Childeric; and that same Bodilo together with the other conspirators fell upon the king and slew him and—I am sorry to say—his pregnant queen, Belechildis, in the Forest of Livry [near Chelles].

Continuation of *The Chronicle of Fredegar* (ca. 736)[21]

Wilfrid Teaches the South Saxons How to Fish (680)

After [bishop] Wilfrid was expelled from his diocese [of York], he travelled over many lands, going to Rome and then back to Britain. Due to the hostility of King Egfrid, he could not return to his own country or diocese, but nothing could keep him from preaching the gospel, so he went instead to the kingdom of the South Saxons [Sussex].... Since the people there were still pagans, Wilfrid taught them the true faith and baptized those that were converted....

Wilfrid's mission not only saved the South Saxons from the misery of perpetual damnation but also from the cruelty of temporal death by calamity. For three years before he came no rain had fallen in the kingdom, and as a result a dreadful famine was cruelly destroying the people.... When the bishop first came into the kingdom and saw the suffering and famine there, he taught the people to get their food by fishing. For although their sea and rivers abounded in fish, the people had no skill at fishing, except for eels. So the bishop's men collected as many eel-nets as they could find and cast them into the sea; with God's help they soon collected three hundred fish of various kinds. They divided their catch into three parts: they gave a hundred to the poor and a hundred to the owners of the nets, keeping the last hundred for their own use. By this good deed, the bishop won the hearts of all, and they were now more inclined to believe his preaching, since it seemed likely that just as he had benefited them in this life so he might in the next.

Bede (d. 735), *Ecclesiastical History*[22]

An Empty Oath (680)

[Duke] Martin and [Mayor] Pippin [II of Heristal] and their [Austrasian] supporters were beaten and put to flight [by the Neustrians]. Ebroin [the mayor of Neustria] followed them up and laid waste most of that region. Martin thereupon entered Laon, barricading himself within the city walls. But Ebroin was behind him, and when he reached the villa of Ecry [in the Ardennes] he sent Aglibert and Bishop Reolus of Rheims as his representatives to Laon, where they gave undertakings but swore falsely upon reliquaries that, unknown to him, were empty. Yet Martin trusted them over this and left Laon with his friends and supporters to go to Ecry. And there, with all his companions they killed him.

Continuation of *The Chronicle of Fredegar* (ca. 736)[23]

God's Gleeman:
The Story of Caedmon (died ca. 680)

There was a certain brother in this monastery [Whitby] ... who had received a special grace from God that enabled him to compose pious and religious songs. Thus whatever was translated for him out of the [Latin] Bible he could quickly turn into moving and delightful poetry in his own tongue, which was English.... To be sure, after him other Englishmen tried to compose religious poems, but none could ever compare with him, for he did not learn the art of poetry from men, but from God. Hence he never could compose any trivial or foolish poem but only those on religious themes that were fit to be uttered by his devout tongue.

Although he was a layman until he was well along in years, he had never learned any songs. Thus he was sometimes embarrassed at a feast when everyone was expected to sing in turn to entertain the others, and when he saw the harp come his way he would get up from the table, leave the feast in the middle, and return home. Once when he did this he left the banquet hall and went out to the stable, where he had to take care of the horses that night. There he lay down and went to sleep when it was time. Presently he dreamed that someone came to him and, greeting him by name, said: "Caedmon, sing me some song." He answered, "I cannot sing, for the reason why I left the feast and came here is because I cannot sing." To which the other replied, "Nevertheless you must sing to me." "What must I sing?" Caedmon answered. "Sing about the beginning of created beings," said the other. Thereupon Caedmon began to sing verses which he had never heard before in praise of God, the gist of which is this:

We are now to praise the Maker of the heavenly kingdom, the power of the Creator and his counsel, the deeds of the Father of glory. How He, being the eternal God, became the author of all miracles, who first, as almighty preserver of the human race, created heaven for the sons of men as the roof of the house, and next the earth.

This is the sense but not the order of the words as he sang them in his sleep, for it is not possible to translate verse word for word from one language into another without considerable loss of beauty and dignity. When Caedmon awoke, he remembered all that he had sung in his dream and he soon added many more verses praising God that were just as good.

In the morning he went to the reeve who was his superior and told him about the gift he had received. The reeve took him to the abbess, who ordered him to tell his dream and recite his verses in the presence of the more learned men so that they might judge whether he had received a gift and from what source it came. They all concluded that heavenly grace had been conferred on him by our Lord. They then translated for him some historical or doctrinal passage from the Bible and told him to put it into verse if he could. He accepted the task, went away, and returned the next morning with the passage turned into most excellent verse.

The abbess now recognized that the man had received a grace from God, so she instructed him to put aside his secular habit and take monastic vows. So he became one of the brothers in her monastery and she ordered that he should be instructed in the Bible from beginning to end. Caedmon remembered what he was told and turned it over in his mind, chewing the cud like some clean animal [Leviticus 11:3], until it became melodious verse. When he recited his lesson in verse, it sounded so sweet that his teachers became his audience.

Bede (d. 735), *Ecclesiastical History*[24]

The Carolingians Unite Frankland:
The Battle of Tertry (687)

Now, too, died Waratto, mayor of the [Neustrian] palace [in 684]. He had had a noble and vigorous wife named Anseflidis, and her son-in-law, Berchar, became mayor of the palace. He was a little fellow of small ability, light-minded and impetuous. Frequently he slighted his Frankish friends and ignored their counsel. This angered Audoramnus, Reolus, and many more of the Franks. So they abandoned Berchar and joined Pippin [II of Heristal, rival mayor of the Austrasian palace] by sending him pledges, and swore friendship with him. They urged an attack upon Berchar and the Franks that remained with him.

Pippin then raised his warbands and set out with speed from Austrasia to do battle with King Theuderic and [his mayor] Berchar. They met near Saint-Quentin at a place called Tertry, and there they fought. Pippin and his Austrasians were the victors: King Theuderic and Berchar were put to flight. The victorious Pippin gave chase and subjugated the region. Shortly afterwards the same Berchar was slain by false and flattering friends at the instigation of his mother-in-law, the lady Anseflidis. Then Pippin secured King Theuderic and his treasure, made all arrangements about the administration of the [Neustrian] palace, and returned to Austrasia.

Continuation of *The Chronicle of Fredegar* (ca. 736)[25]

Speech Therapy in Northumbria (ca. 690)

[John of Beverley, bishop of Hexham, 687-705, always shared his Lenten retreat with some misfortunate person.] In a village not far off, the bishop knew there was a certain dumb youth, who often used to come to him to receive alms and who had never been able to speak one word. Besides this, his head was so scabby and scurfy that no hair could grow on the crown and only a few scattered hairs stuck out around it. The bishop had this young man brought and a little hut made for him within the cathedral close in which he could stay and receive his daily allotment.

On the second Sunday in Lent, he had the young man come in to him and told him to stick out his tongue and show it to him. Then he took hold of his chin and, after making the sign of the Cross on his tongue, told him to pull it back into his mouth and say something. "Say some word," he said; "say *yea*," which in English is the word of assent and agreement, i.e. yes. His tongue was immediately loosed and he said what the bishop told him to say. The bishop then began pronouncing the letters of the alphabet: "Say A," and he said it; then "Say B," and he said that too. When he had repeated all the letters after the bishop, they progressed to syllables, then words, and finally whole sentences. Those who were present say that after that the boy kept talking all that day and night, as long as he could keep awake, expressing his hidden thoughts and wishes to others, which he could never do before....

The bishop rejoiced at this cure and ordered the physician to try to heal the boy's scabby head. This was done with the help of the bishop's blessing and prayers, and when the scalp was healed, the lad grew a fine head of hair. Thus he acquired a clear complexion, ready speech, and beautiful curly hair, whereas before he had been ugly, miserable, and speechless. Although the bishop offered to keep him in his own household, he preferred to return home rejoicing in his newfound health.

Bede (d. 735), *Ecclesiastical History*[26]

The Beginning of the English Mission to the Mainland Germans (690–695)

Egbert [Bede's friend, a priest living in exile in Ireland] planned to bring blessings to many by undertaking the apostolic mission of preaching the word of God to some of those nations that had not yet heard it. He knew there were many such nations in Germany, the country from which the Angles and Saxons had come to Britain. (In fact, their neighbours still call them Germans, or as the British say, "Garmans.") These [mainlanders] include the Frisians, Rugians, Danes, Huns, Old Saxons, and ... there are also many other nations in that country who are still practicing pagan rites.... [But a shipwreck en route discouraged Egbert and] he gave up the project and stayed at home.

One of his companions named Wictbert ... set sail, however, and reached Friesland, where he spent two whole years preaching the news of salvation to the Frisians and their king, Radbod. But all this work among barbarous auditors bore no fruit, so he returned home....

Nevertheless, Egbert still attempted to send some holy and industrious men to preach the Gospel, among whom was Willibrord, a priest outstanding both for his rank and merit. When the twelve missionaries arrived in Germany, they made a detour to visit Pippin [II of Heristal], duke of the Franks, who received them graciously. Since he had recently driven King Radbod out of the part of Friesland closest to Frankland and had taken it over, Pippin sent them there to preach. He gave them the support of his authority, so no one might molest them in their preaching, and he also offerred many benefits to those who were willing to embrace the faith. Thus it was that, aided by divine grace, they quickly converted many from idolatry to the Christian faith....

At the beginning of the mission, however, Willibrord had hurried to Rome [in 693] as soon as he had obtained Pippin's license to preach, because he did not want to start preaching without the pope's permission and blessing. Moreover, he hoped the pope would give him some relics of the blessed apostles and martyrs of Christ, so that when he had destroyed the idols and built churches in the nation to which he was preaching, he might have relics of the saints ready to put into them, in order that each church might be dedicated to the saint whose relics were there. He also wished to obtain and learn other things at Rome that were necessary for his great enterprise. When he got everything he wanted, he returned to preach....

When the English missionaries had spent several years teaching in Friesland, Pippin sent the venerable Willibrord to Rome [in 695] ... with the request, to which the others consented, that he be consecrated archbishop of the Frisians.... For his episcopal see, Pippin gave him a place in his famous fortress ... which the Franks call Utrecht.

Bede (d. 735), Ecclesiastical History[27]

The Eighth Century

Is She Worth the Wergeld? (ca. 700)

50. If any freeman abducts another's wife contrary to law, let him return her and compensate with eight solidi. If, however, he does not wish to return her, let him pay for her with 400 solidi....

53. If anyone takes another's unbetrothed daughter for himself as a wife, let him return her and compensate for her with forty solidi, if her father demands her back....

56. If any free virgin woman goes on a journey between two estates, and anyone meets her [and] uncovers her head, let him compensate with [three] solidi. And if he raises her clothing to the knee, let him compensate with six solidi. And if he exposes her so that her genitalia or posterior appears, let him compensate with twelve solidi. If, however, he fornicates with her against her will, let him compensate with forty solidi. If, however, this happens to an adult woman, let him compensate all things twice what we said above concerning the virgin....

75. If anyone lies with someone's chambermaid against her will, let him compensate with six solidi. And if anyone lies with the first maid of the textile workshop against her will, let him compensate with six solidi. If anyone lies with other maids of the textile workshop against their will, let him compensate with three solidi.

The Laws of the Alamanni (ca. 700)[1]

A Canny King of the Lombards (701-711)

In the days when he held the kingly power, Aripert [II], going forth at night, and wandering about, inquired for himself what was said about him by particular cities, and diligently investigated what kind of justice the various judges rendered to the people.

When the ambassadors of foreign nations came to him, he wore in their presence mean garments and those made of skins, and in order that they not become eager to invade Italy, he never offered them precious wines nor delicacies of other kinds.

Paul the Deacon, *History of the Lombards* (ca. 799)[2]

Why King Roderick Lost Spain (711)

Roderick [king of the Spanish Visigoths] lost Spain in the following way. He ordered Count Julian, who was one of his subjects, to go abroad on an embassy to Haboalim, king of the Saracens, and while Julian was away on the king's business, Roderick went to bed with the count's wife according to some accounts, or with his daughter according to others. At any rate, when the count returned and found out what had happened in his absence, he arranged for the king to lose his kingdom. The result of this conspiracy was that Spain was invaded in the third year of King Roderick's reign, on 11 November 713, by King Haboalim, together with King Abocupra of Morocco, King Ezarich, and twenty-four other Saracen kings. They conquered King Roderick in battle and Spain was completely occupied by the Saracens all the way up to Arles in Provence. This all took place within fourteen months.

Pedro Marfilio (fl. 1370), *Chronicle of San Juan de la Peña*[3]

Saint Boniface Fells Thor's Oak (ca. 723)

[The Anglo-Saxon missionary Boniface, supported by both the pope and Charles Martel, was converting the Germans.] Now at that time many of the Hessians, brought under the Catholic faith and confirmed by the grace of the sevenfold spirit, received the laying on of hands; others indeed, not yet strengthened in soul, refused to accept in their entirety the lessons of the inviolate faith. Moreover, some were wont secretly, some openly to sacrifice to trees and springs; some in secret, some openly practised inspections of victims and divinations, legerdemain and incantations; some turned their attention to auguries and auspices and various sacrificial rites; while others, with sounder minds, abandoned all the profanations of heathenism, and committed none of these things.

With the advice and counsel of these last, the saint attempted, in the place called Gaesmere [Geismar], while the servants of God stood by his side, to fell a certain oak of extraordinary size, which is called, by an old name of the pagans, the Oak of Jupiter [Thor]. And when in the strength of his steadfast heart he had cut the lower notch [to the center of the tree on the side it was to fall], there had gathered a multitude of pagans, who in their souls were most earnestly cursing the enemy of their gods. But when the other side of the tree was notched only a little, suddenly the oak's vast bulk, driven by a divine blast from above, crashed to the ground, shivering its crown of branches as it fell; and, as if by the gracious dispensation of the Most High, it was also burst into four parts, and four trunks of huge size, equal in length, were seen, which had not been split apart by the brethren who stood by. At this sight the pagans who before had cursed now, on the contrary, believed, and blessed the Lord, and put away their former reviling. Then moreover the most holy bishop [Boniface], after taking counsel with the brethren, built from the timber of the tree a wooden oratory, and dedicated it in honour of Saint Peter the Apostle.

Willibald of Mainz, *Life of Saint Boniface* (before 768)[4]

Why King Ini of Wessex Retired (726)

Ini's queen Ethelberga ... was perpetually urging that it was necessary for a Christian to bid adieu to earthly things, at least at the close of life. But since the king just as constantly kept putting her off, she at last tried to get her way by a trick. One day, after they had left a royal manor where they had been revelling with more than usual riot and luxury, one of her attendants, by arrangement with the queen, defiled the palace in every possible manner, both with the excrement of cattle and with heaps of filth; and lastly he put a sow, which had recently farrowed, in the very bed where they had lain. They had hardly proceeded a mile before she attacked her husband with the fondest conjugal endearments, begging that they might immediately return to the place they had just left and saying that his denial would be attended with dangerous consequences. When her request was readily granted, the king was astonished to find that the place, which yesterday might have vied with Assyrian luxury, had become desolate and disgusting with filth. After silently pondering on the sight, his eyes at length turned upon the queen. Seizing the opportunity and pleasantly smiling, she said, "My noble spouse, where are the revellings of yesterday? ... Have they not all passed away? ... Reflect, I beg you, how wretchedly will these bodies decay that we pamper with such unbounded luxury...." Without saying more, she convinced her husband by this striking example to do what she had been vainly trying for years to persuade him to do.... For he now aspired to the highest perfection and went to Rome ... [where] he was tonsured in secret and, wearing simple clothes, grew old in privacy. Nor did his queen, the author of this noble deed, desert him....

William of Malmesbury (d. 1143?), *The Kings of England*[5]

The High Tide of Islam is Turned at Poitiers (October 732)

When [the Christian] Duke Eudo [of Aquitaine] saw that he was beaten [by Charles Martel] and an object of scorn, he summoned to his assistance against Prince Charles and his Franks the unbelieving Saracen people. So they rose up under their king 'Abd ar-Rahman and crossed the Garonne to the city of Bordeaux, where they burnt down the churches and slew the inhabitants. From thence they advanced on Poitiers; and here, I am sorry to say, they burnt the church of the blessed Hilary. Next they were directing their advance towards the like destruction of the house of the blessed Martin [at Tours]; but taking boldness as his counsellor, Prince Charles set the battle in array against them and came upon them like a mighty man of war. With Christ's help he overran their tents, following hard after them in the battle to grind them small in their overthrow, and when 'Abd ar-Rahman perished in the battle he utterly destroyed their armies, scattering them like stubble before the fury of his onslaught; and in the power of Christ he utterly destroyed them. So did he triumph over all his enemies in this his glorious day of victory!

Continuation of *The Chronicle of Fredegar* (ca. 736)[6]

The Venerable Bede's "Heavenly Birthday" (25 May 735)

To his fellow teacher Cuthwin, most beloved in Christ, from his school friend Cuthbert. Health for ever in God.

I was delighted to receive your little gift, and was pleased to read your devout and learned letter in which I learned that, as I had greatly hoped, you are diligently offering masses and holy prayers for our father and master Bede, whom God loved so well. Out of love for him rather than any confidence in my ability to do so, I am glad to give you a short account of his passing from this world, since I understand that you wish and request this....

For nearly a fortnight before the feast of our Lord's resurrection, he was troubled by weakness and breathed with great difficulty, although he suffered little pain. Thenceforward until Ascension Day he remained cheerful and happy, giving thanks to God each hour day and night. He gave daily lessons to us his students, and spent the rest of the day in singing the psalms so far as his strength allowed....

During these days, in addition to the daily instruction that he gave us and his recitation of the psalter, he was working to complete two books worthy of mention. For he translated the Gospel of Saint John into our own [English] language for the benefit of the Church of God, as far as the words "but what are these among so many" [John 6:5]. He also made some extracts from the works of Bishop Isidore [of Seville], saying "I do not wish my sons to read anything untrue, or to labour unprofitably after my death."

But on the Tuesday before our Lord's Ascension his breathing became increasingly laboured, and his feet began to swell. Despite this he continued cheerfully to teach and dictate all day, saying from time to time, "Learn quickly. I do not know how long I can continue, for my Lourd may call me in a short while." It seemed to us that he might well be aware of the time of his departure, and he spent that night without sleeping, giving thanks to God.

When dawn broke on Wednesday, he told us to write diligently what we had begun, and we did this until terce. After terce we walked in procession with the relics of the saints as the customs of the day required; but one of us remained with him, who said, "There is still one chapter missing in the book that you have been dictating; but it seems hard that I should trouble you any further." "It is no trouble," he answered: "Take your pen and sharpen it, and write quickly." And he did so.

But at none he said to me, "I have a few articles of value in my casket, such as pepper, linen, and incense. Run quickly and fetch the priests of the monastery, so that I may distribute among them the gifts that God has given me." In great distress I did as he bid me. And when they arrived, he spoke to each of them in turn, requesting and reminding them diligently to offer masses and prayers for him. They readily promised to do so, and all were sad and wept, grieving above all else at his statement that they must not expect to see his face much longer in this world.... He also told us many other edifying things, and passed his last day happily until evening.

Then the same lad, named Wilbert, said again: "Dear master, there is one sentence still unfinished." "Very well," he replied: "write it down." After a short while the lad said, "Now it is finished." "You have spoken truly," he replied: "It is well finished. Now raise my head in your hands, for it would give me great joy to sit facing the holy place where I used to pray, so that I may sit and call on my Father." And thus, on the floor of his cell, he chanted "Glory be to the Father, and to the Son, and to the Holy Spirit" to its ending, and breathed his last.

Cuthbert, abbot of Wearmouth and Jarrow, *Letter* (735)[7]

Pippin Pops the Question (749)

In the year 750 of the Lord's incarnation, Pippin [mayor of the palace in Frankland] sent ambassadors to Rome to Pope Zacharias, to ask concerning the kings of the Franks who were of the royal line and were called kings, but who had no power in the kingdom, save only that charters and privileges were drawn up in their names. They had absolutely no kingly power, but did whatever the Franks' mayor of the palace desired. But on the [first] day of March [at the spring muster of the army] on the Marchfield, gifts were offered to these kings by the people according to ancient custom. Then the [Merovingian] king himself sat in the royal seat with the army standing round him and the mayor of the palace in his presence, and he commanded on that day whatever was decreed by the Franks, but on all other days of the year he sat at home [and took no part in the affairs of the kingdom].

[Pippin's ambassadors asked the pope whether it was good that the king should simply be a figurehead.] Pope Zacharias therefore in the exercise of his apostolical authority replied to their question that it seemed to him better and more expedient that the man who held power in the kingdom should be called king and be king, rather than he who falsely bore that name. Therefore that pope commanded the king and people of the Franks that Pippin, who was using royal power, should be called king and should be established on the throne. Which was therefore done by the anointing of the holy archbishop [Saint] Boniface in the city of Soissons. Pippin is proclaimed king, and Childeric, who was falsely called king, is tonsured and sent into a monastery.

The Short Lorsch Chronicle (750?)[8]

The Last of the Do-Nothing Merovingian Kings (751)

The family of the Merovingians from which the Franks were accustomed to select their kings was thought to have lasted down to King Childeric, who, by the order of Stephen, the Roman Pontiff, was deposed, tonsured, and thrust into a monastery [in 751]. But this family, though it may be regarded as finishing with him, had long since lost all its strength, and no longer held anything distinguished except the empty royal title. For the wealth and power of the kingdom was in the hands of the prefects of the palace, who were called "mayors of the household," and to whom the whole of supreme authority belonged. The king, contented with the mere royal title, with long hair and flowing beard, used to sit on the throne and give the appearance of ruling, listening to ambassadors, whencesoever they came, and giving them at their departure, as though of his own power, answers which he had been instructed or ordered to give. But this was the only function that he performed, for, besides the useless royal name and the precarious life income which the prefect of the court allowed him at his pleasure, he had nothing of his own except one estate with a very small revenue, on which he had his house, and from which he drew the few servants who performed such services as were necessary and gave him allegiance. Wherever he had to go he went in a wagon, drawn in peasant fashion by yoked oxen, and driven by a ploughman. In this way he used to go to the palace and to the general meetings of the people, which were celebrated annually for the welfare of the kingdom; in this way he returned home. But the prefect of the court looked after the administration of the kingdom and all that had to be done or arranged at home or abroad.

Einhard (fl. 817-836), *Life of Charlemagne*[9]

From Mass Conversion to Massacre (754)

[In 753 Boniface preached to the pagan Frisians, in the present-day Netherlands, and persuaded many to be baptized. The next year he returned to confirm them *en masse*.] Coming to Friesland with a number of his personal followers, he pitched his tents by the bank of the river which is called Boorn, which forms the boundary between the districts of Ostergo and Westergo. But because he had appointed unto the people, already scattered far and wide, a holiday of confirmation of the neophytes, and of the laying on of hands by the bishop upon the newly baptized and of their confirmation, every man went unto his own house, that in accordance with the precise command of the holy bishop all might be presented together on the day set for their confirmation.

Wholly opposite was the event. When the appointed day had dawned, and the morning light was breaking after the rising of the sun, then came enemies instead of friends, new executioners instead of new worshippers of the faith; and a vast multitude of foes, armed with spears and shields, rushed with glittering weapons into the camp.

Then hastily the attendants sprang forth against them from the camp, and betook themselves to arms on either side, and were eager to defend against the crazy host of the mad folk the sainted martyrs that were to be. But when the man of God heard the onset of the tumultuous throng, immediately he called to his side the band of [about fifty] clerics, and, taking the saints' relics which he used to have always with him, he came out of the tent. And at once, rebuking the attendants, he forbade combat and battle, saying: "Stop fighting, lads! Give up the battle! For we are taught by the trustworthy witness of Scripture that we render not evil for evil, but instead give good for evil...."

But also with fatherly speech he incited those standing near, priests and deacons and men of lower rank, trained to God's service, saying: "Men and brethren, be of stout heart, and fear not them who kill the body, since they are not able to slay the soul ... but endure firmly here the sudden moment of death, that you may be able to reign with Christ for all time."

While with such exhortation of doctrine he was kindly inciting the disciples to the crown of martyrdom, quickly the mad tumult of pagans rushed in upon them with swords and all the equipment of war, and stained the saints' bodies with propitious gore.

Willibald of Mainz, *Life of Saint Boniface* (before 768)[10]

Walther: An Aggressively Modest Monk (ca. 765)

[Walther was a soldier who retired to the monastery of Novalesa, near the Mont-Cenis pass in the western Alps. One day the king's servants robbed a convoy of wagons bringing produce to the monastery from its outlying farms. The monks sent Walther to recover the goods, without recourse to violence if possible. Mounting his old war horse, Walther] took with him two or three servants and hastened to meet the aforesaid robbers. When, therefore, he had humbly saluted them, he began to warn them that they should not again do God's servants such harm as they had even now wrought. But they answered him with hard words, whereupon he rebuked them all the more sternly and more frequently.

Moved with wrath at this proud spirit of his, they therefore compelled Walther to strip him of the garments which he wore; and he obeyed them humbly in all things, according to his [monastic] obedience, saying how the brethren had laid this command upon him. They therefore, in the course of stripping him, began to despoil him even of his shoes and his breeches; but when they had come to his breeches, Walther resisted long, saying that the brethren had by no means commanded him to let these garments be taken from him; whereupon they answered that they cared nothing for the bidding of the monks; but Walther withstood them to their face, saying that it was not seemly that he should abandon these garments. When therefore they began to lay violent hands upon him, Walther secretly detached from the saddle the stirrup in which his foot had rested, and with it he so smote one of these ruffians on the head that he fell lifeless to the ground.

Then, seizing his arms, the monk struck right and left.... Many therefore were slain, and the rest took to flight and left all that they had. Walther therefore, having gained the victory, took all that was his and theirs to boot, and returned forthwith to the monastery laden with the spoil.

The Novalese Chronicle (ca. 1025)[11]

The Real Story of Roland at Roncesvalles (778)

While the incessant and almost continuous war with the Saxons was being fought out, Charlemagne placed garrisons at suitable places on the frontier, and then he attacked Spain with the largest military force he could raise. He crossed the Pyrenees, received the surrender of all the towns and fortresses that he attacked, and returned with his army safe and sound, except that as he returned over the summit of the Pyrenees, he experienced for a brief while the treason of the Gascons. While his army was marching in a long line, in the manner permitted by the local terrain and the narrow defiles, the Gascons placed ambushes at the peak of the highest mountain—where the density and the dark shadows of the woods made good opportunities for such actions—and then rushing down into the valley they threw the last part of the baggage train into disorder and also those with the rearguard who were protecting those in advance. When the battle was joined, the Gascons slew them to the last man. Then they seized the baggage, and under the cover of darkness, which was already falling, they scattered swiftly in different directions. The Gascons were aided in this exploit by the lightness of their weapons and by the terrain where the events occurred. On the other hand, due to the weight of their weapons and the difficult terrain, the Franks were no match at all for the Gascons. In this battle there were killed along with many others Eggihard, the steward of the royal table, Anselm, a count of the palace, and Roland, prefect of the Breton frontier. Nor could this assault be avenged at once, because the enemy so completely disappeared after perpetrating the deed that not even a rumour remained of where or among what peoples they might be found.

Einhard (fl. 817-386), *Life of Charlemagne*[12]

Charlemagne's Massacre at Verden (782)

The lord King Charles embarked on a campaign and crossed the Rhine at Cologne. He held an assembly at the source of the river Lippe. All the Saxons came there except the rebel Widukind.... When the assembly was over, the lord King Charles returned to Francia [i.e. France]. As soon as he returned, the Saxons, persuaded by Widukind, promptly rebelled as usual.

Before the lord King Charles knew about this, he sent his agents (*missi*) Adalgis, Gailo, and Worad to lead an army of Franks and Saxons against a few defiant Slavs. When the agents heard en route that the Saxons had revolted, they rushed with the East Frankish [i.e. German] host to the place where they had heard the Saxons were assembling. When they got to Saxony, they were met by Count Theodoric, the king's kinsman, who had with him as many troops as he could hastily gather in Ripuaria [west of the Rhine] after he had heard of the Saxon revolt. He advised them through couriers first to find out by patrols as fast as possible where the Saxons were and what they were doing, and then, if the terrain permitted it, to attack them at the same time. This counsel was found agreeable, and they advanced with the count as far as the Süntel Mountains [near Minden], on whose north side the Saxon camp had been set up.

After Theodoric had pitched camp in this locality, the East Franks, as they had planned with the count, crossed the river, so as to be able to pass more easily around the mountains, and pitched camp on the river bank. When they discussed matters among themselves, they feared that the honour of victory might be Theodoric's alone if they should fight at his side. Therefore, they decided to engage the Saxons without him. They took up their arms and, as if chasing runaways and going after booty instead of facing an enemy lined up for battle, everybody dashed as fast as his horse would carry him for the place outside the Saxon camp where the Saxons were drawn up in battle array.

The battle was as bad as the approach. As soon as the fighting began, they were surrounded by the Saxons and slain almost to a man. Those who were able to get away did not flee to their own camp but to Theodoric's on the other side of the mountain. The losses of the Franks were greater than the number might reveal, since two of the agents—Adalgis and Gailo—as well as four counts and up to twenty other distinguished nobles had been killed, not counting those who had followed them, preferring to perish at their side rather than survive them.

When the lord King Charles heard of this, he rushed to the place with all the Franks that he could gather on short notice and advanced to where the river Aller flows into the Weser [at Verden]. Then all the Saxons came together again, submitted to the authority of the lord king, and surrendered the evildoers who were chiefly responsible for this revolt so they might be put to death—4500 of them. The sentence was carried out. Widukind was not among them, since he had fled into Nord-mannia [i.e. Denmark]. When he had finished this business, the lord king returned to Francia. He celebrated Christmas at the villa of Thion-ville, and Easter too.

Royal Frankish Annals, Revised Version (814-817)[13]

The Twelve Peers of Patristics (ca. 790)

The most glorious Charles [the Great] saw the study of letters flourish-ing throughout his whole realm, but still he was grieved to find that it did not reach the ripeness of the earlier fathers; and so, after super-human labours, he broke out one day with this expression of his sorrow: "Would that I had twelve clerks so learned in all wisdom and so perfect-ly trained as were Jerome and Augustine."

Then the learned Alcuin, feeling himself ignorant indeed in com-parison with these great names, rose to a height of daring that no man else attained to in the presence of the terrible Charles, and said, with deep indignation in his mind but none in his countenance: "The Maker of heaven and earth has not many like to those men and do you expect to have twelve?"

Notker the Stammerer, *Charlemagne* (ca. 884)[14]

Charlemagne's Brand of Caesaropapism (796)

[This letter, written by Alcuin in Charlemagne's name, is addressed to Pope Leo III.] Just as I entered into a pact with the most blessed father your predecessor, so I desire to conclude with your holiness an unbreak-able treaty of the same faith and charity; so that with divine grace being called down by the prayers of your apostolic holiness, the apostolic benediction may follow me everywhere, and the most holy see of the Roman church may always be defended by the devotion that God gives to us. It is *our* part with the help of divine holiness to defend by armed strength the holy Church of Christ everywhere from the outward onslaught of the pagans and the ravages of the infidels, and to strengthen within it the knowledge of the Catholic faith. It is *your* part, most holy father, to help our armies with your hands lifted up to God like Moses, so that by your intercession and by the leadership and gift of God, the Christian people may everywhere and always have the victory over the enemies of his holy name and that the name of our lord Jesus Christ may be glorified throughout the whole world.

Alcuin (d. 804), *Letters*[15]

The Ninth Century

The Coronation of Charlemagne (800)

In the forty-seven years that he reigned, he only went there [to Rome] four times, in order to fulfill his vows and to pray. But these were not the only reasons for his last visit to Rome. For the Romans, in truth, had afflicted Pope Leo with many injuries; they had torn out his eyes and cut off his tongue, and thus had forced him to appeal to the king's solemn promise. Therefore he came to Rome to restore the status of the church, which was very much disturbed, and he spent the whole winter there. On this occasion he received the title of Emperor and Augustus. He resisted this at first to such an extent that he declared that he would not have entered the church that day, though it was one of the principal festivals of the Church, if he could have known the pope's plan in advance.

Einhard (fl. 817-836), *Life of Charlemagne*[1]

When Christmas day arrived, everyone assembled in the basilica of Saint Peter. The reverend and venerable pope with his own hand then crowned him [Charles] with a most precious crown. Next, since all the faithful Roman people saw how Charles was prepared to defend and cherish the holy Roman church and its vicar, they cried out loudly in unison, prompted by God and by Saint Peter, who bears the keys to the kingdom of heaven: "To Charles, most pious augustus, crowned by God, great emperor, bringer of peace—life and victory!" This was said three times in front of the shrine of Saint Peter the Apostle, and many saints were invoked also. Thus everyone participated in establishing Charles as emperor of the Romans. Immediately after this, the most holy bishop and pope [Leo] anointed Charles with holy oil, and he likewise anointed his most excellent son [Louis the Pious] as king, and this on the very day that our lord Jesus Christ was born. Mass was then said, and when the ceremonies were over, the most serene emperor himself presented a silver table, which weighed many pounds, as an offering.

Life of Pope Leo III (816)[2]

Charlemagne's Clock (807)

The envoy of the king of Persia [Harun al-Rashid], Abdallah by name, came to the emperor ... and delivered presents which the king of Persia sent to him, namely ... a brass clock, a marvelous mechanical contraption in which the course of the twelve hours moved as they do in a water clock, with twelve little brass balls that fall down on the hour and in falling ring a cymbal underneath. On this clock there were also twelve horsemen who at the end of each hour stepped out of twelve windows, closing the previously open windows by their movements. There were many other things on this clock which are too numerous to describe now.

Royal Frankish Annals (807)[3]

Charlemagne Portrayed as a Roman Emperor (ca. 742-814)

He was large and powerful in body, prominent in stature though not exceeding proper proportions: for his height measured seven times the length of his feet. The crown of his head was round; his eyes were unusually large and lively. His nose was rather larger than usual; he had beautiful white hair; and his expression was pleasing and cheerful. Thus, whether sitting or standing, he had great authority and dignity. Although his neck seemed rather thick and short and his stomach projected somewhat, nevertheless the good proportions of the other parts of his body concealed this. His step was firm and the whole bearing of his body manly; his voice was clear, it is true, but hardly suited to the appearance of his body. He enjoyed good health, except for four years before his death when he was repeatedly attacked by fevers, and at the end he was lame in one foot. Even then he took his own opinion rather than the advice of his doctors, whom he almost hated, because they urged him to give up the roasted foods to which he was accustomed and to get in the habit of eating boiled foods.

He constantly exercised, both by riding and hunting, for these were part of his heritage; because hardly any people on the earth are found who can match the Franks in these arts. He took delight in the vapours of natural hot springs, and constantly practised swimming, at which he was so skilled that no one rightly was able to surpass him. For this reason he built the royal residence at Aachen, and lived there continuously during the last years of his life until his death. He often invited not only his sons to the bath but also his magnates and friends, and sometimes even a great crowd of his vassals and bodyguards so that on occasion a hundred or more men were bathing together.

He wore the native clothes—that is to say, Frankish. He put linen shirts on his torso and linen pants on his thighs, then came a tunic encircled with a silken border, and hose. His legs were bound in leggings and his feet enclosed in boots. In wintertime he protected his shoulders and chest with a vest made of the skins of otters and ermine. He was wrapped in a blue cloak, and always girded with a sword, whose hilt and belt were either gold or silver. Sometimes he used a jewelled sword, but only on the principal feast days or when the legates from foreign peoples' nations visited him. He disliked foreign garments, however beautiful, and would never allow himself to be clad in them, except at Rome once on the request of Pope Hadrian, and again on the entreaty of his successor, Pope Leo, when he wore the long tunic and chlamys and shoes made according to the Roman custom. On feast days he walked in the procession in clothing of gold cloth, with jewelled boots and with a golden brooch fastening his cloak, and also wearing a diadem of gold embellished with precious stones. On other days, however, his dress differed little from that of the common layman.

He was temperate in eating and drinking, but especially in drinking; for he very much detested drunkenness in any man, but much more so in himself or in his men. He could not in fact abstain from food, and often complained that fasting was harmful to his body. He rarely gave banquets, and then only on the high feast days, for a large number of people. His daily meal was served in four dishes, except for the roast, which the hunters used to bring in on spits, and which he ate with more pleasure than any other food. While eating he would listen either to some entertainment or to a reader. Stories and the deeds of ancient heroes were read to him. He also took delight in the holy books of Augustine, especially those which are entitled *The City of God*. He was so sparing in drinking wine and all other drink that he rarely drank more than three times during the meal.

In summer, after his midday meal, he would take some fruit and another drink, and then, taking off his clothes and boots, just as he was accustomed to do at night, he would rest for two or three hours. At night he slept in such a manner that he would wake up four or five times; and when his sleep was interrupted he even rose.

When he was putting on his boots and clothes, he not only admitted his friends, but if the count of the palace told him of some dispute which could not be settled without his decision, he would have the litigants brought in immediately and hear the case and pronounce judgment just as if he were sitting on his throne. Moreover, at the same time, he would prepare whatever official business had to be done that day or any instructions for one of his ministers.

In eloquence he was fluent and forthright, and could express with the greatest clarity whatever he wished. Not content only with his native tongue, he also took the trouble to learn foreign languages. He learned Latin so that usually he could speak it as well as his native tongue; but he could understand Greek better than he could pronounce it. He had such a command of language, in fact, that he even seemed witty at times.

He cultivated the liberal arts most zealously and showed the greatest respect and bestowed great honours upon those who taught them. For learning grammar he listened to Deacon Peter of Pisa, already an old man; but for all other disciplines Albinus, called Alcuin, also a deacon, was his teacher—a man from Britain, of Saxon origin, and the most learned man anywhere. Under him Charles spent much time and labour learning rhetoric and dialectic, and especially astronomy. He also learned the art of computing and with shrewd purpose examined most carefully the course of the stars. He also tried to learn to write, and for this purpose he used to carry around under the pillows of his couch tablets and notebooks so that when there was some spare time he might accustom his hand to forming letters. But he was not very successful in this absurd labour since he began too late in life.

Einhard (fl. 817-836), *Life of Charlemagne*[4]

Why Charlemagne Wept (ca. 813)

It happened too that on his wanderings Charles once came unexpectedly to a certain maritime city of southern Gaul. When he was dining quietly in the harbour of this town, it happened that some Norman scouts made a piratical raid. When the ships came in sight some thought them Jews, some African or British merchants, but the most wise Charles, by the build of the ships and their speed, knew them to be not merchants but enemies, and said to his companions: "These ships are not filled with merchandise, but crowded with our fiercest enemies." When they heard this, in eager rivalry, they hurried in haste to the ships. But all was in vain, for when the Northmen heard that Charles, "the Hammer," as they used to call him, was there, fearing lest their fleet should be beaten back or even smashed in pieces, they withdrew themselves, by a marvellously rapid flight, not only from the swords but even from the eyes of those who followed them.

The most religious, just, and devout Charles had risen from the table and was standing at an eastern window. For a long time he poured down tears beyond price, and none dared speak a word to him; but at last he explained his actions and his tears to his warlike nobles in these words: "Do you know why I weep so bitterly, my true servants? I have no fear of those worthless rascals doing any harm to me; but I am sad at heart to think that even during my lifetime they have dared to touch this shore; and I am torn by a great sorrow because I foresee what evil things they will do to my descendants and their subjects."

Notker the Stammerer, *Charlemagne* (ca. 884)[5]

Some Prodigies in Frankland (822-825)

A.D. 822. In the land of the Thuringians, in the neighbourhood of a river, a block of earth fifty feet long, fourteen feet wide, and a foot and a half thick, was cut out, mysteriously lifted, and shifted twenty-five feet from its original location. Likewise, in eastern Saxony toward the Sorbian border in the wilderness near Arendsee, the ground was raised into a dam. Within a single night, without any human effort, it formed a rampart-like embankment one Gallic mile in length....

A.D. 824. A few days before the summer equinox of this year, when a sudden change in the air whipped up a storm, an enormous chunk of ice is said to have fallen with the hail in the country around Autun [in France]. It is said to have been fifteen feet long, seven feet wide, and two feet thick....

A.D. 825. In the vicinity of Toul by the village of Commercy, a twelve-year-old girl whose name I don't know, after receiving holy communion from the hand of the priest at Easter, reportedly abstained first from bread and then from all other food and drink. She fasted to such an extreme that she took absolutely no bodily nourishment and lived for three full years without any desire for eating. She began to fast in the year 823, as noted above in the report for that year, and in the present year, 825, at the beginning of November, she ceased to fast and began to take food and to live by eating like the rest of mortals.

Royal Frankish Annals (807)[6]

Why Islam Tolerated Pagan Star-Worship (833)

When, towards the end of his life, [the caliph] al-Ma'mûn was marching through the upper Euphrates valley on his way to make war against Byzantium, the natives came out to greet him and wish him victory. Among them were many people from Harran, who at that time wore close-fitting garments and very long hair that hung down.... Their native dress seemed strange to al-Ma'mûn and he asked them: "Which of the non-Moslem peoples under my protection do *you* belong to?" "We are men of Harran," they answered. "Are you Christians?" "No." "Jews?" "No." "Zoroastrians?" "No." Finally he asked: "Do you have a holy book or a prophet?" To this they gave a vague answer. "So you are heathen idolators," al-Ma'mûn then said to them.... "It is permissable [in Islamic law] to shed their blood, and you have no claim to protection." "But we want to pay for your protection," they said. "Protection money," he replied, "is taken only from those members of non-Islamic religions that God the Sublime—great and powerful is he!—mentions in his holy book [*Koran* 9.29]. They have a holy book of their own and have made a peace treaty with the Moslems. But you are neither Moslems or one of those peoples of the book. Thus you must choose one of these two alternatives: either convert to Islam or to one of the religions that God the Sublime mentions in his holy book. If you do neither, I will have every last one of you beheaded. You must make your decision by the time I come back from this campaign...." Then al-Ma'mûn rode off against Byzantium.

The men of Harran changed their native costume; they cut their hair and discarded all their close-fitting garments. Many of them went over to Christianity and took to wearing a belt; a number converted to Islam; and a small group of them remained true to their old faith. This remnant was anxious and had no idea what to do until a sheik from Harran, a man learned in the law [of Islam], willingly came to their assistance and said to them: "I have found you a way that can save you and keep you from death." Then they brought him much money from their treasury, which they had kept in readiness for just such an emergency.... In return he said to them: "When al-Ma'mûn returns from his campaign, tell him 'We are Sabians,' for this is the name of a religion that God—may his name be praised!—mentioned in the Koran [2.51, 5.73, 22.17]. Call yourselves Sabians and by that means you will be saved."

But it happened by divine judgment that al-Ma'mûn died on that expedition of his, in Badendûn [near Tarsus]. From that time on, they have called themselves Sabians, for previously no one in Harran and surrounding parts had borne that name.

Mohammed ibn Ish'âq al-Nadîm, *Firist-el-U'lûm* (987)[7]

A Viking Who Was Often Converted by Louis the Pious (834)

The terrible race of the Northmen still loyally paid to Louis [the Pious] the tribute which through terror they had paid to his father, the most august Emperor Charles [the Great]. Once the most religious Emperor Louis took pity on their envoys and asked them if they would be willing to receive the Christian religion; and, when they answered that always and everywhere and in everything they were ready to obey him, he ordered them to be baptized.... The nobles of the palace adopted them almost as children, and each received from the emperor's chamber a white robe and from their sponsors a full Frankish attire, of costly robes and arms and other decorations.

This was often done, and from year to year they came in increasing numbers, not for the sake of Christ but for earthly advantage. They made haste to come, not as envoys any longer but as loyal vassals, on Easter Eve to put themselves at the disposal of the emperor; and it happened that on a certain occasion they came to the number of fifty. The emperor asked them whether they wished to be baptized, and when they had confessed he bade them forthwith be sprinkled with holy water. As linen garments were not ready in sufficient numbers, he ordered shirts to be cut up and sewn together into the fashion of wraps.

One of these was forthwith clapped upon the shoulders of one of the elder men; and when he had looked all over it for a minute, he conceived fierce anger in his mind, and said to the emperor: "I have gone through this washing business here twenty times already, and I have been dressed in excellent clothes of perfect whiteness; but a sack like this is more fit for clodhoppers than for soldiers. If I were not afraid of my nakedness, for you have taken away my own clothes and have given me no new ones, I would soon leave your wrap and your Christ as well."

Notker the Stammerer, *Charlemagne* (ca. 884)[8]

French Written for the First Time: The Strasbourg Oath (842)

On the sixteenth of the kalends of March [14 February 842], Louis [the German] and Charles [the Bald] met in the city that formerly was called Argentaria but today is commonly called Strasbourg. And they took the oaths that are reproduced below. Louis swore in the Romance tongue and Charles in German.... [First they explained to their respective armies why they were allying against their elder brother, Lothar.] Then Louis took the oath first because he was the eldest and swore:

"For the love of God and for the Christian people and our common salvation, I shall help this my brother Charles by my aid in all his affairs with such knowledge and power as God may give me, just as by right one ought to help one's brother; and this I shall do on the condition that he shall do the same for me; and I shall never willingly negotiate with Lothar in any way that may be harmful to my brother Charles."

(Pro Deo amur et pro christian poblo et nostro commun salvament, d'ist di in avant, in quant Deus savir et podir me dunat, si salvarai eo cist meon fradre Karlo et in aiudha et in cadhuna cosa, si cum om per dreit son fradra salvar dift, in o quid il mi altresi fazet et ab Ludher nul plaid nunquam prindrai, qui, meon vol, cist meon fradre Karle in damno sit.)

When Louis was done, Charles repeated the same oath in German.... Each people also swore an oath in its own language.... When this was done, Louis and Charles set out for Worms...

Nithard, *History of the Sons of Louis the Pious (after 843)*[9]

How a Moslem Poet
Presented Himself to a Viking King (845)

['Abd-al-Rahman II, emir of Cordova in Spain, sent the poet al-Ghazâl ("the Gazelle") with an embassy to a Viking identified only as "the king of the heathen," probably a Norwegian based in Ireland. The day after the envoys arrived, the king] summoned them to see him and al-Ghazâl made it a condition that he would not prostrate himself and that nothing would ever make them violate their tradition. And he agreed to that. When they proceeded towards him he sat in state for them; and he gave his orders and the entrance which led to him was made so small that no one could enter in to him without bowing down. When al-Ghazâl reached the door, he sat on the ground and advanced his feet and slid once on his buttocks, and when he passed through the door he stood up and saw that the king had decked himself out with a great many arms and a lot of decorations. But that did not awe al-Ghazâl nor did it frighten him, for he stood up presenting himself before the king and [saluted him profusely].... And the interpreter translated to the king what al-Ghazâl had said, and the king held the speech to be good and he said: "This is one of the wise men of the nation and one of their clever men." And he had been astonished at his sitting on the ground and advancing his feet when he entered, and he said: "We wanted to submit him to contempt, but he confronted our face with his shoes; had he not been an ambassador, we would have abhorred that in him!" Then al-Ghazâl presented to him the letter of 'Abd-al-Rahman, and the letter was read and interpreted for him and he regarded it favourably.

Tammam ibn-'Alqamah (9th century)[10]

An Independent Pagan Wife (845)

[After the incident above] when the wife of the king of the heathen heard of al-Ghazâl, she invited him to see her.... [He flattered her] and the wife of the king of the heathen became so fond of al-Ghazâl that she could not bear to go without seeing him each day, so she sent for him every day to stay with her, telling her of the customs of the Moslems and their stories and their land and their neighbouring nations. He rarely departed from her without a gift of clothes, food, or perfume she bestowed on him.

Then their affair became widely known, and his friends disapproved of it. And al-Ghazâl was warned against such conduct, and he became cautious. So he refrained from visiting her for a long time; finally she questioned him about it, and he told her what he had been warned against; she laughed and said: "In our religion we do not have that teaching, and we do not have jealousy; our women stay with our men by the women's own choice. The woman stays with the man as long as she loves him, and she leaves him when she hates him. And the custom of the heathen, before the religion of Rome reached them, had been that no woman would forbid herself the company of any man, although a noble woman would not befriend a man of low class, for then she would be reviled, and her folks would keep him away from her." When al-Ghazâl heard her speech he was delighted with it and returned to his intimacy with her [and wrote poems to amuse her].

Tammam ibn-'Alqamah (9th century)[11]

The Fable of Popess Joan (855-857)

[Pope] John [VIII], of English extraction, but born at Mainz, is said to have arrived at the popedom by evil arts; for disguising herself like a man, whereas she was a woman, she went when young with her paramour, a learned man, to Athens, and made such progress in learning under the professors there, that coming to Rome, she met with few that could equal, much less go beyond her, even in the knowledge of Scriptures; and by her learned and ingenious readings and disputations, she acquired such great respect and authority that upon the death of [Pope] Leo [IV in 855], as Martin says, by common consent, she was chosen pope in his place. But having permitted one of her domestics to lie with her, she hid her big belly a while, till as she was going to the Lateran Church, between the Colosseum (so called from Nero's Colossus) and Saint Clement's, her travail came upon her and she died upon the spot, having sat on the papal throne two years, one month, and four days [855-857], and was buried there without any pomp.

Some say the pope for shame of the thing does purposely decline going through that street when he goes to the Lateran, and that to avoid the like error, when any pope is first placed in the porphyry chair, which has a hole made for the purpose, his genitals are handled by the youngest deacon. As for the first, I deny it not; but for the second, I take the reason of it to be that he who is placed in so great authority may be reminded that he is not a god but a man, and subject to the necessities of nature, such as relieving himself, since that seat is in fact called "the fecal seat" (*sedes stercoraria*). This story is commonly told, but by very uncertain and obscure authors, and therefore I have related it barely and briefly. I have included it lest I should seem obstinate and pertinacious if I had omitted what is so generally talked about, for it is better to be wrong with the rest of the world than alone; and certainly what I have related may be thought not altogether incredible.

Bartolomeo Platina, *Lives of the Popes* (1479)[12]

John the Scot and Charles the Bald (871)

John the Scot came to England at this time. He was a man of penetrating mind and great eloquence who had formerly left his homeland [Ireland] and gone over to France, where he was received with great honour by Charles the Bald [king 843-877], who made him one of his intimate associates. John not only talked seriously to the king but also joked with him; they were inseparable companions both in the king's private quarters and at meals. Many of John's charming and witty remarks are current even today, of which this is an example:

One day at mealtime, John was seated across the table from the king. One round of drinks followed another, and by the time the last course was over, Charles was merrier than ever. As they were talking after dinner, the king noticed John do something that might be offensive in French society, so he rebuked him with a witticism, saying, "What is the difference between a sot and a Scot? (*Quid distat inter sottum et Scottum?*)." But John turned that grave rebuke back on its author with the reply, "Only the table! (*Tabula tantum*)." What could be wittier than this remark? The king was asking about a difference in manners, but John's reply was about the difference between their locations.

William of Malmesbury, *The Bishops of England* (1125)[13]

Martyrdom in the Classroom (878)

At this time John the Scot is supposed to have lived—a man of clear understanding and amazing eloquence. He had long since, from the continued tumult of war around him, retired into France to Charles the Bald [king 843-877], at whose request he had translated the *Hierarchia* of Dionysius the Areopagite word for word out of the Greek into Latin. He also composed a book that he entitled *Peri hyseon merismou*, or *On the Division of Nature*, extremely useful in solving the perplexity of certain indispensable inquiries, if he be pardoned for some things in which he deviated from the opinions of the Latins through too close attention to the Greeks. In after time, allured by the munificence of Alfred [871-899] he came into England, and at our monastery [Malmesbury], as report says, he was pierced with the iron styluses of the boys whom he was instructing, and was even looked upon as a martyr; which phrase I have not made use of to the disparagement of his holy spirit, as though it were a matter of doubt, especially as his tomb on the left side of the altar, and the verses of his epitaph, record his fame. These, though rugged and deficient in the polish of our days, are not so uncouth for ancient times:

> Here lies a saint, the sophist John, whose days
> On earth were graced with deepest learning's praise:
> Deemed meet at last by martyrdom to gain
> Christ's kingdom, where the saints forever reign.

William of Malmesbury (d. 1143?), *The Kings of England*[14]

Alfred and the Cakes (878)

In the *Life of Saint Neot* it is written that Alfred once hid for a long time in the home of one of his cowherds. One day it happened that the country woman who was the cowherd's wife was getting ready to cook some bread, while the king was sitting by the hearth repairing his bow and arrows and other war gear. The loaves had been set by the fire, and when the woman saw they were burning, she ran with haste and moved them. In exasperation, she scolded the invincible king, saying: "Why don't you turn the loaves around when you see they're burning, since you certainly enjoy eating them when they're cooked properly!" That unfortunate housewife had no idea that he was King Alfred who waged so many wars against the pagans and won so many victories over them.

Pseudo-Asser, *Annals of Saint Neot's*[15]

Alfred and Guthram:
An Entertaining Spy Story (878)

Venturing from his concealment [with the cowherds on the island of Athelney in the marshes of Somerset, King Alfred] hazarded an experiment of consummate art. Accompanied only by one of his most faithful adherents, he entered the tent of the Danish king [Guthram] under the disguise of a minstrel; and being admitted as a professional entertainer to the banqueting hall, there was no object of secrecy that he did not minutely attend to both with eyes and ears. Remaining there several days, till he had satisfied his mind on every matter which he wished to know, he returned to Athelney and, assembling his companions, he pointed out the indolence of the enemy and the easiness of their defeat. [Consequently the Danes were defeated and agreed to the treaty of Chippenham (better known as Wedmore) in 878.]

William of Malmesbury (d. 1143), *The Kings of England*[16]

The First Capetian King of France (888)

[From 24 November 885 until May 886, Count Odo of Paris defended the city successfully against the Vikings; then, with victory in sight, he appealled to Emperor Charles the Fat for assistance.]

The future King Odo [founder of the Capetian dynasty] then goes to this emperor of the Franks, Charles, to ask that he help the city quickly! ... Moved deeply in spirit by these words, like the sea stirred up by a storm wind, [the emperor] said to the Franks, "Hurry, go scout near the city, find a place for six hundred tents. Will these thieves dare behave so in my presence?" They obey his orders....

The prince whose tale we recite, surrounded by all sorts of arms, like the heaven with its starry splendors, appears—the Emperor Charles, accompanied by a large, polyglot throng, planting his tents by the tower below Montmartre....

He permits the barbarians to go to Sens, giving them seven hundred pounds of silver as a bribe to go back to their wicked kingdom before next March. Then the world froze in numb November. So Charles went away, shortly to die....

Meanwhile [13 January 888] Charles, stripped of realm and of life, sadly embraced the hidden bosom of rich earth [i.e. he was buried]. Straightway happy Odo takes the name and sanctity of the Frankish throne with much public pleasure and support, and his hand took the sceptre and his head, the crown. Frankland rejoiced, though he is a Neustrian, for he had no peer.

Abbo (fl. 888), *The Siege of Paris*[17]

Ingo's Rise to Feudal Lordship (ca. 890)

[Going up the Dordogne River, an army of Viking pirates had penetrated to Auvergne and were besieging the castle of Montpensier. King Odo of France met them there with a large army, which defeated one band of Vikings only to be attacked by another.] The French were trying to find someone to bear the king's standard because everyone in this great gathering of nobles seemed to be wounded and they all shirked the duty. Then Ingo suddenly sprang into the midst [of the council] and volunteered for the job, saying: "I am the king's groom and of humble birth, but I will carry the royal standard into the enemy ranks, if this does not diminish the honour of the nobility. The risks of war do not frighten me, because I know I can only die once." King Odo replied: "Be standard-bearer by our gift and the will of the princes."

Ingo took the standard and advanced with the army in close array; a wedge was formed with Ingo at the point, and waving the flag he penetrated the opposing host. The barbarians were thrown back with heavy losses. The royal army regrouped, charged again, and struck down more of the enemy. On the third charge almost all of the enemy were wiped out. Since the air was thick with dust raised by the fighting, Catillus [the Viking chief] was able to flee unobserved with a few followers, and he hid in a thicket. But as the victors went about plundering, they found him hiding there and made him prisoner. Those who were hiding with him were run through with the sword; their bodies were despoiled and then brought to King Odo.

Having won the victory, the king led the tyrant Catillus back with him to Limoges and there gave him this choice: he could either live or die, depending on whether he was willing to be baptized or not. The tyrant did not object but immediately asked to be baptized, although there was some doubt as to the sincerity of his faith. As the feast of Pentecost was about to be celebrated and the bishops were holding a council in the king's presence, the bishops decided that the tyrant should fast for three days. On the appointed day, the bishops first celebrated the offices in the basilica of Saint Martial; Catillus was then baptized by triple immersion in the name of the Father, Son, and Holy Spirit; he had just gotten out of the font and was about to be greeted by the king, when Ingo, the former standard-bearer, drew his sword and thrust it through the tyrant, killing him and polluting the sacred font with the blood that flowed from the wound.

The princes trembled with rage at this crime, while the king, filled with righteous anger, ordered that the murderer be seized and slaughtered. But the assassin threw down his sword, fled, and embraced the altar of Saint Martial. Then he shouted again and again that the king and princes should bear with him and give him an opportunity to be heard, until the king commanded that he should stand trial and answer for the crime he had committed.

Ingo spoke thus on his own behalf before the king and princes: "Let God, who knows my intentions be my witness that I care for nothing more than your welfare. Love for you pushed me to do this; concern for your welfare got me into this mess; to save your lives I fearlessly faced great danger. Sure, the deed was a big offense, but its usefulness to you is bigger. I don't deny that I've offended the royal majesty, but my point is that many advantages are to be gained from my crime. This is relevant because you can't judge my intention without considering how useful the crime may be. I noticed that fear caused the captured pirate to request baptism. As soon as he was released, he would have taken revenge for all the injuries done him, and especially for the slaughter of his followers. I turned my sword against him because I saw that this man would cause much bloodshed in the future. That's the motive of my crime...."

Some were sympathetic to this plea.... Some soldiers took his side and did what they could to mollify the king and obtain a pardon. They argued that he had nothing to gain from killing one of his own men; instead one should rejoice at the murder of this tyrant because if he died a true Christian, he would have eternal life, while if he received baptism fraudulently, his trick didn't work. These reasons calmed the king down. He buried the barbarian and restored Ingo to his good graces. Moreover, he gave into his keeping the castle of Blois, the castellan of which had been killed in the war against the pirates, and Ingo also married the man's widow with the king's permission.

Richer, *History of France* (after 995)[18]

A Frankish Prayer for Deliverance from the Vikings (before 900)

O God, deliver us from the cruel Norman people who lay waste our kingdoms, so that our bodies and goods may be preserved by divine grace. For they butcher young men and old alike, and also a multitude of girls and boys. Drive all these evils from us, we pray Thee. We beg Thee, O Lord, to turn us who beseech Thee towards Thee, O King of glory, who art our true peace, holy salvation, and firm hope. Give unto us peace and concord. Bestow upon us unwavering hope together with true faith; grant unto us unceasing and perfect love for our fellow human beings. May our requests be assisted by the prayers of the saints, whose glorious sufferings are an inspiration for us. May the Trinity have the greatest possible praise, peace, and glory throughout all ages. Amen.

Frankish Antiphonary (end of the 9th century)[19]

The Tenth Century

The Foundation of Cluny (910)

At this time the most generous of all leaders was William, duke of Auvergne and Aquitaine, the Celtic province. His household knights often frequented [the abbey of] Baume and were received affectionately by [its] abbot [Berno] and by the brothers of the monastery. Moreover, upon returning to their lord, they noted and reported to him very diligently whatever was good and honourable there. Furthermore, since the duke was a man of conspicuous goodness, he began to think how to find a good site that was suitable for religious use of this kind [i.e. as a monastery]; and straightway he sent to the man of God, Berno, and ordered that he should come to him at a place that God, the giver of all good gifts, had chosen in advance and had predestined to be salubrious forever—namely, Cluny. Berno came, bringing with him Hugo, the most famous monk [of his monastery], whom he consulted in all things. The duke received them with perfect love and disclosed to them the desire of his mind: the construction of a monastery that he wanted to complete if the Lord would grant it to him. Having acutely observed the circumstances of all aspects of the place, the monks could find no place more suitable than this one, namely Cluny. But the duke then said to them that it was not possible because it would spoil the sport of the hunting dogs that were always active in the area. It is reported that the abbot, since he was a wise man, gave this witty and jocular response to the duke. "Take the dogs away from here," he said, "and send in the monks. For you know as well as we do what reward the Lord will give you for dogs and what for monks." And with the greatest exultation the duke joyfully received the words of the man of God and said, "Father, you have given counsel wisely, and prudently without making any pretense. Now, with the cooperation of Christ, let it be done as you have kindly exhorted." And thus the work was begun immediately, pursued quickly, and soon consecrated in honour of Peter, prince of the Apostles.

Life of Saint Hugh (11th century)[1]

A Viking Upsets Charles the Simple (911)

[In 911 the Viking invaders of France made peace with the Franks at Saint-Clair-sur-Epte, where the Norman leader, Hrolf, also known as Rollo, received Normandy as a fief from King Charles the Simple.] At the urging of the Franks, Rollo put his hands between the king's hands—a thing which his father, his grandfather, and his great-grandfather had never done for anyone—and in return the king gave his daughter Giselle to the duke as his wife; and as her dowry, he gave him the land between the Epte river and the sea for a freehold (*in alodo*), and all of Brittany as well, so he would have enough land off of which to live. When Rollo refused to kiss the king's foot, the Franks said to the bishop [Franco of Rouen, who had arranged the alliance], "The recipient of such a gift ought to be glad to kiss the king's foot." But Rollo replied, "I shall never bend my knees to kneel to anyone, nor shall I kiss anybody's foot." But the Franks kept insisting, so he ordered one of his soldiers to kiss the king's foot. The man promptly seized the king's foot, raised it to his mouth, and planted the kiss while he was standing; thus he made the king fall flat on his back. This caused a great deal of laughter and a great uproar among the people.

Dudo of Saint-Quentin, *History of the Normans* (ca. 1000)[2]

A Royal Christmas
at the Monastery of Saint Gall (911)

Not long after, Conrad, who was then king [of Germany, 911-918], spent Christmas with the lord [Bishop Salomon] of Constance. On Christmas day, the bishop told the king about the three-day vespers processions at Saint Gall [20 miles away], which he praised highly. The king said, "I wish I could be there! By my soul! why shouldn't we go there in the morning?" Boats were made ready at once and boarded the next day; by noon the king arrived at our shore with the bishops and the rest of his retinue. He was received gloriously at Saint Gall itself with appropriate celebrations, including the reading of a new poem in praise of the king, and he spent three days and nights there with great good cheer, going back on the fourth day to spend the night at Arbon [on Lake Constance].

It would be a long story to tell in what merriment he spent those days and nights, especially at the children's procession. He ordered apples to be strewn in the middle of the church floor for them, but when he saw that not even the littlest child budged or even seemed to notice them, he marvelled at their discipline.

On children's day he also entered the brothers' dining-room at dinnertime accompanied by two bishops. Everyone stood up and he made many jolly remarks. "Whether you want to or not," he said, "you have to share with us." The dean was getting ready to put the abbot's table at his disposal, but the king embraced him and made him sit down and took the place facing him, while all the onlookers stood round laughing. "Just now *this* is what we'll share." He immediately sent for [Bishop] Salomon, however, so he could eat together with the king and not be slighted.

Next he called for the provost, since nothing had been prepared for the king except what the brothers were eating. "O king," said he, "it is just our luck that you did not wait until the next day, for tomorrow maybe we're going to have bread and plain beans, but that's not the menu today." "Sure," said the king, "and tomorrow God will be able to forgive you, too."

After this, the little children each read a short piece aloud, and as each one came down from the pulpit after his turn was over, he lifted up his mouth to the king, who popped in a gold piece [instead of a sweet]. One of the youngest cried out in surprise and spit out the gold. "If that one survives," the king said, "he'll make a good monk."

Finally, as he got up from the table, he made many good-humoured remarks to the brothers, warning them that as long as he lived he would hope to return and rejoice with them at such banquets. He then went back to his quarters, boasting to Salomon and everyone that he had never been entertained so pleasantly.

Ekkehard IV of St. Gall (ca. 980-1060) *Events at St. Gall*[3]

From Tar to Emperor: A Byzantine Career (913)

In the reign of Leo [VI], father of the present Constantine [VII Porphyrogenitus], the Emperor Romanus [I Lecapenus, an Armenian by birth], although he was *pauvre*, that is, poor, was regarded by everyone as *un homme utile*, that is, as a useful fellow. He was then an ordinary sailor in the emperor's pay serving with the fleet. On several occasions *en bataille*, that is, in battle, he rendered services that were *très utile*, that is, very useful; and finally as a reward his superior officer *donna lui le rang de capitaine*, that is, gave him the rank of captain.... [While reconnoitering the Saracens, he encountered a lion and killed it with his sword.] And so not long afterwards, as a reward for this glorious deed and for his other services, the emperor gave him the rank of admiral and ordered that *tous les bateaux*, that is, all the ships should be under his control and obey his orders.

Finally Leo, the most pious emperor of the Greeks ... [died in 912], leaving as his heirs his brother Alexander and his only son Constantine, who is still alive and happily reigning, he being then an infant *ne pouvant pas parler*, that is, not able to talk. As guardians of the palace and his private estate he appointed, as is the custom there, the eunuch who held the office of high chamberlain and Phocas, commander-in-chief of the land forces. To Romanus, who was not a man of high birth but was of signal courage, he gave the post of lord high admiral of the fleet. Alexander died [in 913] soon after his brother and left the little Constantine sole emperor....

Romanus, being a man of some shrewdness, when he heard of the death of the two emperors Leo and Alexander, got together a body of men from the fleet and collecting his ships made his way to a little island near Constantinople, almost within sight of the imperial palace. He himself, however, never crossed the water and refrained from paying the customary homage to the little emperor who had been born in the purple. This conduct of his caused no small dismay and alarm to the eunuch chamberlain and all the chief men in Constantinople. They therefore sent messengers and inquired the reason of his strange action, asking why he did not pay a visit to the monarch and render him the homage that was his due. Romanus replied that he had avoided the palace because he feared for his own life; and he added that if the chamberlain and the other lords did not come to see him and guarantee him his life and position, he would very soon join the king of the Saracens in Crete, and would help him with all his might to subdue the Greek realm. How cunningly this was said the outcome will declare.

Well, as we have mentioned, the terrified officials, little guessing that a snake was lurking for them in the grass, came in all confidence to see him, anxious and willing to do all that he wanted. But Romanus, following out his clever plan, as soon as they arrived, had them bound and stowed away in the hold, while he himself, free now from all apprehension, hastened with a numerous band of followers to the city. He there purged the palace of all whom he suspected to be against him and replaced them with his own supporters. Governor, superintendents, patricians, accountants, head steward, lord of the chamber, chamberlains, knights of the sword of all three classes, and sea lord were now every one creatures of his own appointment. Finally, to secure the success of his plans completely, he won the affections of Zoë, the little emperor's mother, and was admitted to her intimate favours. All the city was crowned with garlands, and Romanus everywhere was hailed as "father of the emperor." [Eventually, in 919, he had himself crowned emperor as well.]

Liudprand of Cremona, *Tit for Tat* (958-962)[4]

Papal Initiative Cleans Out a Nest of Moslem Pirates (915)

At this time [913] a band of Saracens sailed from Africa to Italy and laid hands on ... almost all the cities belonging to the Romans, so that in every place the Romans held but one half, these Africans the other. Indeed they established a fort on Mount Garigliano [between Rome and Naples], where they kept in security their wives, children, captives, and all their goods and chattels. No one coming from the west or north to make his prayers on the threshold of the blessed apostles [Peter and Paul] was able to get into Rome without being either taken prisoner by these men or only released at a high ransom....

When John [X] was made pope [in 914] ... a certain Landolf, an energetic man and skilful in all military exercises, was the illustrious prince of Benevento and Capua. As the Africans were doing great damage to the country, Pope John consulted this noble prince Landolf and asked him what he had better do in regard to this African business. When the prince got this message, he sent envoys to the pope with the following reply: "My spiritual father, this is a matter that requires careful consideration and a bold policy. Send therefore to the emperor of the Greeks, for these fellows are continually ravaging his territory this side of the [Adriatic] sea just as they do ours. Invite the people of Camerino and Spoleto also to help us, and under God's protection let us all then begin a vigorous campaign...."

As soon as the pope heard this he sent off messengers to Constantinople, humbly asking the emperor for assistance. That latter, being a righteous and God-fearing man, without delay sent off a fleet with an army on board, which passed up the river Garigliano and joined forces with Pope John, Landolf the powerful prince of Benevento, and the people of Camerino and Spoleto. A fierce battle then followed, from which the Africans, seeing that the Christians were the stronger, retreated to the summit of Mount Garigliano and contented themselves with blocking all the narrow paths up it.... Day by day the Greeks and the Latins continued their attacks, and finally by God's grace not a single African remained; they were all either slain by the sword or taken alive.

Liudprand of Cremona, *Tit for Tat* (958-962)[5]

Castile for a Horse and a Hawk (931)

In this year [927] King Sancho [of Leon and Asturias] sent an order to Count Fernán Gonzáles that he should attend the cortes in Leon, and that he should come immediately.... As he journeyed he prayed to God in this manner: "Lord, I ask and beseech you for mercy so that you will wish to help me in such a way that I can take Castile...." The count had with him a very fine molted hawk and an excellent horse that he had gained in battle with Almanzor. When the king saw the horse, it pleased him greatly, and he asked the count to sell it to him. The count replied that he did not want to sell it, but instead the king could just take it as a gift if that pleased him. Then King Sancho said to him that he would have them only if he could buy the hawk and horse and pay the count one thousand marks of silver.... They both agreed to this and set a date when the king should pay the count. If the king had not paid the count by this day, the payment was to be doubled each day thereafter. And then they made a charter in which was written all the details of the arrangement and the testimonies of those who certified it. The king had bought a very fine horse, but the purchase was to cost him very dearly at the end of three years; for he lost the county of Castile because he could not pay the price, which had increased greatly and enlarged his debt to the count....

[In 931] Count Fernán Gonzáles of Castile sent a request to King Sancho of Leon, asking that he pay him for the horse and the hawk he had bought; if he did not, the count said he would make trouble for the king. The king sent no answer as to when payment would be made, so the count assembled all his forces, entered the kingdom, overran the land, stole much livestock, and took many men as prisoners. When King Sancho learned about this, he ordered his steward to collect money for the payment of the debt and to pay the count....

The steward met the count to pay him for the purchase. When they calculated the amount to be paid, they found that, because the debt had doubled each day according to the agreement, it was now so much that all the money in Spain could not have paid the debt. So the steward had to return without accomplishing his task.

When the king heard the news, he was troubled ... because he realized that he had made a bad bargain and he knew he could never pay a debt of that size. So he consulted his vassals, and they agreed that he should give the county of Castile as payment for the debt.... The count was well pleased; he saw that he had won a great prize because he did not have to pay homage to anyone for the county except to the pope as the Lord of Law. And in this way the county came to the Castilians and left the authority and service of Leon and the Leonese.

First Universal Chronicle (13th century)[6]

Women's Rights (929-934)

The hero Theodebald [I] ... was marquess of Camerino and Spoleto. He went to the help of the prince of Benevento against the [Byzantine] Greeks who had pressed him grievously hard [in southern Italy], and attacking them in a regular campaign gained the victory. It happened that he captured a number of the Greeks who had been driven from the countryside but were still holding some forts. These men he castrated, saying to the general who commanded them: "I understand that your holy emperor attaches a special value to eunuchs, and therefore I have hastened to send him a few with my respects, and by God's grace will send him more very soon."

Let me here insert the story of a witty, or rather a clever, trick which a certain woman played on this occasion. One day some Greeks in company with the men of the countryside went out from a fortress to fight against the aforesaid Theodebald, and a certain number of them were taken prisoners by him. As he was taking them off to be castrated, a certain woman, fired by love for her husband and very disturbed for the safety of his members, rushed out in a frenzy from the fortress with her hair all flying loose. Tearing her cheeks with her nails until the blood came, she took her stand before Theodebald's tent and began to cry out and wail aloud. At last Theodebald appeared and said to her: "What is the matter with you, woman, that you are making such a loud and lamentable din?"

To that—a pretence of folly is at the proper time the height of wisdom—she replied: "These are strange and unheard of doings, heroes, to make war against women who cannot attack you back. None of our daughters are descended from the stock of the Amazons. We devote our lives to Minerva's work and are quite ignorant of weapons." Theodebald then said to her: "What hero in his right mind ever made war upon women, except in the days of the Amazons?"

"What more cruel war," she answered, "can you make on women, or what more grievous loss can you inflict upon them, than to seek to deprive their husbands of that member on which the warmth of our bodies depends and in which, most important of all, our hopes of children in the future are centered. By castrating our men you rob them of something which is not theirs but ours. I ask you, did the flocks of sheep and the herds of cattle that you took from me last week bring me as a suppliant to your camp? I willingly agree to give up the animals, but this other loss, so serious, so cruel, and so irreparable, I shudder at, I shrink from, I refuse. May all the gods above protect me from such a calamity!"

At this the whole army burst into a guffaw, and her arguments were received with such favour that they earned for her not only the return of her husband intact but also of the beasts that had been driven away. As she was going off with her belongings, Theodebald sent a page after her to ask what part of her husband he should remove if he came out again from the fortress to fight against him. "My husband," she said, "has a nose, eyes, hands, and feet. If he comes out again, let your master remove those parts that belong to him; but let him leave me, his humble servant, what is mine." Such was the answer she sent back by the messenger, for she realized, by the laughter that her first speech had evoked and by the return of her husband, that she had the favour of the army on her side.

Liudprand of Cremona, *Tit for Tat* (958-962)[7]

A Byzantine Blitzkrieg (941)

The Bulgarians sent word to the [Byzantine] emperor that the Russes were advancing upon Tsargrad [Constantinople] with ten thousand vessels. The Russes set out across the [Black] sea and began to ravage Bithynia [in Asia Minor]. They waged war along the Pontus ... and laid waste the entire region of Nicomedia, burning everything along the gulf. Of the people they captured, some they butchered, others they set up as targets and shot at, some they seized upon, and after binding their hands behind their backs, they drove iron nails through their heads. Many sacred churches they gave to the flames, while they burned many monasteries and villages, and took no little booty on both sides of the sea.

[A Byzantine army arrived, and after an inconclusive battle] the Russes returned at evening to their companions, embarked at night upon their vessels, and fled away. [The Byzantine admiral] Theophanes pursued them in boats with Greek fire, and dropped it through pipes upon the Russian ships, so that a strange miracle was offered to view.

The Russes, upon seeing the flames, cast themselves into the seawater, being anxious to escape, but the survivors returned home. When they came once more to their native land, where each one recounted to his kinsfolk the course of events and described the fire launched from the ships, they related that the Greeks had in their possession the lightning from heaven, and had set them on fire by pouring it forth, so that the Russes could not conquer them.

The Russian Primary Chronicle (ca. 1038)[8]

"Such a Form as Grecian Goldsmiths Make" (949)

[This is an eyewitness account of how envoys from Spain and Italy were introduced to the Byzantine emperor, Constantine VII Porphyrogenitus, at his palace in Constantinople.] Before the emperor's seat stood a tree, made of bronze gilded over, whose branches were filled with birds, also made of gilded bronze, which uttered different cries, each according to its varying species. The throne itself was so marvellously fashioned that at one moment it seemed a low structure, and at another it rose high into the air. It was of immense size and was guarded by lions, made either of bronze or of wood covered over with gold, who beat the ground with their tails and gave a dreadful roar with open mouth and quivering tongue.

Leaning upon the shoulders of two eunuchs I was brought into the emperor's presence. At my approach the lions began to roar and the birds to cry out, each according to its kind; but I was neither terrified nor surprised, for I had previously made inquiry about all these things from people who were well acquainted with them. So after I had three times made obeisance to the emperor with my face upon the ground, I lifted my head, and behold! the man whom just before I had seen sitting on a moderately elevated seat had now changed his raiment and was sitting on the level of the ceiling. How it was done I could not imagine, unless perhaps he was lifted up by some such sort of device as we [in Italy] use for raising the timbers of a wine press.

On that occasion he did not address me personally, since even if he had wished to do so the wide distance between us would have rendered conversation unseemly, but by the intermediary of a secretary he inquired about [my master].... I made a fitting reply and then, at a nod from the interpreter, left his presence and retired to my lodging.

Liudprand of Cremona, *Tit for Tat* (958-962)[9]

The Sword and the Stone (ca. 950)

A knight, Franco, was an exile from Germany in France, and as he came through the midst of the forest of Bihere he saw King Louis [IV d'Outremer, 936-954], the son of Charles [the Simple], sitting alone upon a stone, for his servants had taken a stag in that place, and seeing another stag run by they rushed off and left him and followed it.

Franco wanted to speak to the king, but knew not that this was he, and turning aside to him asked where the king was. Louis, who wished to keep his incognito, said: "He will be here shortly," and when the knight dismounted, the king rose and held the stirrup for him on the other side, as the manner is, lest the saddle should slip over; and seeing the knight girt with a very long sword, asked to look at it, and after admiring the size and beauty of the sword, which he had drawn, he forgot his purposed concealment, and said in a kingly manner: "Bring me a stone to sit upon." Franco, in fear of the sword, brought it, and asked for the sword back again, and when he had it in hand said: "Take that stone back to its place." The king saw the raised sword, feared, and carried the stone back.... The king when rejoined by his men called him back—for he was making off in terror—with great praises, and told his people how bravely and courteously he had made him carry the stone back, and gave him Crêpy-en-Valois for an inheritance.

Walter Map (fl. 1162-1208), *Courtiers' Trifles*[10]

Arcanum Imperii: The Secret of Greek Fire (ca. 950)

Fix, my son [the Byzantine heir apparent], your mind's eye upon my words, and learn those things which I command you, and you will be able in due season as from ancestral treasures to bring forth the wealth of wisdom, and to display the abundance of wit. Know therefore that all the tribes of the north have, as it were implanted in them by nature, a ravening greed of money, never satiated, and so they demand everything and hanker after everything and have desires that know no limit or circumscription, but are always eager for more, and desirous to acquire great profits in exchange for a small service. And so these importunate demands and brazenly submitted claims must be turned back and rebutted by plausible speeches and prudent and clever excuses, which, in so far as our experience has enabled us to arrive at them, will, to speak summarily run more or less as follows: ....

Similar care and thought you must take in the matter of the liquid fire which is discharged through tubes, so that if any shall ever venture to demand this too, as they have often made demands of us also, you may rebut and dismiss them in words like these: "This too was revealed and taught by God through an angel to the great and holy Constantine, the first Christian emperor, and concerning this too he received great charges from the same angel, as we are assured by the faithful witness of our fathers and grandfathers, that it should be manufactured among the Christians only and in the city ruled by them, and nowhere else at all, nor should it be sent nor taught to any other nation whatsoever. And so, for the confirmation of this among those who should come after him, this great emperor caused curses to be inscribed on the holy table of the church of God, that he who should dare to give of this fire to another nation should neither be called a Christian, nor be held worthy of any rank or office; and if he should be the holder of any such, he should be expelled therefrom and be anathematized and made an example for ever and ever, whether he were emperor, or patriarch, or any other man whatever, either ruler or subject, who should seek to transgress this commandment. And he adjured all who had the zeal and fear of God to be prompt to make away with him who attempted to do this, as a common enemy and a transgressor of this great commandment, and to dismiss him to a death most hateful and cruel."

Constantine VII, *Imperial Administration* (ca. 950)[11]

The Adventures of Adelaide (951)

Meanwhile the Italian king, Lothar, fell seriously ill and departed this world [950], leaving the realm to be held as was proper by his lofty queen whom he had joined in love to himself, she who had been the daughter of the great King Rudolf [II of Upper Burgundy], born from a long line of great [Carolingian] kings. The high nobility of her parents determined her brilliant name, Adelaide [= *Adelheit*, "nobility"]. She to be sure shone with such great talent that she could have ruled worthily the kingdom left her, if her people themselves had not presently contrived bitter treachery. When at last, as I said, Lothar was dead, there was a certain part of the people who, already rebellious and perversely hostile toward their own lords, restored to the rule of Berengar [marquess of Ivrea] the realm [of Italy] which had been taken from him forcibly on his father's death....

When he had been elevated to the office he assuredly desired, Berengar revealed whatever rancour he carried in his gloomy heart during the time he mourned the loss of his father's kingdom. His heart being kindled with more bitterness than was proper, he poured out his accumulated rage on the innocent woman, wrongfully using force on

Queen Adelaide who had done him no wrong in her reign. Not only did he take the throne in the lofty hall for himself, but he also straightway unlocked the treasury and with his hand took out from the stores all the gold he found, along with jewels of various kinds and the noble diadem of the royal brow, and he neglected no trifle of the regalia.

And he had no reservation about depriving her of her attendants and of the persons fit for royal service and (alas!) of her royal power. Finally, too, he denied her the liberty of going and staying where she would, entrusting her with a single serving girl to a count obedient to him to guard. He, being constrained by the orders of a king who ordered unjustly, had no qualms about keeping her, who was without taint of guilt and was mistress over him, under lock and key, surrounded by troops of guards as criminals are guarded. But He who freed Peter from Herod's chains mercifully redeemed her when He willed.

When she was distraught in mind with many cares and had no hope of sure comfort, Bishop Adelhard [of Reggio], pitying her wretched state and not tolerating the harm done to his dear lady, sent her quickly a secret message to flee and earnestly advised her to seek the firmly fortified town which was his episcopal see. Here he would provide her the security of a trustworthy garrison and worthy attendants, too. By reason of the kindly messages, the queen, happier now, desired to be released from her bonds. Still, she did not know what to do, for no door lay open which would allow her to leave at night when her guards slept. Moreover, she possessed no person subject to her service in her dungeon who would carry out her orders except only the servant girl I mentioned and one priest of praiseworthy life. When she had with constant lament told them everything she had pondered at length, grieving in her bitter soul, they decided together that they could succeed if they would dig a secret underground passage by which they could escape from their harsh bonds. This it is agreed was readily accomplished by the present help of the merciful Christ, for when the tunnel had been carefully completed according to their plan, a night suitable for gaining freedom again came, a night on which the devout queen with only her two companions escaped all the snares of her guards while sleep crept over the limbs of the people, and she traversed at nighttime as much of the way as her tender feet could. But when presently dark night, its shadows rent, left, and the sky began to pale with the rays of the sun, she hid cautiously in secret caves; now she would wander in forests, now she would hide in the furrows among the ripe stalks of growing grain, until night returning, garbed in her usual darkness, covered again the earth in shadowy mist. Then she eagerly hurried again on the way she had begun.

At last the thoroughly frightened guards, not finding her, reported what had happened to the count who had been assigned the keeping of his lady. He was struck to the quick with great terror and began to hunt her with his many retainers, and when he failed and could not find where the illustrious queen had gone, he fearfully reported the matter to King Berengar. He immediately lapsed into utter rage and at once sent his retainers every which way and ordered them to neglect no place no matter how small, but to inspect carefully all places of concealment lest the queen might be hiding in them.

He himself followed with the multitude of a bold host like one who wants to defeat ferocious enemies in war, and in his rapid course he passed through the very grainfield where the lady then hid in the hollow furrows, she whom he was seeking, covered under the stalks of grain. But though he bustled back and forth about the place where she lay overcome with terror, and though he tried to separate the clumps of wheat stalks by stretching out his spear, still he did not find her whom Christ's grace concealed. But when he was confounded and returned exhausted, the venerable Bishop Adelhard soon arrived and led his lady joyfully within the firm walls of his city. He attended her duly with all honour until by Christ's mercy she received the glory of a royalty greater than the one she had sadly left.

At length our [German] people, then realizing that the queen was bereft of her dear lord—the queen whose sweet piety they had experienced when they began to go through Italy to Rome—reported her manifold piety often to Otto [I, the Great] then already a great king [of Germany], but now [as I write] augustus of the Roman Empire. They said that there was no other woman worthy to be led into the royal bridal chamber since the sad death of his lady Edith. The king, delighted at such a sweet reputation, pondered long in his quiet breast how he might marry this queen who was beset by the intrigues of the king [Berengar]....

[So Otto invaded Italy and seized Pavia while Berengar fled from his captital without resisting. Otto] was quite mindful of noble Adelaide and certainly was eager to see the royal face of one whose goodness he had learned of. Wherefore he sent her secret messengers of peace and sweet love under a seal of faith and urged her by persuasive friends to come quickly to Pavia, a populous city, which she had left with bitter sadness. There, by the holy fidelity of a constant king she would joyfully attain the highest honour where previously she had suffered great grief. The queen yielded to the kindly summons and, with many throngs of subject peoples, came where she was bidden . When the king at whose behest she came learned this, he instructed his dear brother Henry to go back across the Po to meet her so that the collected retinue of the great duke [Henry of Bavaria] could deck out the heiress who was to be exalted with the splendours of royalty. He eagerly carried out the instructions of his elder brother and set out with a royal troop and joyfully sought the respected queen's encampment where she stayed with many retainers. He accompanied her with supreme honour until she came into the king's presence. She immediately and properly pleased the king and was chosen as worthy consort of his realm.

Hrotsvitha of Gandersheim (d. 972), *The Deeds of Otto*[12]

Saint Dunstan Ends a Royal Scandal (955)

In the year of our Lord 955, Edwy, son of Edmund [939-946], the brother of Athelstan, the former king [924-939], taking possession of the kingdom [of England], retained it four years [955-959]. He was a wanton youth, who abused the beauty of his person in illicit intercourse. Finally, taking as his wife a woman nearly related to him [Aelfgifu], he doted on her beauty and despised the advice of his counsellors. On the very day he had been consecrated king, in full assembly of the nobility, when deliberating on affairs of importance and essential to the state, he burst suddenly from amongst them, darted wantonly into his chamber, and rioted in the embraces of the harlot. All were indignant of the shameless deed and murmured among themselves. Dunstan alone, with the firmess implied by his name [hill + stone], regardless of the royal indignation, violently dragged the lascivious boy from the chamber, and on the archbishop's compelling him to repudiate the strumpet [in 958], made him his enemy forever.

William of Malmesbury (d. 1143?), *The Kings of England*[13]

The Conversion of Olga the Wise (955)

[Olga, ruler of the Russian state of Kiev, was the first Russian convert to Christianity.] Olga went to Greece, and arrived at Tsargrad [Constantinople]. The reigning emperor was named Tzimiskes. Olga came before him, and when he saw that she was very fair of countenance and wise as well, the emperor wondered at her intellect. He conversed with her and remarked that she was worthy to reign with him in his city. When Olga heard his words, she replied that she was still a pagan, and that if he desired to baptise her, he should perform this function himself; otherwise, she was unwilling to accept baptism. The emperor, with the assistance of the patriarch, accordingly baptised her....

After her baptism, the emperor summoned Olga and made known to her that he wished her to become his wife. But she replied, "How can you marry me, after yourself baptising me and calling me your daughter? For among Christians that is unlawful, as you yourself must know." The the emperor said, "Olga, you have outwitted me." He gave her many gifts of gold, silver, silks, and various vases, and dismissed her, still calling her his daughter.

The Russian Primary Chronicle (ca. 1038)[14]

"He is Only a Boy":
John XII, A Worldly Pope (963-964)

[Pope John XII, who was also hereditary duke of Rome, was elected pope at the age of 18. In 962, when he was 25, he crowned the king of Germany, Otto I the Great, as emperor. After Otto left Rome, however, John began to plot against him, so Otto sent agents to Rome to discover the reason for the young pope's change of heart.] On his messengers' arrival they got this answer, not from a few chance informants, but from all the citizens of Rome: "Pope John hates the most sacred emperor ... [who] knows, lives by, and loves the things of God.... Pope John is the enemy of all these things.

"What we say is a tale well known to all. As witness to its truth, take the widow of Rainer his own vassal, a woman with whom John has been so blindly in love that he has made her governor of many cities and given to her the golden crosses and cups that are the sacred possessions of

Saint Peter himself. Witness also the case of Stephana, his father's mistress, who recently conceived a child by him and died of an effusion of blood. If all else were silent, the palace of the Lateran, which once sheltered saints and is now a harlot's brothel, will never forget his union with his father's wench, the sister of the other concubine Stephania. Witness again the absence of all women here save Romans: they fear to come and pray at the threshold of the holy apostles, for they have heard how John a little time ago took women pilgrims by force to his bed—wives, widows, and virgins alike.... Witness the women he keeps, some of them fine ladies who, as the poet says, are as thin as reeds by dieting [Terence, *Eunuchus* 2.3.5-6], while others are everyday buxom wenches. It is all the same to him whether they walk the pavement or ride in a carriage and pair [Juvenal, *Satires* 6.350-351]. That is the reason why there is the same disagreement between him and the holy emperor as there is of necessity between wolves and lambs [Horace, *Epodes* 4.1.5]...."

When the envoys on their return gave this report to the emperor, he said: "He is only a boy, and will soon alter if good men set him an example. I hope that honourable reproof and generous persuasion will quickly cure him of these vices...."

[But the pope persisted in his intrigues against the emperor, so in November 963 Otto returned to Rome and called a church council to try John XII *in absentia*, since he had fled to Tivoli. At the trial] Benedict cardinal deacon with his fellow deacons and priests said that ... as regards his adultery, though they had no visual information, they knew for certain that he had carnal acquaintance with Rainer's widow, Stephana his father's concubine, the widow Anna, and his own niece, and that he had turned the holy palace into a brothel and resort for harlots. He had gone hunting publicly; ... he had caused the death of cardinal subdeacon John by castrating him; he had set houses on fire and appeared in public equipped with sword, helmet, and cuirass. To all this they testified; while everyone, clergy and laity alike, loudly accused him of drinking wine for love of the devil. At dice, they said, he asked the aid of Jupiter, Venus, and the other demons; he did not celebrate matins nor observe the canonical hours nor fortify himself with the sign of the cross....

[After hearing this testimony, Otto wrote to John, inviting him to come and purge himself of the charges. But when the messengers] arrived at Tivoli, they could not find the pope: he had gone off into the country with bow and arrows, and no one could tell them where he was. [So he was deposed, and eventually] the Lord decreed that every age should know how justly Pope John had been repudiated by his bishops and all the people.... One night [in May 964] when John was disporting himself with some man's wife outside Rome, the devil dealt him such a violent blow on the temples that he died of the injury within a week. Moreover at the prompting of the devil, who had struck the blow, he refused the last sacraments, as I have frequently heard testified by his friends and kinsmen who were at his deathbed.

Liudprand of Cremona, *History of Otto* (964)[15]

A Wandering Scholar: Gerbert of Aurillac (967-972)

Born in Aquitaine [in the 940s], Gerbert was raised since boyhood in the monastery of Saint-Géraud in Aurillac, where he learned [Latin] grammar. He was still pursuing his studies there when Count Borrel of Barcelona came to the monastery on a pilgrimage [in 967]. The count was received with the utmost hospitality by the abbot, who asked him in the course of conversation whether they had anyone in Spain who was deeply learned in the liberal arts. When the count promptly replied in the affirmative, the abbot soon persuaded him to take someone from the abbey back with him to be instructed in the arts. Far from refusing, the count generously agreed to the request, and with the consent of the brothers he took Gerbert and entrusted his education to Bishop Hatto [of Vich, near Barcelona]. Under his direction, Gerbert successfully studied most of mathematics [probably at the monastery of Ripoll].

But God wanted France, which was then still in darkness, to be illuminated again with great light, so He gave the count and the bishop the idea of going to Rome on a pilgrimage [in 970]. They got ready and set out with the young man who had been placed in their care. When they arrived in the city, first they prayed at the tomb of the holy apostles, and then they went and presented themselves to the pope [John XIII], to whom they offered anything of theirs that he cared to have.

The pope did not fail to notice the young man's intelligence and his eagerness to learn. Since music and astronomy were at that time almost completely unknown in Italy, the pope soon sent a legate to Otto [the Great], the king of Germany and Italy, informing him of the arrival of this young man who knew mathematics better than anyone else and could teach it to the king's subjects effectively. The king soon replied to the pope that the young man should be kept at Rome and by no means be allowed to go home. The pope tactfully explained to the count and bishop who had come from Spain with Gerbert that the king wished to retain the young man for a while and that he would be sent home presently with honour and, moreover, that they would then be compensated for the favour. Thus the count and the bishop were persuaded to leave the young man behind under these terms, while they returned to Spain.

The young man was therefore left with the pope, who presented him to the king. When questioned about his knowledge of the liberal arts, he replied that he knew mathematics well enough but that he wanted to learn the science of logic. Since this was his goal, his stay in Rome as a teacher was not long.

At that time, Gerannus, the archdeacon of Rheims, had the greatest reputation as a logician. Lothar, the king of France, sent Gerannus as his ambassador to Otto, king of Italy, [who was then in Rome for his son's wedding on 14 April 972]. Overjoyed at the archdeacon's arrival, Gerbert went to the king and obtained permission to study under Gerannus. For some time he was his constant companion and accompanied him back to Rheims; from him he learned the science of logic, mastering it completely in a short period of time. Garannus tried to learn mathematics at the same time but was overcome by the difficulties of the subject, even though he never tried to master musical theory [which was part of mathematics]. In the meantime, the excellence of Gerbert's scholarship brought him to the attention of the archbishop [Adelbero of Rheims], who valued him above all others for his learning and asked him to take charge of teaching the liberal arts to classes of pupils [at the cathedral school of Rheims].

Richer, *History of France* (after 995)[16]

The Childhood of Ethelred the Unready (born ca.969)

In the year of our Lord's incarnation 979, Ethelred, son of Edgar and Elfthrida, obtaining the kingdom [of England], occupied, rather than governed, it for thirty-seven years. The career of his life is said to have been cruel in the beginning, wretched in the middle, and disgraceful in the end....

[Saint] Dunstan [archbishop of Canterbury] had indeed foretold his worthlessness, having discovered it by a very filthy token. For when Ethelred was quite an infant and the bishops were standing round as he was being immersed in the baptismal font, he defiled the sacrament by a natural evacuation. Dunstan, being extremely angered at this, exclaimed, "By God and his mother, this will be a sorry fellow."

I have read that when he was ten years of age and heard the report that his brother [Edward the Martyr] was killed, he so irritated his furious mother by his weeping that she, not having a whip at hand, beat the little innocent with some candles she snatched up, nor did she desist until he was drenched with tears and nearly lifeless. For this reason he dreaded candles for the rest of his life, so much so that he would never let their light be brought into his presence.

William of Malmesbury (d. 1143?), *The Kings of England*[17]

A Nest of Moslem Highwaymen in the Alps (973)

A huge multitude of the cruellest Saracens poured forth from Spain by sea and reached the frontiers of Italy and Provence. In each kingdom they indiscriminately slaughtered both males and females of all ages, afterwards destroying and pillaging monasteries, cities, villages, and manors. Then these Saracens moved rapidly along the Julian Alps until they came to the upper slopes of the Pennine Alps, where for a long time their impieties went unbridled. From there they raided the Christians and afflicted them with various calamities: some they killed, others they kidnapped, while yet others were robbed of all their goods; in short, they expressed their impiety by tyrannical conduct of every kind.

Among the other evil deeds of this abominable people was the kidnapping of the most blessed father Maiolus [the grand abbot of Cluny, the second most important churchman in Christendom]. He was returning from Rome, where he had been visiting the pope, when [in the summer of 972] they seized him by deceit and ambush, despoiled him of all his goods, put him in chains, and afflicted him with hunger and thirst. He was freed with God's help: in the end, the money of his monastery paid his ransom, and, because God was protecting him, he escaped unharmed from their hands .

Because the Saracens captured the abbot unjustly, they were cast out and ruined forever. Just as the Jews were expelled from their lands after the passion of Christ, so the Saracens were driven out from Christian lands following the capture of Christ's most faithful servant, Maiolus. And just as the Lord used the Roman emperors Titus and Vespasian to carry out his vendetta against the Jews, so he used William [count of Provence], a man of distinction and a most Christian prince, to lift the yoke of the Saracens from the Christians' shoulders. For the sake of the blessed Maiolus, God's mighty power rescued from the tyranny of the Saracens much territory that they held unrighteously.

Saint Odilo (d. 1049), *Life of Saint Maiolus*[18]

The Narrow Escape of Emperor Otto II (982)

Meanwhile the Caesar [Otto II] ruled the [Western] Roman Empire so that he maintained all the former property of his father [Otto the Great], bravely resisting the Saracens' attack and forcing them far back from his territory [in southern Italy]. When he heard that Calabria suffered greatly from frequent [Byzantine] Greek invasions and Saracen plunder, he called out the Bavarians and the battle-hardened Alemanni [or Swabians].

He and Duke Otto [of Swabia], the son of his brother Liudulf, hurried to the city of Taranto, which the Greeks had secured by an occupation force, and he was shortly able to subdue them in a courageous raid.

In order to put down the Saracens, who had covered the territory with numerous troops, he sent out trained spies to collect information about the enemy. First he bottled them up in a town and forced them to flee, totally beaten, and afterwards meeting them in an open field, he killed countless of them in a brave attack and now hoped to destroy them.

But unexpectedly they collected themselves once more, proceeded in closed ranks against our troops, and on 13 July defeated them [at Cortone in Calabria] since our side put up very little resistance—what a disaster! Among the [4000] slain was Richer, the lance-bearer, and Duke Udo, my mother's uncle; Count Thietmar, Bezelin, Gebhard, Gunther, Ezelin and his brother Bezelin, with Burkhard, Dedi, Conrad, and many others, whose names God only knows.

The emperor, however, fled with the aforesaid [Duke] Otto and others by way of the sea, and seeing in the distance a [Byzantine] ship of the "Salandria" type, he tried to reach it on the horse of the Jew Calonimus. But it refused to take him aboard and passed by. Upon his return to dry land he saw the Jew, who was apprehensive and wanted to await the fate of his beloved lord. And when the emperor saw that the enemy was approaching, he was upset and asked him what would become of him now; but then he saw a second Salandria and recognized a friend among the crew on whose help he could count, so he plunged once more into the sea on horseback, reached the ship, and was taken on board.

Only his knight Henry (with the Slavic name Zolunta) knew who he was; they laid him on the bed of the ship's commander, who finally recognized him and asked if he was the emperor. After a lengthy disclaimer he finally had to admit it. "It's me," said he: "my sins have rightly brought me to this misfortune. But listen to what we should do now together. Miserable me, I have just lost the best men of my empire, and driven by this grief, I can not and will not ever set foot on these lands again nor see their friends again. Let's go to Rossano where my wife [the Greek princess Theophano] awaits my return. We will pick her up and all the money—a vast sum—and look up your emperor, my brother. Surely he will be a good friend in need to me, or so I hope." The commander of the ship agreed, delighted over such pleasant conversation, and hurried day and night to reach that place.

When they were near, the knight with the double name [Henry-Zolunta] was sent ahead by the emperor to get the empress, together with Bishop Dietrich, who was with her, and the many pack animals laden with much gold. When the Greeks saw the empress leave the town with the aforesaid gifts, they anchored and let Bishop Dietrich on board with a few attendants. On the advice of the bishop, the emperor took off his poor clothes and put on better ones. Standing on the prow of the ship, he suddenly trusted to his strength and agility and jumped into the sea. One of the Greeks standing around wanted to grab him by his garment and hold him fast; but transfixed by the sword of the good knight Liuppo, he fell down backwards.

Then they fled to the other side of the ship, but our forces went into the boats with which they had come, following undisturbed behind the caesar, who was waiting on the dry land and was ready to fulfil the promised reward to the Greeks by means of rich presents. But since they were greatly frightened and full of mistrust, they went home, contrary to their promises.... With what joy the emperor was greeted by those present and the ones coming later, I need not describe.

Thietmar of Merseburg (975-1018), *Chronicle*[19]

"We Cannot Exist Without that Pleasure" (986)

Vladimir [Olga's grandson] was visited by Bulgarians of Mohammedan faith, who said, "Though you are a wise and prudent prince, you have no religion. Adopt our faith and revere Mohammed." Vladimir inquired what was the nature of their religion. They replied that they believed in God, and that Mohammed instructed them to practice circumcision, to eat no pork, to drink no wine, and, after death, promised them complete fulfillment of their carnal desires. "Mohammed," they asserted, "will give each man seventy fair women. He may choose one fair one, and upon that woman will Mohammed confer the charms of them all, and she shall be his wife. Mohammed promises that one may then satisfy every desire, but whoever is poor in this world will be no different in the next." They also spoke other false things which out of modesty may not be written down. Vladimir listened to them, for he was fond of women and indulgence, regarding which he heard with pleasure. But circumcision and abstinence from pork and wine were disagreeable to him. "Drinking," said he, "is the joy of the Russians. We cannot exist without that pleasure."

The Russian Primary Chronicle (ca. 1038)[20]

Pomp and Circumstance Convert Russia (987)

[Olga's grandson, Vladimir, was urged to convert to Islam, Judaism, and several kinds of Christianity. In order to make an informed decision, he sent ten emissaries to observe the leading contenders.] They returned to their own country, and the prince called together his boyars and the elders. Vladimir then announced the return of the envoys who had been sent out, and suggested that their report be heard. He thus commanded them to speak out before his vassals.

The envoys reported: "When we journeyed among the Bulgarians, we beheld how they worship in their temple, called a mosque, while they stand ungirt. The Bulgarian bows, sits down, looks hither and thither like one possessed, and there is no happiness among them, but instead only sorrow and a dreadful stench. Their religion is not good. Then we went among the Germans, and saw them performing many ceremonies in their temples; but we beheld no glory there. Then we went on to Greece, and the Greeks led us to the edifices where they worship their God, and we knew not whether we were in heaven or on earth. For on earth there is no such splendour or such beauty, and we are at a loss how to describe it. We know only that God dwells there among men, and their service is fairer than the ceremonies of other nations. For we cannot forget that beauty. Every man, after tasting something sweet, is afterward unwilling to accept that which is bitter, and therefore we cannot dwell longer here."

Then the boyars spoke and said: "If the Greek faith were evil, it would not have been adopted by your grandmother Olga, who was wiser than all other men." Vladimir then inquired where they should all accept baptism, and they replied that the decision rested with him. [He was baptised next year at Kherson.]

The Russian Primary Chronicle (ca. 1038)[21]

Richer's Difficult Trip from Rheims to Chartres (991)

In my preoccupation with liberal studies, I was eager to learn the science of Hippocrates [medicine], when one day on the streets of Rheims I bumped into a knight from Chartres. I asked him who he was, who he served, where he had come from and why. He answered that he had been sent by Heribrand, a cleric of Chartres, to seek out Richer, a monk of Saint-Remi. When I heard the purpose of the mission and my friend's name, I immediately admitted that I was the one he was looking for; we exchanged the kiss of peace and went off together. He promptly handed over a letter that urged me to study the *Aphorisms* [of Hippocrates], and filled with joy at the prospect, I engaged the services of a boy and got ready to set out with the knight for Chartres [150 miles away].

My abbot helped by providing me with a palfrey, and I departed without money, changes of clothes, and other necessaries. I arrived at Orbais, a monastery famous for its great hospitality, and there I enjoyed the conversation of the lord abbot D. no less than the ample refreshments. The next day I set out for Meaux, but my two companions and I did not avoid misfortune as we passed along the path that wound through the woods. At a crossroads we took the wrong turn and made a detour of six leagues. After we went through Château-Thierry, the palfrey Bucephalus began to go rather slowly, like a baby ass. It was past noon and rain was falling everywhere when that mighty Bucephalus, exhausted after making his utmost effort, fell down between the legs of the boy, who was riding him, and expired there six miles from the city as if struck by lightning. You can appreciate how worried we were if you have had such an accident yourself or if you can draw an analogy to some similar one. The boy, who was not used to difficult trips like this, was tired to the bone; having lost his horse, he just lay on the ground. The baggage lay there, too, without a carrier. The rain simply poured down in great torrents; the sky was covered over with clouds; the sun was already threatening to leave us in darkness as it set.

God did not leave me in doubt about all this but sent the gift of counsel. I left the boy there together with the baggage, told him how he should answer any passers-by who questioned him, and cautioned him to resist the urge to sleep. Then, accompanied only by the knight of Chartres, I went on to Melun. I started to cross the bridge there, though I could scarcely see it in the poor light, and found I was in trouble again, for there were so many big gaps in the bridge that traffic supplying the daily needs of the citizens could scarcely pass over it. My knight, who was a man of action experienced in dealing with the emergencies of travel, looked all around for a boat, but finding none, he returned to confront the perils of the bridge. Thank heaven he found a way to get the horses safely across: he filled in the gaps under the horses' feet, sometimes with his shield, sometimes with ripped-off planks; after much running back and bending over, he got all the way across with the horses, and I kept him company.

The night had become frightening and had covered the world with a veil of mist by the time I entered the basilica of Saint-Faron, just as the brothers were preparing spiced wine for travellers. That day they were late in doing this because the monks had read the [especially long] chapter [in *The Rule of Saint Benedict*] on the cellarer of the monastery, after which they had had a formal dinner. They greeted me like a brother with kind words, and I was made comfortable with enough to eat. I sent the knight from Chartres with the horses back to the boy we had left behind; he had to undergo again the perils of the bridge we had just escaped. He crossed as skillfully as before, and proceeding with some uncertainty, in the second watch of the night he finally reached the place where we had left the boy; he only found him by calling loudly and often. Having recovered the boy and the baggage, he returned to the city, but not wanting to face the perils of the bridge yet again, which he knew too well by experience, he took refuge in some shack with the boy and the horses. Although they had not eaten all day, they spent the night there where they could rest but not eat.

What a sleepless night I spent! and what torments I suffered during that night! Those who have had to keep watch for dear ones can imagine what I went through. Finally the dawn I longed for arrived, and soon after came my famished companions. They were given food, and the horses got grain and straw. Since the boy would have had to walk, I left him with Abbot Augustine and, setting out with only the knight from Chartres, I quickly arrived at Chartres itself. Then I immediately sent the horses back to the city of Meaux for the boy I had left there, and when he had been brought back, all my problems were solved.

So I settled down to study the *Aphorisms* of Hippocrates carefully with dom Heribrand, a man of great knowledge and liberal education. After I had learned what that book says about the diagnosis of diseases, I felt that I wanted to learn more than just how to recognize sicknesses, so I asked if I might also read with him the book entitled *A Concordance to Hippocrates, Galen, and Soranus*, and he agreed, because pharmacy, botany, and surgery held no secrets for a man so well versed in the art of medicine.

Richer, *History of France* (after 995)[22]

The Conversion of
"Christ's Best Hatchet-Man" (994)

While Olaf Tryggvason [a Viking] lay in the Scilly Isles [off the coast of Cornwall], he heard of a seer, or fortune teller, on the islands, who could tell beforehand things not yet done, and what he foretold many believed was really fulfilled. Olaf became curious to try this man's gift of prophecy. He therefore sent one of his men, who was the handsomest and strongest, clothed him magnificently, and bade him say he was the king; for Olaf was known in all countries as handsomer, stronger, and braver than all others, although, after he had left Russia, he retained no more of his name than that he was called Ole, and was Russian. Now when the messenger came to the fortune teller and claimed to be the king, he got the answer: "You are not the king, but I advise you to be faithful to your king." And more he would not say to that man.

The man returned and told Olaf, and his desire to meet the fortune teller was increased; and now he had no doubt of his being really a fortune teller. Olaf visited him himself, and, entering into conversation, asked him if he could foresee how it would go with him with regard to his kingdom, or of any other fortune he was to have. The hermit replied in a holy spirit of prophecy: "You will become a renowned king and do celebrated deeds. Many men will you bring to faith and baptism, and both to your own and others' good; and that you may have no doubt of the truth of this answer, listen to these tokens: when you return to your ships, many of your people will conspire against you, and then a battle will follow in which many of your men will fall, and you will be wounded almost to death and will be carried upon a shield to your ship; yet after seven days you will be well of your wounds, and immediately you will let yourself be baptised."

Soon after Olaf returned to his ships, where he met some mutineers and people who would destroy him and his men. A fight took place, and the result was just what the hermit had predicted, that Olaf was wounded and carried upon a shield to his ship, and that his wound was healed in seven days. Then Olaf perceived that the man had spoken truth—that he was a true fortune teller and had the gift of prophecy. Olaf went once more to the hermit and asked particularly how he came to have such wisdom in foreseeing things to be. The hermit replied that the

Christians' God himself let him know all that he desired, and he brought before Olaf many great proofs of the power of the Almighty. In consequence of this encouragement, Olaf agreed to let himself be baptised forthwith. He remained here a long time, took the true faith, and got with him priests and other learned men. [He then returned to Norway, became king, and began the conversion of Norway to Christianity.]

Snorri Sturluson (d. 1241), *King Olaf Tryggvason's Saga*[23]

The Eleventh Century

The Revival of the Latin West (1002)

A couple of years after the turn of the millenium, people began to rebuild their cathedral churches all over the world, but especially in Italy and in France, even though the buildings were well situated and structurally sound, for the peoples of Christendom were competing with one another to have more pleasing places of worship. It was as if the very world, having reviewed its wardrobe and thrown out the oldest things, was clothing itself in a white robe of churches.

Raoul Glaber, *History of His Time* (ca. 1044)[1]

How to Uproot a Mandrake (early 11th century)

This is the way to take [a mandrake root, which has a human shape]. When you come to it, you will recognize it because at night it shines just like a lamp. When you first see its head, then instantly scratch it with an iron implement lest it escape from you. Its power is so great and so excellent that it will immediately flee from an unclean man when he comes to it, so you should scratch it with iron, as we said before. Next you should dig around it, but dig the earth hard with an ivory stick so you will not touch the mandrake again with iron. And when you see its hands and feet, then tie it up. Then take the other end and tie it to the neck of a dog that is hungry. Next put some meat in front of the dog where he cannot reach it unless he jerks up the root he is tied to. It is said that this plant has the power to betray whatever uproots it [because one can die from hearing its screams]. Therefore, as soon as you see it has been jerked up and have it in your possession, take it immediately in hand and twist it and wring the ooze out of its leaves into a glass container.

Anglo-Saxon Herbal (early 11th century)[2]

A Martyr Almost Escapes (1012)

[Alphage, Elphege, or Aelfheah, archbishop of Canterbury, was being held hostage by the Danes in a prison at Greenwich.] And the Friday in the Easter week the devil appeared to this holy man in the prison in the likeness of an angel and said to him that it was our Lord's will that he should go out of prison and follow him. And this holy man believed him, went out, and followed the wicked angel by night, and he brought this holy man into a dark valley, and there he waded over waters and ditches, mires and hedges, and ever this holy man followed him as he might for weariness, till at the last he had brought him into a foul mire that was set about with great waters, and there the devil left him, and vanished away.

And then this holy man knew well that he was deceived by his enemy the fiend, and then he cried God mercy and prayed him for help. And then our Lord sent to him his holy angel, who aided him out of the mire and water and said it was the will of God that he should return again to the prison that he came from, "for tomorrow you shall suffer martyrdom for our Lord's sake." And as he went again towards the prison at Greenwich early the next morning, his keepers that had sought him all the night met him, and immediately they threw him down on the ground and there they wounded him most piteously. And then they brought him again to prison, and ... [the next day] the wicked tormentors stoned him to death....

Osbern (died ca. 1100), *Life of Saint Elphege*[3]

The Death of Ethelred the Unready (1016)

The richest and bravest of all kings at that time was Cnut, king of the Danes. He, summoned by the nobles of England and enticed by their frequent letters—the English not opposing but inviting him and receiving him with joy—landed with a very large force [on the coast of Essex].... This was occasioned by shameful oppression, for with kings it is the rule that the worse coward any is, the crueller he is. Such and so savage was Ethelred, and being very cowardly and in fear of every one, he set traps for all, and caught not all at once, but the foremost one by one, and reduced freedom to slavery, and vice versa: the necks of the nobles he gave to serfs to trample on.... He liked no one whom in his wrath he could not charge with servile birth, treason, or some other crime....

When the news of Cnut's arrival was noised abroad, [Ethelred] was in his chamber at Westminster in company with serfs whom he had chosen, and at whose beck he raged against the free. He took to flight in a boat, and at London town died of fear in the midst of his serfs, and, deserted by them, was carried by the current of the river "thither where Numa's gone and Ancus too" [Horace, *Epodes* 1.6.27]. Though my soul naturally loathes serfs, this point about them does please me, that in the end or in an emergency they show plainly how much they deserve affection. There is an English proverb about them: *"Have hund to godsib ant steng in thir oder hond"*; that is, "Take a dog for companion and a stick in your other hand."

Walter Map (fl. 1162-1208), Courtiers' Trifles[4]

The End of Edmund Ironside (1016)

[King] Edmund sought in his pleasures one similar in his own character, or rather in his faults, and set over the freemen of his court a man of servile and low condition [Edric Streona]. This person obtained from him many pieces of emolument which he had not hoped for and which were wholly unsuited to his low origin; but one vill in particular belonging to the crown attracted him.... This he asked for, and in the king's answer received, not a refusal but a postponement. He conceived an anger at once rapid and rabid, and this man [plotted to kill his master in revenge and thereby win the favor of King Cnut, who ruled the rest of England].... [So] this serf ... put into the hole of his master's privy a large, sharp iron spit, and, preceding him as he came with a strong light of candles, suddenly turned them in another direction, so that his master might fall into the snare unawares. He fell into it, and was pierced with a mortal wound [in the posterior], and had himself carried thence, and died at Ross....

The serf hastened to appear before Cnut and said: "Hail to you, whole king, who were yesterday but half a king; and may you recompense the author of your wholeness by whose hand your enemy has been removed and your one foe rooted out of the earth." The king, though much saddened, replied with unmoved face: "Good God! who has been so much my friend that I may set him on high above all his fellows?" "I," said the serf. Then the king had him caught up on high and hung on the tallest oak: the due and proper end of such serfs.

Walter Map (fl. 1161-1208), *Courtiers' Trifles*[5]

A Royal Miracle of Robert the Pious (1022)

[Helgaud, a monk of Fleury, was sent by his abbot to the court of Robert II the Pious, king of France (996-1031), along with some other monks to conduct business with the king.] In order to celebrate Lent at Poissy, the king speeded up his journey and ordered us to leave with him so we could wind up the business we had been sent on. Presently we came to a river port on the Seine called Charles's *venna* (i.e. fishpond), where the crossing was difficult. By the king's holy command, we monks were put into a little boat by ourselves while the king himself watched anxiously from the opposite bank, where he hoped we would arrive safe and sound. Because he prayed for us, God, who is praised, blessed, and adored everywhere, was with us poor mortals. During the crossing we were towing our horses by the bridle behind the boat, and when we reached midstream one of the war horses, who was poorly trained and had never done a crossing like this before, got his two front feet up into the back of the boat. His crazy thrashing about threatened to tip the boat over and send us to the bottom. The king and his people cried out with loud voices, beseeching God most high and the heavenly powers to save us from peril. The king shouted at us to untie the bridles and keep the horses at a safe distance from the boat. We slackened the reins just as the voice that we loved had ordered, and when we had gotten the horse's feet out of the boat as well, we began to move towards the shore. With his eyes full of tears, the king himself called Saint Denis, Saint Benedict, and all the saints to help us. God, who is blessed world without end, heard his prayer and it was done as he wished: our boat reached land and by the grace of God he received us safe and sound, as both he and we praised God for this miracle (and we still continue to praise Him for it). We remained with this man of God for three days in that place, enjoying his sweet speech and pleasant expression.

Helgaud of Fleury, *Life of Robert the Pious* (before 1041)[6]

Benedict of Clusa: A Renaissance Ego (1028)

I am the nephew of the abbot of Clusa. He led me about through many places in Lombardy and France for the sake of grammar. My learning cost him two thousand solidi, which he paid to my masters. For nine years I stood at grammar and now am become a *scholasticus*. We were nine *scholastici* who learned grammar, and I indeed am thoroughly learned. I have two large houses filled with books, and at this moment I have not read them all, but I meditate upon them daily. There is not in the whole earth a book that I have not. After I have left the schools, there will be no one under heaven so learned as I. I shall be abbot of Clusa after the death of my uncle. I am already chosen by all, and but for the malice of some evil monks who care for nothing but hypocrisy and rusticity, I should have been consecrated abbot long ago. I *am* the prior of Clusa, and I know well how to make discourse and how to write. [Here] in Aquitaine there is no learning, they are rustics all: and if any one in Aquitaine has learned any grammar, he straightway thinks himself Virgil. In France there is learning, but not much. But in Lombardy, where I mostly studied, is the fountain of learning.

Ademar of Chabannes (988-1034), *Martial's Apostolate*[7]

The Charity of Robert the Pious (died 1031)

Although [Robert II, king of France 996-1031] was robbed by the poor, the clergy, and the laity, it was plainly done with his consent, even when gold, silver, and the most precious ornaments were involved. When some wanted to investigate the thefts, the king threatened them in strong terms, swearing by the Lord's faith that the thieves would not lose what they had taken. At the castle of Etampes, Queen Constance had a fine palace with an oratory [or chapel] constructed. The king was delighted and merrily sat down to dine there with his followers; for the occasion he ordered the house to be filled with God's poor. One of them seated himself at the king's feet, where he glutted himself with the best morsels, which the king passed to him under the table; but he did not fail to notice an ornamental fringe hanging about the king's knees. It contained six ounces of gold, so he quickly cut it off with a knife and hid it even more quickly. When the crowd of paupers had emptied the palace and the king had ordered his followers, who by then were stuffed with food and drink, to withdraw from his presence, he himself got up from the table. The queen immediately noticed that her lord had been deprived of the ornament that was his glory, and she was mightily upset, so much so that Constance became inconstant and cried out to her saintly husband: "Alas, my good lord! What enemy of God has dishonoured you by spoiling your handsome gold garment?" "Me?" he said, "no one has dishonoured me. But may it be God's will that he profit from that which he took and which he needs more than we do." With these soothing words, the king went to the oratory, where God give him the grace to rejoice over his loss and his wife's remark.

*   *   *   *   *

One day the king returned to his room after being united with God in prayer, since he needed to rest his humble body after having poured forth torrents of tears while praying. There he found that his queen, in her vainglory, had had his lance nicely decorated with silver. He looked at it for a while and then went outside to see if he could find someone who might need the silver. He found a very poor man and cautiously inquired whether he had any tool with which he could remove the silver. Thus the poor man did not know why the king asked this question; God's servant [the king] simply told him to find such a tool as fast as possible, and then he prayed while he was waiting for the man to return. Presently the pauper came back with a tool that would do the job and handed it over. The two went inside, and behind closed doors the king removed the silver from the lance with the poor man's help. Then he gave it to the poor fellow, putting it into the beggar's bag with his own holy hands. As he did so, he ordered him—as was his custom—to be careful not to let the queen see him as he was leaving. The poor man's need was great, and he did not need to be told twice; he did as the king commanded. Soon after he had left, the queen arrived. She was astonished to find what had been done to the lance that she had hoped would be her lord's pride and joy—now it was ruined. In response to her complaints, the king as a joke swore by the Lord's faith that he didn't know how it happened; *that* led to a friendly argument between them.

Helgaud of Fleury, *Life of Robert the Pious* (before 1041)[8]

Inheritance by Couvade in Aragon (ca. 1035)

[At the end of his reign, Sancho the Great (died 1035) divided up his kingdom between his sons. The biggest shares were to go to his three legitimate sons by Queen Urraca; to a fourth son] Ramiro he gave an out-of-the-way part of the kingdom, namely [the county of] Aragon, because Ramiro [being a bastard] was not equal to his brothers on his mother's side, and hence they would only allow him a smaller share in the inheritance. But with the cunning of an evil enemy, Garcia [one of the legitimate borthers] disrespectfully slandered his own mother [Urraca] and spread it about that she had wronged her husband by committing adultery. But he was answered by Ramiro, who defended her steadfastly and truthfully and freed her from danger and disgrace by proving the charge to be false. Consequently the queen flared up in such anger against Garcia that she cursed him and made it possible for Ramiro to hold a portion of the kingdom independently. She adopted him in the presence of the court by taking Ramiro under her dress and thrusting him out from under the dress as if she were giving birth. [Thus Ramiro became equal in status with his brothers, and his county of Aragon was accordingly raised to the rank of a kingdom.]

Anonymous (fl. 1152-57), *Crònica Najerense*[9]

King Canute and the Tide (1035)

When at the summit of his power [Canute, king of England, 1016-1035] ordered a seat to be placed for him on the seashore when the tide was coming in. Thus seated, he shouted to the flowing sea: "You, too, are subject to my command, as the land on which I am seated is mine; and no one has ever resisted my commands with impunity. I command you, then, not to flow over my land, nor presume to wet the feet and robe of your lord." The tide, however, continuing to rise as usual, dashed over his feet and legs without respect to his royal person. Then the king leaped backwards, saying: "Let all men know how empty and worthless is the power of kings, for there is none worthy of the name, but He whom heaven, earth, and sea obey by eternal laws." From thenceforth King

Canute never wore his crown of gold, but placed it for a lasting memorial on the image of our crucified Lord, to the honour of God the almighty king.

Henry of Huntington (fl. 1130), *History of the English*[10]

How Lady Godiva Tricked Her Husband (ca. 1043)

In the same year [1057] died Leofric earl of Chester, a man of praiseworthy life; he was buried in the monastery which he had founded at Coventry ... by the advice of his wife the noble countess Godiva.... The countess Godiva, who was a great lover of God's mother, longing to free the town of Coventry from the oppression of a heavy toll, often with urgent prayers besought her husband that from regard to Jesus Christ and his mother he would free the town from that service and from all other heavy burdens. The earl sharply rebuked her for foolishly asking what was so much to his damage and always forbade her ever more to speak to him on the subject; while she, on the other hand, with a woman's pertinacity, never ceased to exasperate her husband on that subject. At last he made her this answer, "Mount your horse and ride naked before all the people through the market of the town, from one end to the other, and on your return you shall have your request." On which Godiva replied, "But will you give me permission, if I am willing to do it?" "I will," said he. Whereupon the countess, beloved of God, loosed her hair and let down her tresses, which covered the whole of her body like a veil, and then mounting her horse and attended by two knights, she rode through the marketplace without being seen, except her fair legs; and having completed the journey, she returned with gladness to her astonished husband and obtained of him what she had asked; for Earl Leofric freed the town of Coventry and its inhabitants from the aforesaid service, and he confirmed what he had done by a charter.

The Flowers of History (1202)[11]

Lay Investiture as a Lesson for Lechers (ca. 1050)

Frequently, when disengaged from the turmoils of his empire, Henry [III the Black, emperor 1039-56] gave himself up to good fellowship and merriment, and was replete with humour.... He was so extremely fond of his sister, who was a nun, that he never let her leave his side, and her chamber was always next to his own. One winter, when he was detained for a long time in the same place due to remarkably severe ice and snow, a certain clerk attached to the imperial court became too familiar with the girl and often passed the greatest part of the night in her chamber.... On one particular night, however, as they were enjoying their fond embraces and continuing their pleasures longer than usual, the morning dawned upon them and behold! snow had completely covered the ground. The clerk, fearing that he should be discovered by his track in the snow, persuaded his mistress to extricate him from his difficulty by carrying him on her back. She, regardless of modesty so she might escape exposure, took her paramour on her back and carried him out of the palace. It happened at that moment that the emperor had risen for a necessary purpose, and looking out of the window of his chamber, he beheld the clerk mounted. At first he was stupified by the sight, but observing still more closely, he became mute with shame and indignation. While he was hesitating whether he should pass over the crime unpunished or openly reprehend the delinquents, an opportunity occurred for him to give a vacant bishopric to the clerk, which he did: but at the same time he whispered in his ear, "Take the bishopric, but be careful you do not let women carry you any more." At the same time he gave his sister rule over a company of nuns. "Be an abbess," said he, "but carry clerks no longer." Both of them were greatly embarrassed, and feeling themselves grievously stricken by so grave an injunction, they desisted from a crime which they thought had been revealed by God.

      William of Malmesbury (d. 1143?), *The Kings of England*[12]

The Boy Who Seduced a Convent (ca. 1050)

Berkeley by Severn, a vill of £500 value, belonged to certain nuns who dwelt there and had a noble and comely abbess. Now [Godwin, earl of Wessex, fl. 1018-1053], the man of whom I tell, took stock of all with subtle craft and conceived desire not of the abbess but of her property, and as he passed by the place, he left in her care his nephew, a very handsome lad, on pretence of his illness, till he should return, and enjoined the invalid not to recover completely until he had made a conquest of the abbess and as many of the nuns as he could, and to give the youth the means of finding favour with them, he supplied him with rings, girdles, and fawnskins, starry with gems, to be presented to the nuns in traitorous wise. He accordingly entered with alacrity and good will on the path of pleasure, and learned it easily, for "easy is the descent to Avernus," [*Aeneid* 6.126] and fooled wisely in that which was to his taste. In him dwelt all that foolish virgins could desire—beauty, delights of luxury, and kind address; and the devil was agog to find an abode in each one of them; so he drove out Pallas and brought in Venus, and made a church that was sacred to the Saviour and the saints into a cursed Pantheon, and a sanctuary into a brothel, and the ewe-lambs into she-wolves. So, when the shame of the abbess and many of the nuns was past concealment, their seducer fled and speedily brought to his lord the conquering eagles that had earned the reward of iniquity. Godwin at once approached the king [Edward the Confessor], informed him that the abbess and her nuns were wantons, sent men to investigate, and on their return proved the truth of all he had said. The nuns were cast out, and he asked for and received Berkeley from his lord [the king], who might better be called his fool.

Walter Map (fl. 1162-1208), *Courtiers' Trifles*[13]

How the Welsh Penalized a Dream (ca. 1050)

[Gruffydd ap] Llewelyn, king of Wales [1039-63], a man faithless as were most of his forebears and successors, had a very beautiful wife, whom he loved more ardently than she loved him, for which reason he gave his whole energies to spying on her chastity, and, burning with suspicion and jealousy, cared for nothing but that no one else should touch her.

It chanced to come to his ears that a young man of those parts, most exalted in reputation, nobility of character, race, and beauty, and most prosperous in affairs and person, had dreamed that he had married the queen. The king said he had been deceived, was as enraged as if the thing had been real, was in agony, seized the innocent man by guile, and, had not respect for his kindred and fear of vengeance restrained him, would have tortured him to death.

As is the custom, the whole clan offered themselves as bail for the youth and protested against his being brought to trial. The king refused bail, and demanded instant judgment. The repulsed party complained of their repulse but deferred vengeance as long as the youth was in prison. On many occasions, numbers were summoned to try the matter, now at the king's order, now by invitation of the other side, but, baffled in every discussion, they went on to summon more sages from all parts. Finally, they consulted one whom report described as pre-eminent and whom his position proved no less; and to them he said:

"We must follow the laws of our land and can by no means annul what our fathers ordained and what has been established by long use. Let us then follow them and not produce anything new until a public decree directs us to the contrary. It has been promulgated in our oldest laws that he who outraged the consort of the king of Wales should pay a thousand kine to the king and go free and unharmed. With regard to the wives of princes, and every class of magnates in like manner, a penalty was appointed according to the rank of each, with a certain number specified. This man is accused of dreaming that he abused the queen and does not deny the charge. Had the offence confessed been real, it is certain that a thousand kine would have had to be paid. But because it was a dream, our judgment is that this young man shall set a thousand kine in the king's sight on the bank of the lake of Behthen, in a row in the sunlight, so that the reflection of each may be seen in the water, and that the reflections shall belong to the king, and the kine to him who owned them before, inasmuch as a dream is the reflection [or shadow] of the truth [i.e. of reality]." This decision was approved by all and ordered to be put in execution, in spite of the angry protests of Llewelyn.

Walter Map (fl. 1162-1208), *Courtiers' Trifles*[14]

The Just Desert of Earl Godwin (1053)

[After the death of King Canute, Earl Godwin of Wessex had played the kingmaker; in 1041 he had been responsible for the death of the Anglo-Saxon claimant to the English crown, Alfred, whose younger brother, Edward the Confessor, was put on the throne the next year with Godwin's help. But Edward refused to be Godwin's puppet and exiled him for some time.] When Godwin was back in the king's grace, they were relaxing together at a feast and the conversation turned to the king's [late] brother Alfred. "Listen here, king," said the earl, "I can see that you give me an angry look whenever you think of your brother Alfred. But God forbid that I should swallow this bite if I was party to anything that put him in danger or you at a disadvantage." Just after saying this, he choked on the bite he had put into his mouth and closed his eyes in death. He was pulled out from under the table by his son Harold [the Saxon], who stood near the king, and was buried in Winchester cathedral.

William of Malmesbury (d. 1143?), *The Kings of England*[15]

Wales Pays Homage to Humility (1056?)

In the midst of his works of wickedness there is one thing [Gruffydd ap Llewelyn, king of Wales, 1039-63] is recorded to have done nobly and courteously. In his time he was so oppressive and obnoxious to his neighbours that it became necessary for Edward [the Confessor], then king of England [1042-66], either to use entreaty on behalf of his subjects or to take up arms in their defence.

Ambassadors were sent from both sides, and then they negotiated from opposite banks of the Severn, Edward being at Austclive, Llewelyn at Beachley. The nobles went to and fro between them in boats, and after many exchanges of messages, the question was long debated which of them ought to cross over to the other. It was a difficult crossing owing to the roughness of the water, but that was not the ground of the dispute. Llewelyn alleged his precedence, Edward his equality: Llewelyn took the position that his people had gained all England, with Cornwall, Scotland, and Wales, from the giants, and affirmed himself to be their heir in a direct line. Edward argued that his ancestors had got the land from its conquerors.

After a great deal of quarrelsome contention, Edward got into a boat and set off to Llewelyn. At that point the Severn is a mile broad. Llewelyn seeing and recognizing him cast off his state mantle—for he had prepared himself for a public appearance—went into the water up to his breast, and throwing his arms lovingly about the boat, said: "Wisest of kings, your modesty has vanquished my pride, your wisdom has triumphed over my foolishness. The neck which I foolishly stiffened against you, you shall mount and so enter the territory which your mildness has today made your own." And taking him to shore on his shoulders, he seated him upon his mantle, and then with joined hands did him homage.

Walter Map (fl. 1162-1208), *Courtiers' Trifles*[16]

151

Ralph the Ill-Tonsured: A Man of Parts (died 1060)

Ralph was the fifth [son of Giroie, a Norman knight]. Surnamed "the clerk" on account of his knowledge of letters and skill in other arts, he was also called "the ill-tonsured" (*malacorona*) because in his youth he was much given to military exercises and other frivolities.... He was studious from his childhood and learned the secrets of science with signal success in the schools of France and Italy, being deeply skilled in astronomy as well as in grammar and dialectics, and also in music. He was so complete a master of the art of medicine that at Salerno, where the most ancient school of medicine had long flourished, he was unrivalled except by one wise woman. But although his learning was so extensive and profound, he did not abandon himself to a peaceful life but served in the wars and often distinguished himself among his comrades, both in council and in the field. The natives of Montreuil still relate many things which appear to us wonderful concerning his skill in treating cases of disease and other accidents, such as they were witnesses of themselves or heard from their fathers, to whom he was well known by his long residence among them.

At last, apprehending the destruction of a tottering world and taking the precaution of a prudent retirement, he despised its luxury and betook himself to Marmoutier, a cell dependent on the abbey of Saint Martin at Tours, where for seven years he lived in submission to the monastic rule under Albert its venerable abbot. After he had been confirmed in that order, he came to Saint-Evroul by permission of his abbot [in 1059], to assist his nephew [Abbot Robert] who had recently undertaken the government of the new monastery [which Giroie's family had founded in 1050].

This noble soldier having obtained from the Lord by earnest prayers the disease of leprosy to expiate the multitude of sins which burdened his conscience, his nephew gave him a chapel [at the source of the river Ouche] that he had built in honour of Saint Evroul, where he lived for a considerable time, having the monk Goscelin for his own comfort and the service of God, and did much good by his counsels to numbers who flocked to him on account of his deep wisdom and high rank....

[But when his uncle the abbot fled to Rome because Duke William the Bastard was persecuting him, Ralph] withdrew from the chapel ... and retired to Marmoutier, the monastery where he had first made his monastic profession, and there he soon afterwards made a glorious end on January 19 [1060].

Ordericus Vitalis (d. ca. 1142), *Ecclesiastical History*[17]

Mabel the Poisoner (1063)

[The Norman lord] Viscount Roger of Montgomery ... married Mabel, niece of the bishop [of Séez], with whom he acquired a large portion of the domains of [the bishop] William of Bellême.... Now this Mabel was both powerful and worldly, cunning and glib, but extremely cruel....

[She procured the exile of Arnold of Echauffour and her husband received Echauffour as a fief, but when Duke William the Conqueror forgave Arnold and promised to restore his fief in 1063] Mabel poisoned the refreshments which she ordered to be set before Arnold as he was returning from the court of the duke to [the county of] France. But a friend of Arnold's gave him notice of the treachery she intended. Therefore, while he was conferring with some of his friends at Echauffour and was earnestly invited by Mabel's attendants to partake of the entertainment, he would on no account consent, remembering the friendly warning, so he utterly refused all meat and drink, which he suspected to be poisoned. But Gilbert, the brother of Roger of Montgomery, who had conducted him there and was quite unaware of the treacherous plan, took a cup without dismounting from his horse, and having drunk the poisoned cup, died in consequence on the third day afterwards at Rémalard. Thus this perfidious woman, in attempting to destroy her husband's rival, caused the death of his only brother, who was in the flower of his youth and much distinguished for his chivalrous gallantry.

Not long afterwards, lamenting the failure of her first attempt, she made another no less deadly effort to accomplish the object of her desires. By means of prayers and promises she worked on Roger Goulafré, Arnold's chamberlain, till she had bent the false retainer to her nefarious wishes. She then prepared the poisoned drink, which the chamberlain presented to his master [and two other knights].... Thus the three nobles imbibed the venom of the poison at Courville [near

Chartres] at one and the same time. But Giroi and William, who were carried to their own homes where they could command all necessary care, recovered by God's mercy aiding the skill of the physician; whereas Arnold, who was far from home, had no means of securing proper care in the house of a stranger; he languished for some days as the disorder increased until he breathed his last on the first of January [1064].

Ordericus Vitalis (d. ca. 1142), *Ecclesiastical History*[18]

William the Conqueror's Claims to England (1064)

About the same time, Edward, king of the English, who loved William [duke of Normandy] as a brother or a son, established him as his heir with a stronger pledge than ever before. The king, who in his holy life showed his desire for a celestial kingdom, felt the hour of his death approaching and wished to anticipate its inevitable consequences. He therefore dispatched Harold [Godwinson, "the Saxon"] to William in order that he might confirm his promise by an oath. This Harold was of all the king's subjects the richest and the most exalted in honour and power, and his brother and his cousins had previously been offered as hostages in respect of the same succession. The king, indeed, here acted with great prudence in choosing Harold for this task, in the hope that the riches and the authority of this magnate might check disturbance throughout England if the people with their accustomed perfidy should be disposed to overturn what had been determined.

While travelling upon this errand Harold only escaped the perils of the sea by making a forced landing on the coast of Ponthieu, where he fell into the hands of Count Guy, who threw him and his companions into prison. He might well have thought this a greater misfortune even than shipwreck, since among many peoples of the Gauls there was an abominable custom utterly contrary to Christian charity, whereby, when the powerful and rich were captured, they were thrown ignominiously into prison and there maltreated and tortured even to the point of death, and afterwards sold as slaves to some magnate.

When Duke William heard what had happened he sent messengers at speed, and by prayers and threats he brought about Harold's honourable release. As a result Guy in person conducted his prisoner to the castle of Eu, although he could at his pleasure have tortured or killed him, or sold him into slavery. Since, moreover, he did this very

honourably without the compulsion of force or bribes, William in gratitude bestowed upon him rich gifts of land and money, and then took
Harold with proper honour to Rouen. This was the chief city of the
Norman duchy, and there William sumptuously refreshed Harold with
splendid hospitality after all the hardships of his journey. For the duke
rejoiced to have so illustrious a guest in a man who had been sent him
by the nearest and dearest of his friends: one, moreover, who was in
England second only to the king, and who might prove a faithful medi-
ator between him and the English.

When they had come together in conference at Bonneville, Harold
in that place swore fealty to the duke, employing the sacred ritual recognized among Christian men. And as is testified by the most truthful
and most honourable men who were there present, he took an oath of
his own free will in the following terms: first, that he would be the representative of Duke William at the court of his lord, King Edward, as
long as the king lived; secondly that he would employ all his influence
and wealth to ensure that after the death of King Edward the kingdom
of England should be confirmed in the possession of the duke.... The
duke on his part, who before the oath was taken had received cere-
monial homage from him, confirmed to him at his request all his lands
and dignities. For Edward in his illness could not be expected to live
much longer.

William of Poitiers (fl. 1071), *The Deeds of William*[19]

Breaking Byzantium: The Battle of Manzikert (1071)

[The Emperor Romanus IV] Diogenes decided to fight the next day
using the troops he had with him and in the morning started preparing
for battle. But in the meantime envoys came from the sultan [of the Seljuk Turks, Alp Arslan] to discuss peace. The emperor, however, did not
receive them courteously, though he did grant them an audience, telling them to go back to their master and report thus: "If he wants to talk
about peace, let him leave the place where he is camped and tent some-
where far off so that I can camp with the Roman army where the barbarian emplacement is now."

When he had spoken in this boastful way to the envoys, he abruptly
ordered them away. Now they reported the emperor's words to the sultan, who consulted with those around him about peace. But the

emperor was arrogant and trusted his domestics, who said that the sultan was afraid because he had not brought a battleworthy force and so sought peace in order to delay the fight and bring up reinforcements. [Romanus] did not wait for the return of the ambassadors, nor did he consider anything else but ordered the trumpeters to sound the battle call. The suddenness of it upset the barbarians, but they formed up their ranks and, when the Romans came on, did not return the charge but gave way without turning their backs or fighting.

In the late afternoon, as the emperor saw that the guard around the camp was insufficient and feared that it would be plundered by the enemy, he decided to break up the battle and move up around the camp. After he had turned the imperial standard around and was going back, he ordered the army to do the same. Those who were close calmly carried out the order, but those who held positions at a distance assumed that the withdrawal of the emperor was flight, for Andronicus [Ducas], the son of the caesar [John Ducas], spread the notion among the ranks. Now the caesar and his sons always schemed and plotted secretly against the emperor. Accordingly, Andronicus started out with the men around him (beginning thereby no small part of the rout) and at a gallop returned to camp.

[The emperor] along with his retinue received the assault and up to a point held out vigorously. Then when some of his men fell and others were captured, he was surrounded by the barbarians. But he did not give up even then. After he had wounded and killed many, he was wounded himself in the hand and so grew weary and was unable either to ward off his attackers or to flee, because his horse had fallen from blows of missiles. The emperor of the Romans was captured and led off by the barbarians as a prisoner.

When the capture of the emperor was reported to the sultan, he was of course pleased but ... he did not believe the capture of the emperor because of the sheer good luck of it. Even seeing him he did not accept the report as true until the ambassadors he had sent recognized him, and Basilakes, who was being held there, on seeing him threw himself at Romanus's feet wailing. Then [the sultan] bounded up from his throne as though divinely possessed and, placing him on the ground, stepped on him acccording to custom.

John Zonaras (fl. 1200), Epitome of History[20]

The Love of Learning: A Striking Example (ca. 1076)

[Guibert, a knight's son, was being tutored at home.] Once [when I was about twelve] I had been beaten in school—the school being simply the dining-hall in our house.... When, at a certain hour in the evening, my studies—such as they were—had come to an end, I went to my mother's knee after a more severe beating than I had deserved. And when she, as she used to do, began to ask me repeatedly whether I had been whipped that day, I, not to appear a tattle-tale, entirely denied it. Then she, whether I liked it or not, threw off the inner garment that they call a vest or shirt and saw my little arms blackened and the skin of my back everywhere puffed up with cuts from the twigs. And being troubled, agitated, weeping with sorrow, and grieved to the heart by the very savage punishment inflicted on my tender body, she said: "You shall never become a clerk nor any more suffer so much to get learning." At that I, looking at her with what reproach I could, replied: "If I had to die on the spot, I would not give up learning my book and becoming a clerk."

Now she had promised that if I wished to become a knight, when I reached the age for it, she would give me the arms and equipment. But when I had, with a good deal of scorn, declined all these offers, she ... accepted this rebuff so gladly and was made so cheerful by my scorn of her proposal that she repeated to my master the reply with which I had opposed her. Then both rejoiced that I had such an eager longing to fulfil my father's vow [that Guibert should become a cleric].

Guibert of Nogent, *Memoirs* (1115)[21]

The Assassination of Mabel the Poisoner (1077)

For twenty-six years after the fall of the family of Giroie, Roger of Montgomery possessed all their patrimony of Echauffour and Montreuil [in Normandy], and at first—as long as his wife Mable lived—he was, at her instigation, a very troublesome neighbour ... she having always been opposed to the family of Giroie, the founders of the [writer's] abbey of Saint-Evroul. At last the righteous Judge, who spares repentant sinners but exercises vengeance on the impenitent, punished that cruel woman, who had caused many great lords to be disinherited and to beg their bread in foreign lands. [See above at the year 1063.]

She herself fell by the sword of Hugh, from whom she had wrested his castle *Ialgeium*, thus unjustly depriving him of the inheritance of his fathers. In the extremity of his distress, he undertook a most audacious enterprise; for with the assistance of his three brothers, who were men of undaunted courage, he forced an entry by night into the chamber of the countess at a place called Bures on the river Dive, and there, in revenge for the loss of his inheritance, he cut off her head as she lay in bed just after enjoying the pleasures of a bath.

The death of this cruel lady caused much joy to many persons, and the perpetrators of the bold deed instantly took the road for Apulia. Hugh of Montgomery, who was then in the place with sixteen men-at-arms, on hearing of his mother's murder, instantly pursued the assassins, but he was unable to catch up with them, as they had taken the precaution of breaking down the bridges behind them as they crossed the rivers.... It was the winter season, the night was dark, and the streams were flooded, so there were such obstacles in the way of pursuit that the assassins, having satiated their revenge, were able to escape out of Normandy.

Ordericus Vitalis (d. ca. 1142), *Ecclesiastical History*[22]

Pope and King at Canossa (1077)

[In February 1076, Pope Gregory VII excommunicated Henry IV because the king would not give up his right of lay investiture. Hoping to weaken the monarchy, some of the German nobles threatened to elect a new king if Henry was not absolved within a year, and they invited Gregory to come to Germany to preside over the election. As the deadline approached and the pope was travelling northward, Henry decided to seek absolution before his enemies could join forces; therefore he crossed the Alps in the dead of winter and intercepted Gregory at Canossa in January 1077. Gregory's apologetic letter to the disappointed rebel nobles describes the meeting.]

For the love of justice, you have made common cause with us and have taken the same risks in fighting in Christ's service. Therefore, with sincere affection, we have taken care to write you about how the king humbly did penance, how he obtained absolution, and how the whole affair has progressed since his entry into Italy up to the present time....

Before he entered Italy [the king] sent us ambassadors who promised that he would render satisfaction in all things to God, to Saint Peter, and to us. And he renewed his promise that he would not only mend his ways but would also obey us if only he might obtain from us absolution and the apostolic benediction. For a long time we postponed our reply and frequently took counsel, while conveying to him through the messengers who were passing between us our bitter reproaches for his outrageous conduct. Finally he came of his own accord, with a few followers and showing no hostility or defiance, to the castle of Canossa where we were staying. There he stood before the gate of the castle on three successive days with none of the trappings of royalty but rather with bare feet and clad simply in wool. With many tears he kept begging for the pope out of his mercy to aid and console him, until all who were present or who heard of it were so moved by pity and compassion that they interceded for him with many prayers and tears. Indeed, everyone marvelled at our unusual hardness of heart, and some even exclaimed that we were acting, not like a responsible pope, but like a cruel and savage tyrant.

Finally we were overcome by his persistent show of repentance and by the constant appeals of all present, so we released him from the bond of excommunication and received him back into communion and into the bosom of holy mother church. He gave us written promises, which are confirmed by the signatures of the abbot of Cluny, of our daughters the countesses Matilda and Adelaide, and of other princes, bishops, and laymen....

Pope Gregory VII, *Letter* (1077)[23]

How Anselm Found the Ontological Argument (1078)

After I had published, at the solicitous entreaties of certain brethren [at the monastery of Bec, in Normandy, of which Anselm was at this time prior] a brief work [the *Monologion*] as an example of meditation on the grounds of faith, in which the writer impersonates one who, in a course of silent reasoning with himself, investigates matters of which he is ignorant. Considering that this book was knit together by the linking of many arguments, I began to ask myself whether there might be found a single argument that would require no other argument for its proof than itself alone and that would suffice by itself alone to demonstrate that God truly exists and that there is a supreme good requiring nothing else, which all other things require for their existence and well-being; in short, it would prove whatever we believe regarding the divine Being.

Although I often and earnestly directed my thought to this end, and although at some times that which I sought seemed to be just within my reach, while again it wholly evaded my mental vision, at last in despair I was about to cease, as if from the search for a thing which could not be found. But when I wished to exclude this thought altogether, lest, by busying my mind to no purpose, it should keep me from other thoughts in which I might be successful, then more and more, though I was unwilling and shunned it, it began to force itself upon me with a kind of importunity. So one day when I was exceedingly wearied with resisting its importunity, in the very conflict of my thoughts the proof of which I had despaired offered itself, so that I eagerly embraced the thoughts which I was strenuously repelling.

Thinking, therefore, that what I rejoiced to have found, would, if put in writing, be welcome to some readers of this very matter and of some others, I have written the following treatise ... [which at first was entitled] *Faith Seeking Understanding* [but later it was re-titled] ... the *Proslogion.*

Saint Anselm, *Proslogion* (ca. 1084)[24]

How Anselm Almost Lost the Ontological Argument (1078)

[After writing the *Monologion*] it came into his mind to try to prove by one single and short argument the things which are believed and preached about God.... And this, as he himself would say, gave him great trouble, partly because thinking about it took away his desire for food, drink, and sleep, and partly—and this was more grievous to him— because it disturbed the attention which he ought to have paid to matins and to divine service at other times. When he was aware of this, and still could not entirely lay hold on what he sought, he supposed that this line of thought was a temptation of the devil, and he tried to banish it from his mind. But the more vehemently he tried to do this, the more this thought pursued him. Then suddenly one night during matins the grace of God illuminated his heart, the whole matter became clear to his mind, and a great joy and exultation filled his inmost being.

Thinking therefore that others also would be glad to know what he had found, he immediately and ungrudgingly wrote it on writing tablets and gave them to one of the brethren of the monastery for safekeeping. After a few days he asked the monk who had charge of them for the tablets. The place where they had been laid was searched, but they were not found. The brethren were asked in case anyone had taken them, but in vain. And to this day no one has been found who has confessed that he knew anything about them.

Anselm wrote another draft on the same subject on other tablets, and handed them over to the same monk for more careful keeping. He placed them once more by his bed in a more secret place, and the next day—having no suspicion of any mischance—he found them scattered on the floor beside his bed and the wax which was on them strewn about in small pieces. After the tablets had been picked up and the wax collected together, they were taken to Anselm. He pieced together the wax and recovered the writing, though with difficulty.

Fearing now that by some carelessness it might be altogether lost, in the name of the Lord he ordered it to be copied onto parchment. From this, therefore, he composed a volume small in size but full of weighty discourse and most subtle speculation, which he called the *Proslogion* because in this work he speaks either to himself or to God.

Eadmer (d. 1124), The Life of Saint Anselm25

How Bishop Benno Avoided Extremes (1080)

[Benno was a royal administrator whom Emperor Henry IV made bishop of Osnabrück. In 1080 he was present at a council held at Henry's command in the cathedral of Brixen for the purpose of deposing Pope Gregory VII.] Not knowing how things would turn out, Benno began to consider whether he could find a way to avoid taking sides without compromising his integrity. He happened to notice that in the church where the meeting was being held there was an altar which had been hollowed out, with a hole at the back through which a man could barely enter, and this hole was hidden by the altar cloth that hung down.... Accordingly, while the others were singing psalms, as is the custom [at the opening of a church council], he left his seat near the altar, slipped behind it, and investigated whether that would be a good place to hide. Unobserved he cautiously experimented to see whether he could get inside. Although it was hard to pass through the opening, once inside he found that the cavity itself was big enough to accomodate his body. Giving thanks to God, he carefully covered the hole with the hanging altar cloth and spent the whole day hiding in there with simply no one aware of his whereabouts.... When the time came for everyone to assemble for the business meeting, Bishop Benno of Osnabrück was not to be found. So the king sent men to look for him everywhere in the church and also in the house in which he was staying, which the searchers almost tore apart, but he was nowhere to be found.... When vespers was near, after the pope had been deposed and replaced with the bishop of Ravenna ... and after many other things had been enacted to which the bishop would hardly have consented had he been present, Benno emerged from his hiding place while no one was watching and suddenly was seen sitting in his original seat near the altar. Everyone was dumbfounded, not to say amazed, and kept asking where he had been. Benno assured them he was willing to swear by the saints, who certainly knew where he had been, that he had not left the church during the entire day. He was immediately brought before the king and fully purged himself of any disloyalty.... Ever since, either by exceptionally good luck or by his own prudence, he remained on good terms with both popes—which has been possible for only a very few in these stormy times—and he also never offended the king. Thus he practiced the precept of the Apostle: "insofar as in you lies, be at peace with all men" [Romans 12:18].

Norbert, Life of Bishop Benno of Osnabrück[26]

Why Henry I Was Called "Beauclerc" (ca. 1080)

Henry, the youngest son of William the Great [the Conqueror], was born in England the third year after his father's arrival [1068].... The early years of instruction he passed in liberal arts, and so throughly imbibed the sweets of learning that no warlike commotions, no pressure of business could ever erase them from his noble mind—although he neither read much openly, nor displayed his attainments except sparingly. To speak the truth, however, his learning, though obtained by snatches, assisted him much in the art of governing, according to that saying of Plato, "Happy would be the state if philosophers governed, or kings would be philosophers." Not slenderly tinctured by philosophy, then, he learned by degrees in the process of time how to restrain the people with lenience; nor did he ever permit his soldiers to fight unless he saw a pressing emergency. In this manner, by strengthening himself with learning in his youth, he became the hope of the kingdom. And in his father's hearing he often made use of the proverb: "An illiterate king is a crowned ass" (*Rex illiteratus, asinus coronatus*).

William of Malmesbury (d. 1143?), *The Kings of England*[27]

A Chase Scene:
The Emperor Alexius Eludes the Normans (1081)

[The imperial Byzantine army was defeated at Durazzo—now Dorrës in Albania—by the Italian-based Norman, Robert Guiscard, who wanted Emperor Alexius I Comnenus taken alive.] The soldiers pursued the emperor very smartly to a place the natives call "the Bad Bank"; its situation is this—a river, named Charzanes, flows below, and a high cliff rises up on one side. Between these the pursuers overtook him; some of them thrust him with their spears on the left side (they were nine altogether) and thus made him lean to the right. And he certainly would have fallen had he not managed to fix the sword, which he carried in his right hand, in the ground and support himself upon it. Moreover the rowel of the spur on his left foot caught in the edge of his saddlecloth (often called *hypostoma*) and made it more difficult for the rider to move; with his left hand, too, he grasped the horse's mane and thus held on. And he was succored by divine interposition, which unexpectedly brought him aid from his enemies themselves.

For providence produced some more Franks on the right side who also raised their spears at him, and thus by thrusting the tips of their spears against his right side, they lifted the soldier and set him upright in their midst. And a strange sight it was to behold! For those on the left strove to overthrow him while those on the right fixed their spears against his right side as if opposing the others, and by spears set against spears, they kept the emperor upright.

When he had settled himself more firmly in the saddle and held his horse and also the saddlecloth tightly between his thighs, the horse gave a signal proof of its mettle. (Alexius had once received this horse and a purple saddlecloth as a gift from Bryennius, after he had taken him captive in battle at the time when Nicephorus Botaniates was still emperor.) This horse, besides being very fiery and supple in the legs, was also remarkably strong and warlike, and now to put it briefly, inspired by divine providence, he suddenly leaped through the air and stood on the top of the cliff, springing up lightly like a bird, or, as the myth would say, with the wings of Pegasus. (Bryennius used to call this horse "Sgouritzes" [Dark Bay].)

Some of the barbarians' spears were hurled into the empty air as it were, and fell from their hands, while others remained sticking in parts of the emperor's clothes and, borne aloft, followed the horse. Alexius at once cut off the clinging spears. Not even now, when in such dire peril, was he disturbed in soul or confused in his calculations, but swiftly saw his best course and unexpectedly freed himself. The Franks on their side stood gaping, awestruck at what they had seen, and certainly it might well cause consternation; but when they saw Alexius riding off down another road, they recommenced their pursuit. After showing his pursuers his back for some considerable time, he turned upon them and encountering one of them, ran his spear through his chest, and the man fell backwards to the ground. Then the emperor turned his horse again and held on his former way.

And so he met a number of the Franks who before had been chasing the Roman troops. When they saw him in the distance, they formed in close order and halted, partly to wind their horses, but also because they were anxious to take him alive and carry him off as booty to Robert. But when he saw that besides the men pursuing him there were now others in front as well, he had well-nigh despaired of safety; nevertheless he collected himself and noticing a man amongst the foe whom from his stature and gleaming weapons he judged to be Robert himself, he set his horse straight at him, and the other aimed his spear at him.

So both joined combat and launched themselves the one against the other in the intervening space. The emperor first directing his hand aright, struck at his opponent with his spear, which passed right through his breast and out at the back. Straightway the barbarian fell to the ground and gave the the ghost on the spot, for the wound was mortal.

And next the emperor dashed right through the middle of the company and rode away, for by slaying that one barbarian he had gained safety for himself. As soon as the Franks saw their hero wounded and hurled to the ground, they crowded round the fallen man and busied themselves about him. And when those who had been pursuing the emperor saw them, they too dismounted and, on recognizing the dead man, began beating their breasts and wailing. However, the man was not Robert, but one of the nobles, second only in rank to Robert. While they were thus occupied, the emperor continued his flight.

Anna Comnena (born 1083), *The Alexiad*[28]

Fatherly Advice from Persia (1082)

Let it be clear to you, my son, that if you fall in love with a person, you should not indulge in sexual congress indiscriminately, whether you are drunk or sober....

As between women and youths, do not confine your inclinations to either sex; thus you may find enjoyment from both kinds without either of the two becoming inimical to you.... During the summer let your desires incline towards youths and during the winter towards women....

[If you are in the slave market] do not have a slave girl brought before you when your appetites are strong upon you; when desire is strong, it makes what is ugly appear good in your eyes. First abate your desires and then engage in the business of purchasing....

Do not purchase a house in the neighbourhood of sages or of philosophers, because it is difficult to maintain the duty of revering them....

When you seek a wife, do not demand her possessions also; and look well to her character, refusing to be enslaved by beauty of face—for prettiness, men take a mistress. A wife, to be good, should be chaste and of sound faith, capable in household management and fond of her husband, modest and God-fearing, brief-tongued, sparing and economical of materials....

Never sell your daughter—that is conduct which your own sense of honour should not permit—yet lavish all you possess in the endeavour to prevent your daughter from remaining in your house; quickly hand her to a husband and, as speedily as you can, rid yourself of trouble. Give all your friends this same advice, for much profit lies in it....

No merchant should permit goods to leave his hands before completion of a sale and there should be no shame about bargaining; wise men declare that moderation reduces a man's fortune: one should not make a practice of restraint in demanding more....

If you are a poet, see to it that your verses are, within limits, easy of comprehension, and guard against making your utterances too profound. There may be subjects familiar to you but not to other people, who will need a commentary; these subjects are to be avoided, because poetry is composed for the benefit of the general public and not for oneself alone.... When you are looking for a patron, do not go about the bazaar with a gloomy countenance and soiled garments, but rather be ever of an agreeable and smiling appearance. Learn anecdotes, rare quips, and amusing tales in abundance and repeat them to your patron. It is an exercise indispensable to the poet.....

[If you are a secretary] commit no forgery for a trivial object, but [reserve it] for the day when it will be of real service to you and the benefits substantial. Then too, if you practice it [rarely], no one will suspect you....

Kai Kâ'ûs ibn Iskandar, A Mirror for Princes (1082)[29]

Why Odo of Bayeux Hated Lanfranc (1083)

[William the Conquerer's brother Odo was both bishop of Bayeux and earl of Kent. He hated Lanfranc, the archbishop of Canterbury] because, he said, it was by his advice that his brother had cast him into chains. Nor was this assertion false: for [in 1083] when William [I] the elder formerly complained to Lanfranc that he was deserted by his brother, Lanfranc said: "Seize him and cast him into chains." "What!" replied the king, "he is a clergyman!" Then the archbishop with playful archness, as Persius says: "balancing the objection with nice antithesis" [*Saturae* 1.85], rejoined: "You will not seize the bishop of Bayeux but confine the earl of Kent."

William of Malmesbury (d. 1143?), The Kings of England[30]

The Last Words of Pope Gregory VII (1085)

[When Emperor Henry IV occupied Rome, Pope Gregory VII was taken into protective custody by his Norman allies and died in exile at Salerno.] The blessed Pope Gregory, when asked if he wished to give dispensation [before he died] to those whom he had excommunicated, responded: "Except for Henry who is called king and [his antipope] Guibert who sits in usurpation, and all those who counselled and aided their wickedness and impiety, I absolve and bless all who believe without doubt that I act as the special agent of the apostles Peter and Paul."

In addition to this, he gave the following command: "Acting as God's agent by the authority of the blessed apostles Peter and Paul, I warn you that no one should hold the Roman pontificate unless he be elected as canon law prescribes and elected and ordained by the authority of the holy fathers."

When he was just about to die, his last words [echoing Psalm 44:8] were: "I have loved justice and hated iniquity, therefore I die in exile." It is told that a certain venerable bishop countered this by replying: "Lord, it is not possible for you to die in exile, for you, as the agent of Christ and his apostles, have received the nations as your heritage and the ends of the earth are yours to possess."

Paul Bernried, Life of Gregory VII (1128)[31]

See Jerusalem and Die (1085)

Robert Guiscard [first Norman duke of Apulia], after having done many and noble things in Apulia, purposed and desired, by way of devotion, to go to Jerusalem on pilgrimage; and it was told him in a vision that he would die in Jerusalem. Therefore, having commended his state to Roger, his son, he embarked by sea for the voyage to Jerusalem, and arriving in Greece, at the port which was afterwards called after him Port Guiscard, he began to sicken of his malady; and trusting in the revelation which had been made to him, he in no wise feared to die. There was over against the said port an island [Cephalonia], to which he caused himself to be carried so he might repose and recover his strength, and after being carried there he grew no better but rather grievously worse. Then he asked what this island was called, and the mariners answered that of old it was called "Jerusalem." Having heard this he knew his death was imminent, so he devoutly fulfilled all those things which appertain to the salvation of the soul and died in the grace of God ... having reigned in Apulia thirty-three years.

Giovanni Villani (d. 1348), *Florentine Chronicle*[32]

The Extravagance of William Rufus (ca. 1090)

[King William II of England] was a man who knew not how to take off from the price of anything, or to judge of the value of goods; but a trader might sell him his commodity at whatever rate, or a soldier demand any pay he pleased. He was anxious that the cost of his clothes should be extravagant, and angry if they were purchased at a low price. One morning, indeed, while putting on his new boots, he asked his chamberlain what they cost; and when he replied, "Three shillings," indignantly and in a rage he cried out: "You son of a whore, how long has the king worn boots of so paltry a price? Go, and bring me a pair worth a mark of silver." He went, and bringing him a much cheaper pair, told him, falsely, that they cost as much as he had ordered. "Aye," said the king, "these are suitable to royal majesty." Thus his chamberlain used to charge him what he pleased for his clothes, acquiring by these means many things for his own advantage.

William of Malmesbury (d. 1143?), *The Kings of England*[33]

The Pope's Call to the First Crusade: Clermont, 1095

[At the Council of Clermont, Pope Urban II preached this sermon to a vast crowd of French laymen:] "From the confines of Jerusalem and the city of Constantinople a horrible tale has gone forth and very frequently has been brought to our ears, namely, that a race from the kingdom of the Persians, an accursed race [i.e. the Seljuk Turks], a race utterly alienated from God, a generation forsooth which has not directed its heart and has not entrusted its spirit to God, has invaded the lands of those Christians and has depopulated them by the sword, pillage, and fire; it has led away a part of the captives into its own country, and a part it has destroyed by cruel tortures; it has either entirely destroyed the churches of God or appropriated them for the rites of its own religion....

The kingdom of the Greeks is now dismembered by them and deprived of territory so vast in extent that it cannot be traversed in a march of two months.

"On whom therefore is the labour of avenging these wrongs and of recovering this territory incumbent, if not upon you? You [Frenchmen], upon whom above other nations God has conferred remarkable glory in arms, great courage, bodily activity, and strength to humble the hairy scalp of those who resist you. Let the deeds of your ancestors move you and incite your minds to manly achievements....

"Let none of your possessions detain you, no solicitude for your family affairs, since this land which you inhabit, shut in on all sides by the seas and surrounded by the mountain peaks, is too narrow for your large population; nor does it abound in wealth; and it furnishes scarcely food enough for its cultivators. Hence it is that you murder one another, that you wage war, and that frequently you perish by mutual wounds. Let therefore hatred depart from among you, let your quarrels end, let wars cease, and let all dissensions and controversies slumber. Enter upon the road to the Holy Sepulchre; wrest that land from the wicked race, and subject it to yourselves....

"From you [Jerusalem] especially asks succor, because, as we have already said, God has conferred upon you above all nations great glory in arms. Accordingly undertake this journey for the remission of your sins, with the assurance of the imperishable glory of the kingdom of heaven."

When Pope Urban had said these and very many similar things in his urbane discourse, he so influenced to one purpose the desires of all who were present, that they cried out, "It is the will of God! It is the will of God!" *(Deus le volt!)* When the venerable Roman pontiff heard that, with eyes uplifted to heaven he gave thanks to God and, with his hand commanding silence, said: ... "Let then this be your war-cry in combats, because the word is given you by God. When an armed attack is made upon the enemy, let this one cry be raised by all the soldiers of God: It is the will of God! It is the will of God!"

Robert the Monk (eyewitness), *The Jerusalem Story*[34]

The Norman Crusaders Pass Through Italy (1096)

After leaving Gaul [September 1096], we Western Franks came as far as Lucca, a most renowned city. Near there we met Pope Urban [II]; and [Count] Robert the Norman and Stephen, count of Blois, and others of us who wished spoke with him. Having received his blessing [26 October], we went on our way joyfully to Rome.

When we had entered the church of Saint Peter, we met, before the altar, men of Wibert, the pseudo-pope [named by Emperor Henry IV], who, with swords in their hands, wrongly snatched the offerings placed on the altar. Others ran up and down on the roof of the church itself, and from there threw stones at us as we were prostrate praying. For when they saw anyone faithful to Urban, they straightaway wished to slay him.

In one of the towers of the church were Lord Urban's men, who carefully guarded it in fidelity to him, and withstood their adversaries as well as they could. We were very grieved when we saw such a great atrocity committed there, but we earnestly wished for nothing to be done except as punishment by the Lord. Thereupon, without hesitation, many who had come this far with us, now weak with cowardice, returned to their homes.

Fulcher of Chartres (born 1059), *The Jerusalem Story*[35]

The Best of Both Worlds (1096)

The abbot of Bourgueil [near Angers] came to the court [of King Philip I of France] at Christmas in order to receive the bishopric [of Orleans], which the queen had promised to him. The abbot talked and spent freely at court, acting as if his success were assured; but his claim was set aside and his rival [Sanctio] was given the office because his friends had noticeably more moneybags in store, and fuller ones, than the abbot had. And when the abbot complained to the king, asking why he had been thus deceived, Philip replied: "Bear with me for a while until I make my profit from that fellow; afterwards accuse him [of simony] so he can be deposed, and then I will do what you want."

Ivo of Chartres (d. 1116), *Letters*[36]

Why the Normans Diverted the First Crusade (1097)

In 1091 [the Franks] attacked and conquered the island of Sicily and turned their attention to the African coast.... In 1097 the Franks attacked Syria. This is how it all began: Baldwin, their king, a kinsman of Roger [I of Hauteville], the Frank who had conquered Sicily, assembled a great army and sent word to Roger saying: "I have assembled a great army and now I am on my way to you, to use your bases for my conquest of the African coast. Thus you and I shall become neighbours."

Roger called together his companions and consulted them about these proposals. "This will be a fine thing both for them and for us!" they declared, "for by this means these lands will be converted to the Faith!" At this Roger raised one leg and farted loudly, and swore that it was of more use than their advice. "Why?" "Because if this army comes here it will need quantities of provisions and fleets of ships to transport it to Africa, as well as reinforcements from my own troops. Then, if the Franks succeed in conquering this territory they will take it over and will need provisioning from Sicily. This will cost me my annual profit from the harvest. If they fail, they will return here and be an embarrassment to me here in my own domain. As well as all this Tamim [the emir of Tunisia] will say that I have broken faith with him and violated our treaty, and friendly relations and communications between us will be disrupted. As far as we are concerned, Africa is always there. When we are strong enough we will take it."

He summoned Baldwin's messenger and said to him: "If you have decided to make war on the Muslims, your best course will be to free Jerusalem from their rule and thereby win great honour. I am bound by certain promises and treaties of allegiance with the rulers of Africa." So the Franks made ready and set out to attack Syria.

Ibn al-Athir (1160-1233), *The Perfect History*[37]

The Holy Lance Saves the Crusaders at Antioch (1098)

After taking Antioch the Franks camped there for twelve days without food. [Soon after they took the city, a Moslem army had arrived from Mosul and besieged them.] The wealthy ate their horses and the poor ate carrion and leaves from the trees. Their leaders, faced with this situation, wrote to Kerbuqâ [general of the besieging army] to ask for safe conduct through his territory but he refused, saying: "You will have to fight your way out." ... There was a holy man [Peter Bartholomew] who had great influence over them, a man of low cunning, who proclaimed that the Messiah had a lance buried in the Qusyân, a great building in Antioch [the church of Saint Peter]. "And if you find it you will be victorious, and if you fail you will surely die." Before saying this he had buried a lance in a certain spot and concealed all trace of it. He exhorted them to fast and repent for three days, and on the fourth day he led them all to the spot with their soldiers and workmen, who dug everywhere and found the lance as he had told them. Whereupon he cried: "Rejoice! For victory is secure." ... When all the Franks had come out and not one was left in Antioch, they began to attack strongly, and the Moslems turned and fled.... The Franks killed them by the thousand and stripped their camp of food and possessions, equipment, horses and arms, with which they re-equipped themselves.

Ibn al-Athir (1160-1233), *The Perfect History*[38]

William Gregory the Good Monk (fl. 1099)

On the feast of All Saints [1061, Guy, a well-to-do Norman knight] placed his son William, a boy about nine years old, in the monastery of Saint-Evroul to serve God under the monastic rule.... By the grace of God, the boy William grew up in the way of virtue and was diligent in his studies, so that his superiors gave him the surname of Gregory. Carefully nurtured in the bosom of holy mother church and entirely shut out from the tumults of the world and carnal indulgences, he made great advances in those pursuits which are so especially fitting the sons of the Church, being an excellent reader and chanter, and exceedingly skilled in copying and illuminating books. The works executed by his own hands are still very useful to us in reading and chanting, and they serve as examples to deter us from idleness by the exercise of similar diligence. Assiduous from his very childhood at the offices of devotion and vigils, and submitting with moderation even in his old age to fastings and other macerations of the flesh, he was a strict observer of monastic discipline himself and a zealous monitor of those who infringed the holy rule. He had committed to his tenacious memory the Epistles of Saint Paul, the

Proverbs of Solomon, and other portions of sacred scripture, which he quoted in his daily conversations for the benefit of those with whom he talked. Devoted to these pursuits, he has already spent fifty-four years in the order of monks and still continues the practice of good works in his usual manner under Abbot Roger [1091-1123], so that by ending well he may attain to the assurance of eternal rest.

Ordericus Vitalis (d. ca. 1142), *Ecclesiastical History*[39]

The Twelfth Century

The Death of William Rufus (2 August 1100)

Being greatly moved [by ominous dreams the night before, the king] hesitated a long while whether he should go out to hunt as he had planned. His friends urged him not to let the truth of the dreams be tried at his own risk. In consequence, he abstained from the chase before dinner, dispelling the uneasiness of his unregulated mind by serious business.

They relate that, having plentifully feasted in royal fashion that day, he soothed his cares with more than the usual quantity of wine. After dinner he went into the forest, tended by few persons, of whom the most intimate with him was Walter, surnamed Tirel, who had been induced to come from France by the liberality of the king. This man alone had remained with him while the others employed in the chase were dispersed as chance directed. The sun was now declining when the king, drawing his bow and letting fly an arrow, slightly wounded a stag which passed before him. As it ran, he followed it for a long time with his eyes, gazing keenly and holding up his hand to keep off the power of the sun's rays. At this instant Walter conceived a noble exploit, which was to bring down another stag that by chance came near the king while his attention was otherwise occupied. But—good God!—Tirel shot his deadly arrow into the unwitting king's defenseless breast.

On receiving the wound, the king uttered not a word but broke off the shaft of the arrow where it projected from his body and fell upon the wound, by which he brought on his own death all the more quickly. Walter immediately ran up, but as he found him senseless and speechless, he leaped swiftly upon his horse and escaped by spurring it to top speed. Indeed there was none to pursue him: some did not question his flight, others were filled with pity, and all were intent on other matters. Some began to fortify their dwellings, others to plunder, and the rest to look around for a new king. The body was placed on a horsecart and conveyed by a few countrymen to the cathedral at Winchester with blood dripping from it all the way. Here it was buried within the tower, attended by many of the nobility, though lamented by few.

William of Malmesbury (d. 1143?), *The Kings of England*[1]

Thomas of Marle:
A Truly Atrocious Feudal Lord (1113)

Thomas, lord of the castle of Marle ... from early youth preyed on the poor and on pilgrims to Jerusalem, and the proceeds provided him with the means to destroy hosts of other people. So unheard-of in our times was his cruelty that men considered cruel seem more merciful in killing cattle than he in murdering men. For he did not merely kill them outright with the sword and for definite offences, as is usual, but by butchery after horrible tortures. For when he was compelling prisoners to ransom themselves, he hung them up by their testicles, sometimes with his own hands, and these often breaking away through the weight of the body, there followed at once the breaking out of their vital parts. Others were suspended by their thumbs, or even their private parts, and were weighted with a stone placed on their shoulders, and he himself walking below them, when he failed to extort what he could not get by other means, beat them madly with cudgels until they promised what satisfied him or perished under punishment.

No one can tell how many expired in his dungeons and chains by starvation, disease, and torture. But it is certain that ... [in 1110] when he had gone to Le Mont de Soissons to give aid against some peasants, he went to the entrance of a cave in which three of these fellows had hidden themselves, and taking his lance, he drove the weapon into the mouth of one of them with so hard a thrust that the iron point of the lance tore through the entrails and passed out by the anus. Why go on with instances that have no end? The two left in the cave both perished by his hand.

Again, one of his prisoners being wounded could not march. He asked the man why he did not go faster. He replied that he could not. "Stop," said Thomas, "I will make you hurry and be sorry for it." Leaping down from his horse, he cut off both his feet, and of that the man died....

[In 1113 he helped his father, the feudal lord of Amiens, to put down that city's independence movement.] In one of his manors, Thomas set up a strong garrison by means of which he wasted the rest with fire and sword. Having carried off from one of them a very great number of prisoners and much money, he burned the rest of the people—a large group of both sexes and all ages that had taken refuge in a church, which he set on fire....

Some of the prisoners travelled too slowly and he ordered the bones under their necks, called the collarbones, to be pierced and had cords inserted through the holes in five or six of them, and so made them travel in terrible torture; and after a little while they died in captivity. Why prolong the story? In that affair he slew with his own sword thirty persons.

Guibert of Nogent, *Memoirs* (1115)[2]

The Rise of Courtly Love (1060–1115)

[Guibert, a professional preacher, contrasts the current fashion in courtly love with the mores of nobles in his mother's day.] O God, Thou knowest how hard, how almost impossible it would be for women of the present time to keep such chastity as this; whereas there was in those days such modesty that hardly ever was the good name of a married woman smirched by ill report. Ah! how wretchedly have modesty and honour in the state of maidenhood declined from those times to these, and both the reality and the show of a mother's chaperon shrunk to naught! Therefore coarse mirth is all that may be noted in their manners and naught but jesting heard, with sly winks and ceaseless chatter. Wantonness shows in their gait, only silliness in their behaviour. So much does the extravagance of their dress depart from the old simplicity that in the enlargement of their sleeves, the narrowness of their skirts, the distortion of their shoes of cordovan leather with their curling toes, they seem to proclaim that everywhere shame is a castaway. A lack of lovers to admire her is a woman's crown of woe! On her crowds of thronging suitors rests her claim to nobility and courtly pride. In the old days—I call God to witness—there was greater modesty in married men, who would have blushed to be seen in the company of such women, than there is now in married women.

Women by such shameful conduct encourage men to seek an affair and drive them to haunt the marketplace and the public street. Indeed, such women have caused far-reaching changes in male mores. No man now blushes for his own levity and licentiousness because he knows that all are tarred with the same brush, and seeing himself in the same case as all others, why should he be ashamed of pursuits in which he knows all others engage? But why do I say "ashamed" when such men only feel shame if they are not conspicuous in their example of lustfulness, nor is a man's private boastfulness about the number of his loves, or his choice of the beauty which he prefers, any reproach to him, nor is he scorned for vaunting his love affairs. Rather does his part in furthering the general corruption meet with the approval of all. Listen to the cheers when, with the inherent looseness of his unbridled passions that deserve the doom of eternal silence, he shamelessly broadcasts what ought to have been hidden in shame, what should have burdened his soul with the guilt of ruined chastity and plunged him into the depths of despair. In this and in like manner is this age corrupt and corrupting, bespattering men with its evil imaginations, while the filth thereof, spreading to others, goes on increasing without end.

Guibert of Nogent, *Memoirs* (1115)[3]

The First Troubadour (ca. 1115)

[Duke William IX of Aquitaine (1071–1127) was] a joker and a lecher who ... wallowed as completely in the sty of vice as though he had believed that all things were governed by chance and not by providence. Moreover, he rendered his absurdities pleasant by a kind of satirical wit, exciting the loud laughter of his hearers. Finally he erected, near a castle called Niort, certain buildings after the form of a little monastery, and he used to talk idly about placing therein an abbey of prostitutes, naming several of the most abandoned courtesans, one as abbess, another as prioress, and declaring that he would fill up the rest of the offices in like manner.

Repudiating his lawful consort, he carried off the wife of a certain viscount [de Chatellerault], of whom he was so desperately enamoured that he placed the figure of this woman on his shield, affirming that he was desirous of bearing her in battle in the same manner as she bore him at another time.

Being reproved and excommunicated for this by Girard, bishop of Angoulême, and ordered to renounce this illicit amour, he said, "You shall curl with a comb the hair that has forsaken your forehead ere I repudiate the viscountess"—thus taunting a man whose scanty hair required no comb.

Nor did he less when Bishop Peter of Poitou, a man of noted sanctity, rebuked him still more freely and began to excommunicate him publicly when he proved contumacious. The duke seized the prelate by the hair and, flourishing his drawn sword, said, "You shall die this instant unless you give me absolution." Pretending to be afraid, the bishop asked leave to speak and boldly completed the rest of the excommunication formula. Having done what he thought was his duty and eager to become a martyr, he stretched out his neck, saying, "Strike, strike." But William, becoming somewhat softened, regained his usual pleasantry and said, "Certainly I hate you so cordially that I will not dignify you by the effects of my anger, nor shall you ever enter heaven by the agency of my hand."

After a short time, however, tainted by the infectious insinuations of his meretricious girlfriend, he drove the rebuker of his incest into banishment. The bishop died in exile [1115] and made manifest to the world by great and frequent miracles how gloriously he survives in heaven. On hearing this, William abstained not from his inconsiderate speeches but declared openly that he was sorry he had not dispatched him before, so that his pure soul might chiefly have to thank him through whose violence he had acquired eternal happiness.

William of Malmesbury (d. 1143?), *The Kings of England*[4]

Lust Exemplified by Two Wives and a Mute Troubadour (ca. 1115)

In Auvergne, beyond Limousin,
I was walking alone, on the sly,
I met the wives of En Garin
and En Bernard.

They greeted me modestly in the name
of Saint Leonard.

One of them says to me with her high-class speech:
"God save you, my lord pilgrim,
you look to me like a gentleman,
as far as I can tell;
but we all see crazy fools too often
walking through the world."

Now you are going to hear how I answered them:
I didn't say but or bat to them,
didn't mention a stick or a tool,
but only this:
"Babariol, babariol,
barbarian."

Then Agnes says to Ermessen:
"We've found what we are looking for.
Sister, for the love of God let us take him in,
he is really mute,
with this one what we have in mind
will never get found out.

One of them took me under her mantle
and brought me to her chamber, by the fireplace.
Let me tell you, I liked it,
and the fire was good,
and I gladly warmed myself
by the big coals.

To eat they gave me capons,
and you can be sure I had more than two,
and there was no cook or cook's boy there,
but just the three of us,
and the bread was white, and the wine was good,
and the pepper plentiful.

"Sister, this man is tricky,
he's stopped talking just for us.
Let us bring in our red cat
right now,
it'll make him talk soon enough,
if he's fooling us."

Agnes went for that disgusting animal,
and it was big, it had a big long mustache,
and I, when I saw it, among us, there,
I got scared,
I nearly lost my courage
and my nerve.

When we had drunk and eaten,
I took my clothes off, to oblige them.
They brought the cat up behind me,
it was vicious.
One of them pulls it down my side,
down to my heel.

She gets right to it and pulls the cat down
by the tail, and it scratches:
they gave me more than a hundred sores
that time;
but I wouldn't have budged an inch
if they killed me.

"Sister," Agnes says to Ermessen,
"he's mute, all right.
So, sister, let us get ourselves a bath
and unwind."
Eight days and more I stayed
in that oven.

I fucked them, you shall hear how many times:
one hundred and eighty-eight times.
I nearly broke my breeching strap

and harness.
And I cannot tell the vexation,
it hurt so bad.

No, no, I cannot tell the vexation,
it hurt so bad.

Duke William IX of Aquitaine (1071–1127)[5]

Abelard and Heloise (1118)

Now there was in this city of Paris a certain young maiden by the name of Heloise, the niece of a certain canon who was called Fulbert, who, so great was his love for her, was all the more diligent in his zeal to instruct her, so far as was in his power, in the knowledge of letters. While she was not inferior to other women in face, she was supreme in the abundance of her learning. Since this advantage of literary knowledge is rare in women, so much the more did it commend the girl and had won her the greatest renown throughout the realm.

Seeing in her, therefore, all those things which usually attract lovers, I thought it suitable to join her with myself in love, and I believed that I could effect this most easily. For I then had such renown, and so excelled in grace of youth and form, that I feared no refusal from whatever woman I might think worthy of my love. I believed this girl would consent to me all the more readily because I knew her both to possess and to delight in the knowledge of letters; even in absence it would be possible for us to reach one another's presence by written intermediaries, and, to express many things more boldly in writing than in speech, and thus ever to indulge in pleasing discussions.

So, being wholly inflamed with love for this girl, I sought an opportunity whereby I might make her familiar with me in intimate and daily conversations, and so might the more easily lead her to consent. With this purpose in mind, I made an agreement with her uncle, with the help of some of his friends, whereby he should take me into his house, which was near our school, at whatever price he might ask. I claimed as my pretext that the management of my household gravely hindered my studies and that the expense of it was too great a burden on me. Now he was avaricious and most anxious that his niece should continue to progress in the study of letters. For these two reasons I easily secured his consent and obtained what I desired, since he was eager to get my money and he believed that his niece would profit from my teaching. In fact he begged me to be her tutor, and the arrangement he proposed furthered my love more than I dared hope for: he committed her wholly to my mastership, so that as often as I returned from my school, whether by day or by night, I might devote my leisure to her instruction, and, if I found her idle, I might punish her severely. His simplicity in this amazed me no end; I could not have been more astonished if he had entrusted a tender lamb to a ravening wolf. For in giving her to me, not only to be taught but to be severely disciplined, what else was he doing than giving free rein to my desires and providing an opportunity, whether I wanted it or not, whereby I might bend her to my will by threats and blows if I could not move her by blandishment. But there were two things which chiefly kept him from ignoble suspicions, namely his love for his niece and my fame for continence in the past.

Need I say more? First we were united in one house, then in one mind. So, under the pretext of studying, we abandoned ourselves utterly to love, and the study of texts provided the seclusion that love requires. And so, with our books lying open before us, more words of love rose to our lips than of literature; kisses were more frequent than speech. My hands went more often to her breasts than to the pages. Loving turned our eyes more frequently to gaze at one another than reading kept them fixed on the textbook. And to avert suspicion all the better, sometimes I struck her, not through anger or frustration, but out of love and affection, and these blows were beyond the sweetness of any balm. No stage of love was omitted by us in our cupidity, and, if love could elaborate anything new, that we took in addition. The less experienced we were in these joys, the more ardently we persisted in them and the less satiety did they bring us.

And the more this pleasure occupied me, the less leisure could I find for my philosophy and to attend to my school. Most tedious was it for me to go to the school or to stay there; it was hard work, too, spending my nights in love and my days in study. I now was so negligent and lukewarm at my studies that I produced nothing from my mind but everything from memory; nor was I anything now save a reciter of things learned in the past, and if I found time to compose a few verses, they were about love and not the secrets of philosophy.

Peter Abelard, *The Story of My Misfortunes* (ca. 1132)[6]

Fulbert's Revenge on Abelard (1119)

Few could fail to perceive a thing so manifest [as my affair with Heloise], and none, I believe, did fail save he to whose shame it principally reflected, namely the girl's uncle [Fulbert] himself. Indeed, when various persons had suggested this to him now and again, he had been unable to believe it.... "But [in the words of Saint Jerome] what one is the last to know one does at any rate come to know in time...." And thus, several months having elapsed, it happened to us also. Oh, what was the uncle's grief at this discovery! ...

[The lovers were separated but] not long after this, the girl found that she had conceived, and with the greatest exultation wrote to me on the matter at once, consulting me as to what I should decide to do; and so on a certain night, her uncle being absent, I took her by stealth from her uncle's house, as we had planned together, and carried her to my own country [Brittany] without delay. There, in my sister's house, she stayed until such time as she was delivered of a male child whom she named "Astrolabe."

After her flight, her uncle was almost driven mad with grief and shame.... And, that I might conciliate him beyond all that he could hope, I offered him the satisfaction of marrying her whom I had corrupted, provided that this were done in secret lest I should injure my reputation. He assented, and with his own word and kiss, as well as with those of his household, he sealed the agreement that I had required of him—the more easily to betray me.

I immediately returned to my country to bring back my mistress so that I might make her my wife.... And so, leaving our infant in the care of my sister, we returned secretly to Paris, and a few days later, having kept a secret vigil of prayer by night in a certain church, there at daybreak, in the presence of her uncle and several of our own friends and his, we were joined together by the nuptial benediction. Afterwards we left [the church] separately and in secret, and after that we saw each other only seldom and by stealth, concealing as far as possible what we had done.

Her uncle and his servants, however, sought to mitigate their disgrace by making our marriage public, thus breaking the promise they had given me in that regard. But Heloise swore with mighty curses that what they said was a lie. This greatly provoked her uncle, who retaliated by subjecting her to a continual stream of verbal abuse. When I learned of this, I removed her [from his house] to a certain convent of nuns near Paris, which is called Argenteuil, where she herself had been brought up and schooled as a young girl. I had a religious habit made for her, of the kind novices wear, and had her assume all but the veil. When the uncle and his friends and relatives heard of this, their view of it was that I had played a trick on them, and by making her a nun I had found an easy way to rid myself of Heloise.

Therefore they were greatly indignant and conspired together against me. They corrupted a servant of mine with money, and then, one night while I was sound asleep in an inner room of my lodging, they punished me with a most cruel and shameful revenge, and one that shocked everyone who heard of it by its barbarity, for they cut off those parts of my body with which I had committed the act they resented. Although they fled immediately, two of them were caught and deprived of their eyes and testicles; one of them was that servant of mine who was led by greed to betray me while in my service.

Peter Abelard, *The Story of My Misfortunes* (ca. 1132)[7]

Clerical Celibacy Causes a Riot at Rouen (1119)

Geoffrey, the archbishop, having returned to Rouen from attending the council at Rheims [where the pope insisted that the policy of clerical celibacy be enforced], held a synod in the third week of November, and stirred up by the late papal decrees, dealt sharply and rigorously with the priests of his diocese. Among other canons of the council which he promulgated was one that forbade them from having sexual intercourse with females of any description, and against such transgressors he launched the terrible sentence of excommunication.

As the priests shrank from submitting to this grievous burden, and in loud mutterings among themselves vented their complaints of the struggle between the flesh and the spirit to which they were subjected, the archbishop ordered one Albert, a man free of speech, who had used some offensive words—I know not what—to be arrested on the spot, and he was presently thrust into the common prison....

The other priests, witnessing this extraordinary proceeding, were utterly confounded; and when they saw that, without being charged with any crime or undergoing any legal examination, a priest was dragged like a thief from a church to a dungeon, they became so exceedingly terrified that they knew not how to act, doubting whether they had best defend themselves or take to flight. Meanwhile, the archbishop rose from his seat in a violent rage, and hastily leaving the synod, summoned his guards, whom he had already posted outside with instructions as to what they were to do. The archbishop's retainers then rushed into the church with arms and staves and indiscriminately began striking the assembled clergy, who were conversing together.

Some of these ecclesiastics ran to their lodgings through the muddy streets of the city, though they were robed in their albs; others snatched up some rails and stones which they chanced to find and defended themselves; whereupon their cowardly assailants fled and took refuge in the sacristy, followed closely by the indignant clergy. The archbishop's people, ashamed of having been routed by an unarmed, tonsured band, summoned to their aid, in the extremity of their fury, all the cooks, bakers, and scullions they could muster in the neighbourhood and had the effrontery to renew the conflict within the sacred precincts. All whom they found in the church or cemetery, whether engaged in the broil or innocently looking on, they beat and cuffed or inflicted on them some other bodily injury....

[Finally all the priests] made their escape from the city as soon as they could, together with their friends who had before fled, without stopping to receive the bishop's licence and benediction. They carried the sorrowful tidings to their parishioners and concubines, and, to prove the truth of their reports, exhibited the wounds and livid bruises on their persons.

Ordericus Vitalis (d. ca. 1142), *Ecclesiastical History*[8]

The Wreck of the White Ship (1120)

A large fleet having been fitted out in the port of Barfleur, and the gallant company who were to accompany the king having assembled there, the king [Henry I Beauclerc of England] and his attendants embarked on November 25 in the first watch of the night with a south wind blowing; the sails being hoisted up, they put to sea, and in the morning those whom God permitted embraced the shore of England.

In this voyage a sad disaster happened that caused much lamentation and innumerable tears to flow. Thomas, the son of Stephen, had obtained an audience of the king, and offering a gold mark [as feudal relief], said to him: "Stephen, the son of Airard, was my father, and during his whole life he was in your father's service as a mariner. He it was who conveyed your father to England in his own ship when he crossed the sea to make war on Harold. He was employed by your father in services of this description as long as he lived and gave him such satisfaction that he honoured him with liberal rewards, so that he lived in great credit and prosperity among those of his own class. My lord king, I ask you to employ me in the same service, having a vessel called the White Ship (*Blanche Nef*), which is fitted out in the best manner and perfectly adapted to receive a royal retinue." The king replied: "I grant your request; but I have already selected a ship that suits me, and I shall not change; however, I entrust to you my sons, William and Richard, whom I love as myself, with many of the nobility of my realm."

The mariners were in great glee at hearing this, and greeting the king's son with fair words they asked him to give them something to drink. The prince gave orders that they should have three muids [about 100 litres]. No sooner was the wine delivered to them than they had a great drinking bout and became intoxicated.

By the king's command many barons with their sons embarked in the White Ship, and there were in all, as far as I can learn, three hundred souls on board the ill-fated ship. But two monks ... and a count ... with two knights ... the chamberlain ... and several others came on shore, having left the vessel upon observing that it was overcrowded with riotous and headstrong youths. The crew consisted of fifty experienced rowers, besides an armed marine force who were very disorderly and as soon as they got on board insolently took possession of the benches of the rowers and, being very drunk, forgot their station and scarcely paid respect to any one.... They even drove away with contempt, amidst shouts of laughter, the priests who came to bless them together with the other ministers who carried the holy water; but they were speedily punished for their mockery. Besides the king's treasure and some casks of wine, there was no cargo in Thomas's ship, which was full of passengers; and they urged him to use his utmost endeavours to overtake the royal fleet which was already plowing the waves. In his drunken folly, Thomas, confident in his seamanship and the skill of his crew, rashly boasted that he would soon leave behind him all the ships that had started before them.

At last he gave the signal for departure; the sailors seized the oars without a moment's delay, and, unconscious of the fate which was imminently impending, joyously handled the ropes and sails, and made the ship rush through the water at a great rate. But as the drunken rowers exerted themselves to the utmost in pulling the oars, and the luckless pilot steered at random and got the ship out of its due course, the starboard bow of the White Ship struck violently on a huge rock, which every day is left dry when the tide is out and is covered by the waves at high water. Two planks having been shattered by the crash, the ship, alas! filled and went down.

At this fearful moment, the passengers and crew raised cries of distress, but their mouths were soon stopped by the swelling waves, and all perished together.... But Berold [a butcher of Rouen], who was the poorest man of all the company and wore a sheepskin dress, was the only one among so many who survived till the dawn of another day.... [He clung to a spar and] in the morning, three fishermen took him into their skiff, and thus he only reached the land.....

The people [like the king and his court] also mourned for Prince William, whom they considered the lawful heir to the throne of England, and who thus suddenly perished with the flower of her highest nobility. The young prince had at this time almost reached his seventeenth year; he had just married the lady Matilda, who was near of his own age....

Ordericus Vitalis (d. ca. 1142), *Ecclesiastical History*[9]

The Origin of "Plantagenet" (ca. 1129)

[Geoffrey V, count of Anjou (1129–1151) and father of King Henry II Plantagenet of England, was surnamed by contemporary chroniclers "Plantegenet," "Plantegenest," or "Plantagenest." Later historians guessed this was because he wore a sprig of the *genêt* plant, which can be any member of the genus *Genista*, but especially the broom plant. Quite a different origin is suggested, however, by a variant of his soubriquet that appears in several contemporary charters from the chartulary of Fontevrault Abbey, where the early Plantagenets were buried. One document, for example, was enacted "on the advice of Geoffrey the Fair, count of the Angevins, Heather-planting" (*miricem plantantis*). Here he is represented as planting quite a different species named *myrice* in Latin, *bruyère* in French, and "heather" in English. From this it has been surmised that Geoffrey earned his nickname—or rather nicknames—because he somehow caused fields to be fallow or waste land in which broom and heather flourished. Perhaps, it has been suggested, he preserved such lands to hunt on; but he might have laid them waste in war or might have preferred the two-field to the newer three-field system of crop rotation.]

Fontevrault Abbey, *The "Pancarta" Chartulary*[10]

The Courtly Fashion of Long Hair (ca. 1130)

A circumstance occurred in England which may seem surprising to our long-haired gallants, who, forgetting what they were born, transform themselves into the fashion of females by the length of their locks. A certain English knight, who prided himself on the luxuriancy of his tresses, being stung by conscience on the subject, seemed to feel in a dream as though some person strangled him with his ringlets. Awaking in a fright, he immediately cut off all his superfluous hair. The example spread throughout England; and, as recent punishment is apt to affect the mind, almost all military men allowed their hair to be cropped in a proper manner without reluctance. But this decency was not of long continuance, for scarcely a year had expired before all who thought themselves courtly relapsed into their former vice; they vied with women in length of locks, and if these were not long enough, they put on false tresses. Thus they were forgetful, or rather ignorant, of the saying of the Apostle: "If a man nurture his hair, it is a shame to him" [1 Cor. 11:14].

William of Malmesbury (d. 1143?), *Recent History*[11]

For Whom the Bell Tolls (1134)

[When Alfonso I of Aragon died childless in 1134, he left his kingdom to the military orders; but his will was disregarded, and instead his brother, Ramiro II the Monk, left his monastery to assume the crown. Some of the Aragonese nobility challenged his claim to the crown, so] King Ramiro sent notice to all nobles, knights, and incorporated communities of his realm, ordering them to be at Huesca on the day assigned for holding his court there. The king let it be spread far and wide that he meant to have a bell made at Huesca by French masters, whom he had [in his service], and they would make a bell the sound of which would reach to all parts of the kingdom. And when the nobles and knights heard about the bell, they discussed it among themselves, saying: "Let us go and see the folly that our king wishes to do." And they who said such a thing were the ones who thought their king was next to nothing.

When they were at Huesca, the king ordered some of his confidants to be armed in his chamber and to do whatever he told them to. When the knights and nobles arrived at the council, the king ordered each of them to be called one after the other to give counsel. And when they entered his chamber, he ordered his men inside to behead them immediately. The knights and nobles who were called into the chamber, however, were only those guilty of opposing Ramiro. And in this way the king had twelve of the knights and nobles beheaded before dinner. And in fact the king would have decapitated all of the nobles and knights had not those who were outside somehow or other sized up the situation and decided to flee.

Pedro Marfilo (fl. 1370), *Chronicle of San Juan de la Peña*[12]

A Thirsty King: Henry I of England (1100–1135)

Rather than emperor or king, this pleasant and kindly man should be called the father of England. We cannot relate his great traits of courtesy, but who can keep back the little ones? His chamberlain, Payne fitz John, customarily used to draw a sexterce of wine every night to allay the royal thirst. It would be asked for only once or twice a year, or not at all. So Payne and the pages had no scruple about drinking it all up, and often did so early in the night. One night in the small hours it happened that the king called for wine, and there was none. Payne got up, called the pages, and found nothing. The king discovered them hunting for wine and not finding it. So he summoned Payne, all trembling and afraid, and said: "What is the meaning of this? Do you not always have wine with you?" He timidly answered: "Yes, lord, we draw a sexterce every night, and by reason of your rarely being thirsty or calling for it, we often drink it either in the evening or after you have gone to sleep. Now we have confessed the truth and we beg you to forgive us out of your mercy." The king: "Did you draw only one measure for the night?" Payne: "Yes." "That was very little for the two of us. In the future draw two measures every night from the butlers, the first for yourself, the second for me."

Walter Map (d. 1208), *Courtiers' Trifles*[13]

A Superficial Conversion (ca. 1139)

Ludwig the Landgrave [of Thuringia, fl. 1139] was a very great tyrant.... When he was at the point of death, he gave this order to his friends: "Just as I am about to die, put the cowl of the Cistercian order on me and take the greatest care that this is done while I am still alive." They obeyed him; he died dressed in a cowl. When a certain knight saw it he said ironically to his companions: "Truly, my lord is unique in the variety of his virtues! When he was a knight, he had no equal in military prowess; now when he has become a monk, he is a model to all of discipline. See how carefully he keeps the rule of silence; not a single word does he speak." But when his soul was drawn from his body, it was presented to the chief of the devils....

Caesarius of Heisterbach (d. 1223), *Dialogue on Miracles*[14]

Consultants for Love and War (ca. 1140)

Robert, earl of Gloucester [d. 1147], the [natural] son of Henry I [and the chief supporter of Queen Matilda], was a man of great cleverness and much learning, though, as often happens, he had a weakness for love affairs. He often preferred the company of Stephen of Beauchamp, a man beset by the same fault, rather than that of his knights whose conduct was more noble. One time he was preparing for battle: the trumpet was already stirring the spirits; both sides had donned helmets, put their lances in place, raised their shields, and held their horses tightly reined in. At the last minute the earl was hurriedly seeking aid and counsel from his nobles, not Stephen, who for the moment was of no use to him. But one of the nobles said to him: "Call Stephen." The earl felt the force of the rebuke and blushed; then, to all whom he had summoned to council, he said: "Pity me, and do not be slow to forgive one who confesses his fault. I am a man of strong passions, and when my lady Venus calls me, I call her servant Stephen, who is the best helper in such a case. But when Mars calls, I turn to you, his pupils. Since my ear is almost always attentive to her, her call is usually in my mouth, so you are right to reproach me. For I serve Venus as a volunteer, but for Mars I fight only when I must." All laughed and granted him pardon and gave him their aid.

Walter Map (d. 1208), *Courtiers' Trifles*[15]

A Complaisant Cuckold (ca. 1140)

[A Moslem observer of Christian morals in the crusaders' kingdom of Jerusalem reported:] The Franks are void of all zeal and jealousy. One of them may be walking along with his wife. He meets another man who takes the wife by the hand and steps aside to converse with her while the husband is standing on one side waiting for his wife to conclude the conversation. If she lingers too long for him, he leaves her alone with the conversant and goes away.

Here is an illustration which I myself witnessed [at Nâblus, north of Jerusalem, where a certain Frank, or western European, lived across the street].... One day this Frank went home and found a man with his wife in the same bed. He asked him, "What could have made you enter into my wife's room?" The man replied, "I was tired, so I went in to rest." "But how," asked he, "did you get into my bed?" The other replied, "Well, I found a bed that was spread, so I slept in it." "But," said he, "my wife was sleeping together with you!" The other replied, "Well, the bed is hers. How could I therefore have prevented her from using her own bed?" "By the truth of my religion," said the husband, "if you should do it again, you and I would have a quarrel." Such was for the Frank the entire expression of his disapproval and the limit of his jealousy.

Usâmah ibn Murshid, *Learning by Example* (ca. 1182)[16]

Why Bernard of Clairvaux was Stoned (ca. 1140)

I was once present at the table of Blessed Thomas [Becket], then archbishop of Canterbury [1162-1170]. Next to him were sitting two white [Cistercian] abbots who were telling of many wonders done by Bernard. Their tales were prompted by a letter that had just been read aloud, written by Dom Bernard, abbot of Clairvaux, to Pope Eugenius [III]....

In that letter it was said that Master Peter [Abelard] was as proud as Goliath, and Arnold of Brescia was his standard-bearer, with much more to the same vicious effect. The two abbots seized the occasion to praise Bernard and extolled him to the stars. So John Planeta [one of Becket's clerks], hearing things that vexed and pained him being said of his good master [Abelard], remarked: "I saw a miracle at Montpellier which made many men marvel." He was asked to relate it, and said he:

"The great man, whom you so justly extol, had one who was possessed by a demon brought to him at Montpellier to be healed. The man's arms had been bound and he stood before the abbot, who was seated on a great she-ass. While the assembled crowd kept silence, Bernard commanded the unclean spirit to depart; then he said, 'Loose the man and let him go.' But the madman, on feeling himself freed, began to throw stones at the abbot as hard as he could. He chased him through the streets, and even when the people caught him, he still kept glaring at Bernard though his hands were held."

The archbishop [Becket] was not pleased with the tale and said threateningly to John: "These are your miracles, are they?" "Well," says John, "those who were present said it was a very memorable miracle because the madman was gentle and kind to everyone and only vicious to charlatans; and it still seems to me that it was a judgment on presumptuousness."

Walter Map (d. 1208), Courtiers' Trifles[17]

The Origin of Guelfs and Ghibellines (1140)

The accursed names of the Guelf and Ghibelline parties are said to have arisen first in Germany by reason that two great barons of that country were at war together, and each had a strong castle the one over against the other, and the one had the name of Guelf ["Welf" in German], and the other of Ghibelline [Waibling], and the war lasted so long that all the Germans were divided, and one held to one side, and the other to the other; and the strife even came as far as to the court of Rome, and all the court took part in it, and the one side was called that of Guelf and the other that of Ghibelline; and so the said names continued in Italy.

Giovanni Villani (d. 1348), Florentine Chronicle[18]

The Devil's Tail (1150)

Henry [bishop of Winchester] was believed to be instigating his brother [Stephen] the king [of England] against the church.... [While Henry was in Rome] it chanced meanwhile that the king oppressed the church with fresh persecutions, and when the news was brought to the pope the bishop of Winchester, who happened to be with him, exclaimed: "How glad I am that I am not there now, or this persecution would be laid at my door."

Smiling, the pope gave tongue to the following fable: "The devil and his dam were chatting with each other, as friends do, and whilst she was endeavoring to curb her son's evil-doing by rebuking him and chiding him for his misdeeds, a storm arose in their sight and many ships were sunk. 'See,' said the devil, 'if I had been there you would have blamed me for this mischief.' Said she, 'Even if you were not actually on the spot, you have certainly trailed your tail there beforehand.'" And, turning the moral against the bishop, he added, "Ask yourself, my brother, if you have not been trailing *your* tail in the English sea."

John of Salisbury, *Memoirs of the Papal Court* (ca. 1164)[19]

Bernard of Clairvaux:
An Absent-Minded Saint (ca. 1150)

Once, when he [Bernard, abbot of the Cistercian monastery of Clairvaux, 1115–1153] had gone to [the rival Carthusian monastery] La Chartreuse and edified the monks by his virtue, the prior of La Chartreuse was nonetheless somewhat scandalized to see that the saddle of Bernard's horse was rather elegant and hardly in accordance with the saint's vow of poverty. But when the prior's remark was brought to Bernard's attention, the saint inquired with surprise what sort of a saddle it was, for he had ridden from Clairvaux to La Chartreuse [200 miles] without even noticing what he was sitting on. Another time, after he had been travelling all day along the lake of Lausanne [Lake Geneva], when his companions were talking about the lake that evening, he asked them where it was. On hearing this, they marvelled greatly.

Jacobus de Voragine (d. 1298), *The Golden Legend*[20]

Saint Bernard Abstains from Abstinence (died 1153)

I have heard it told of the blessed Bernard of Clairvaux that in his youth he so afflicted his flesh as to be unable to bear the common [monastic] life in his old age. For this reason his abbot-superior commanded him to obey, in his bodily diet, certain brethren that were assigned to him.

It came to pass, therefore, that King Louis VII [of France] once came to Clairvaux when the saint was already an old man dwelling in the infirmary. When the king heard this, he sent him a present of fish. But his messengers found Saint Bernard sitting down to eat a roast capon, and they reported the matter to the king, who would not believe it of so great a man. Therefore, somewhat later when the king was visiting with the saint, he told him what his servants had said. Then the saint confessed it to be true, saying that, so long as he was in health and had felt the power of endurance in his body, he had worn it down with abstinence; until, being unable to bear its accustomed burdens, it must now be supported and sustained, and he was being compelled to do so by his superior. The king was much edified by these words.

Stephen of Bourbon (1261), *Stories for Sermons*[21]

A Wit at the Dull Court of Louis VII (1154)

Waleran of Effria was a knight without letters but had a most pleasant gift of speech, and he was known and loved by the king [Louis VII of France, 1137-1180]. And the king had three ministers who were set over the whole of France—Walter the chamberlain, Bucard the mastiff, and William de Gournai, the provost of Paris. Walter reaped at will almost all the profits of France; Bucard, who was next after him, some part of them; William none; Louis, in his simplicity, whatever they allowed him. Waleran saw this and knew what went on, and guessing that such immense losses befell the treasury through the power of these underlings, he made a rhyme about it in French in these words:

> *Gautier vendange et Buchard grappe*
> *Et Willelmus de Gournay happe*
> *Louis prend ce que leur échappe.*

As Buchard gleans where Walter reaps,

The provost nippers from the heaps;
Whatever's left, King Louis keeps.

When the rhyme was noised abroad, these men saw that their frauds were being discovered and their connivances revealed. They smarted accordingly and armed themselves for revenge; they gathered against him everything that could injure him, set traps for him, accused him of crime to the king, whom, by frequently stirring him up, they put away from kindly feeling.

Finally a very rich and noble woman, but one of slippery reputation, in the intoxication of her spite and pride, accused Waleran in the king's presence of having sung ribald songs not only about her but about the king. The king was pricked by this and said: "Waleran, I can bear abuse of myself patiently, but abuse of this my cousin I must not pass over, since she is of my blood and one of my own members." Waleran answered: "A very sick member." Even this saying the king bore with temper. The rest laughed, but the lady smarting at the taunt said: "Lord king, leave his punishment to me; I will suit him. I know well enough how clowns ought to be corrected; I will find three harlots to whip him as he deserves." "Madam," said Waleran, "you have little more to do; you only have two to get." At this she wept and begged for vengeance for these injuries, and the three men whom he had offended added their complaints to hers, and the poor man was exiled. So Waleran took refuge with our lord, [Henry II] the king of England, and was kindly received. [Eventually Louis relented, recalled Waleran, and made amends.]

Walter Map (d. 1208), *Courtiers' Trifles*[22]

The Sutri Episode:
Barbarossa Takes the Wrong Side (1155)

[Frederick I Barbarossa, already king of Germany, was on his way to Rome for his coronation as emperor.] The king sent Adrian, the lord pope, ambassadors of the highest rank to invite him to take counsel in his camp [at Sutri, 30 miles north of Rome].... When the pope arrived at the camp, the king hastened to meet him, held the stirrup as he got off the horse, took his hand, and led him into the tent. [In a welcoming speech, the bishop of Bamberg stressed the honour that had been thus shown to the pope.] ... To this the lord pope replied, "Brother, what you have spoken are mere words. You say that your ruler has shown appropriate reverence to Saint Peter. But instead Saint Peter seems to have been dishonoured because he held the left stirrup when he should have held the right one!"

When an interpreter told this to the king, Frederick humbly said: "Tell him it was not for lack of devotion but of knowledge. For I have not given very much attention to the holding of stirrups. In fact, as I recall, he is the first for whom I have performed such a service."

To which the lord pope replied: "If through ignorance he has been negligent in a simple matter, how do you think he will handle great matters of state?"

The king was somewhat provoked at this, and he said: "I would like to be better informed about this custom. Is it based on good will or on duty? If it is an expression of good will, then the lord pope has no grounds for complaint if the service varies, because it depends on what I want to do, not on what I am legally obliged to do. But if you say that this act of reverence is due to the pope as an obligation of long standing, then what difference does it make whether the right stirrup or the left is held, just so long as the ruler shows his humility and bows at the pope's feet?"

Therefore they disputed bitterly for a long time. In the end each went his way without the kiss of peace. The king's chief nobles were afraid, however, that the whole expedition might prove to be in vain if things remained at an impasse. So after much persuasion, they overcame the king's feelings, and he called the pope back to the camp. When the pope returned [two days later], the king performed the reception ceremony without a flaw.

Helmold of Bosau (fl. 1167-1172), *Chronicle of the Slavs*[23]

Henry the Lion and the Slavs: "You Be Our God" (1156)

Gerold, our bishop [of Oldenburg-Lübeck] after this went to the duke [of Saxony, Henry the Lion] for the provincial conference which had been proclaimed to meet in Artlenburg, and the rulers of the Slavs who were called came there at the time of the assembly. Then, on the persuasion of the bishop, the duke addressed the Slavs regarding Christianity. Niclot, the ruler of the Abodrites, said to him: "Let the god, who is in heaven be your God; you be our god, and 'it sufficeth us' [John 14:8]. You honour Him; in turn we shall honour you." And the duke reproved him for the blasphemous speech. Nothing more, however, was at this time done in furtherance of the bishopric and of the church because our duke, lately returned from Italy, was entirely absorbed with gain. For the chest was void and empty.

Helmold of Bosau (fl. 1167-1172), *Chronicle of the Slavs*[24]

The Besançon Incident: Legalism in Eruption (1157)

[This manifesto of Emperor Frederick I Barbarossa relates his grievance against the papacy.] Recently, while we were holding court at Besançon [in Burgundy] ... there came apostolic legates [from the pope] asserting that they brought a message to our majesty that would considerably increase the honour of our empire. On the first day of their coming we had received them honourably, and, on the second day, as is the custom, we sat together with our princes to listen to their report. They—as if swollen with the spirit of greed, out of the height of their pride, from the summit of their arrogance, in the execrable elation of their hearts— did present to us a message in the form of an apostolic letter [from the pope], the gist of which was that we should always keep it before our mind's eye how the lord pope had "conferred" upon us the distinction of the imperial crown and that he would not regret it if our highness were to receive from him even greater "benefices" (*beneficia*).

This was that message of paternal sweetness which was to foster the unity of church and empire, which strove to bind together both with a bond of peace, which enticed the minds of the hearers to the concord and obedience of both! Of course that message, blasphemous and devoid of all truth, not only kindled righteous indignation in our imperial majesty, but also filled all the princes who were present with such fury and wrath that without doubt they would have condemned those two wicked priests to death had not our presence prevented them.... We made the legates return to Rome by the way they had come.

The rule of the empire is ours because we received it, through election by the princes, from God alone. By the passion of His Son Christ, God subjected the world to the rule of two swords, both of which are necessary. Whoever says that we received the imperial crown as a benefice from the lord pope is guilty of a lie because he contradicts a divine institution and the teaching of Peter, who taught this doctrine to the world: "Fear God, honour the king" [1 Peter 2:17].

Frederick I Barbarossa, *Manifesto* (1157)[25]

Barbarossa's Argument from Roman Law (1158)

Once when the lord emperor [Frederick I Barbarossa], mounted on his favorite palfrey, was riding between the lords Bulgarus and Martinus [two famous professors of Roman law at the university of Bologna], he inquired of them whether *de jure* he was lord of the world (*dominus mundi*). And lord Bulgarus replied that the emperor did not have lordship over the world as far as property was concerned; the lord Martinus, however, said that the emperor was lord of the world pure and simple. And then, when the emperor dismounted from the palfrey on which he had been sitting, he made a present of it to Martinus. On hearing this, however, Bulgarus made this elegant remark: "I lost a horse because I said what is right, which was not right (*Amisi equum, quia dixi equum, quod non fuit equum*)."

Otto Morena, *History of Frederick I*, revised version (13th century)[26]

Barbarossa and the Monk's Needle (ca. 1158)

Some time ago in the days of the Emperor Frederick [I, 1152-1190] ... one of the imperial abbeys fell vacant; two men were elected, and when the monks could not agree, one of them took a large sum of money, which he had collected in the monastery, and offered it to Frederick, that he might take his side. The emperor took the money and gave his promise, and afterwards he learned that the other candidate was a man of good life and simple and well-ordered, and he began to take counsel with his friends, how he might get rid of the unworthy candidate and confirm the election of him who had been chosen for his virtues. And one of his counsellors said to him: "Sire, I have heard that every monk is bound by his rule to carry a needle. When you are sitting in the chapter house, say to that candiadate of irregular life that you wish him to lend you his needle in order to take a splinter out of one of your fingers, and when he proves to have none, you will find an occasion of disallowing him, owing to his irregularity." Now when this was done and the man had no needle, the king said to the other, "Sir, lend me your needle," and when he immediately produced it, perhaps having been forewarned, the emperor went on: "You are a monk, upright in keeping the rules of your order and so you are worthy of this great honour. I had intended to give the honour to your opponent, but his irregularity has shown him to be unworthy. He that is careless in that which is least will be careless in important matters." By such sophistry did the emperor get rid of the worldly-wise monk and promote his simple brother to be abbot.

Caesarius of Heisterbach (d. 1223), *Dialogue of Miracles*[27]

Foiled by Feudalism (1159)

In the war and siege of Toulouse, in which England, Normandy, Aquitaine, Anjou, and Brittany sent all their knightly bravery and warlike prowess to the assistance of the English king [Henry II], the chancellor [Thomas Becket] had handpicked seven hundred knights from his own household for the king's forces. And certainly, if the chancellor's advice had been heeded, this army, because it was so large, would have invaded and taken Toulouse as well as the king of France [Louis VII], who on behalf of his sister, the Countess Constance [who had married the lord of Toulouse], had rashly placed himself in Toulouse with inadequate strength. But from vain superstition and reverence, the king followed the counsel of others and did not wish to attack the city in which his lord, the king of France, was. The chancellor argued, to the contrary, that the king of France had given up his position of lord because he opposed the king as an enemy in violation of their feudal contract. Soon afterwards an army of the French king, having been called and assembled, arrived at the city, and the English king, with the king of the Scots [Malcolm IV] and his army, left without accomplishing his goals.

William Fitzstephen, *Life of Saint Thomas* (ca. 1191)[28]

A King Caught Napping (ca. 1160)

It was the habit [of Louis VII, king of France] that wherever he felt sleep coming on he would take his rest on or near the spot. As he was slumbering by a wood in the shade, attended only by two knights (for the rest were hunting), the Count Theobald [of Blois], whose sister he had married [in 1160], found him and reproved him for sleeping so solitarily; it was not right, he said, for a king to do so. He answered: "I may sleep alone quite safely, for no one bears me any grudge." It was a simple answer, the utterance of a pure conscience. What other king can claim so much for himself!

Walter Map (d. 1208), *Courtier's Trifles*[29]

Frederick Barbarossa Envies Alexander the Great (1164)

[On his third expedition to Italy in 1163-64, Emperor Frederick I took a small army and found himself outnumbered.] And since he knew that the army he had with him was not sufficient ... he resolved to cross over into Germany in order to return from there with a greater number of people.... And in 1164 at the end of September he returned to Germany. And it is clear that he left with his spirit greatly angered, for when on his journey he was having a light meal and, as was his custom, listened to a recital of the great success of the deeds of Alexander the Great, he said, sadly as it were, "Happy was Alexander, who never saw Italy, and happier I would be had I crossed over to Asia."

Ricobaldo of Ferrara (fl. 1297), *Imperial History*[30]

Henry II Rages Against Thomas Becket (1170)

[While King Henry of England was spending Christmas in his hunting lodge at Bures, near Bayeux in France] three bishops informed him that the archbishop of Canterbury [Thomas Becket] would not release them from the excommunication he had laid on them. Henry flew into a fit of rage that deserves to be cursed for centuries to come. Like a skillet heated up for frying, he became hotter and hotter until he was no longer able to keep from bursting out into flame; then he complained loudly of the archbishop as if he were an enemy and did so openly in front of everyone, although he was worse in private when only his close associates were present, whom he had brought up and to whom he had given many honors and goods. Inflamed by wrath, he burst out cursing in a dreadful voice, damning everyone in his service who was obliged to him for the favour of his friendship and for benefits he had given them, because they would not avenge him on one priest who kept him and his kingdom in turmoil and who was trying to deprive him of his inheritance and the rights of his office.

In his fury he said these things over and over again until four knights of the king's bedchamber took his words to be what he wished. They thought there could be no doubt that if they killed the archbishop they would render the king a service for which he would be most grateful, and so they swore to kill the archbishop.... These four household knights of the king's bedchamber, although not of noble birth, were well brought up, made famous by honours, and great among the great. The four conspirators set out right away for England.

Herbert of Bosham, *Life of St. Thomas* (1184-1186)[31]

The Raven of Corvey (ca. 1170)

In the time of the last Emperor Frederick [Barbarossa], this monastery [of Corvey in Saxony] was ruled by one Conrad, who, according to the pompous custom of prince-abbots, among other gauds of worldly glory, wore gold rings—in a spirit far different to that of the truly poor and humble-minded abbot-founder of Clairvaux [Bernard], who (we find it written) delighted more in rake and hoe than in mitre and ring.

Now it came to pass one day, when he sat at meat and in courtly fashion had laid down a precious golden ring for the sake of washing his hands, that some trifle or some serious matter intervened, and the ring was left, somewhat too negligently, on the table. Meanwhile a tame raven, whom the abbot's courtiers kept as a pet, watching an unguarded moment, caught the ring in his beak and flew away swiftly to his nest without conscience of his own guilty theft. When, therefore, the feasters' hunger was satisfied and the meats were removed, and the guests had arisen from the table, then the abbot learned his loss, blamed his servants' negligence, and bade them seek the ring forthwith in every corner; however, nowhere could it be found nor could the thief be discovered.

Whereupon the abbot, suspecting both guests and servants and stirred to fervent indignation, sent word to the parish priests of the great and wealthy town which was situated hard by the abbey and subjected to its rule, bidding them publicly launch the most grievous sentence of excommunication upon him who had not feared to defile himself with this crime. The sentence was proclaimed; and, as all rational beings in those parts found in their guiltless conscience a crown of innocence, so the irrational creature itself could not escape the temporal penalties of that curse, whereof the eternal pains could take no hold upon his fragile and shortlived condition. For this thief, guilty yet unaware of his own guilt, began to sicken little by little, to loathe his food, to cease more and more from his droll croakings and other irrational follies whereby he was wont to delight the minds of fools who neglect the fear of God; then he began even to droop his wings, and at last his very feathers fled from the corruption of his decaying flesh, exposing him as a miserable and marvellous spectacle to all beholders.

It came to pass one day that, as the abbot's household disputed one with the other in his presence concerning this portentous change in the bird and concluded that so great a marvel must have some cause, one of them said half in jest to the abbot: "You ought to consider, my lord, whether by chance this be the thief whom you seek, and whether this loathsome plague which you behold is not the token of the curse wherein he is involved." At which word all were astonished, and the abbot bade one of his servants straightway to climb the tree wherein this bird had his nest and to turn over diligently his couch of straw and woven twigs. The servant climbed, found the ring forthwith, cleansed it from the filth that disfigured it, and laid it within the abbot's hands, to the amazement of all that stood by....

Then the lord abbot, by the advice of prudent men, sent word to the priests who had pronounced this sentence of excommunication, to proclaim that the ring was now restored and the curse was invalid. Whereupon, even as at first the aforesaid bird had sickened by slow degrees and visibly languished from day to day under that insidious disease, even so he now began slowly to revive and to recover his former strength, until at last by a plain miracle of God he was wholly restored to his first health and beauty.

Origins of the Cistercian Order (after 1190)[32]

The Perils of Episcopacy (ca. 1170)

It is told of a certain prior of Clairvaux, Geoffrey by name, that when he had been elected bishop of Tournai [in 1149], and Pope Eugene [III] as well as the blessed Bernard, his own abbot, was urging him to take the office, he cast himself down at the feet of the blessed Bernard and his clergy, lay prone in the form of a cross, and said: "An expelled monk I may be, if you drive me out; but I will never be a bishop."

At a later time [between 1166 and 1172], as this same prior lay breathing his last, a monk who loved him well adjured him in the name of God to bring him news of his state beyond the grave, if God would permit it. Some time after, as the monk was praying prostrate before the altar, his friend appeared and said that it was he. When the monk asked him how he was faring, he replied: "Well, by the grace of God. Yet verily it has been revealed to me by the blessed Trinity that had I been in the number of bishops, I should have been in the number of the reprobate and the damned."

Stephen of Bourbon, *Stories for Sermons* (ca. 1250)[33]

The Power of the Purse (1174)

Jocelin, bishop of Salisbury [1141-1184], made this answer to his son, Reginald, who had been elected by coercion to the see of Bath but was refused consecration by [the archbishop of] Canterbury and was complaining: "Fool, be off quick to the pope, bold, without a flinch. Give him a good smack with a heavy purse, and he will tumble which way you like." He went: one smote, the other tumbled; down fell the pope, up rose the bishop. And straightway he wrote a lie to God at the head of every one of his letters, for where there should have stood "by the grace of the Purse," he said "by the grace of God."

Walter Map (d. 1208), Courtiers' Trifles[34]

A Lapful of York (1176)

In the month of March, about Mid-Lent, the king [Henry II Plantagenet] came to London with his son Henry and the Lord Huguccio, the papal legate, who had called together the clergy of England in order to hold a council [in Westminister Abbbey].

At the opening of the council, when the papal legate had taken his seat on a raised throne in the midst, and Richard, the archbishop of Canterbury, had sat down on his right hand by right of his primacy [in the Church of England], then Roger, the archbishop of York, puffed up with his own innate arrogance, rejected the left-hand throne that was destined for him and strove instead to sit down between the legate and the archbishop of Canterbury, pressing down with his buttocks so that he was sitting on the lap of his own primate [Canterbury]. Yet scarce had he struck my lord of Canterbury with the weapon of his choice, when he was ignominiously seized by certain bishops, clerics, and laymen, torn from the archbishop's lap, and cast upon the floor. But, when staves and fists were now wielded on both sides, the archbishop of Canterbury sprang up and returned good for evil, snatching away from this disastrous conflict his own rival and the inveterate enemy of his see. At length the contumacious archbishop of York, rising from the pavement with his cape ignominiously torn by the struggle, fell down at the king's feet and belched forth lying calumnies against the archbishop of Canterbury.

Gervase of Canterbury (1145–1210?), Chronicle[35]

Fair Rosamund (died 1176)

[Henry II Plantagenet], who had imprisoned his wife, Queen Eleanor [of Aquitaine] and had broken his marriage vows secretly, now [ca. 1173] broke them openly and was not ashamed to fornicate with the wench

Rosamund. For this fair girl the king had made [in the royal palace] at Woodstock a room like the labyrinth that Daedalus built, lest the queen should find and take Rosamund; but the girl soon died and was buried in the chapter house at Godstow [the convent where she was educated] near Oxford with this inscription on her tomb:

Hic iacet in tumba rosa mundi, non rosa munda.
Non redolet, sed olet, quae redolere solet.

["Here in the tomb lies the rose of the world, but not a perfect rose; it is not fragrant as it once was, but now stinks."] This wench had a little coffer, scarcely two feet long, made by a wonderfully skilled craftsman, on which it seems that giants fight, beasts run off, fowls flee, and fishes move, not as puppets are moved but of their own accord....

In the year A.D. 1192, Saint Hugh, bishop of Lincoln, while inspecting the religious houses in his diocese, came to the convent of Godstow near Oxford. When he entered into the church to make his prayers, the bishop saw a tomb in the midst of the choir before the high altar covered with cloths of silk, and placed around it were lamps and tapers burning. The bishop presently inquired what person was buried there, and some bystanders told him that it was Rosamund, friend to King Henry II, for whose sake the king had done many great benefits to their church. Then the bishop commanded that she should be buried outside of the church with the other common people, lest Christian morals suffer from this glorification of her. She was a whore, he said, and if she were no longer honoured, those women who were tempted to imitate her example would learn to avoid the sins of adultery and lechery.

Ralph Higden (d. 1364), *Polychronicon*[36]

Barbarossa's Final Submission to the Papacy (1177)

When the lord emperor [Frederick I Barbarossa] disembarked [at Venice to make his peace with the papacy in 1177], he proceeded with honour to the church of Saint Mark, where he was met by the pope [Alexander III]. The emperor showed him due reverence and honour by prostrating himself at the pope's feet, whereupon the pope touched the emperor with his foot and repeated this verse of David: "You shall walk upon the asp and the basilisk: and you shall trample under foot the lion and the dragon" [Psalm 90:13]. To this the lord emperor replied: "I do this, not to you, but to Saint Peter (*non tibi sed Petro*)." In response, the pope said: "To Saint Peter and to me acting in Peter's place (*et Petro et mihi gerenti vices Petri*)."

Bonincontrus de Bovis (fl. 1313-1346), *History*[37]

France and her Royal Rivals (1179)

It happened that when I was making some long stay with the king [Louis VII] at Paris [in 1179], and he was talking with me of the riches of kings, among other matters, he said: "As the wealth of kings is diverse, so it is marked out by many differences. The riches of the king of the Indians are in precious stones, lions and pards and elephants; the emperor of Constantinople and the king of Sicily boast themselves in cloth of gold and silver, but they have no men who can do anything but talk, for in warlike matters they are useless. The Roman emperor, whom they call the emperor of the Germans, has men fit for arms, and war horses, but no gold or silk or other splendour. For Charlemagne, when he had won that land from the Saracens, gave everything except the castles and forts to the archbishops and bishops whom he had established in all the cities he had converted. But your lord, the king of England, who wants for nothing, has men, horses, gold, silk, jewels, fruits, game, and everything else. We in France have nothing but bread and wine and gaiety." This saying I took note of, for it was merrily said, and truly.

Walter Map (d. 1208), *Courtiers' Trifles*[38]

John and Fulk Play Chess: Boys Will Be Boys (ca. 1180)

After the death of the father [Henry II Plantagenet] reigned Richard [the Lionhearted, Henry's son], and after Richard came John, his brother [born 1167], who for the whole of his life was wicked, contrary, and envious. Fulk ["a baronial Robin Hood" from whose legend this story comes] was brought up with King Henry's four sons, and was much loved by all of them except John, with whom he had frequent quarrels. It happened one day that John and Fulk were sitting all alone in a chamber playing at chess. John took the chess board and struck Fulk a great blow with it. Feeling himself hurt, Fulk raised his foot and gave John a blow in the midst of his chest; his head struck against the wall so that he became giddy and fainted. Fulk was frightened but was glad that there was no one in the room but the two of them. He rubbed John's ears until he recovered consciousness. John went to his father the king and made a great complaint. "Hold your tongue, you good-for-nothing," said the king, "you are always quarrelling. If Fulk has done all that you say, it is your own fault." He called John's tutor and caused the boy to be well and soundly whipped for his complaint. John was very angry with Fulk, and never afterwards did he love him in his heart.

The Legend of Fulk Fitz-warin (13th century)[39]

Kissing the Cat: An Improbable Heresy (1182)

There is also another old heresy newly sprouted forth to a great extent [during the last century] ... called Publicans or Paterines.... Men and women live together, but no sons or daughters issue of the union. Many, however, have dropped their errors and returned to the faith, and these relate that about the first watch of the night, after their gates, doors, and windows have been shut, each congregation sits waiting in silence in each of their synagogues, and there descends by a rope which hangs in the midst a black cat of wondrous size. On sight of it they put out the lights, and do not sing or distinctly repeat hymns, but hum them with closed teeth and draw near to the place where they saw their master, feeling after him, and when they have found him they kiss him, each one according to the degree that his madness makes him more humble: some the feet, more under the tail and the most shameful parts. Then, as if the stench of the cat's private parts had excited their lust, each seizes his or her neighbour—the sex of the partner doesn't matter—and they do together whatever appeals to the wantonness of either party. For they say that their masters teach the novices that perfect charity consists in doing or accepting whatever a brother or sister might desire and ask in order to mutually extinguish the flames of lust; and from such contracting *(paciendo)* they are called "Paterini."

Walter Map (d. 1208), *Courtiers' Trifles*[40]

Welsh Archery Makes an Impression on the English (1182)

The people of Gwentland [Monmouthshire] are more accustomed to war, more famous for valour, and more expert in archery, than those of any other part of Wales. The following examples prove the truth of this assertion. In the capture of Abergavenny Castle [1182], as two soldiers were passing over a bridge to take refuge in a tower built on a mound of earth, the Welsh shot at them from behind and their arrows penetrated the tower's oaken door, which was four fingers thick. The arrows were left in the gate as a permanent reminder of the force of such arrows.

William de Braose [lord of that castle] also testifies that one of his soldiers, in a conflict with the Welsh, was wounded by an arrow, which passed through his thigh and the armour with which it was cased on both sides and through that part of the saddle which is called the *alva*, or seat, mortally wounding the horse.

Another soldier had his hip, equally sheathed in armour, penetrated by an arrow quite to the saddle, and on turning his horse around, received a similar wound on the opposite hip, which fixed him on both sides of his seat.

What more could be expected from a balista? Yet the bows used by this people are not made of horn, sapwood, or yew, but of wild elm; unpolished, rude, and uncouth, but stout; they are not calculated to shoot an arrow to a great distance but to inflict very severe wounds in close fight.

Gerald of Wales, *Journey through Wales* (1191)[41]

A Rebellious Son (1183)

Now this Henry [the son and heir of Henry II Plantagenet] ... departed this life at Martel [on the Dordogne in France] ... in the year [1183] ... and in the twenty-seventh year of his birth.... This Absalom [2 Samuel 17–18] had stirred up all Aquitaine and Burgundy, as well as many of the French, against our lord his father, and all of them of Maine and Anjou and the Bretons. Of those who were fighting on our side the greater part deserted to him.... And when the power of all the world was flocking to this Absalom, he took an oath against his father at Martel, and on that same day he was smitten with the hammer (*martellum*) of death by the all-righteous avenging Hand, and he was not. Riot was turned to quiet, and so the world was at rest.... This hammer, smitten at Martel, died, they say, penitent, yet no admonition could bend him to make peace with his father. "If I die, I will be quiet; if not, I will attack him," was what he said. He had war in his heart.

Walter Map (d. 1208), *Courtiers' Trifles*[42]

A Nun Becomes Empress-Mother (1186)

Constance [1154-1198] shone forth from the highest pinnacle onto the lands of the Romans as empress.... She was the daughter of William [II] the Good, the former [Norman] king of the Sicilians. At her birth, as many say, Joachim [of Flora], a Calabrian abbot endowed with a prophetic spirit, told William that she would be the ruin of the realm of Sicily. The king was stupified and frightened by this declaration. Since he had believed the prophecy, he pondered how that could happen with a woman. Seeing that it could happen only through a husband or a son, and having pity on his kingdom, he decided to avoid it if he could by planning. And he compelled the little girl to be shut up in a convent and vow to God perpetual virginity so as to remove hope of marriage and offspring. It would not have been a bad scheme had it succeeded....

At the time of the death of her revered father and brother, with no other legitimate heir to the throne left other than herself, she had passed all her youth and had now become an old woman. And after the death of William [II], Tancred, his illegitimate nephew, had taken the royal crown, and after him his son William [III], still a young man. Because of the frequent or unworthy change of kings, matters had reached the point that, as factions of nobles burst forth in wars everywhere, the kingdom seemed to be drawn utterly toward ruin. Therefore as certain men pitied the unfortunate state, an idea occurred to them which subsequently was realized, namely for Constance to be married to some illustrious prince so that the pestilential disorders could be settled by his resources and power. Nor was this goal obtained without great cunning and effort, with the pope [Lucius III] agreeing that Constance consent to the idea of marrying although she remained steadfast in her proposed profession and although her advanced age seemed an obstacle.

But, though she still resisted, since matters had advanced to the point that their course could not easily be reversed, she was espoused to Henry [VI Hohenstaufen] the Roman emperor, son of the late Frederick I [Barbarossa in 1186]. And so a wrinkled old hag left the cloister, laid aside the veil of her order, and appeared in public dressed as a royal bride and empress. And she who had vowed perpetual virginity gave it up unwillingly upon entering the royal bedchamber.

As a consequence of this, it happened to the amazement of all that in her fifty-fifth year she became pregnant. And since all were reluctant to accept this sort of pregnancy, and since many suspected trickery, as the time of her delivery approached it was prudently enacted by an imperial decree, designed to remove suspicion, that all the married women of the realm of Sicily who wanted could be present at the forthcoming birth. When they had gathered even from afar, a tent was erected in the fields outside Palermo, or according to others, in the city. As everyone watched, the decrepit empress bore a baby, namely Frederick [II Hohenstaufen, in 1194], who afterward turned into a monstrous man and a plague to all Italy, let alone Sicily, so that the Calabrian abbot's prophecy was not idle.

Giovanni Boccaccio (d. 1375), *Famous Women*[43]

Frederick Barbarossa Drowns in Turkey (1190)

The whole army of crusaders suffered [on the journey across the Taurus Mountains in southern Turkey], both from the hard life and from the rocky cliffs, which were hardly accessible except to birds and wild mountain goats. The rich were as affected as the poor, and those who seemed to be well as much as the sick. The emperor [Frederick I, then about 67] was unterrified at all the dangers, however; [on June 10] he wanted to alleviate the immoderate heat and to avoid the peaks of the mountains, so he tried to swim across the bed of an extremely rapid river, the Saleph [the Gök-su]. Everyone tried to dissuade him, because one who is wise in most things uses his powers foolishly against the current and stream of the river, as Ecclesiasticus said: "Do not strive against the stream of the river" [4:32]. But Frederick entered the water anyway, and although he had often escaped from great perils before, he sank into the troubled water and perished miserably.... The other nobles who were around him hastened to his assistance but they were too late and could only raise him up and bring him to the shore. [The body was taken to Antioch and buried there.]

Ansbert, *History of Frederick's Crusade* (ca. 1200)[44]

*   *   *   *   *

While on pilgrimage in the thirty-ninth year of his reign, the emperor Frederick ended his life submerged in the river Saleph, and he is said to have exclaimed: "O blessed, crucified son of God, may the water that regenerated me and made me a Christian [at baptism] now receive me and make me a martyr!" And thus he expired.

Albert of Stade, *Annals* (ca. 1256)[45]

The Kyffhäuser Legend: Barbarossa Underground (after 1190)

Many folk have seen the Emperor Frederick sitting in his underground hall [beneath the Kyffhäuser mountain in Thuringia], sometimes alone, sometimes surrounded by his men-at-arms, sometimes with the princess, his daughter. To many a shepherd a dwarf has appeared, to many others, the daughter herself.

A shepherd boy was playing a courtly song on his bagpipe when a venerable old man's head raised itself behind him and asked in a gentle voice: "For whom was this song meant, boy?" And the boy boldly cried: "It was meant for the Emperor Frederick!" And then the old man beckoned the boy to follow him, and the boy was led by the old man down below, where treasure lay about everywhere and men-at-arms were standing. Then the shepherd bowed himself low before the elder because he saw with terror who his guide was, and the emperor spoke: "This boy has honoured us!" As he was showing him the magnificence and splendour of the underground hall, he broke a foot off a vase, gave it to the boy, and spoke: "Go and let this be known above: when the time is fulfilled that the Lord God releases us from this enchantment, then will the German realm be free!" The shepherd boy came up out of there, but how it happened he did not know. The Emperor Frederick's gift in his hand was of pure gold.

Ludwig Bechstein, *Legends of the Kyffhäuser* (1835)[46]

Saladin Discovers the Crusaders' Hypocrisy (1191)

Saladin, at the time of his sultanate [1174-1193], ordered a truce between himself and the Christians [on the Third Crusade], and said he would like to behold our customs, and if they pleased him, he would become a Christian. The truce was made.

Saladin came in person to study the habits of the Christians; he beheld the tables set for eating with dazzlingly white cloths, and he praised them exceedingly. And he beheld the disposition of the table where the king of France [Philip II Augustus] ate, set apart from the others, and he praised it highly. He saw the places where the great ones of the realm ate, and he praised them highly. He saw how the poor ate on the ground in humility, and of this he disapproved greatly. Moreover, he blamed them because the lord's retainers ate more lowly and further down the table.

Then the Christians went to see the customs of the Saracens, and saw that they ate on the ground grossly. The sultan had his pavilion, where they ate, richly draped and the ground covered with carpets which were closely worked with crosses. The ignorant Christians entered, stepping with their feet on these crosses and spitting upon them as on the ground. The sultan spoke and took them to task harshly: "Do you preach the Cross and scorn it thus? It would seem then that you love your God only with show of words and not with deeds. Your behaviour and your manners do not meet with my liking." The truce was broken off, and the war began again.

The Hundred Old Tales (compiled at end of 13th century)[47]

The Crusaders' Camp Followers:
A Moslem Rabelais (ca. 1192)

[During the Third Crusade, 1189-1193] there arrived [in Syria] by ship three hundred lovely Frankish women, full of youth and beauty, assembled from beyond the sea and offering themselves for sin. They were expatriates come to help expatriates, ready to cheer the fallen and sustained in turn to give support and assistance, and they glowed with ardour for carnal intercourse. They were all licentious harlots, proud and scornful, who took and gave, foul-fleshed and sinful, singers and coquettes, appearing proudly in public, ardent and inflamed, tinted and painted, desirable and appetizing, exquisite and graceful, who ripped open and patched up, lacerated and mended, erred and ogled, urged and seduced, consoled and solicited, seductive and languid, desired and desiring, amused and amusing, versatile and cunning, like tipsy adolescents, making love and selling themselves for gold, bold and ardent, loving and passionate, pink-faced and unblushing, black-eyed and bullying, callipygian and graceful, with nasal voices and fleshy thighs, blue-eyed and grey-eyed, broken-down little fools.

Each one trailed the train of her robe behind her and bewitched the beholder with effulgence. She swayed like a sapling, revealed herself like a strong castle, quivered like a small branch, walked proudly with a cross on her breast, sold her graces for gratitude, and longed to lose her robe and her honour.

They arrived after consecrating their persons as if to works of piety, and offered and prostituted the most chaste and precious among them. They said that they set out with the intention of consecrating their charms, that they did not intend to refuse themselves to bachelors, and they maintained that they could make themselves acceptable to God by no better sacrifice than this. So they set themselves up each in a pavilion or tent erected for her use, together with other lovely young girls of their age, and opened the gates of pleasure.

They dedicated as a holy offering what they kept between their thighs; they were openly licentious and devoted themselves to relaxation; they removed every obstacle to making of themselves free offerings. They plied a brisk trade in dissoluteness, adorned the patched-up fissures, poured themselves into the springs of libertinage, shut themselves up in private under the amourous transports of men, offered their wares for enjoyment, invited the shameless into their embrace, mounted breasts on backs, bestowed their wares on the poor, brought their silver anklets up to touch their golden ear-rings, and were willingly spread out on the carpet of amourous sport.

They made themselves targets for men's darts, they were permitted territory for forbidden acts, they offered themselves to the lances' blows and humiliated themselves to their lovers. They put up the tent and loosed the girdle after agreement had been reached. They were the places where tent-pegs are driven in, they invited swords to enter their sheaths, they razed their terrain for planting, they made javelins rise toward shields, excited the plow to plow, gave the birds a place to peck with their beaks, allowed heads to enter their ante-chambers, and raced under whoever bestrode them at the spur's blow. They took the parched man's sinews to the well, fitted arrows to the bow's handle, cut off sword-belts, engraved coins, welcomed birds into the nest of their thighs, caught in their nets the horns of butting rams, removed the interdict from what is protected, withdrew the veil from what is hidden.

They interwove leg with leg, slaked their lovers' thirsts, caught lizard after lizard in their holes, disregarded the wickedness of their intimacies, guided pens to inkwells, torrents to the valley bottom, streams to pools, swords to scabbards, gold ingots to crucibles, infidel girdles to women's zones, firewood to the stove, guilty men to low dungeons, money-changers to *dinar*, necks to bellies, motes to eyes. They contested for tree trunks, wandered far and wide to collect fruit, and maintained that this was an act of piety without equal, especially to those who were far from home and wives.

'Imad ad-Din (1125–1201), *Saladin's Conquests*[48]

How Blondel Found Richard the Lionhearted (1193)

Now we shall tell you how King Richard was held prisoner by the duke of Austria; no one except the duke and his counsellors knew what had happened to him. Now there was a minstrel named Blondel who had grown up in the king's household. He decided that he would seek through every land until he found out what had happened to the king, so he set out and travelled for a year and a half through many foreign countries, but he was not able to gather any news about the king.

It happened that by chance he went to Austria and soon came to the castle [Durrenstein] where the king was in prison. Blondel lodged with an old woman, and he asked her who was lord of this castle that was so fine and strong and well situated. His hostess replied that it belonged to the duke of Austria. "Good hostess," said Blondel, "is there at present any prisoner in the castle?" "No doubt about it," said the good woman. "Yes, there is one, who has been there a good four years. But we haven't been able to find out who he is; I can tell you for certain that he is guarded carefully and well, and we have good reason to believe that he probably is a nobleman and a great lord."

Blondel rejoiced to hear these words, for in his heart he felt he had found what he had been looking for, but he hid his feelings from his hostess. That night he relaxed and slept until dawn; when he heard the watchman blow his horn, he got up and went to church to pray for God's help, and then he went to the castle, where he introduced himself to the castellan, who was in charge. Blondel said he was a minstrel and would be most willing to stay with him if he wished; the castellan, who was a fine young knight, said he did indeed wish to retain him.

So Blondel was happy and went back to the inn to get his viol and his instruments; and he served the castellan so well that he pleased him greatly, and he was well rewarded by the castellan and the whole household. Thus Blondel spent the whole winter there, but he was not able to discover who the prisoner was until one day at Eastertime he went all alone into a garden that was beside the tower and looked around, thinking that by some chance he might be able to see the prisoner. While Blondel was lost in thought, the king looked out through a loophole and saw him and wondered how he could make himself known to him; and he remembered a song that they both had made together and that no one else knew.

So he began to sing the first line loud and clear, for he was a good singer. When Blondel heard it, he knew for certain that it was his lord, and his heart was far happier than it had been for many a day; so he left the garden and went to his room and took his viol and began to play a tune out of sheer delight at having found his lord. Thus Blondel remained at the castle until Pentecost, and he contained himself so well that no one there guessed what his business there was.

Finally Blondel went to the castellan and said to him, "My lord, if it please you, I would like to go to my own country, for I have been away for a long time." "Blondel, my brother, don't do it if you believe me but stay here still, and I shall reward you greatly." But Blondel replied, "My lord, be assured there is no way I can stay here." When the castellan saw that he could not retain him, he gave him leave to go and sent him off with a pack horse and a new robe. After taking his leave of the castellan, Blondel went straight to England and told the king's friends and the barons that he had found the king and told them where he was. [Then they were able to ransom him.]

A minstrel from Rheims (ca. 1260)[49]

The Tumbler of Our Lady (late 12th century)

Now I will tell and repeat to you what happened to a minstrel. So much had he travelled to and fro to so many places, and so irregular had been his way of life, that he became weary of the world and became a monk [at Clairvaux].... And when this tumbler, who was so graceful and fair, so handsome and well-formed, became a monk, he did not know how to perform any of the monks' duties, for indeed he had lived only to spring and tumble, to dance and turn somersaults. He knew how to leap and jump, but nothing else, for indeed he had learned nothing else, neither the *Pater noster*, nor the psalms, nor the *Credo*, nor the *Ave Maria*, nor anything else that would further his salvation.... He was very sad and pensive in the monastery because everywhere he saw the monks and novices each serving God in the duty assigned to him. He saw the priests at the altars, for such was their duty, and the deacons at the gospels, and the subdeacons at the epistles, while the acolytes rang the bell at the proper time during mass. One recited a verse and another a lesson; the young priests worked at the psalter, the novices at the *Miserere*, and the least experienced learned the *Pater noster*, for each had his appointed task....The tumbler observed each as closely as he was able. One made lamentation, another wept, and another groaned and sighed. And he could not understand what ailed them. "Holy Mary," he said at last, "What troubles these people that they act thus and show such grief in this manner? ... I suppose they are asking God's grace.... But I shall never render any service here, for I can neither do nor say anything...."

And he went prying about the church until he entered a crypt ... and above the altar was the image of our lady, the blessed Mary.... And when he heard the bell ring for mass ... he said: "Now everyone will be saying his response, and here I am... What shall I do? What shall I say? ... I will do what I have learned, and thus, in my own way, I will serve the mother of God in her monastery."

And he took off his habit and laid his garments beside the altar, but not wanting his body to be naked, he kept on an undershirt, which was very clinging and close fitting.... Then he began to turn somersaults, now high, now low, first forwards, then backwards, and then he fell on his knees before the image and bowed his head. "Ah, most gentle queen!" said he, "of your pity and your generosity, despise not my service." Then he tumbled, leaped, and gaily turned the somersault of Metz. And he bowed to the image and venerated it, for he honoured it as much as he was able. Presently he turned the French somersault, next the somersault of Champagne, and after that those of Spain and of Brittany, and then that of Lorraine. After that he did the Roman somersault, and then, with one hand before his face, he danced gracefully.... Then he put his feet in the air and walked about on his two hands. His feet danced in the air and his eyes wept as he said: "Lady, I worship you with heart, with body, feet, and hands, for I understand nothing else. Let me be your minstrel. Upstairs they are singing, but I have come down here to divert you. My lady, do not despise me." ... Then he turned and gave another leap. "Lady," he said, "as God is my Saviour, I've never turned that somersault before; in fact, no tumbler has ever done it, and really it's not half bad...."

As long as the mass went on, he kept on dancing, jumping, and leaping until he almost fainted and could not stand up, and thus he fell to the ground and dropped from sheer exhaustion. And just as grease drops from the spitted meat, so sweat poured from him all over, from head to foot. "Lady," said he, "I can do no more just now, but I promise to come back again...."

.   .   .   .

[He visited the crypt every day, until finally a curious monk discovered what the tumbler was doing and brought the abbot to watch.] And as the abbot was looking, he saw a lady descend from the vaulting, and she was so glorious that another so shining or so richly dressed never lived, and none has ever been so fair.... And the sweet and noble queen took a white cloth, and with it she very gently fanned her minstrel before the altar. And the noble and gracious lady fanned his neck and body and face to cool him, and greatly did she concern herself to aid him and gave herself up to his care; but of this the good man took no heed, for he neither perceived nor did he know that he was in such fair company.

The Tumbler of Our Lady (13th century)[50]

Robin Hood and Little John (ca. 1195)

[This sample of the Robin Hood legends comes from the earliest known ballad about the famous highwayman. He and Little John are setting out for Nottingham on an adventure.]

"Of all my merry men," said Robin
"By my faith I will have none.
But Little John shall bear my bow
Til I may wish to draw."

"You shall bear your own," said Little John,
"Master, and I will bear mine,
And we will shoot for pennies," said Little John,
"Under the green wood fine."

"I will not shoot for pennies," said Robin Hood,
"In faith Little John with thee,
But for the one you shoot," said Robin,
"In faith I will hit three."

Thus shot they forth these yeomen two
Both at busk and broom [staff and target]
Til Little John from his master won
Five shillings for hose and shoon [shoes].

A sudden strife between them rose
As they went by the way;
Little John said he had won five shillings,

And Robin Hood said, "Nay."

With that Robin Hood lied Little John,
And smote him with his hand;
Little John waxed wroth therewith,
And pulled out his bright brand [sword].

"Were you not my master," said Little John,
"You would be hit full sore,
Get you a man wherever you can, Robin,
For you have me no more."

Then Robin goes to Nottingham
Himself, mourning alone,
And Little John to merry Sherwood,
The paths he knows along.

Robin Hood and the Monk (ca. 1400)[51]

The Death of Richard the Lionhearted (1199)

Guidomar, viscount of Limoges, having found a great treasure of gold and silver on his lands, sent to Richard, king of England, his liege lord, no small part of the same; but the king refused it, saying that he ought by right to have the whole of this treasure [since the viscount was his vassal], but the viscount would by no means agree to this. Accordingly, the king brought a large force to Limoges to attack the viscount, and he laid siege to his castle, which was called Chalus, in which he hoped that the treasure was concealed....

When the king and [the captain of his mercenaries] Marchadès were reconnoitering the castle on all sides and examining in which spot it would be most advisable to make the assault, a certain arbalister, Bertram de Gurdun by name, aimed an arrow from the castle and struck the king on the arm, inflicting an incurable wound. The king, on being wounded, mounted his horse, rode to his quarters, and issued orders to Marchadès and the whole of the army to make assaults on the castle without intermission until it was taken, which was done. After its capture, the king ordered all the people to be hanged, him alone excepted who had wounded him, whom, as we may reasonably suppose, he would have condemned to a most shocking death if he had recovered.

After this, the king gave himself into the hands of a physician of Marchadès, who, after attempting to extract the iron head, extracted the wood only, while the iron remained in the flesh; but after this butcher had carelessly mangled the king's arm in every part, he at last extracted the arrow. When the king was now in despair of surviving, he left the kingdom of England and all his other territories to his brother John....

He then ordered Bertram de Gurdun, who had wounded him, to come into his presence and said to him: "What harm have I done to you, that you have killed me?" On which he made answer: "You slew my father and my two brothers with your own hand, and you had intended now to kill me; therefore, take any revenge on me that you may think fit, for I will readily endure the greatest torments you can devise so long as you have met with your end after having inflicted so many and so great evils on the world." On this, the king ordered him to be released and said: "I forgive you my death." ... And then, after being released from his chains, he was allowed to depart, and the king ordered one hundred shillings of English money to be given him. Marchadès, however, the king not knowing of it, seized him, and after the king's death, first flaying him alive, had him hanged.... The king ... departed this life ... the twelfth day after he had been wounded....

Roger of Hoveden, Chronicle (ca. 1201)[52]

Better than the Tooth Fairy (ca. 1199)

While Abbot William [of the Danish church of Roskilde, near Copenhagen] was yet in this corruptible body and weighed down with old age, two teeth were torn from his head, which he committed to brother Saxo saying: "Keep these two teeth in your charge and see that you don't lose them." He did as the abbot had ordered, pondering in his own mind why this command had been laid on him.

When however the Lord had taken him away from before our face [i.e. William died in 1203], then his surviving disciples, in memory of so holy a father, each sought to acquire some of his possessions or garments. One of them—Brice the sacrist—complained that nothing had fallen to his share save a fur cap which the saint used to wear on his head. To these complaints, that brother to whom these teeth had been entrusted made answer: "I will give you no small gift—nay, a mighty one, a pearl of great price, no less than a tooth of our father, who in his lifetime loved you not only with a special love but above all others." With these words he delivered to him the tooth; and the sacrist, rendering manifold thanks for this grace conferred upon him, took the tooth and held it in that dear veneration which it deserved. Oh what gifts did God afterwards confer upon mortal men through that tooth!—gifts which, if they were written down, man's weak intellect would never be content to believe!

Life of Saint William (after 1203)[53]

The Thirteenth Century

The Fifth Gospel:

A Parody of the Bible (ca. 1200?)

Here beginneth the Holy Gospel according to Marks of silver. At that time the pope said unto the Romans, "When the Son of Man shall have come to the throne of our majesty, say unto him, first, 'Friend, wherefore art thou come?' But if he shall continue knocking without giving you any present, thrust him out into outer darkness."

And it came to pass that a certain poor clergyman came to the court of our lord the pope and cried out, saying, "Have pity upon me, O doorkeepers of the pope, because the hand of poverty has been laid upon me. I am poor and needy and beseech you to turn away my misfortune and my misery." But when they heard him they were exceeding wroth and said, "Friend, thy poverty perish with thee! Get thee behind me, Satan, because thou savourest not what the pieces of money savour. Verily, verily, I say unto thee, thou shalt not enter into the joy of thy Lord until thou shalt have given the uttermost farthing."

So the poor man departed, sold his cloak and his tunic and all that he had, and gave unto the cardinals and the doorkeepers and the chamberlains. But they said, "What is this among so many?" and they cast him out, and going forth he wept bitterly and would not be comforted.

Then there came unto the court a certain clergyman, who was rich, fat, sleek, and puffed up, and he had killed a man in a riot. He gave, first to the doorkeeper, next to the chamberlain, then to the cardinals. But they thought among themselves that they ought to get more. Then the lord pope, hearing that the cardinals and servants had received many gifts from the clergyman, fell sick even unto death; but the rich man sent him a medicine of gold and silver, and straightway he was healed. Then the lord pope called unto him the cardinals and the servants and said to them, "Brethren, see to it that no one seduce you with empty words; for, lo! I give you an example that just as I receive, so ye receive also."

Carmina Burana (late 13th century)[1]

Life in a Monastery is No Picnic (ca. 1200)

A certain abbot of black monks [Benedictines], a good man and a lover of discipline, had monks under him who were somewhat wayward and undisciplined. It happened one day that some of these monks had prepared for themselves a feast of special kinds of meat and choice wines, which they dared not eat in any part of the house for fear of the abbot; therefore they gathered together to enjoy that which they had prepared in a vast empty container for wine, which in common speech is called a *tun*.

Now the abbot was told that such and such monks were enjoying their feast in that wine tun. He therefore hurried to the spot immediately in much bitterness of spirit and, by his presence, turned the joy of the feasters into sorrow. Seeing how frightened they were, he pretended to be merry himself, saying: "Ha! brethren, would you eat and drink thus without me? I think this is not fair. Believe me, I will dine with you!" So he washed his hands and ate and drank with them, allaying their fears by his example.

Next day (having forewarned the prior and instructed him what to do) the abbot arose at the chapter meeting in the presence of these monks; and, begging for pardon with much humility and feigned fear and trembling, he let these words burst forth: "I confess to you, my lord prior, and to all my brethren here assembled that, sinner as I am, yesterday I was overcome by the sin of gluttony and that I ate flesh in a secret place and as it were by stealth—in fact in a wine tun—contrary to the precept and rule of our father Saint Benedict." Whereupon he sat down and began to bare his body for the discipline; and when the prior would have forbidden him, he answered, "Let me be whipped, for it is better that I pay the penalty here than in the other world."

When he had therefore taken his chastisement and his penance and had returned to his place, then those other monks who dined with him were afraid that they would be accused by him if they hid their fault, so they rose of their own accord and confessed the same transgression. The abbot therefore caused them to be whipped soundly and well by a monk whom he had already chosen for that purpose, rebuking them bitterly and commanding that they should never again presume to transgress thus, under pain of a punishment still more severe.

Caesarius of Heisterbach (d. 1223), *Dialogue on Miracles*[2]

How a Clerk Confounded the Jews (ca. 1200)

As we have been speaking of Jews, would you like to hear another ... story to the honour of our faith and of all Christian folk and to the confusion of the Jews? ... In the city, I think of Worms, there lived a Jew who had a beautiful daughter; and close by lived a young clerk, who fell in love with her, seduced her, and got her with child; for their houses were so near together that the clerk could enter unnoticed whenever he wished and talk with the maiden at his pleasure. When she discovered that she had conceived, she said to the youth, "I am with child! What shall I do? If my father should find out, he will kill me." The clerk answered, "Have no fear; I will make you perfectly safe. If your father or mother tell you that they suspect anything, simply say that you know nothing about it, that all you know is that you are a maiden and have never known a man; I will so deal with them that they will surely believe you."

For he had pondered diligently how best he could save the girl, and this was the device he had hit upon. He took a hollow reed, and at dead of night approached the room in which he knew her parents were sleeping, and putting the end of the reed in at the window, he spoke through it words like these, "O upright souls, beloved of God"—and here he spoke their names—"rejoice, for behold, your virgin daughter has conceived a son who shall be the deliverer of your people Israel." Then he carefully withdrew the reed.

The Jew, who had awakened at the first sound of this voice, shook his wife and said, "Did you not hear what the heavenly voice said to us?" And when she answered, "No," he said, "Let us pray that you too may be found worthy to hear it." While they were praying, the clerk, who was standing by the window and listening attentively to all they were saying, after a little delay repeated the same words as before and added, "You must show great honour to your daughter, tend her with the greatest care, and preserve diligently the boy who shall be born from her virgin body, for he is the Messiah, whose coming you have so long expected."

Since this repetition confirmed the revelation, they in their exultation could scarcely wait for the dawn. Looking at their daughter and seeing by her shape that she had conceived, they said to her: "Tell us, daughter, by whom you are with child." She replied just as she had been instructed; and they, almost beside themselves with joy, could not refrain from telling their friends what they had heard from the angel. These told the story to others, and it was bruited abroad through cities and towns that this maiden would give birth to the Messiah.

When the time of her delivery drew near, many Jews flocked to the girl's house, eager to share in the rejoicings over this new nativity so long hoped for. But ... [when] the hour came in which the unhappy one should be delivered and there ensued the usual pain, groans, and cries, at last she brought forth an infant, not indeed the Messiah, but a daughter. When this became known, there was much confusion and trouble among the Jews, and one of them, wild with indignation, seized the poor baby by the foot and dashed it against the wall....

Her father [the Jew], overcome with anger at his shame, treated [his daughter] cruelly and extracted from her by torture a confession of the whole fraud.... It was a miserable ending, that an infidel maiden who had been seduced and ruined by a Christian man should not have been brought to baptism.... Perhaps the clerk was really unable to bring this about, or more likely perhaps took no pains to do it but rejoiced more in the confounding of the Jews than in the enlightenment of the maiden.

Caesarius of Heisterbach (d. 1223), *Dialogue on Miracles*[3]

They Were Expendable (1203)

The king of France [Philip Augustus] went to Conches [in Normandy] and besieged it [in July 1203. The English castellans of Andeli and Le Vaudreuil surrendered their castles to him without a fight.] King John [of England] sent William Marshall to Philip to negotiate a peace at any price. But King Philip kept raising difficulties because he wanted to keep on fighting until he had conquered the whole of Normandy. [As a pretext, Philip refused to turn over the castellans, whom John wanted to punish for their disloyalty, because—Philip claimed—they had lordship over the castles and could dispose of them as they saw fit.] When the marshall realized that there was no hope of coming to terms, he said to Philip: "Good sir, there is one thing I would like to know, if it please you to tell me. Up to now in France, traitors have been held in disgrace; they have been burned, drawn, and quartered. Why are they no longer held to their obligations now, but instead are treated as if they were their own lords and masters?" "On my honour," replied the king, "nothing is more natural! We have just been haggling over terms, and these men are like rags that are used to wipe oneself and then are cast into the latrine after they have served their purpose." The marshall dropped the subject, took his leave of the king, and returned to John's headquarters at Falaise, where he made his report.

The Story of William Marshall (after 1219)[4]

How Saint Francis Was Disowned by his Father (ca. 1205)

[Francis's father] brought his son before the bishop of the city [Assisi], so that by a formal renunciation of all his property in the bishop's presence he might give up all he had. And Francis not only did not refuse to do this but rejoicing greatly made haste with ready mind to perform what had been demanded of him. When brought before the bishop, Francis would brook no delay nor hesitation in anything; nay, without waiting to be spoken to and without speaking, he immediately put off and cast aside all his garments and gave them back to his father. Moreover he did not even keep his drawers but stripped himself stark naked before all the bystanders. But the bishop, observing his disposition and greatly wondering at his fervour and steadfastness, arose forthwith, gathered him into his arms, and covered him with the mantle which he himself was wearing.

Thomas of Celano (d. 1260), *First Life of St. Francis*[5]

Pope Innocent III: A Judicial Wit (1205–1206)

[Innocent III presided in person at the trial of the famous case between the bishop of Worcester and the abbey of Evesham. The abbey's attorney, Thomas of Marlborough, reported back that he had hired the four best lawyers in Rome to assist him.] And when our adversary complained that I had diminished his access to counsel, the pope replied with a smile: "There's never been a shortage of lawyers at the Roman curia."

*　　　*　　　*　　　*

[Some weeks later, at the second hearing, the abbey's lawyer began to read documents proving that his client had excercised jurisdiction over the disputed territory by customary right (*praescriptio*).] This bored the lord pope, so he turned to our adversary [the bishop's lawyer] and said, "Is it necessary to read these proofs? Don't they have the right by custom?" And Master Robert replied, "They certainly do have it by custom." "Then what are we doing here?" the pope asked. And our adversary replied: "Holy Father, [in England] we have been taught in our schools, and this still is the opinion of our masters, that a bishop's rights cannot be invalidated by custom." To which the lord pope replied: "You and your teachers had surely been drinking English beer when you were taught that!" And when Master Robert insisted he was not mistaken, he received the same response again.

Thomas of Marlborough, *Letter to Evesham Abbey* (1206)[6]

King John Profits from his Clergy's Amours (1208)

[During the Great Interdict, when King John of England] sent knights and royal officials to confiscate the goods of churches and clergymen, he ordered them to arrest any concubines, housekeepers, or sweethearts of priests or clerics that they might find and to detain them until they were ransomed by a money payment from the priests and clerics; and this was done.

Waverley Annals (before 1291)[7]

"God Will Know His Own" (1209)

In the year of our Lord 1210 [sic], a crusade was preached against the Albigenses throughout Germany and France, and in the following year [the crusaders assembled] ... and the preacher and leader of them all was Arnold, abbot of Cîteaux, afterward [arch]bishop of Narbonne. When they came to the great city of Béziers, which is said to have contained more than a hundred thousand men, they laid siege to it [and took it by storm].... When they discovered from the admissions of some of them that there were Catholics mingled with the heretics, they said to the abbot: "Sir, what shall we do, for we cannot distinguish between the faithful and the heretics." The abbot, like the others, was afraid that many, in fear of death, would pretend to be Catholics, and after their departure would return to their heresy, and he is said to have replied: "Kill them all; for the Lord knows them that are His!" [2 Tim. 2:10]. And so countless numbers in that town were slain.

Caesarius of Heisterbach (d. 1223), *Dialogue on Miracles*[8]

Saint Francis and Otto of Brunswick (1209)

The blessed Francis with the other brethren went to live at a place called Rivo Torto by the city of Assisi. Here there was a forsaken hovel beneath whose shelter those most strenuous despisers of large and beautiful houses made their abode and thereby protected themselves from storms of rain. For, as the saint says, one ascends to Heaven quicker from a hovel than from a palace....

When at that time the Emperor Otto [IV of Brunswick] was passing through those parts with great stir and pomp to receive the crown of the earthly empire [at Rome], the most holy father [Francis] and his companions in the said hovel were close to the road by which the emperor was passing; but Francis did not go out to look, nor did he allow any to do so, save one who was ordered to announce unflinchingly to the emperor that this glory of his would endure but for a short time.

Thomas of Celano (d. 1260), *First Life of St. Francis*[9]

Saint Francis and the Birds (ca. 1210)

During the time [after 1210] when ... many joined themselves to the brethren, the most blessed father Francis was journeying through the valley of Spoleto and came to a spot near Bevagna [and three miles south of Assisi] where a very great number of birds of different sorts were gathered together, namely doves, rooks, and those other birds that are called in the vulgar tongue *monade* [jackdaws]. When he saw them, being a man of the most fervent temper and also very tender and affectionate toward all the lower and irrational creatures, Francis, the most blessed servant of God, left his companions in the way and ran eagerly toward the birds. When he was come close to them and saw that they were awaiting him, he gave them his accustomed greeting. But, not a little surprised that the birds did not fly away (as they are wont to do), he was filled with exceeding joy and humbly begged them to hear the word of God.

After saying many things to them, he concluded: "My brother birds, much ought you to praise your Creator and ever to love him who has given you feathers for clothing, wings for flight, and all that you had need of. God has made you noble among his creatures, he has given you a habitation in the purity of the air, and, whereas you neither sow nor reap, he himself does still protect and govern you without any care of your own."

On this (as he himself and the brethren who had been with him used to say) those little birds, rejoicing in wondrous fashion after their nature, began to stretch out their necks, to spread their wings, to open their beaks, and to gaze on him. And then he went to and fro amidst them, touching their heads and bodies with his tunic. At length he blessed them and, having made the sign of the Cross, gave them leave to fly away to another place.

But the blessed father went on his way with his companions, rejoicing and giving thanks to God whom all creatures humbly acknowledge and revere. By grace being now become simple (though he was not so by nature) he began to blame himself for neglecting to preach to the birds before, since they listened so reverently to God's word. And so it came to pass that from that day he diligently exhorted all winged creatures, all beasts, all reptiles, and even creatures insensible, to praise and love the Creator, since calling daily on his Saviour's name, he had knowledge of their obedience by his own experience.

Thomas of Celano (d. 1260), *First Life of St. Francis*[10]

King John Freed from his Last Restraint (1213)

That year [1213] Geoffrey Fitzpeter, justiciar of all England and a man of great power and authority, died on October 14 to the great detriment of the kingdom, for he was the realm's firmest pillar, inasmuch as he was a generous man, learned in law, related to all the magnates of England by either blood or friendship, and well supplied with treasure, income, and goods of every kind. Hence the king had no love for him but dreaded him more than any other person. And hence after his death England was like a ship without a rudder in a storm. That storm began with the death of Hubert Walter, the archbishop of Canterbury, a distinguished and faithful man [who died in 1205]; and after the death of those two, England was not able to breathe again.

When Fitzpeter's death was announced to King John, he gave a big laugh and said: "When he gets to hell, let him greet Archbishop Hubert of Canterbury, whom no doubt he will find there." And turning to those who were seated around him, he added: "By God's feet, now I am king and lord of England for the first time!"

Matthew Paris (d. 1259), *Major Chronicle*[11]

The Mendicant Mission
as Envisioned by Innocent III (1215)

In the time of the said Pope Innocent [III] began the holy order of the Friars Minor, the founder of which was the blessed Francis, born in the city of Assisi in the Duchy [of Spoleto]; and by this pope the said order was accepted and approved and given privileges because it was altogether founded on humility, love, and poverty, following in all things the holy gospel of Christ and shunning all human delights. And this pope saw in a vision Saint Francis supporting the church of Lateran [the pope's cathedral] upon his shoulders, as he afterwards similarly beheld Saint Dominic. These visions prophesied in a figurative way how Holy Church and the faith of Christ would be supported by these saints.

And still in the time of this pope, the order of the Preaching Friars began in the same manner. Its founder was the blessed Dominic, who was born in Spain. But in this pope's time the order was not confirmed, although in a vision it seemed to that pope that the church of the Lateran was falling upon him and the blessed Dominic sustained it on his shoulders. And by reason of this vision he proposed to confirm the order, but death overtook him, and afterwards his successor, Pope Honorius [III], confirmed it in the year of Christ 1216.

The visions of the aforesaid Innocent concerning Saints Francis and Dominic were true, for the Church of God by not fearing God was falling into many errors and many licentious sins; and the blessed Dominic, through his holy learning and preaching, corrected it and was the first exterminator of heretics therefrom; and the blessed Francis, through his humility and apostolic life and penitence, corrected the wanton life and brought back Christians to penitence and to the life of salvation.

Giovanni Villani (d. 1348), *Florentine Chronicle*[12]

The Buondelmonte Murder Polarizes
Florentine Politics (1216)

Messer Buondelmonte dei Buondelmonti, a noble citizen of Florence, had promised to take to wife a maiden of the house of the Amidei, who were honourable and noble citizens. Afterwards, as the said Messer Buondelmonte, who was very charming and a good horseman, was riding through the city, a lady of the house of the Donati called to him, reproaching him as to the lady to whom he was betrothed, maintaining that she was not beautiful or worthy of him, and saying: "I have kept this my daughter for you." She showed him the girl, and she was most beautiful; and immediately by the inspiration of the devil he was so taken by her that he was betrothed and wedded to her.

In consequence, the kinsfolk of the first betrothed lady, being assembled together and grieving over the shame which Messer Buondelmonte had done to them, were filled with the accursed indignation whereby the city of Florence was destroyed and divided. For many houses of the nobles swore together to bring shame upon the said Messer Buondelmonte in revenge for these wrongs. And while taking counsel among themselves as to what way they should punish him, whether by beating or killing, Mosca de' Lamberti said the evil word: "Thing done has an end," by which he meant that he should be slain; and so it was done [on Easter 1216]....

As a result, the city rose in arms and tumult; and this death of Messer Buondelmonte was the cause and beginning of the accursed parties of Guelfs and Ghibellines in Florence, albeit long before this there were factions among the noble citizens and the said parties existed by reason of the conflicts and disputes between the church and the empire; but by reason of the death of this Messer Buondelmonte, all the families of the nobles and the other citizens of Florence were divided, and some held with the Buondelmonti, who took the side of the Guelfs and were the leaders of that party, and some sided with the Uberti, who were the leaders of the Ghibellines, whence followed much evil and disaster to our city ... and it is believed that it will never have an end if God does not cut it short.

Giovanni Villani (d. 1348), *Florentine Chronicle*[13]

Saint Francis and the Sultan at Damietta (1219)

[In the thirteenth year of his conversion], when severe and daily combats were raging between Christians and pagans [during the Fifth Crusade], he took a companion [Illuminato] with him and went to the regions of Syria [Egypt, to be precise]; nor did he fear to present himself to the sight of the sultan of the Saracens [al-Kamil]. But who can tell with what steadfastness of mind he stood before him, with what power of spirit he spoke to him, with what eloquence and confidence he answered those who were reviling the Christian law? For before he came to the sultan he had been seized by the [sultan's] associates, insulted and beaten, yet he was not afraid, nor feared the threat of torments, nor blenched at the menace of death. But though he was shamefully treated by many who were moved with bitter hostility and dislike, he was most honourably received by the sultan. For he paid him what honour he could and tried to sway his mind toward worldly riches by the offer of many gifts. But when the sultan saw that he most stoutly held all such things in contempt like dung, he was filled with the utmost amazement and gazed on him as a man unlike almost all men. He was deeply stirred by his words and heard him very willingly. But in all this the Lord did not fulfil Saint Francis's desire [for martyrdom].

Thomas of Celano (d. 1260), *First Life of St. Francis*[14]

An Excess of Affirmative Action (1219)

In the year of our Lord 1219 and the thirteenth year of his conversion, Brother Francis [of Assisi] held a general chapter at Santa Maria della Porziuncola [Portiunula], and sent brethren to France, Germany, Hungary, Spain, and those provinces of Italy which the brethren had not yet reached....

The German mission was led by Brother John of Parma with some sixty or more brethren. When they were come into Germany, not knowing the language, and when men asked whether they desired lodging or meat or any such thing, they answered *Ja*, and thus received kindly welcome from some folk. Seeing therefore that this word procured them humane treatment, they resolved to answer *Ja* to all questions whatsoever.

Wherefore, being once asked whether they were heretics, come now to infect Germany after the same fashion wherewith they had already perverted Lombardy, they answered *Ja*; so that some were cast into prison, and others were stripped of their raiment and led to the common dancing place, where they were held up for a laughingstock to the inhabitants.

The brethren therefore, seeing that they could make no fruit in Germany, came home again; and this deed gave the brethren so cruel a report of Germany that none dared return thither but such as aspired to martyrdom.

Jordan of Giano, Chronicle (ca. 1262)[15]

A Contest in Humility: Francis vs. Dominic (1220)

Those two bright lights of the world, Saint Dominic and Saint Francis, were once at Rome with the lord cardinal [bishop] of Ostia, who was afterwards pope [Gregory IX]. And as in turn they uttered honeyed words concerning God, the bishop at last said to them: "In the primitive church the pastors of the church were poor, and men glowed with charity and not with greed. Why (he said) do we not make bishops and prelates of your brethren, who excel other men in teaching and example?" There was a contention between the saints as to which of them should answer; each strove not to anticipate but to give way to the other; nay, each was urging the other to answer. Each, therefore, was foremost in respect of the other, while each paid honour to the other. At length humility conquered Francis so that he did not put himself forward, and it also conquered Dominic so that in humble obedience he answered first. Blessed Dominic, therefore, gave this answer to the bishop: "My lord, my brethren, if they only recognize it, have been raised to a good degree, nor, so far as I can, will I allow them to acquire any other mark of dignity." After he had finished this brief reply, blessed Francis bowed down before the bishop and said: "My lord, my brethren have been styled Lesser [i.e. Friars Minor] so that they should not presume to become greater...."

Thomas of Celano (d. 1260), *Second Life of St. Francis*[16]

A Form Letter for University Students (ca. 1220)

B. to his venerable father A., greeting. This is to inform you that I am studying at Oxford with the greatest diligence, but the matter of money stands greatly in the way of my progress, as it is now two months since I spent the last of what you sent me. The city is expensive and makes many demands; I have to rent lodgings, buy necessaries, and provide for many other things which I cannot now specify. Wherefore I respectfully beg your paternity that by the promptings of divine pity you may assist me so that I may be able to complete what I have well begun. For you must know that "without Ceres and Bacchus, Apollo grows cold." Therefore act now so that with the means you provide I can finish well what I have begun. Farewell.

Collection of Form Letters (ca. 1220)[17]

A Student Song (13th century)

Omittamus studia;
Dulce est desipere,
Et carpamus dulcia
Iuventutis tenerae;
Res est apta senectuti
Seriis intendere.

Let's give up our studies now;
Far more fun to be carefree,
And let's study only how
Loving sweet young things can be;
Time enough when old and gray to
Talk of working seriously.

Carmina Burana (late 13th century)[18]

Saint Francis Strikes a Bad Bargain (ca. 1225)

Saint Francis ... had grown almost blind [at the end of his life] by the rigour of his penance and incessant weeping, so that he saw poorly. Once upon a time he departed from the place where he was and went to a place where [his first convert] brother Bernard [of Quantavalle] was, in order to speak with him of divine things. When he arrived, he found that brother Bernard was at prayer in the woods, wholly lifted up and united with God. Then Saint Francis went into the woods and called him. "Come," he said, "and speak with this blind man." And brother Bernard answered him not a word; for being a man great in contemplation, his soul was lifted up and raised to God.... After a while, Saint Francis called him a second and a third time in the same way, and both times brother Bernard did not hear him, so he neither answered nor came to him.

Being somewhat disconsolate at this, Saint Francis departed, marvelling within himself and grieving that brother Bernard had not come to him although he had been called three times. Saint Francis turned away with these thoughts in his mind, and when he had gone a little way he said to his companion: "Wait for me here." And he went into a solitary place nearby and prostrated himself in prayer, asking God to reveal to him why brother Bernard did not answer him. And as he remained thus in prayer there came to him a voice from God, saying: "O poor little one, why are you troubled? Should a man forsake God for his creature? When you called, brother Bernard was united with me, and therefore he could neither come to you nor answer you. Do not be surprised if he could not respond, for he was so lifted out of himself that he heard none of your words."

Having heard these words from God, Saint Francis immediately returned with great haste to brother Bernard in order to accuse himself humbly before him of the evil thoughts he had nursed concerning him. And when brother Bernard saw him coming, he came and cast himself at his feet. Then Saint Francis made him rise up and with great humility related to him the thoughts he had had, the tribulation he had suffered concerning him, and how God had answered his prayer. And he concluded thus: "I command you by holy obedience that you do whatever I command you." Brother Bernard feared that Saint Francis might lay some excess of penance on him, as he often did, and desiring with all sincerity to escape such obedience, he answered him thus: "I am ready to do your obedience if you will promise to do what I shall command you." And Saint Francis gave him the promise.

Then brother Bernard said: "Go on, father; what would you have me do?" And Saint Francis answered him, saying: "I command you by holy obedience to punish the arrogance and rashness of my heart. I am going to lie down on the ground and I want you to put one foot on my neck and the other on my mouth as you walk across me three times. At the same time I want you to revile and shame me, especially by saying, 'Lie there, you boor, son of Peter Bernadone! how can so vile a creature as you be so proud?'" On hearing this, brother Bernard performed in holy obedience what Saint Francis had commanded him, although it was very hard for him to do, and he did it as gently as he could.

After that was over, Saint Francis said: "Now order me to do what you want, for I have promised holy obedience to you." Then brother Bernard said: "I command you by holy obedience that every time we are together you shall rebuke and correct me harshly for all my faults." This surprised Saint Francis very much since brother Bernard was of such great sanctity that he held him in great reverence and in no way thought he deserved a scolding. And from then on Saint Francis was careful to avoid being with him very much, because of the said obedience, lest he might have to utter one word of reproach against one whom he knew to be of such great holiness. But whenever they met, after Saint Francis had heard him speak of God, he made haste to leave him and depart from him. And it was a fine thing to see what great charity and reverence and humility Saint Francis, the father, used towards Bernard, his first-born son, when he spoke with him.

The Little Flowers of Saint Francis (ca. 1322)[19]

Frederick II in Jerusalem (1229)

[Having made a truce with the sultan al-Kamil that gave Jerusalem to the Christians but left the Moslems in possession of their holy places in the city] the emperor entered Jerusalem.... During his visit various curious incidents occurred. One was that when he went into the [Moslem] Dome of the Rock he saw a [Christian] priest sitting near the imprint of the [Prophet's] Holy Foot and taking some pieces of paper from the Franks. The emperor went up to him as if he wanted to ask a benediction of him and struck him a blow that knocked him to the ground. "Swine!" he cried. "The sultan has done us the honour of allowing us to visit this place, and you sit here behaving like this! If any of you comes in here again in this way I shall kill him!"

The scene was described by one of the custodians of the Dome of the Rock. They said too that the emperor looked at the inscription that runs round the inside of the sanctuary, saying: "Saladin purified this city of Jerusalem of the polytheists..." and asked, "Who would these polytheists be?"

He also asked the custodians, "What are these nets at the doors of the sanctuary for?" They replied, "So that the little sparrows should not come in." He said, "God has brought the giants [*jabbarîn*, also magnates, big shots] here instead."

When the time came for the midday prayer and the muezzins' cry rang out, all his pages and valets rose, as well as his tutor, a Sicilian with whom he was reading [Aristotle's] logic in all its chapters, and offered the canonic prayer, for they were all Moslems.

The emperor, as these same custodians recall, had a red skin and was bald and short sighted. Had he been a slave he would not have been worth two hundred *dirham*. It was clear from what he said that he was a materialist and that his Christianity was simply a game to him.

Al-Kamil had ordered the qadi of Nablus, Shams ad-Din [whom he provided as Frederick's official escort] to tell the muezzins that during the emperor's stay in Jerusalem they were not to go up into their minarets and give the call to prayer in the sacred precinct. The qadi forgot to tell the muezzins, and so the muezzin 'Abd al-Karîm mounted his minaret at dawn and began to recite verses from the Koran about Christians, such as "God has no son" [Koran 23.93], referring to Jesus son of Mary, and other such texts. In the morning the qadi called 'Abd al-Karîm to him and said, "What have you done? The sultan's command was thus and thus." He replied, "You did not tell me; I am sorry." The second night he did not give the call. The next morning the emperor summoned the qadi, who had come to Jerusalem as his personal adviser and had been responsible for handing the city over to him, and said "O qadi, where is the man who yesterday climbed the minaret and spoke these words?" The qadi told him of the sultan's orders. "You did wrong, qadi; would you alter your rites and law and faith for my sake? If you were staying in my country, would I order the bells to be silenced for your sake? By God, do not do this; this is the first time that we have found fault in you!"

Then he distributed a sum of money among the custodians and muezzins and pious men in the sanctuary—ten *dinar* to each. He spent only two nights in Jerusalem and then returned to Jaffa, for fear of the Templars, who wanted to kill him.

Sibt ibn al-Jauzî (1186–1256), *The Mirror of the Times*[20]

Frederick II and the Mongol Khan (1230)

In the year 1238, the king of the Tartars [Ughetai] wrote to Emperor Frederick ordering that he should advise him whether there might be some office at the khan's court in which the emperor would choose to serve so that in return for this service he could hold his land from the khan. The emperor is reported to have replied that he knew enough about birds and should do well as the falconer.

Aubry of Troisfontaines (fl. before 1241), *Chronicle*[21]

The Disgrace of Christian Profanity (1230s)

A Jew once was playing dice with a Christian. When he heard the Christian swearing and blaspheming God because he was losing, the Jew stopped up his ears, got up from the game, and fled, leaving his money behind. For the Jews neither blaspheme God nor wish to hear others doing so. O miserable tavernkeepers, who for a little profit let men who are worse than Jews curse God with such blasphemies in their establishments! If the foul things that are said of the blessed Virgin were said of their wives, they would not stand for it but would fly into a rage. If such things as are said of God were said of their father or mother or any of their relatives, they would not stand for it but would throw the speaker out of the place.

Jacques de Vitry (d. ca. 1240), *Examples*[22]

The Brother of the Horn: An Italian Revivalist (1233)

[A religious revival swept Italy when Salimbene was twelve.] First came Brother Benedict to Parma, who was called the brother of the horn, a simple man and unlearned, and of holy innocence and honest life, whom also I saw and knew familiarly, both at Parma and afterwards at Pisa. This man had joined himself unto no religious congregation but lived after his own conscience and busied himself to please God; he was a close friend of the Friars Minor. He was like another John the Baptist to behold, as one who should go before the Lord and make ready for him a perfect people. He had on his head an Armenian cap, his beard was long and black, and he had a little horn of brass wherewith he trumpeted; terribly did his horn bray at times, and at other times it would make dulcet melody. He was girt with a girdle of skin, his robe was black as sackcloth of hair, and fell even to his feet. His rough mantle was made like a soldier's cloak, adorned both before and behind with a broad and long red cross from the collar to the foot, even as the cross of a priest's chasuble. Thus clad he went about with his horn, preaching and praising God in the churches and the open places; and a great multitude of children followed him, often with branches of trees and lighted tapers. Moreover I myself have often seen him preaching and praising God, standing upon the wall of the bishop's palace, which at that time was being built. And thus he began his praises, saying in Italian, "Praised and blessed and glorified be the Father." Then would the children repeat in a loud voice that which he had said. And again he would repeat the same words, adding "be the Son"; and the children would repeat the same, and sing the same words. Then for the third time he would repeat the same words, adding "be the Holy Ghost"; and then "Alleluia, alleluia, alleluia!" Then he would play his trumpet, and afterwards he preached, adding a few good words in praise of God. And lastly, at the end of his preaching, he would salute the blessed Virgin with the hymn *Ave Maria clemens et pia* [by Adam of Saint-Victor].

Salimbene di Adam (1221–1289), *Chronicle*[23]

The Election of Pope Innocent IV (1241)

It came to pass afterwards, as it pleased God, that there was elected pope Messer Ottobuono dal Fiesco, of the counts of Lavagna of Genoa, who was cardinal and was made pope because he was the greatest friend and confidant whom the Emperor Frederick [II] had in Holy Church, so that there might be peace between the Church and the emperor; and he was called Pope Innocent IV.... And when he was elected pope, the tidings were brought to the Emperor Frederick with great rejoicing, knowing that he was his great friend and protector. But the emperor, when he heard it, was greatly disturbed, whence his barons marvelled much, and he said: "Marvel not; for this election will be of much hurt to us; for he was our friend when cardinal, and now he will be our enemy as pope." And so it came to pass....

Giovanni Villani (d. 1348), *Florentine Chronicle*[24]

Saint Thomas and the Temptress (1244)

[In 1244, when Thomas Aquinas was nineteen, his brothers tried to dissuade him from being a Dominican friar. They took him to a castle where] he was shut up alone in a room. While he was sleeping there, they sent in a very beautiful girl who, being an accomplished prostitute, might be able to attract him into sinning by means of her appearance, caresses, fun and games, and other delights. But Thomas had already pledged himself to take God's Wisdom as his wife, for love of which he was burning. So when he saw her and felt himself coming under the influence of the stimulus of the flesh, which he had always kept subject to reason, ... he seized a burning firebrand from the hearth and indignantly chased the young girl from the room. Then, still filled with spiritual fervour, he went to a corner of the room and burned the sign of the Cross onto the wall with the tip of the firebrand. After this he fell to the ground and begged God with tears to grant him perpetual virginity, which was given to him.

William of Tocco, *History of St. Thomas* (written 1316-1321)[25]

The Deposition of Frederick II (1245)

When Pope Innocent [IV] was at Lyons, he called a general council in that place and invited bishops and archbishops and other prelates from throughout the whole world, who all came thither.... And this done, the pope summoned the [Emperor] Frederick to this council, as to a neutral place, to excuse himself of thirteen articles proved against him of things done against the faith of Christ and against Holy Church. The emperor would not appear there but sent thither his ambassadors and representatives ... [including] the wise clerk and master Piero delle Vigne of the Regno, who, making excuses for the emperor that he was not able to come by reason of sickness and suffering in his person, prayed the pope and his brethren to pardon him, and averred that he would ask the pope for mercy and would restore that which he had seized of the Church; and they offered, if the pope would pardon him, that he would bind himself to arrange it so that within one year the sultan of the Saracens should render up to his command the Holy Land overseas.

And the pope, hearing the endless excuses and vain offers of the emperor, demanded of the ambassadors if they had an authentic mandate for this, whereon they produced a full authorization, under the golden seal of the emperor, to promise and undertake it all. And when the pope had it in his hand, in full council, the ambassadors being present, he denounced Frederick on all the said thirteen criminal articles, and to confirm it he said: "Judge, faithful Christians, whether Frederick betrays Holy Church and all Christendom or no, for according to his mandate he offers within one year to make the sultan restore the Holy Land, very clearly showing that the sultan holds it through him, to the shame of all Christians." And this said and declared, he caused the process against the emperor to be published; he condemned him and excommunicated him as a heretic and persecutor of Holy Church, laying to his charge many foul crimes proved against him; and he deprived him of the lordship of the empire, of the realm of Sicily, and of that of Jerusalem, absolving from all fealty and oaths all his barons and subjects, excommuicating whoever should obey him, or should give him aid or favour, or further should call him emperor or king. And this sentence was passed at the said council at Lyons on the Rhone on July 17, 1245.

Giovanni Villani (d. 1348), *Florentine Chronicle*[26]

Money Talks (1246)

I have heard how a certain bishop of Grenoble commanded his priests, when they came to the synod, to come decently clad in stole and alb or surplice; which they scorned to obey. Then he commanded it under pain of suspension; yet even thus they obeyed not. Then he made his hand yet heavier, proclaiming at the next synod that they should come [properly dressed] under pain of excommunication; yet few obeyed even then. Then the bishop said: "Come tomorrow as I have bidden, under pain of five shillings." Then all the clergy, fearing this fine aforesaid, sought out albs and surplices, or even hired them; so that all came attired as they had been bidden. Wherefore the bishop rebuked them in that synod, showing plainly how they feared more to lose a little money than to lose their souls.

Stephen of Bourbon (d. 1261), *Stories for Sermons*[27]

The Heretics' Crucifix: Realism and Reaction

(before 1249)

The heretics have another method of deceiving by means of pictures. We do not think it is proper to pass over that method in silence, as the faithful should know it in order to be the more cautious to avoid it. For the heretics often paint or carve ill-shapen images of saints, so that by gazing on such images the devotion of simple Christian folk may be turned to loathing. Thus, in derision and scorn of Christ's Cross, they carve images of our Lord with one foot laid over the other, so that both are pierced by a single nail, thus striving by adding these variations and novelties either to annul or to render doubtful men's faith in the holy Cross and the traditions of the sainted fathers, .

Bishop Luke of Tuy (d. ca. 1249), *The Other Life*[28]

Emperor Frederick II (1194–1250): A Guelf Portrait

This Frederick reigned thirty years as emperor, and he was a man of great capacity and of great valor, wise in books, and of natural intelligence, universal in all things; he was acquainted with the Latin tongue and our [Italian] vernacular, with German and French, Greek and

Arabic; he was of abounding talents, liberal and courteous in giving, courageous and prudent in arms, and much feared. And he was dissolute and licentious after divers fashions, and had many concubines and catamites after the manner of the Saracens, and he sought indulgence in all bodily pleasures and led an epicurean life, not taking account that there were ever another life. This was one chief cause why he became the enemy of the clergy and of holy Church; the other was his greed in taking and sequestrating the revenues of Holy Church, to squander them evilly.

Giovanni Villani (d. 1348), *Florentine Chronicle*[29]

The Corruption of the Papal Court (ca. 1250)

In Paris ... as I have heard tell, there was once a great merchant, a large dealer in textiles, a good man, very honest and righteous, his name Jeannot of Chevigny, who was close friends with a Jew named Abraham, also a merchant, and a man of great wealth, and likewise very honest and righteous. Now Jeannot, observing Abraham's honesty and rectitude, began to worry lest the soul of one so worthy and wise and good should perish for want of faith. Therefore he began to plead with him in a friendly manner, urging that he should leave the errors of the Jewish faith and turn to the truth of Christianity, which, because it was sound and holy, he might see daily prospering and gaining ground, whereas, on the contrary, his own religion was dwindling and was almost come to nothing.

The Jew replied that he believed that there was no faith sound and holy except the Jewish faith, in which he was born and in which he meant to live and die, nor would anything ever turn him from it. Undaunted, however, Jeannot began some days later to ply Abraham with similar arguments, explaining to him in such crude fashion as merchants use the reasons why our faith is better than the Jewish. And though the Jew was a great master in the Jewish law, yet, whether it was by reason of his friendship for Jeannot or that the Holy Spirit dictated the words that the simple merchant used, at any rate the Jew began to be much interested in Jeannot's arguments, though still too staunch in his faith to let himself be converted.

But Jeannot was no less assiduous in plying him with argument than Abraham was obstinate in adhering to his law, so that at length the Jew, overcome by such incessant appeals, said: "Listen, Jeannot, you want me to become a Christian, and I am disposed to do so, provided I first go to Rome and there see the man you call God's vicar on earth and observe what manner of life he leads, and his brother cardinals with him. After that, if what you have been saying—that your faith is better than mine—still seems true, I will do as I have said; otherwise, I will remain as I am a Jew."

When Jeannot heard this, he was greatly distressed, saying to himself: "I thought I could convert him, but now I see that my good efforts were all in vain; for, if he goes to the court of Rome and sees the iniquitous and foul life which the clergy lead there, it would be enough to make him relapse into Judaism if he had already been converted." [Jeannot tried to dissuade Abraham but the Jew persisted.] … "Go then," said Jeannot, seeing that his mind was made up, "and good luck go with you." …

Abraham took horse and posted with all possible speed to Rome, where on his arrival he was honourably received by his fellow Jews. He said nothing to any one of the purpose for which he had come but began circumspectly to acquaint himself with the ways of the pope and the cardinals and the other prelates and all the courtiers. And from what he saw for himself, being a man of great intelligence, or learned from others, he discovered that without distinction of rank they were all sunk in lust of the most disgraceful kind, sinning not only in the way of nature but after the manner of the men of Sodom without any restraint of remorse or shame, in such sort that, when any great favour was to be procured, the influence of the whores and boys was of no small moment. Moreover he found them one and all gluttonous, wine-bibbers, drunkards, and, next after lust, most addicted to the shameless service of the belly, like brute beasts. And, as he probed the matter still further, he perceived that they were all so greedy and avaricious that human, indeed Christian, blood and sacred things of every kind—spiritualities no less than temporalities—they bought and sold for money, which commerce was greater and employed more brokers than the textile trade and all the other trades of Paris put together. What was plainly simony the Romans called "procurement," and gluttony went under the name "sustenance," as if God could not penetrate the thoughts of even the most corrupt hearts, to say nothing of the signification of words, and would suffer Himself to be misled after the manner of men by the names of things. Our modest and sober-minded Jew found these matters, and many others which are not to be mentioned, by no means to his liking, so that, when his curiosity was fully satisfied, he decided to return to Paris and did so.

On his arrival there, he was met by Jeannot and the two celebrated his return. Since Jeannot hardly expected Abraham's conversion, he allowed him some days of rest before he asked what he thought of the holy father and the cardinals and the other courtiers. To which the Jew promptly replied:

"It seems to me that they deserve evil from God. I tell you, as far as I could find out, no holiness, devotion, good works, or exemplary living of any kind was to be found in any cleric; but only lust, avarice, gluttony, and the like, and worse, if worse may be, appeared to be held in such honour by all, that (to my mind) the place is a center of diabolical rather than of divine activities. To the best of my judgment, your shepherd, and in consequence all that are around him, devote all their zeal and ingenuity and subtlety to devise how best and most speedily they may bring the Christian religion to nought and banish it from the world. And because I see that what they so zealously endeavour to do does not come to pass, but that on the contrary your religion continually grows and shines more and more clear, therein I seem to discern a very evident token that it, rather than any other, has the Holy Spirit for its foundation and support and is thus more true and holy than any other faith. For this reason, although I formerly resisted your exhortations and would not become a Christian, now I frankly tell you that I would on no account fail to become one. Let us go to church, then, and let me receive baptism there according to the traditional rite of your holy faith."

Jeannot, who expected just the opposite conclusion, was the best pleased man that ever was in the world when he heard these words. So taking Abraham with him to Notre Dame he asked the clergy there to baptize him, and when they heard that it was his own wish, they forthwith did so, and Jeannot raised him from the sacred font and named him Jean, and afterwards he caused teachers of great eminence to instruct him thoroughly in our faith, which he readily learned and afterwards practised in a good, virtuous, and holy life.

Giovanni Boccaccio (d. 1375), *Decameron*[30]

Second Thoughts on the Sixth Crusade (1250)

[The Sixth Crusade fizzled out when King, and subsequently Saint, Louis IX of France was captured in Egypt and had to be ransomed. The negotiations were conducted by Husâm ad-Din, who told this story.] The king of France was an extremely wise and intelligent man. In one of our conversations I said to him: "How did your majesty ever conceive the idea—a man of your character and wisdom and good sense—of going on board ship and riding the back of this sea and coming to a land so full of Moslems and soldiers, thinking that you could conquer it and become its ruler? This undertaking is the greatest risk to which you could possibly expose yourself and your subjects." The king laughed but did not reply. "In our land," I added, "when a man travels by sea on several occasions, exposing himself and his possessions to such a risk, his testimony is not accepted as evidence by a court of law." "Why not?" "Because such behaviour suggests to us that he lacks sense, and a man who lacks sense is not fit to give evidence." The king laughed and said: "By God, whoever said that was right, and whoever made that ruling did not err."

Ibn Wasil (1207-1298), *History of the Ayyubids*[31]

The First Florins: A Golden Opportunity (1252)

The city [of Florence] increased greatly in state and in riches and lord-ship and in great quietness. Hence the merchants of Florence, for the honour of the commune, ordained with the people and commune that golden coins should be struck at Florence; and they promised to furnish the gold, for before the custom was to strike silver coins of 12 pence the piece [i.e. soldi]. And then began the good coins of gold, 24 carats fine, which are called golden florins, and each was worth 20 soldi. And this was in ... 1251. These florins weighed eight to the ounce, and on one side was the stamp of the lily and on the other the stamp of Saint John [the Baptist, patron of Florence].

By reason of the new money of the golden florin, there fell out a pretty story and one worth telling. The said new florins having begun to circulate through the world, they were carried to Tunis in Barbary; and being brought before the king of Tunis, who was a worthy and wise lord, they pleased him much, and he caused them to be tried; and finding them to be of fine gold, he much commended them, and having caused his interpreters to translate the imprint and legend on the florin, he found that it said, "Saint John the Baptist," and on the side of the lily, "Florence." Perceiving it to be Christian money, he sent to the Pisan merchants who then enjoyed a privileged status in the city and were much with the king (and even the Florentines traded in Tunis through the Pisans) and asked them what manner of city among Christians was this Florence that made these florins. "They are our inland Arabs," which is to say, "our mountain rustics." Then answered the king wisely: "It does not seem to me the money of Arabs. O you Pisans, what manner of golden money is yours?" Then were they confused and knew not how to answer.

He asked if there were among them any one from Florence, and there was found there a merchant from Oltrarno, by name Pera Balducci, discreet and wise. The king asked him of the state and condition of Florence, whom the Pisans called their Arabs. He answered wisely, showing the power and magnificence of Florence, and how Pisa in comparison had neither half the power nor half the inhabitants of Florence, and that they had no golden money, and that the florin was the fruit of many victories gained by the Florentines over them. Thus the Pisans were shamed, and the king, by reason of the florin and by the words of our wise fellow citizen, gave the freedom of the city to the Florentines and allowed them a place of habitation and a church in Tunis, and he gave them the same privileges as the Pisans.

Giovanni Villani (d. 1348), *Florentine Chronicle*[32]

Robert Grosseteste Rebels Against
Papal Provisions (1253)

[In 1253 Grosseteste had been ordered as bishop of Lincoln to provide a lucrative position in his cathedral for the pope's nephew. In reply he sent this refusal to the pope's agent in England] It is not possible that the apostolic see, to which has been handed down from Christ himself power for edification and not for destruction, can issue a precept so hateful and so injurious to the human race as this; for to do so would constitute a falling off, a corruption and abuse of its most holy and plenary power. No one who is subject and faithful to the said see in immaculate and sincere obedience, and who is not cut off from the body of Christ and the said holy see by schism, can obey commands or precepts such as this, even if it emanated from the highest order of angels; but he must of necessity and with his whole strength, contradict and rebel against them.... Therefore it is out of filial reverence and obedience that I disobey, resist, and rebel....

To sum up, the holiness of the apostolic see can only tend to edification and not to destruction; for the plenitude of its power consists in being able to do all things for edification. These "provisions," however, as they are called, are not for edification but for manifest destruction. They are not, therefore, within the power of the apostolic see: they owe their inspiration to "flesh and blood" which "shall not inherit the kingdom of God" [Matt. 16:17], and not to the Father of our Lord Jesus Christ who is in heaven.

Robert Grosseteste (d. 1253), Letters[33]

Saint Louis and the Snob (ca. 1254)

[Saint Louis, king of France] asked me if I washed the feet of the poor on Holy Thursday. "Sire," said I, "it would make me sick! The feet of these villains will I not wash." "In truth," said he, "that was ill said, for you should never disdain what God did for our teaching. So I pray you, for the love of God first, and then for the love of me, that you accustom yourself to wash the feet of the poor."

Jean de Joinville (d. 1317), Life of St. Louis[34]

"Wise Is The Child That Knows Its Father" (ca. 1254)

[Saint Louis, king of France] said that the Christian faith and creed were things in which we ought to believe firmly, even though we might not be certain of them except by hearsay. On this point he asked me what was my father's name? And I told him his name was Simon. And he asked how I knew it. And I said I thought I was certain of it and believed it firmly because my mother had borne witness thereto. Then he said, "So ought you to believe all the articles of the faith to which the Apostles have borne witness, as also you chant of a Sunday in the Creed."

Jean de Joinville (d. 1317), *Life of St. Louis*[35]

How Saint Louis Did Justice in Person (ca. 1254)

[In 1254 a Franciscan friar urged Louis IX, king of France, to] "do justice well and speedily among his people, so that our Lord suffer his kingdom to remain in peace all the days of his life...." The king forgot not the teaching of the friar but ruled his land very loyally and godly, as you shall hear. He had so arranged that my lord of Nesle, and the good count of Soissons, and all of us who were about him should go after we had heard our masses and hear the pleadings at the gate which is now called the Gate of Requests.

And when he came back from church, he would send for us, and sit at the foot of his bed and make us all sit round him, and ask if there were any whose cases could not be settled save by himself in person. And we named the litigants, and he would then send for such and ask, "Why do you not accept what our people offer?" And they would make reply, "Sire, because they offer us very little." Then would he say, "You would do well to accept what is proposed, as our people desire." And the saintly man endeavoured thus, with all his power, to bring them into a straight and reasonable path.

Ofttimes it happened that he would go, after his mass, and seat himself in the wood of Vincennes, and lean against an oak, and make us sit round him. And all those who had any cause in hand came and spoke to him without hindrance of usher or of any other person. Then would he ask, out of his own mouth, "Is there any one who has a cause in hand?" And those who had a cause in hand stood up. Then would he say, "Keep silence all, and you shall be heard in turn, one after the other." Then he would call my lord Peter of Fontaines and my lord Geoffry of Villette and say to one of them, "Settle me this cause."

And when he saw that there was anything to amend in the words of those who spoke on his behalf, or in the words of those who spoke on behalf of any other person, he would himself, out of his own mouth, amend what they had said. Sometimes have I seen him go in summer to do justice among his people in the garden of Paris, clothed in a tunic of camlet, a surcoat of tartan without sleeves, and a mantle of black taffeta about his neck, his hair well combed, no cap, and a hat of white peacock's feathers upon his head. And he would cause a carpet to be laid down, so that we might sit round him, and all the people who had any cause to bring before him stood around. And then would he have their causes settled, as I have told you before he used to do in the wood of Vincennes.

Jean de Joinville (d. 1317), *Life of St. Louis*[36]

How a Christian Knight Disputed With a Jew

(ca. 1254)

[Saint Louis, king of France] told me that there was once a great disputation between clergy and Jews at the monastery of Cluny. And there was at Cluny a poor knight to whom the abbot gave bread at that place for the love of God; and this knight asked the abbot to let him speak the first words, and they let him, not without doubt. So he rose, leaned upon his crutch, and asked that they should bring to him the greatest scholar and most learned rabbi among the Jews; they did so. Then he asked the Jew a question, which was this: "Master," said the knight, "I ask you if you believe that the Virgin Mary, who bore God in her body and in her arms, was a virgin mother and is the mother of God?"

And the Jew replied that of all this he believed nothing. Then the knight answered that the Jew had acted like a fool when—neither believing in her nor loving her—he had yet entered into her monastery and house. "And verily," said the knight, "you shall pay for it!" Whereupon he lifted his crutch and smote the Jew near the ear and beat him to the earth. Then the Jews turned to flight and bore away their rabbi sore wounded. And so ended the disputation.

The abbot came to the knight and told him he had committed a deed of very great folly. But the knight replied that the abbot had committed a deed of greater folly in gathering people together for such a disputation, for there were a great many good Christians there who, before the disputation came to an end, would have gone away misbelievers through not fully understanding the Jews. "And I tell you," said the king, "that no one, unless he be a very learned scholar, should dispute with them;

but a layman, when he hears the Christian law slandered, should not defend the Christian law unless it be with his sword, and with that he should pierce the slanderer in the midriff so far as the sword will enter."

Jean de Joinville (d. 1317), *Life of St. Louis*[37]

Some Royal Phobias (1258)

The fears and anxieties of the [English] barons were increased by the coming of the month of July with its pestilence-bearing constellation Leo and the scorching Dog Star, whose deadly barking usually disturbs the atmosphere. More than anything else they were alarmed at the fickleness and inscrutable duplicity of the king [Henry III], which they discovered from a certain ominous speech.

One day the king had left his palace at Westminster and gone down the Thames in a boat to take his dinner out of doors, when the sky clouded over and a thunderstorm came on, attended with lightning and heavy rain. Now the king feared a storm of this kind more than anything else, so he directed them to land him at once; and the boat was opposite to the stately palace of the bishop of Durham, where [Simon de Montfort] the earl of Leicester was then staying. On knowing of his arrival, the earl goes gladly to meet him and, greeting him with proper respect, says by way of consolation, "What is it that you fear? The storm is now passed." To this the king answered, not in jest but seriously, with a severe look: "The thunder and lightning I fear beyond measure, but by the head of God, I fear you more than all the thunder and lightning in the world." The earl gently replied: "My lord, it is unjust and incredible that you should fear me, your firm friend, who am ever faithful to you and yours, and to the kingdom of England. It is your enemies, those who lie and are destructive, that you ought to fear."

Everyone suspected that the king blurted out these astounding words because the earl of Leicester manfully and boldly persevered in carrying out the Provisions [of Oxford] by which the barons might coerce the king and all their adversaries to assent to their wishes and might entirely banish his brothers, who were corrupting the whole kingdom.

Matthew Paris (d. 1259), *Major Chronicle*[38]

The Death and Burial of Manfred (1265)

[In 1265, the battle of Benevento was fought for the possession of the Italian Regno. King Manfred, Frederick II's illegitimate son, was defeated by the French challenger, Charles of Anjou, because most of Manfred's vassals deserted at the critical moment.] Manfred, being left with few followers, did as a valiant lord who would rather die in battle as king than flee with shame; and ... immediately entered into the battle without the royal insignia, so as not to be recognised as king, but like any other noble, he struck bravely into the thickest of the fight. Nevertheless, his followers endured but a little while, for they were already turning; and straightway they were routed and King Manfred slain in the midst of his enemies, it was said by a French squire, but it was not known for certain....

At his end, search was made for Manfred for more than three days, and he could not be found, and it was not known if he were slain, or taken, or escaped, because he had not borne royal insignia in the battle. At last, by sundry marks on his person he was recognised in the midst of the battlefield by one of his own camp followers, and his body being found by the said camp follower, he threw it across an ass he had and went his way crying, "Who buys Manfred? Who buys Manfred?" And one of the king's barons chastised this fellow and brought the body of Manfred before the king [Charles of Anjou], who caused all the barons who had been taken prisoners to come together, and having asked each one if it were Manfred, they all timidly said "Yes." When Count Giordano came, he smote his hands against his face, weeping and crying, "Alas, alas, my lord," wherefore he was commended by the French.

Some of the barons begged the king that he give Manfred the honor of burial, but the king made answer: "I would do it willingly if he were not excommunicated." But since he was excommunicated, King Charles would not have him laid in a holy place, but he was buried at the foot of the bridge of Benevento, and upon his grave each one of the host threw a stone; whence there arose a great heap of stones.

But by some it was said that afterwards, by command of the pope, the bishop of Cosenza [who was papal legate] had him taken from that tomb and expelled him from the Regno, which was Church land, and he was buried beside the river of Verde [i.e. the Garigliano] on the borders of the Regno and Campagna. This, however, we do not affirm.

Giovanni Villani (d. 1348), *Florentine Chronicle*[39]

An Absent-Minded Professor: Thomas Aquinas (ca. 1269)

It is told that once [Thomas Aquinas] was invited to dine with the famous King Louis [IX, the saint] at his table. Thomas humbly wanted to excuse himself because he was preoccupied with study and writing, but the prior [of the Dominican convent] of Paris wanted to oblige the king and forced him to go. When he left his study, he was turning over in his mind an idea he had had to oppose the Manichaean heresy, which he was attacking at that time. While he was sitting next to the king at the table, the truth came to him by divine inspiration, and, striking the table with his hand, he said, "Now the argument against the Manichaean heresy is proved!" And he called his secretary by name and said, "Get up, write!" as if he were studying in his office or his cell. However, the prior touched him with his hand and said, "Master, notice that now you are at the king of France's table and not in your cell." Thomas came to himself, noticed where he was, blushed, and said, as he bowed humbly to the king, "Excuse me, my lord king, because I believed I was in my study where I had begun to think out an argument against that heresy." The holy king was amazed and edified that a man's mind could be so enraptured by the spirit that none of the body's senses could disturb it. Then the holy and helpful king called a scribe, however, and ordered him to write down immediately what had been divinely revealed to this teacher.

Bernard Gui (1260-1331), *Life of St. Thomas*[40]

The English Theodora (1270-1272)

Eleanor, wife to King Edward the First, a most virtuous and wise woman, when he took his long and dangerous voyage into the Holy Land, would not be dissuaded to tarry at home but would needs accompany him, saying: "Nothing must part them whom God has joined, and the way to Heaven is as near in the Holy Land (if not nearer) as in England or Spain." ...

When King Edward the first was in the Holy Land, he was stabbed with a poisoned dagger by a Saracen, and through the rancour of the poison, the wound was judged incurable by his physicians. This good Queen Eleanor his wife, who had accompanied him in that journey, endangering her own life in loving affection, saved his life and eternized her own honour. For she daily and nightly sucked out the rank poison, which love made sweet to her, and thereby effected that which no art durst attempt—to his safety, her joy, and the comfort of all England.

So that well worthy was she to be remembered by those crosses as monuments, which instead of statues were erected by her husband to her honour [at the places where her funeral procession stopped in 1290] at Lincoln, Grantham, Stanford, Geddinton, Northampton, Stony-Stratford, Dunstable, Saint Albans, Waltham, and that of Westminster (called Charing Cross)—all adorned with [her] arms of Castile, Leon, and the county of Ponthieu, which by her right was annexed to the crown of England.

William Camden, Remains (1657)[41]

Thomas Aquinas in Ecstasy (1273)

While brother Thomas was saying his mass one morning in the chapel of Saint Nicholas at Naples, something happened which profoundly affected and altered him. After mass he refused to write or dictate; indeed he put away his writing materials. He was in the third part of the *Summa* [*theologica*], at the questions on penance.

And brother Reginald [his secretary], seeing that he was not writing, said to him: "Father, are you going to give up this great work, undertaken for the glory of God and to enlighten the world?" But Thomas replied: "Reginald, I cannot go on." Then Reginald, who began to fear that much study might have affected his master's brain, urged and insisted that he should continue his writing; but Thomas only answered in the same way: "Reginald, I cannot—because all that I have written seems to me so much straw."

Then ... brother Thomas went to see his sister, the countess of San Severino, whom he loved in all charity. When he arrived, after hastening there with great difficulty, the countess came out to meet him, and he could scarcely speak. The countess, very much alarmed, said to Reginald: "What has happened to brother Thomas? He seems quite dazed and hardly spoke to me?" And Reginald answered: "He has been like this since about the feast of Saint Nicholas [December 6]—since then he has written nothing at all."

Then again brother Reginald began to beseech Thomas to tell him why he refused to write and why he was so stupefied; and after much of this urgent questioning and insisting, Thomas at last said to Reginald: "Promise me ... that as long as I live you will never reveal what I shall tell you." Then he added: "All that I have written seems to me like straw compared with what has now been revealed to me."

So Thomas, leaving the countess very sad, returned to Naples; and then he set out for the council [of Lyons] to which he had been summoned. And on the way, at the castle of Maenza in the Campagna, he fell ill of the sickness of which he was to die [on March 7, 1274].

Bartholomew of Capua, *First Canonization Inquiry* (1319)[42]

A Beam in the Bishop's Eye (ca. 1275)

[In Scotland] there was a certain vicar who was notorious for his lewd behaviour, for although often penalized on account of a concubine whom he kept, he did not on that account desist from sinning. But when the bishop [of Saint Andrews, William Wischard, 1271-79] arrived on his ordinary visitation, the wretch was suspended and made subject to the prelate's mercy. Overcome with confusion, he returned home and beholding his paramour, poured forth his sorrows, attributing his mishap to the woman. Inquiring further, she learned the cause of his agitation and became bitterly aware that she was to be cast out. "Put away that notion," said she to cheer him up, "and I will get the better of the bishop."

The next day as the bishop was hastening to the vicar's church, she met him on the way laden with pudding, chickens, and eggs, and, on his drawing near, she saluted him reverently with bowed head. When the prelate inquired where she was coming from and going to, she replied:

"My lord, I am the vicar's concubine, and I am hastening to the bishop's sweetheart, who was lately brought to bed [with child], and I wish to be as much comfort to her as I can."

This pricked the bishop's conscience; straightway he resumed his progress to the church and, meeting the vicar, desired him to prepare for celebrating mass. The other reminded him of his suspension, and the bishop stretched out his hand and gave him absolution. The sacrament having been performed, the bishop hastened away from the place without another word.

The Lanercost Chronicle (1346)[43]

An Eccentric Parish Priest (1282)

About this time, in Easter week, the parish priest of Inverkeithing [in Scotland], named John, revived the profane rites of Priapus, collecting young girls from the villages and compelling them to dance in circles to honour Father Bacchus. When he had these females in a troop, out of sheer wantonness he led the dance, carrying in front on a pole a representation of the human organs of reproduction; and singing and dancing himself like a mime, he ogled them all and stirred them to lust by filthy language. Those who held respectable matrimony in honour were scandalised by such a shameless performance, although they respected the parson because of the dignity of his rank. If anybody remonstrated kindly with him, the priest became worse than before and violently reviled him.

But the iniquity of some men brings manifestly just retribution on them. In the same year, when his parishioners assembled according to custom in the church at dawn in Penance Week, at the hour of discipline he would insist that some persons should strip for penance and others should prick them with goads. The townsmen, resenting the indignity inflicted upon them, turned on its author. The same night, as he was defending his nefarious innovation, he was pierced by a knife and died. Thus God's punishment fit the crime.

The Lanercost Chronicle (1346)[44]

The Sicilian Vespers (1282)

On Easter Monday ... a Frenchman in his insolence laid hold of a woman of Palermo to do her villainy. When she began to cry out, the retainers of the barons of the island began to defend the woman because the people were already irritated and all moved with indignation against the French. Thus arose a great battle between the French and the Sicilians, and many were wounded and slain on either side, but those of Palermo came off worst. But then all of the people [of Palermo who had been away celebrating the holiday] returned in haste, and the men flew to arms, crying, "Death to the French!" ... And all the Frenchmen who were in the city were slain in the houses and in the churches without any mercy.... And each one in his own city and country did the like, slaying all the Frenchmen who were in the island [of Sicily]....

Giovanni Villani (d. 1348), *Florentine Chronicle*[45]

A Profitable Sideline to Gardening (1283)

There was a lady at Perelada [in Spain] whom I knew and saw: men called her Marcadera because she sold merchandise (*mercadaria*); she was a very doughty woman, stout and big-boned. One day while the French host lay encamped before Perelada [which they were besieging], she went forth to fetch herbs from her garden outside the walls. She put on a man's quilted doublet and armed herself with sword and shield and lance, and thus went forth into her garden. And as she stooped in the garden she heard a sound of bells, and thinking it strange, she stopped picking colewart and went to see what this might be. And lo! on the path between her garden and her neighbour's she saw a French knight in full armour riding on his horse, which had little bells hanging on his breastband; he rode hither and thither trying to find an exit from that path. When she saw what was going on, she strode forward a step and dealt him so shrewd a thrust with her lance through the cuisses [his thigh armor] that she drove through thigh and saddle and even wounded the horse as well. When the beast felt the hurt, he reared and kicked, and the rider would surely have been thrown had he not been chained to the saddle. What more shall I say? She drew her sword and ran round by a little gate and smote the beast so hard on the head that it staggered. What more? She seized the reins and cried to the knight, "Give yourself up or you are a dead man!" He thought he was as good as dead, so he cast away his sword and surrendered himself to be her prisoner. She therefore took up the sword, drew the lance from his side, and led him into Perelada. The king [Peter of Aragon] and the Infante made merry over this story and would oftentimes bid the lady tell them how she had taken that knight. To conclude: the knight and his armor were hers; he ransomed himself for two hundred gold pieces, which fell to her share. Thereby you may know God's anger against the French [who were there on a crusade against Christians].

Don Ramón Muntaner (1265-1336), *Chronicle*[46]

The First English Prince of Wales (1284)

On Saint Mark's day, or the five-and-twentieth day of April [1284] at Carnarvon in Wales was born the king's son named Edward upon this occasion. King Edward [I], albeit he had brought all Wales under his subjection, and a statute made at Rhuddlan in the twelfth year of his reign [1284] incorporated and united the same unto England, yet could he never win the goodwill of the common people of the country to accept him for their prince, unless he would remain himself in that country among them; neither could he bring them to yield obedience to any prince except he were of their own nation. For the Welshmen having experience of the government of the English officers and knowing that the king would rule the country by his deputies, could not abide to have any Englishman to be their ruler. Wherefore oftentimes upon the king's motion they answered that they were contented to take for their prince any man whom he name, so that he were a Welshman, and other answer could he never get of them by any means.

Whereupon, having secretly sent for the queen, being then great with child, caused her to remain at Carnarvon, and when she was nigh her time of deliverance, the king being at Rhuddlan, sent for all the barons and best men of Wales to come to him to consult concerning the weal public of their country; and when they were come, he deferred the consultation until he were certified that the queen were delivered of a son. Then sending certain lords to the christening, he called the Welshmen together, declaring unto them that whereas they were oftentimes suitors unto him to appoint a prince, he now having occasion to depart out of the country would name them a prince if they would attend and obey him whom he should name. To the which they answered that they would so do if he would appoint one of their nation. Whereunto the king replied that he would name one that was born in Wales and could speak never a word of English, whose life and conversation no man was able to detect [i.e. to fault]. And when they all had granted that such a one they would obey, he named his own son Edward, born at Carnarvon Castle a few days before.

John Stow (d. 1605), *Annales of England*[47]

Stonewalling the Ghibellines: The Battle of Campaldino (1289)

The Florentine [Guelf] army set out to invade the [Ghibelline] enemy's territory ... and arriving near Bibbiena, at a place called Campaldino, where the enemy was, they halted there and set themselves in battle array. The captains of the war placed the picked cavalry in front of the main body, and those armed with large shields bearing the red lily on a white ground [the Florentine arms] were drawn up to support them.

Then the bishop [in the opposing camp], who was shortsighted, asked, "What walls are those?" and received the answer, "The enemy's shields."

Baron de' Mangiadori of San Miniato, a bold knight and experienced in deeds of arms, assembled the [Guelf] men-at-arms and addressed them thus: "Sirs, the wars in Tuscany used to be won by attacking well.... But now things have changed, and victory comes by standing your ground. Therefore I advise you to stand firm and leave the attack to them." [The tactic worked, chiefly because the enemy was greatly outnumbered, and the Florentine Guelfs won the battle.]

Dino Compagni, *Chronicle* (1312)[48]

An Unpardonable Word (1291)

Roger of Portland, clerk of the sheriff of London, complained to ... the warden of the city of London ... that Robert of Sutton, in the full court of ... the sheriff of the same city, which the said Roger was then holding in the name of his master ... cast vile contempt upon him, the said Roger, in contempt of our lord the king, by saying these words in English—*Tprhurt, Tprhurt*—because he would not allow him, the said Robert, to plead in his court until he had reformed his conduct toward the warden of the city aforesaid, by whom he had been previously suspended for certain trespasses alleged against him, and because he would not submit to being forbidden by the said Roger; and thereupon he uttered the aforesaid word—*Tprhurt, Tprhurt, Tprhurt*—to his damnifying and in manifest contempt of our lord the king.

[Robert denied the charge, but the court found to the contrary] that the said Robert did say in full court that he would care nothing, for all the forbidding of the said Roger; also, still further speaking in manifest contempt, he uttered these words in English—*Tphurpt, Tphurt*—at the same time raising his thumb in contempt for his suspension aforesaid. Therefore, he was to be committed to prison for the contempt aforesaid.

London court record (1291)[49]

A Hermit Saint Resigns the Papacy (1294)

In the year of Christ 1294, in the month of July, the church of Rome had been vacant ... for more than two years by reason of the discord of the cardinals, who were divided, each party desiring to make one of themselves pope. And the cardinals ... [compromised and] agreed not to name one of their own college, and they elected a holy man who was called brother Peter of Morrone in the Abruzzi. This man was a hermit and of austere life and penitence.... He, being elected and brought and crowned pope [Celestine V], made in the following September, for the reformation of the Church, twelve cardinals, for the most part [Frenchmen] from beyond the mountains....

But because he was simple, knew no letters, and did not occupy himself willingly with the pomps of the world, the cardinals held him in small esteem, and it seemed to them that they had made an ill choice for the well-being and status of the Church. The said holy father perceiving this, and not feeling himself sufficient for the government of the Church, as one who loved the service of God and the weal of his soul more than worldly honour, sought every way how he might renounce the papacy.

Now, among the other cardinals of the court was one Master Benedetto Caetani of Anagni, very learned in books and much practised and sagacious in the things of the world, who had a great desire to attain to the papal dignity; and he had laid plans, seeking and striving to obtain it by the aid of King Charles [of the Italian Regno] and the cardinals, and they had already promised to elect him, as they afterwards did. He put it before the holy father, hearing that he was desirous to renounce the papacy, that he should make a new decretal to the effect that for the good of his soul any pope might renounce the papacy....

And even as the said cardinal gave counsel, Pope Celestine made the said decretal; and this done, on the day of Saint Lucy in the following December, in a consistory of all the cardinals, in their presence he took off the crown and papal mantle and renounced the papacy; then he departed from the curia and returned to his hermit life and to do his penance. And thus Pope Celestine reigned in the papacy five months and nine days.

Giovanni Villani (d. 1348), Florentine Chronicle[50]

How to Convince a Mystic (1294)

[Cardinal Caetani's influence on Pope Celestine, described above in a matter-of-fact way by Villani, was embellished by this rumor.] It is reported that this crafty man [the cardinal] devised a way by which he might make him [the pope] even more ardent [in his desire to resign]. During the night [at the hour] when the pope was aroused from sleep so he might contemplate God, the cardinal often spoke to him through a hole that he had cunningly contrived, saying in a low voice that he was a heavenly messenger who had come to him so that the pope might arrange to serve only God by giving up the enticements of the false world.

Ferreto de' Ferreti (d. 1337), History of Italy[51]

A Mad Scientist (1295)

Master Thaddeus [d'Alderotto, professor at Bologna, who died in 1295], as he was instructing his medical scholars, argued that whoever should continue for nine days to eat eggplant (*Solanum insanum*) would go mad. And he proved it according to the law of physic. One of his students, hearing this lesson, decided to put it to the test. He began to eat eggplant, and at the end of nine days went before his master and said: "Master, that lesson you read us is not true, because I have put it to the test, and I am not mad." And he rose and showed him his behind. "Write," said the master, "that all this about the eggplant has been proved." And he wrote a learned article on the subject.

The Hundred Old Tales (before 1300)[52]

An English Pun of King Edward I (1297)

[In 1297, Edward I wanted to send some of his English vassals to Gascony while others would sail to Flanders under his personal command. The king held his parliament at Salisbury, where] he asked certain magnates to sail to Gascony, and they began to excuse themselves one by one. Filled with indignation, the king warned some of them that they would either go or he would give their lands to others who were willing to go. Many were scandalized by this remark, and discord began to arise among them. The earl of Hereford [Humphry Bohun, the constable] and the marshal [Roger Bigod, earl of Norfolk] excused themselves by saying that they would willingly perform their duties, which belonged to them by hereditary right, by going with the king himself [to Flanders]. But when the king continued to press the earl marshal to go [to Gascony instead], the vassal said, "Willingly shall I go with you, O king; I shall lead the first rank of the army that is under your personal command, just as is my duty by hereditary right." The king replied, "I insist that you shall go with the others without me." But the earl answered, "I am not obligated, nor is it my wish, O king, to campaign overseas without you." And it is said that the king burst out in anger with these words: "By God, O earl [Bigod], either you shall go or you shall hang." And the earl replied, "By the same oath, O king, I will neither go nor will I hang." And without the king's permission he left the council, which thereupon adjourned.

Walter of Guisborough (fl. 1300-15), *Chronicle*[53]

The Fourteenth Century

Papal vs. Royal Power:
A Pragmatic Approach (1300)

The King of France [Philip IV the Fair] sent an envoy named Pierre Flote to the lord pope [Boniface VIII]. In the presence of the pope and his whole court, Pierre pressed the king's case as hard as he could. The pope was finally exasperated with Pierre's audacity and said to him: "But we have both powers" [i.e. the temporal as well as the spiritual]. Pierre promptly replied on his lord's behalf: "Be that as it may, my lord, but your power is verbal while ours is real." This response so inflamed the pope's wrath that he said he would move heaven and earth against him.

Continuator of Rishanger's *Chronicle* (before 1335)[1]

Dante and the Blacksmith (ca. 1300)

After dinner, Dante went out from his house, and started on his way.... As he passed by the Porta San Piero [in Florence], a blacksmith was hammering iron on his anvil and at the same time bawling out some of Dante's verses, leaving out lines here and there and putting in others of his own, which seemed to Dante a most monstrous outrage. Without saying a word he went up to the blacksmith's forge where were kept all the tools he used to ply his trade, and seizing the hammer, he flung it into the street; then he took the tongs and flung them after the hammer, and the scales after the tongs; and he did the same with a number of other tools. The blacksmith, turning round to him with a coarse gesture, said: "What the devil are you doing? are you mad?" Dante replied: "What are you doing?" "I am about my business," said the smith, "and you are spoiling my tools by throwing them into the street." Dante retorted: "If you do not want me to spoil your things, don't you spoil mine." The smith replied: "And what of yours am I spoiling?" Dante said: "You sing out of my book [the *Vita nuova*] and do not give the words as I wrote them. That is my business, and you are spoiling it for me." The blacksmith, bursting with rage but not knowing what to answer, picked up his things and went back to his work. And the next time he wanted to sing, he sang of Tristan and Lancelot and let Dante's book alone.

Franco Sacchetti (ca. 1330—ca. 1400), *Tales*[2]

An Affluent Society (1301)

At the end of the month of May [1301], [the French] King Philip [IV the Fair] with his wife, Queen Joan of Navarre, came to Flanders with a great retinue and much pomp .... Then he summoned as much of Flanders as he had inherited to his court, which was called a parliament. Here he established laws and conceded privileges, although lesser matters, such as judgments and appointments, were done elsewhere; here, too, he received fealty and homage from the nobility and royal officials. The king was received with joyous feasts and effusive good-will; no honour or formality was spared. Since festive games were in order, tournaments were held in his honour. Gifts were exchanged on a lavish scale, and the citizens competed with one another in the display of wealth and luxury.... Likewise the king was received with great honour at Bruges.... The pride and splendour of the women of Bruges irked the queen so much that she is supposed to have said: "I thought that I alone was the queen, but here I see before me sixty of them."

Jacques de Meyer (d. 1552), *Annals of Flanders*[3]

Greed is a Cardinal Sin (1302)

This Anthony [Bek, bishop of Durham 1283–1311] was magnanimous, second to none in the realm, save the king only, in pomp and bearing and might of war, busy rather about the affairs of the kingdom than of his diocese.... Nothing was too dear for him, if only it might magnify his glory.... He bought cloth of the rarest and costliest and made it into horsecloths for his palfreys because someone had said that he believed Bishop Anthony dared not buy so precious a stuff....

[When the bishop was in Rome on business] a cardinal desired one of his palfreys (for he had the fairest in the world), and he sent two so the cardinal might take his choice; but the cardinal was seduced by their beauty and kept them both. When this was reported to the bishop, he said: "So save me God! he has not failed to choose the better of the two!"

Robert Graystanes, *Chronicle of Durham* (1336)[4]

Drinking at the Florentine Fountain of Gold (1302)

[Pope Boniface VIII appointed Charles of Valois, a French prince, as peacemaker in Tuscany. The pope wanted Charles to weaken the party of White Guelfs that controlled Florence, first by recalling their rivals, the Black Guelfs, from exile, and then by exiling the leaders of the Whites. The first phase was completed in 1301.]

After Charles had restored the Black party to Florence, he went to Rome; and when he demanded money from the pope, the latter answered that he had put him in the fountain of gold....

After Charles returned from the curia, one night in Florence he assembled a secret council of seventeen citizens, which decided certain citizens were guilty and should be seized and beheaded....

The next day [after some had fled] Charles caused them and several others to be cited, and by virtue of his office of peacemaker he condemned them as contumacious and as traitors, and he burnt their houses and confiscated their goods to the public use.... By this means he got 24,000 florins from the city, and he gave receipts to the government for all that he had confiscated in the exercise of his office of peacemaker [because he kept the money as compensation for his services].

In the month of April 1302, having issued citations to many citizens, both Ghibellines and White Guelfs, he condemned [eight Ghibelline families] ... and he banished or placed under house arrest [many other leaders of the Whites, including Dante Alighieri] ... and many others—more than 600 men in all—who wandered about the world in need, some in one place and some in another.

Dino Compagni, *Chronicle* (1312)[5]

The Outrage at Anagni (1303)

After strife had arisen between Pope Boniface [VIII] and King Philip [IV the Fair] of France, each one sought to abase the other by every method and guise that was possible.... The king of France ... sent one Master William of Nogaret of Provence, a wise and crafty clerk ... into Tuscany, furnished with much ready money.... They conducted secret negotiations to take Pope Boniface prisoner in Anagni, spending much money and corrupting the barons of the country and the citizens of Anagni.

And as it had been purposed, so it came to pass; for Pope Boniface being with his cardinals and with all the curia in the city of Anagni, in Campagna, where he had been born and was at home ... in the month of September 1303, Sciarra della Colonna, with his mounted followers to the number of three hundred and many of his friends on foot, paid by money of the French king ... one morning early entered into Anagni with the ensigns and standards of the king of France, crying: "Death to Pope Boniface! Long life to the king of France!" And they rode through the city without any hindrance ... and when they came to the papal palace, they entered without opposition and took the palace, forasmuch as the present assault was not expected by the pope and his retainers, and they were not on their guard.

Pope Boniface, hearing the uproar and seeing himself forsaken by all his cardinals, who had fled and were hiding, ... and by most of his servants, ... gave himself up for lost, but like the high-spirited and valourous man he was, he said: "Since, like Jesus Christ, I am willing to be taken and needs must die by treachery, at the least I desire to die as pope." And straightway he caused himself to be robed in the mantle of Saint Peter, and with the crown of Constantine on his head and with the keys and the cross in his hand, he seated himself upon the papal chair....

And when Sciarra and his other enemies came to him, they mocked at him with vile words and arrested him and his household, which had remained with him.... William of Nogaret ... threatened him, saying that he would take him bound to Lyons on the Rhone and there in a general council would cause him to be deposed and condemned....

But afterwards ... no man dared to touch him, nor were they pleased to lay hands on him, but they left him robed under gentle ward and thought to rob the treasure of the pope and of the Church.... But ... on the third day ... the people of Anagni ... drove out Sciarra della Colonna and his followers ... and freed the pope and his household.

Giovanni Villani (d. 1348), *Florentine Chronicle*[6]

Robert Bruce and the Spider (1306)

The news of the taking of Kildrummie, the captivity of his wife, and the execution of his brother [all done by the English], reached [Robert] Bruce [king of Scotland, 1306-29] while he was residing in a miserable dwelling at Rachrin [or Rathlin, an island off the northern coast of Ireland], and reduced him to the point of despair. It was about this time that an incident took place, which, although it rests only on tradition in families of the name of Bruce, is rendered probable by the manners of the times.

After receiving the last unpleasing intelligence from Scotland, Bruce was lying one morning on his wretched bed, and deliberating with himself whether he had not better resign all thoughts of again attempting to make good his right to the Scottish crown, and, dismissing his followers, transport himself and his brothers to the Holy Land, and spend the rest of his life in fighting against the Saracens; by which he thought, perhaps, he might deserve the forgiveness of Heaven for the great sin of stabbing Comyn in the church at Dumfries. But then, on the other hand, he thought it would be both criminal and cowardly to give up his attempts to restore freedom to Scotland, while there yet remained the least chance of his being successful in an undertaking which, rightly considered, was much more his duty than to drive the infidels out of Palestine, though the superstition of his age might think otherwise.

While he was divided betwixt these reflections, and doubtful of what he should do, Bruce was looking upward to the roof of the cabin in which he lay; and his eye was attracted by a spider, which, hanging at the end of a long thread of its own spinning, was endeavouring, as is the fashion of that creature, to swing itself from one beam in the roof to another, for the purpose of fixing the line on which it meant to stretch its web. The insect made the attempt again and again without success; and at length Bruce counted that it had tried to carry its point six times, and been as often unable to do so. It came into his head that he had himself fought just six battles against the English and their allies, and that the poor persevering spider was exactly in the same situation with himself, having made as many trials, and been as often disappointed in what it aimed at. "Now," thought Bruce, "as I have no means of knowing what is best to be done, I will be guided by the luck which shall attend this spider. If the insect shall make another effort to fix its thread, and shall be successful, I will venture a seventh time to try my fortune in Scotland; but if the spider shall fail I will go to the wars in Palestine, and never return to my native country more."

While Bruce was forming this resolution, the spider made another exertion with all the force it could muster, and fairly succeeded in fastening its thread to the beam which it had so often in vain attempted to reach. Bruce, seeing the success of the spider, resolved to try his own fortune; and as he had never before gained a victory, so he never afterwards sustained any considerable or decisive check or defeat. I have often met with people of the name of Bruce, so completely persuaded of the truth of this story, that they would not on any account kill a spider; because it was that insect which had shown the example of perseverance, and given a signal of good luck to their great namesake.

Sir Walter Scott, *Tales of a Grandfather* (1828)[7]

The Destruction of the Knights Templars (1307)

In the year 1307 ... the king of France [Philip IV the Fair] ... accused and denounced to the pope, incited thereto by his officers and by desire of gain, the master and the order of the Temple, charging them with certain crimes and errors whereof the king had been informed the Templars were guilty.... The king ... made secret arrangements with the pope and caused him to promise to destroy the order of the Templars.... The pope ... to please the king promised that he would do this; and ... on a day named in his letters, he caused all the Templars to be seized throughout the whole world, and all their churches and mansions and possessions, which were almost innumerable in power and in riches, to be sequestered.

All those in the realm of France the king caused to be occupied by his court, and at Paris the master of the Temple was taken, who was named Jacques of the lords of Molay in Burgundy, with sixty knights, friars, and gentlemen. And they were charged with certain articles of heresy and certain vile sins against nature that they were said to practise among themselves; it was also charged that at their profession they swore to support the order right or wrong, and that their worship was idolatrous, that they spat upon the Cross, and that when their master was consecrated it was secretly and in private, and none knew the manner; moreover it was alleged that their predecessors had caused the Holy Land to be lost by treachery and King Louis [IX] and his followers to be taken at Mansourah [in 1250]. And when sundry proofs had been given by the king of the truth of these charges, he had them tortured with divers tortures that they might confess, and it was found that they would not confess nor acknowledge anything.

Giovanni Villani (d. 1348), *Florentine Chronicle*[8]

The Legend of William Tell (1307)

Now it happened one day that Gessler, the bailiff [of Albert of Austria], went to [the Swiss canton of] Uri with something new in mind. He put up a pole under the lime tree in Uri and set up a hat upon the pole, and he had a servant near it and ordered that whoever passed by there should bow before the hat as though the lord were there; and he who did it not, him would he punish and cause to repent heavily, and the servant was to watch and tell of such a one.

Now there was there an honest man called Tell [who had already sworn to oppose the bailiff's tyranny].... Now he went rather often to and fro before the hat. The servant who watched by it accused him to the lord. The lord went and had Tell sent for, and he asked him why he was not obedient to his bidding and did not do as he was bidden. Tell spoke: "It happened without malice, for I did not know that it would vex your grace so highly; for were I clever, then I would be called something else, and not the Simpleton" [*der Tall*, a pun on his name].

Now Tell was a good archer; he also had fine children. These the lord sent for, and setting an apple on the head of one of them, he decreed that Tell must shoot the apple off the head. Now Tell saw he had no choice, for the lord had many servants present, so he took an arrow and put it into his quiver; he took another arrow in his hand. Then he bent his crossbow, prayed God that he might save his child, and shot the apple from the child's head.

The lord liked this well and asked him what he meant by taking an extra arrow. Tell replied that he would rather not answer, but the lord insisted that he wanted to know what he meant by it. Tell feared the lord and was afraid he would kill him. The lord understood his fear and spoke: "Tell me the truth; I will make your life safe and not kill you." Then Tell spoke: "Since you have promised me, I will tell you the truth, and it is true: had the shot failed me, so that I had shot my child, I would have shot the other arrow into you or one of your men." Then spoke the lord: "Now this also is true, that I have promised you not to kill you." And he had him bound and said he would put him into a place where he would nevermore see sun or moon. [But Tell eventually escaped and killed Gessler.]

The White Book of Sarnen (ca. 1470)[9]

The Bones of Edward I: Two Tales (1307–1308)

In such a manner did these two kings [Robert Bruce and Edward I], who were looked upon as the two most gallant knights of their time, bear themselves until the death of King Edward at Burgh-on-the-Sands [7 July 1307]. When he perceived he could not recover, he called to him his eldest son, who was afterwards king [Edward II], and made him swear by the saints in the presence of all his barons that, as soon as he should be dead, he would have his body boiled in a large caldron until the flesh should be separated from the bones; that he would have his flesh buried and the bones preserved; and that every time the Scots should rebel against him, he would summon his people and carry with him the bones of his father: for he believed most firmly that as long as his bones should be carried against the Scots, those Scots would never be victorious. His son, however, did not fulfill what he had sworn but had his father carried to London and buried—for which much evil befell him.

Jean Froissart (fl. 1338–1410), *Chronicles*[10]

Meanwhile, Robert Bruce of Scotland invaded many of the English king's towns and dealt roughly with those who were siding with that king [Edward II]. Consequently, on the advice of the king's counsellors, the counts of Gloucester and of Hereford were sent to Scotland with a large force in order to resist Robert, who by now was raging cruelly. But, before they reached Scotland, the king of England and the tyrant of

Scotland made a truce which lasted till the following All Saints' Day [1308]. Many received the news of the truce with shock and indignation. This tyrant, among the many insults he spewed out reproachfully at the king of England, was saying that he was more afraid of the dead king's bones than he was of the living king; and that it would be a more magnificent feat of war for an invader to have conquered half a foot of territory from King Edward [I] while he lived than to conquer a whole kingdom from his present successor.

St. Paul's Annals (1307–1341)[11]

The Execution of the Knights Templars (1310)

After keeping them a long time in prison in great misery [1307–1310] and not knowing how to put an end to their trial, at last outside Paris at Saint Antoine ... in a great park enclosed by wood, fifty-six of the Templars were bound each one to a stake, and they began to set fire to their feet and legs little by little, admonishing them one after the other that whosoever of them would acknowledge the error and sins wherewith they were charged might escape; and during this martyrdom, exhorted by their kinsfolk and friends to confess and not to allow themselves to be thus vilely slain and destroyed, yet would not one of them confess, but with weeping and cries they defended themselves as being innocent and faithful Christians, calling upon Christ and Saint Mary and the other saints; and all burning to ashes they ended their lives by the said martyrdom.

And the master [Jacques de Moulay] was reserved as well as ... other leaders of the order who had been officers and treasurers of the king of France, and they were brought to Poitiers before the pope, the king of France [Philip IV the Fair] being present, and they were promised forgiveness if they would acknowledge their error and sin, and it is said that they confessed something thereof.

And when they had returned to Paris there came thither two cardinal legates to give sentence and condemn the order upon the said confession and to impose some discipline upon the said master and his companions. And when they had mounted a great scaffold opposite the church of Notre Dame, and had read the indictment, the said master of the Temple [de Moulay] rose to his feet, demanding to be heard; and when silence was proclaimed, he denied that ever such heresies and sins as they had been charged with had been true and maintained that the rule of their order had been holy and just and catholic, but that he certainly was worthy of death and would endure it in peace, since through fear of torture and by the persuasions of the pope and of the king, he had by deceit been persuaded to confess some part thereof. And the discourse having been broken off and the sentence not having been fully delivered, the cardinals and the other prelates departed from that place.

And having held counsel with the king, the said master and his companions, in the Isle de Paris and before the hall of the king, were put to martyrdom after the same manner as the rest of their brethren, the master being burned slowly to death while he continually repeated that the order and their religion were catholic and righteous, and he commended himself to God and Saint Mary.... And note that the night after the said master and his companions had been martyred, their ashes and bones were collected as sacred relics by friars and other religious persons and carried away to holy places.

Giovanni Villani (d. 1348), *Florentine Chronicle*[12]

The End of the World (1312)

And thus the day following, September 19, 1312, the emperor [Henry VII] came with his host to the city of Florence, his followers setting fire to everything they came across; and thus he crossed the river Arno opposite the place where the Mensola enters it, and abode at the monastery of Santo Salvi with perhaps a thousand horsemen.... The emperor lay sick many days at Santo Salvi, and perceiving that he could not gain the city by agreement and that the Florentines would not give battle, he departed, not yet recoverd.

And while he was still at Santo Salvi, the count of Savoy was discoursing with the abbot and certain monks of that place concerning the emperor, how he had heard from his astrologers or by some other revelation that he was to conquer as far as to the world's end. Then said the abbot, smiling: "The prophecy is fulfilled, for near where you are dwelling there is a road that has no exit, which is called the World's End (*Via Capo di Mondo*)." This coincidence showed the count and the other barons who heard this that their hope had been in vain. And for this reason wise men ought not to put faith in any prophecy or pronouncement of astrologers, which can lie and have a double meaning.

Giovanni Villani (d. 1348), *Florentine Chronicle*[13]

A Secular Judge Does Not Recognize the Two Laws (1313)

In Venice there came up once before a secular court a case in litigation of a will. The attorneys for both sides were present and presented briefs in defense of the interests of their clients. One of these, a priest, made reference in his argument to the *Clementina* and the *Novella* and quoted passages therefrom. Upon this, one of the judges, a very old man who nevertheless had little in common with Solomon and to whom these names were utterly unknown, assailed the speaker with great scorn: "Are you not ashamed, sir, to bring the names of these sluts before the court?"

Poggio Bracciolini (1380–1459), *Facetiae*[14]

The Death of Philip the Fair (1314)

In the year 1314, in the month of November, King Philip [IV] of France, who had reigned twenty-nine years, died by an ill adventure; for, being at a chase, a wild boar ran between the legs of the horse on which he was riding and caused him to fall, and shortly thereafter he died. He was one of the most comely men in the world, of the tallest in person, and well proportioned in every limb. He was a wise man in himself and good after layman's fashion, but by reason of pleasure seeking, especially in the chase, he did not devote his powers to ruling his realm but rather allowed them to be played upon by others, so that he was generally swayed by bad counsel, which he was too ready to believe; whence many perils came to his realm.

He left three sons.... All these sons one after another in a short while became kings of France, one succeeding on the death of the other [1314–1328]. And a little while before King Philip, their father, died, there fell upon them great and shameful misfortune, for the wives of all three were found to be faithless....

Giovanni Villani (d. 1348), *Florentine Chronicle*[15]

Birds of a Feather Flock Together (ca. 1316)

Dante Alighieri, my fellow citizen some years ago, was a man greatly accomplished in the vulgar tongue [Italian]; but on account of his pride he was somewhat more free in his manners and speech than was acceptable to the sensitive eyes and ears of the noble princes of our country. Thus, when he was exiled from his native city and was a guest at the court of Can Grande [della Scala in Verona, 1312–1318], at that time the refuge and resort of all who were in misfortune, he was at first held in high honour; but afterwards by degrees he began to lose favour, and day by day became less pleasing to his host. Among the guests at the same time were, according to the custom of those days, mimics and buffoons of every description, one of whom, an impudent rascal, by means of his coarse remarks and broad jests made himself a universal favorite and a person of considerable influence. Can Grande, suspecting that this was a cause of vexation to Dante, sent for the buffoon, and, after lavishing praise upon him, turned to Dante and said: "I wonder how it is that this man, fool though he be, understands how to please us all and is petted by everyone; while you, for all your reputed wisdom, can do nothing of the kind!" Dante replied: "You would hardly wonder at that if you remembered that like manners and like minds are the real causes of friendship" [as Aristotle says in book 8 of his *Nicomachean Ethics*].
Francis Petrarch, *Memorable Things* (1345)[16]

Dante's Epochal Gymnastics (ca. 1321)

The fourteenth century grows out of the thirteenth as the thirteenth grows out of the twelfth, so that there is no real break between the medieval renaissance and the Quattrocento. Dante, an undergraduate once declared, "stands with one foot in the Middle Ages while with the other he salutes the rising star of the Renaissance"!
C. H. Haskins, *Renaissance of the Twelfth Century* (1927)[17]

The Lack-Latin Bishop of Durham (1318–1333)

This Louis [de Beaumont, bishop of Durham] was of noble birth, sprung from the kings of France and Sicily; he was fine of face but feeble in his feet, for he limped with both legs; so liberal that many called him prodigal; covetous of gain but not very scrupulous about the means whereby he procured it.... He was chaste but unlearned, for he understood not Latin and could scarce pronounce it. When therefore at his consecration [1318] he should have made his formal profession, he could not read it, though he had been instructed therein for many days beforehand; and having at last arrived, with many promptings from others, at the word *Metropolitan*, which after many gasps he yet could not pronounce, at length he said in the French tongue, "Let that be taken as read!" Another time, when he was conferring Holy Orders and could not pronounce the phrase *in aenigmate* [1 Cor. 13:12, "darkly"], he said in French to those that stood by, "By Saint Louis, he who wrote this word was no gentleman!"

Robert Graystanes, *Chronicle of Durham* (1336)[18]

Lese Majesty:
The Horrible Murder of Edward II (1327)

After King Edward II of England abdicated, he was imprisoned in Berkeley Castle in Gloucestershire.] Then began the lethal persecution of Edward that was designed to kill him. First he was enclosed in a tightly sealed room, and they tortured him almost to the point of suffocation with the fumes from corpses in the cellar underneath his room. One day this holy man complained to carpenters who were working beside his window that the intolerable stench was the worst punishment he had ever endured. When his oppressors saw that this exceedingly robust man could not be killed by that hideous stink, they suddenly seized him on September 22 while he was lying in bed and held him down and immobilized him with big pillows and the weight of more than fifteen strong men. Then plumbers burned the vital organs, which are located above the intestines, with a white-hot iron rod, which they passed through a flexible tube that was inserted into his anus. They employed this method because they feared that, if the royal body were wounded anywhere that one might normally expect wounds to be, some friend of justice might discover them and his torturers would be held responsible for inflicting a manifest injury and be punished accordingly. However, it was evident enough that he suffered a violent death, for the cries of this most vigorous knight as he was thus overwhelmed were heard inside and outside of the castle.

Thomas de la More, *Life and Death of Edward II* (1356)[19]

If I Were King (ca. 1330)

[While in Naples] Giotto made many works in the Castel dell'Uovo, and in particular the chapel, which much pleased the king [Robert, 1309-1343], by whom he was so greatly beloved that many times, while working, Giotto found himself entertained by the king in person, who took pleasure in seeing him at work and in hearing his discourse. And Giotto, who had ever some jest on his tongue and some witty repartee in readiness, would entertain him with his hand, in painting, and with pleasant discourse, in his jesting.... Thus one day the king said, "Giotto, if I were you, now that it is hot I would stop painting for a while." And he answered, "And in faith I would too, if I were you."

Giorgio Vasari (1511-1174), *Lives of the Painters*[20]

Giotto's Political Cartoon (ca. 1330)

[From 1330 to 1333, Giotto was court painter to Robert, king of Naples.] While Giotto was painting a room where he left his own portrait among those of various famous men, King Robert asked him, for some reason or another, to include an image of the kingdom of Naples. So it is said that Giotto depicted an ass saddled with a pack that was marked with a crown and scepter. At his feet lay another pack saddle that also bore royal insignia. The ass was sniffing at this new burden and seemed eager to have it put on his back in place of the one that was there. When the king asked what this allegory meant, Giotto explained that the ass was an appropriate image for the kingdom of Naples, which constantly desired to have a new master.

Giorgio Vasari (1511-1574), *Lives of the Painters*[21]

"Handsome Is As Handsome Does" (ca. 1335)

[There were two citizens of Florence.] The one, Master Forese da Rabatta [d. 1348?] by name, had a short and deformed body, with a pug nose and flat face ... but he knew Roman law so well that he had the reputation of being a veritable storehouse of civil jurisprudence. The other, whose name was Giotto [d. 1337], was an artist of such genius that ... with his stylus and pen and pencil he could depict nature so well that men often mistook what he drew for the real thing.... But although he was a great artist, he was no better looking than Master Forese in any way.

But to come to the story: It was in Mugello [ten miles or so north-east of Florence] that Master Forese had his country house, as did Giotto as well. Forese was returning from a stay that he had made there during the summer vacation of the courts, and being mounted on a poor, broken-down draft horse, he met Giotto, who was also on his way back to Florence after a similar stay on his own estate, and he was neither better mounted nor in any other way better equipped than Master Forese. And so, both being old men, they jogged along together at a slow pace; and being surprised by one of those sudden showers that are common in summer, they presently took shelter in the house of a farmer who knew both of them and was their friend. But after a while, as the rain gave no sign of ceasing and as they wanted to be at Florence that same day, they borrowed from the farmer two old cloaks of rough, Romagnole cloth and two hats much the worse for the wear, for the man had nothing better, and resumed their journey.

They had not proceeded far when, taking note that they were soaked through and through and liberally splashed with the mud cast up by their nags' hooves (circumstances which are not of a kind to add to one's dignity), they began to converse after a long silence, as the sky was beginning to brighten a little. And Master Forese, as he rode and listened to Giotto, who was an excellent talker, surveyed him sideways, and from head to foot, and all over, and seeing how disreputable and unsightly he appeared (but giving no thought to himself), started laughing and said: "Giotto, if any stranger met us who had not seen you before, do you think he would believe that you were the greatest painter in the world?"

To which Giotto promptly replied: "Well, your honor, I think he might believe it if he were able to believe that you, looking as you do now, knew so much as the alphabet." When Master Forese heard this, he recognized his error and saw that he had been paid in his own coin.

Giovanni Boccaccio (d. 1375), Decameron[22]

The First Step in the Hundred Years War (1336)

Then the king [Edward III of England] caused a great navy of ships to be ready in the haven of Hampton and caused all manner of men of war to draw thither.... When the king's navy arrived in [Saint-Vaast de] la Hogue [in Normandy] and was securely anchored at the beach, the king came out of his ship, and as soon as he set his foot on land, he fell down so hard that the blood burst out of his nose. The knights that were with him lifted him up and said: "Sir, for God's sake enter again into your ship and do not come on land today, for this is surely some sort of sign for you." Then the king answered quickly and with ready wit: "Why? This is a good token for me, for the land desires to have me." This answer caused all of his men to rejoice.

Jean Froissart (fl. 1338–1410), Chronicles[23]

The Countess of Montfort Defends Her City (1342)

[During the Hundred Years War, while the French and English were fighting over Brittany, the French general decided] to set out for Hennebon, where the countess of Montfort resided. Since her husband [whom the English were backing as heir to the duchy of Brittany] was imprisoned in Paris, the general reckoned that the war would be over if he could only get possession of her person and her son.... When the countess and her knights heard that the enemies were coming to besiege them and were almost there, they ordered that the alarm bells be rung and that every one should arm himself to defend the town.... [After a day of skirmishing, the French assaulted the walls in earnest on the second day.]

The countess, who had clothed herself in armour, was mounted on a war horse and galloped up and down the streets of the town urging her people to make a good defense. She ordered the ladies and other women to unpave the streets, carry the stones to the ramparts, and throw them on their enemies. She also had bombs and pots of quick-lime brought to throw on the attackers.

The same day the countess performed a very gallant deed: she as-cended a high tower to see how her people were doing; and, having ob-served that all [the French] ... had left their tents and joined the assault, she immediately descended, and being already armed, she mounted her horse, collected three hundred horsemen, sallied out at their head by another gate that was not under attack, and galloping up to the tents of her enemies, cut them down and set them on fire, all without any loss, for there were only servants and boys in the camp, who fled when she approached. As soon as the French saw their camp on fire and heard the cries, they immediately hurried back, bawling out, "Treason! trea-son!" so that none remained at the assault. The countess, seeing this, got her men together, and, finding that she could not re-enter Henne-bon without great risk, rode straight for the castle of Brest, which was nearby, ... where they were received with great joy....

[Five days later] the countess had been so active that she assembled five or six hundred men, well armed and mounted, and went out from Brest with them about midnight and came straight to Hennebon about sunrise, riding along one side of the enemy's host until she came to the gates of the castle, which were opened to her. She entered with great triumph to the sound of trumpets and bagpipes, and the French host was astounded. [She continued to hold Hennebon until an English fleet arrived to relieve the siege.]

Jean Froissart (fl. 1338–1410), *Chronicles*[24]

The Catcher in the Rye (1343)

At that time there befell a marvel in the northern parts [of England] in the matter of a certain youth who had been of the household of the baron of Graystock. He, riding one day through a rye field, and mark-ing how the rye rippled like a sea, suddenly saw a little red man raise his head from the grain. As the youth gazed upon him, the man seemed to grow bigger and bigger in stature. Then this apparition drew nigh and caught his bridle and led him against his will into the rye, to a place where it seemed to him that a lady of wondrous beauty was seated with many maidens like unto herself. Then the lady bade them take him from his horse and tear his skin and flesh, and at last she commanded that he should be flayed alive. Then the said lady cut his head through the midst and (as he thought) took out his brain and closed up the empty skull; after which she bade them lift him upon his steed and dismissed him. With that he straightway lost his senses and began to rave and play the madman.

When therefore he was come to the nearest town, then a certain maiden came and cared for him, who had been of the same lord's household and had loved him well; and, lest he should harm those who waited upon him, she let him be bound in chains. Thus she led him to many saints beyond the sea for the restoration of his health; until, seeing that all was in vain, she brought him back to England. All this while that red man with the red hair ceased not to haunt him but stood everywhere before his eyes just as he had first appeared to him; and, even though men bound him with three or four chains, he kept getting loose.

At length, after six years of this misery, he was wholly cured at the shrine of Saint John at Beverley; where, falling into a quiet sleep, he seemed to see that comely lady cleave his head once more and replace the brain even as she had first taken it away. Therefore, finding himself restored to health, he wedded that same maiden who had led him from shrine to shrine, by whom he had fifteen sons. After her death he took holy orders, was made a priest, and received the benefice of Thorpe Basset. While therefore he sang mass with much devotion and, according to custom, raised the body of Christ in his hands for the people to see, then the same red man appeared to him and said: "Let Him whom you have in your hands be your guardian from now on, for He can keep you better than I can."

Thomas Walsingham, *English History* (after 1422)[25]

An Incredible Collection of Relics (1346)

[In 1346 the chapel in the marketplace (*Chapelle du Marché*) at Saint-Omer, near Calais, made an inventory of its relics, which included the following mementos from biblical times.]

A piece [each] of the sign from the Lord's cross, of his lance, and his column. Of the manna which rained from heaven. Of a stone whereon Christ's blood was spilt. Item, another little cross of silvered wood, containing pieces of the Lord's sepulchre and of Saint Margaret's veil. Of the Lord's cradle in a certain copper reliquary.

... In a certain crystal vessel, some portions of the stone tables whereon God wrote the law for Moses with his finger. Item, in the same vessel, of the stone upon which Saint James crossed the sea. Item, part of the Lord's winding-sheet. Item, pieces of Aaron's rod, of the altar at which Saint Peter sang mass, of Saint Boniface; and all this in a glass tube.

Portions of the hairs of Saint Mary; item, of her robe; item, a shallow ivory box without any ornament save only a knob of copper, which box contains some of the flower which the blessed Virgin held [at the Annunciation] ... and of the window through which the angel Gabriel entered when he saluted her.... Item, a fragment of the blessed Mary's sepulchre in [the vale of] Jehoshaphat, in a certain leaden case enclosed in a little ivory casket.

Inventory of the Market Chapel, Saint-Omer (1346)[26]

Cola Di Rienzo Restores the Empire to Italy and Rome (1347)

In order that the gifts and favour of the Holy Ghost may be shared by all the Italians, from ancient times brothers and sons of the sacred Roman people, we have made one and all the citizens of the states of sacred Italy Roman citizens, and we admit them to the election of the empire which has devolved rationally upon the sacred Roman people. And we have decreed that the election is to be conducted in the City with solemnity and maturity by the voices of twenty-four elders acting as electors.... We desire, indeed, to renew more firmly the ancient union with all the magistrates from the cities of sacred Italy and with you [the Florentines]. And sacred Italy, now for a long time prostrated and degraded by those [German emperors] who ought to govern her in peace and justice, ... we desire to free from all its risk of degradation and lead it back to its former condition of ancient glory, and so to augment it that, having tasted the sweetness of peace, it may flourish by the grace of the Holy Ghost better than ever a nation has flourished in other parts of the world. For we intend, the Holy Ghost granting success ... happily to promote, through the sacred Roman people and those to whom we give the votes of the imperial election, some Italian whom unity of race and suitability of nation may induce to a zeal for Italy according to the inspiration of the Holy Ghost, who has deigned piously to regard sacred Italy itself, so that through the pleasing action of accomplished facts we may honour the title of augustus which the Roman people has granted and assigned with truly divine inspiration.

Cola di Rienzo, *Letter to the Florentines* (1347)[27]

"... And Everything in its Place" (before 1348)

Giovanni Andrea, a law professor of Bologna who was widely reputed for his wisdom, was surprised by his wife as he lay with the housemaid. Utterly astounded by his unexpected infidelity, she cried: "Where is your famous wisdom now, Giovanni?" To which the professor answered laconically: "In this girl's vulva, which is a place quite suitable for wisdom" [since a Latin proverb says: "A woman's mind is in her uterus"].

Poggio Bracciolini (1380–1459), *Facetiae*[28]

Tournaments and Transvestites (1348)

In those days there arose a great clamour and outcry among the people, seeing that in almost every place where tourneys were held [in England] they were attended by a band of ladies who formed part, as it were, of the spectacle. These came in divers and marvellous men's garments, to the number sometimes of forty, sometimes of fifty ladies, of the fairest and comeliest in the whole realm, yet not of the most virtuous. They were clad in motley tunics, half of one colour and half of another, with short hoods and liripipes wound like cords round their heads, and richly studded girdles of silver or gold, nay, even across their bodies they wore pouches containing those knives that are commonly called "daggers"; and thus they rode forth to the place of tourney on choice chargers or richly decked palfreys, thus wasting their own goods and debasing their bodies with folly and, as it was commonly reported, scurrilous wantonness. Thus they neither feared God nor blushed for the modest outcries of the people but made nought of their marriage vows.... But herein, as in all other matters, God brought a wondrous remedy by scattering their dissolute concourse; for upon the places and times that had been appointed for such vain sports he showered rain and thunder and flashes of lightning, with all discomforts of wind and tempests.

Henry Knighton (fl. 1400), *Chronicle*[29]

The Black Death in England (1348–1349)

In this year [1348] and in the following one there was a general mortality of men throughout the whole world.... At this same time the pestilence became prevalent in England, beginning in the autumn in certain places. It spread throughout the land, ending in the same season of the following year.... That most grievous pestilence penetrated the coastal regions by way of Southampton and came to Bristol, and people died as if the whole strength of the city were seized by sudden death. For there were few who lay in their beds more than three days or two and a half days; then that savage death snatched them about the second day. In Leicester, in the little parish of Saint Leonard, more than 380 died; in the parish of the Holy Cross, more than 400, and in the parish of Saint Margaret in Leicester, more than 700. And so in each parish, they died in great numbers.

And the price of everything was cheap because of the fear of death; there were very few who took any care for their wealth or for anything else.... And the sheep and cattle wandered about through the fields and among the crops, and there was no one to go after them or to collect them. They perished in countless numbers everywhere in secluded ditches and hedges, for lack of watching, since there was such a lack of serfs and servants that no one knew what he should do.... In the following autumn [1349] one could not hire a reaper at lower wage than eight pence with food, or a mower at less than twelve pence with food. Because of this, much grain rotted in the fields for lack of harvesting, but in the year of the plague, as was said above, among other things there was so great an abundance of all kinds of grain that no one seemed to have concerned himself about it....

At this same time there was so great a lack of priests everywhere that many widowed churches had no divine services, no masses, matins, vespers, sacraments, or sacramentals. One could hardly hire a chaplain to minister to any church....

After the aforesaid pestilence, many buildings, both large and small, in all cities, towns, and villages had collapsed and had completely fallen to the ground in the absence of inhabitants. Likewise many small villages and hamlets were completely deserted; there was not one house left in them, but all those who had lived in them were dead. It is likely that many such hamlets will never again be inhabited.

Henry Knighton (fl. 1400), *Chronicle*[30]

A Satire on Ludicrous Relics (ca. 1350)

[In this imaginary tale, Boccaccio satirizes those preachers who traded on the credulity of the gullible by displaying improbable relics. The speaker, Fra Cipolla—"Brother Onion"—is explaining to an Italian audience how he acquired his wares in Palestine.]

And there I found the venerable father Dontblamemeifyouplease, the most worshipful patriarch of Jerusalem; who out of respect for the habit that I have ever worn, namely that of Baron Master Saint Antony, was pleased to let me see all the holy relics that he had by him, which were so many that, were I to enumerate them all, I should not come to the end of them in some miles. However, not to disappoint you, I will tell you a few of them. In the first place, then, he showed me the finger of the Holy Spirit, as whole and entire as it ever was, and a tuft of feathers from the wing of the seraph that appeared to Saint Francis, and one of the nails of the cherubim, and one of the ribs of the Verbumcarohowsaboutadate, and some of the vestments of the Holy Catholic Faith, and some of the rays of the star that appeared to the Magi in the East, and a phial of the sweat of Saint Michael as he battled with the Devil, and the jaws of death of Saint Lazarus, and other relics.

And because I gave him a liberal supply of the acclivities of Monte Morello *in vulgo* and some chapters of Caprezio, of which he had long been in quest, he gave me in return one of the teeth of the Santa Croce, and in a small phial a bit of the sound of the bells of Solomon's temple, and this feather of the angel Gabriel, whereof I have told you, and one of the clogs of San Gherardo da Villa Magna, which not long ago at Florence I gave to Gherardo di Bonsi, who holds him in prodigious veneration. The patriarch also gave me some of the coals with which the most blessed martyr, Saint Lawrence, was roasted. All of these things I devoutly brought back with me and have them all safe. It's true that up to now my superior has not permitted me to show them publicly, until he could be certain that they are genuine. Now, however, their authenticity is shown by certain miracles they have done, as the patriarch assured us in a letter, so I now have permission to show them.

Giovanni Boccaccio (1375), *The Decameron*[31]

Francesco Ordelaffi: "The Dog Captain of Forli" (ca. 1355)

There was a perfidious dog in the Romagna, who was a heretic and a rebel against the Church. He had been excommunicated for thirty years and the region under his control had been placed under an interdict, so mass was not sung there. At that time he held many lands that belonged to the Church [as part of the Papal States], including Forlì, Cesena, Forlimpopolo, Castrocaro, Bertinoro, Imola, and Giaggiolo, as well as many other castles and communities in the area—all of which he ruled as a tyrant. This Francesco was a desperate man: he had a mortal hatred for all high officials of the Church ... and moreover he refused to let priests tell him how to live. In short, he was an obstinate and traitorous tyrant.

When this Francesco heard the bells being rung, to excommunicate him, he immediately had other bells rung and then he excommunicated the pope and the cardinals. Worse than that, he had the pope and cardinals burned in the public square, or rather paper images of them that were stuffed with hay. When chatting with his gentlemen friends, he used to say: "See, we are excommunicated; still, for all of that, the bread, the meat, and the wine we consume tastes no less good and is no less nourishing." This is how he treated priests and monks: the bishop who proclaimed his excommunication was insulted and and left town. Then the Captain [Francesco] forced the clergy to celebrate mass.... The people of Forlì were like family to Francesco; they loved him dearly. The way he treated them would, if done by another man, be called pious charity: he arranged marriages for orphan girls, he gave dowries so that young girls could marry, and in general he helped poor little girls of common birth, who were utterly devoted to him.

Fragments of Roman History (1358)[32]

How to Persuade a Pope (after 1362)

When Pope Urban [V, 1362-1370] was in Avignon, the people of Perugia sent three ambassadors to him, and when they arrived, they found the pope seriously ill. His holiness, reluctant to keep them waiting, gave them audience, begging them, however, before they began to speak, to be brief. A learned doctor, who during the voyage had learned by heart a long speech to deliver to the pope, had no respect for his malady and launched into an interminable and tiresome discourse. When the doctor had finally ended his wearying address, Urban courteously asked the other two what was their wish. One of the other two ambassadors, who had realized the stupidity of his companion and the annoyance he had caused the pope, said: "Holy Father, we have instructions from our people that, if your holiness does not do all you can for us in this matter, my colleague here will deliver his address all over again." The jest made the pope laugh, and he ordered that what the Perugians wanted should be done.

Poggio Bracciolini (1380–1459), *Facetiae*[3]

Official Honesty is not Medieval Policy (after 1366)

There was once a duke of Burgundy, a most excellent prince, who prepared, as was often his custom, to journey throughout the greater part of his territory and visit his officers who were in those places, but more especially his treasurers, and to see what they did and how they fared. And coming to the mansions of six of his treasurers who were in various places, by the first five he was received richly and honourably in very fine palaces, but by the sixth, who was the oldest and had been there the longest time, he was received very meanly in a little house. Seeing this the duke marvelled, and he described to this treasurer the palaces of the others and the honour they had done him and asked what was the reason why he acted thus.

Then the treasurer answered: "Monseigneur, if I had wished to steal and cheat, as the others may happen to have done, I should also have a rich and beauteous mansion; but I have lived with perchance too much loyalty to desire to live richly, as do those of whom you tell me." Said the duke: "But now I desire that you should steal and do as the others do in order that I may find you in a fine mansion when next I come here." Then the treasurer answered: "Since that is your pleasure, I will do it."

Upon the next day the duke departed and returned unto his own house. And after the space of a year and a half or more, he went again in the same manner to visit his treasurers. And when he came to the house of the sixth treasurer, after having seen all the others, he found that none was to be compared with this one, and so likewise with the life that he led. Wherefore the duke called the treasurer and said:

"I now understand that you know how to obtain both fine palaces and a fine life with the permission which I gave you; but, reflecting that such a thing may be to the hurt of many, and perchance more to my hurt than that of others, I desire that henceforth you steal no more nor get yourself more things. You have a fine mansion and are richer than any of the others; with this you can rest content, and with this, as my treasurer, you can receive me richly at all times."

Replied the treasurer: "Monseigneur, formerly I led the life which now you desire I should lead, and it was your pleasure that I should lead that life no longer but that I should do just the contrary; to this in a short time I have become so accustomed that now I could not by any manner of means return unto my former life."

So then the duke said that he desired that he would at least no longer cheat or steal, but the treasurer answered that he could not promise that. He begged, however, that it might please the duke to take from him his palace and all the treasures and possessions which he had and appoint another treasurer, because he was grown old and was no longer fitted to serve him. And, notwithstanding all that the duke could say, he turned not from his resolve, so that the duke dismissed him, let him depart by himself with few possessions, and took another treasurer.

Franco Sacchetti (ca. 1330—ca. 1400), *Tales*[34]

The Most Honoured Knight (1367)

[Bertrand du Guesclin, the constable of France, was captured by the English at the battle of Navarette.] We will now relate how Sir Bertrand du Guesclin obtained his liberty. After the [Black] Prince of Wales returned [from Spain] to Aquitaine ... Sir Bertrand du Guesclin remained prisoner to the prince and to Sir John Chandos, and they would neither set his ransom nor release him on any other terms....

Now it happened (as I was informed both then and later) that one day, when the prince of Wales was in great good humor, he called Sir Bertrand du Guesclin and asked him how he was. "My lord," replied Sir Bertrand, "thanks to God I was never better; and I can hardly be otherwise, for I am the most honoured knight in the world, even though I remain your prisoner. Why and how this can be is simple: They say in France, and in other countries as well, that you are so much afraid of me and have such a dread of my gaining my liberty that you dare not set me free."

The prince, on hearing these words, thought Sir Bertrand had spoken them with much good sense, for in truth his council were unwilling he should have his liberty.... So he answered, "What, Sir Bertrand, do you imagine that we keep you a prisoner for fear of your prowess? By Saint George, it is not so; for my good sir, if you will pay one hundred thousand francs, you shall be free." Sir Bertrand was eager to gain his liberty; now having heard upon what terms he could obtain it, he took the prince at his word and replied, "My lord, through God's will I will never pay a lesser sum."

The prince, when he heard this, began to repent of what he had done. It is said that some of his council went further and told him, "My lord, you have acted very wrong in granting him his ransom so easily." And they wanted him to break his agreement; but the prince, who was a prudent and loyal knight, replied, "Since we have granted it, we will keep to it and not act in any way contrary, for it would be a shame, and we should be blamed by every one for not agreeing to his ransom, when he has offered to pay so largely for it as one hundred thousand francs."

From the time of this agreement, Sir Bertrand worked hard to obtain the settlement money from his friends, and he was so effective that in less than a month he paid the hundred thousand francs by the assistance of the king of France and the duke of Anjou, who loved him well. And he went to the aid of the duke of Anjou with two thousand fighting men....

Jean Froissart (1337–1410), *Chronicles*[35]

The Accounts of a Conquering Cardinal (1367)

Cardinal Giles [Albornoz subdued the Papal States for the popes while they lived at Avignon, but he] was accused of maladministration of the revenues of the Church because he did not send larger payments to Avignon. Being asked to render an account, he called for a wagon, piled a great quantity of keys upon it, and presented himself before the cardinals and the pope [Urban V, when he landed at Corneto in 1367 on his way back to Rome] and the cardinals, saying that he could give no better account than that he had recovered for him the aforementioned provinces and that here were the keys of the towns!

Guerriero da Gubbio (d. 1481), *Chronicle*[36]

"Turn Again Whittington" (1379)

[Richard Whittington was a poor country boy who came to London seeking work.] Well at length he was admitted and made a member of the family [of a merchant, Hugh Fitzwarren], in which he demeaned himself so well by his willingness to run or go or do any service how mean so ever that he had got the good will of all the household, only the kitchen maid being a damned shrew, and knowing him to be an under-servant to her, domineered over him and used him very coarsely and roughly, of which he would never complain, though he had cause enough.... [Eventually he became] as weary of his life as of his service, for she (usurping upon his plainness and modesty) would be quarrelling with him upon every small occasion or none at all, sometimes beating him with the broom, sometimes laying him over the shoulders with a ladle, the spit or what came next to her hands, being of so dogged a disposition that she still continued her cruelty towards him; and therefore he resolved with himself to run away, and for that purpose he had bundled up those few clothes which he had, and before day broke he got as far as Bunhill, and then he sat down to consider with himself what course was best for him to take. Then by chance (it being All-Hallows day) a merry peal from Bow Church began to ring, and the tune that the bells played seemed to be singing this song to him:

> Turn again Whittington, Lord Mayor of London,
> Turn again Whittington, Lord Mayor of London.

This made such a great impression on him that finding how early it was and that he might yet come back in his master's house before any of the family were stirring, he resolved to go back and found everything according to his own wishes and desires, inasmuch as when the household got up no one could claim he had been missing. And thus he continued as before in his first plainness and honesty, well beloved of all save the kitchen drudge....

The History of Sir Richard Whittington (1656)[37]

The Death of Wat Tyler (1381)

[During the Peasants' Revolt, the insurgents marched on London to present their demands to the king, Richard II, then fourteen years old. After several days of rioting and negotiation] the king caused a proclamation to be made that all the commons of the country who were still in London should come to Smithfield, to meet him there; and so they did.

And when the king and his train had arrived there, they turned into the eastern meadow in front of Saint Bartholomew's, which is a house of canons, and the commons arrayed themselves on the west side in great troops. At this moment the mayor of London, William Walworth, came up, and the king bade him go to the commons and make their chieftain come to him. And when he was summoned by the mayor, by the name of Wat Tyler of Maidstone, he came to the king with great confidence, mounted on a little horse, so that the commons might see him.

And he dismounted, holding in his hand a dagger which he had taken from another man, and when he had dismounted he half bent his knee, and then took the king by the hand and shook his arm forcibly and roughly, saying to him, "Brother, be joyful and of good comfort, for you shall have, in the fortnight that is to come, praise from the commons even more than you have yet had [for promising to free the serfs], and we shall be good companions."

And the king said to Walter [Wat], "Why will you not go back to your own country?" But the other answered with a great oath that neither he nor his fellows would depart until they had got their charter such as they wished to have it.... [Wat then presented a long list of demands.] To this the king gave an easy answer and said that he should have all that he could fairly grant, reserving only for himself the regality of his crown. And then he bade him go back to his home without making further delay....

Presently Wat Tyler, in the presence of the king, sent for a flagon of water to rinse his mouth because of the great heat that he was in, and when it was brought he rinsed his mouth in a very rude and disgusting fashion before the king's face. And then he made them bring him a jug of beer and drank a great draught, and then, in the presence of the king, climbed on his horse again....

[At this point one of the king's valets called Wat "the greatest thief and robber in all Kent" and incited him to attack.] And for these words Wat tried to strike him with his dagger and would have slain him in the king's presence; but because he strove so to do, the mayor of London, William Walworth, called the said Wat to account for his violent behaviour and contempt done in the king's presence, and he arrested him. And because he arrested him, the said Wat stabbed the mayor with his dagger in the stomach in great wrath. But, as it pleased God, the mayor was wearing armor and took no harm, but like a hardy and vigorous man drew his cutlass and struck back at the said Wat and gave him a deep cut on the neck and then a great cut on the head. And during this scuffle one of the king's household drew his sword and ran Wat two or three times through the body, mortally wounding him. And Wat spurred his horse, crying to the commons to avenge him, and the horse carried him some four score paces, and then he fell to the ground half dead.

And when the commons saw him fall, and knew not how for certain it was, they began to bend their bows and to shoot, wherefore the king himself spurred his horse and rode out to them, commanding them that they should all come with him to Clerkenwell Fields.... [So assuming leadership of the rebels, the king led them away, gaining time until the mayor could assemble a counterforce to restrain the mob.]

[Then the mayor] returned with a company of lances to Smithfield to make an end of the captain of the commons. And when he came to Smithfield he found not there the said captain Wat Tyler, at which he marvelled much and asked what was become of the traitor. And it was told him that he had been carried by some of the commons to the hospital for poor folks by Saint Bartholomew's and was put to bed in the chamber of the master of the hospital. And the mayor went thither, found him, and had him carried out to the middle of Smithfield and there beheaded in the presence of his fellows. And thus ended his wretched life. But the mayor had his head set on a pole and borne before him to the king, who still abode in the fields.

Anonimalle Chronicle (1381)[38]

The Condottiere as War Profiteer (1384)

Very diverting was the answer given by Sir John Hawkwood to two Brothers Minor [of the order of Saint Francis]. These friars went to visit him, upon some errand of their own, at a castle of his where he was then sojourning, which was called Montecchio and was about a mile this side of Cortona. And when they were come into his presence they said, as was their custom: "My lord, may God grant you peace." And he instantly replied: "May God take away all the alms you have received." The monks were astonished and cried: "Lord, why do you say that?" "And why do you say that to me?" returned Sir John. "We thought it was well said," answered the friars. And Sir John replied: "How could you think it was well said to come to me and pray that God would make me die of hunger? Do you not know that I live by war and that peace would ruin me? And as I live by war, so you live by alms, so the reply that I gave you was like the greeting you gave me."

Franco Sacchetti (ca. 1330—ca. 1400), *Tales*[39]

A Royal Nervous Breakdown:
Charles VI Goes Berserk (1392)

[Charles VI, king of France] set out from Le Mans between nine and ten o'clock in the morning ... to march to Angers [on the way to Brittany].... The day the king left Le Mans was excessively hot, as was to be expected for it was the middle of August when the sun is in its greatest force.... He had been feeble in body and mind all that summer, scarcely eating or drinking anything and was almost daily attacked with fever, to which he was naturally inclined, and this was increased by any contradiction or fatigue....

A strange accident happened to him as he was riding through the forest of Le Mans.... A man, bareheaded, with naked feet, clothed in a jerkin of white russet, who seemed to be more mad than otherwise, rushed out from among the trees and boldly seized the reins of the king's horse. Having thus stopped him, he said, "King, ride no further, but return, for you are betrayed!" [The man was then chased away.] ... This speech impressed the king more than it should have, however, because his mind was weakened....

The king and his army passed on, and at about noon they left the forest and entered a broad, sandy plain; the sun was so strong and bright that hardly anyone could endure the heat. The horses suffered greatly, and even experienced campaigners complained of the heat. To have less dust, each of the lords took a different route apart from the others, so the king rode by himself....

The king rode over this sandy plain that reflected the heat.... Moreover, he was dressed in a jacket of black velvet that added to the warmth.... He was followed by one of his pages who had a Montauban cap of polished steel on his head that glittered in the sun, and behind him rode another page on horseback carrying a lance ... the head of which was broad, sharp, and bright.... As they were thus riding, the pageboys grew negligent of themselves and their horses; the one who bore the lance fell asleep, and, forgetful of what he had in his hand, let it fall on the steel helmet that the other page was wearing. They were riding just behind the king, who being so near was startled and shuddered, for he still had in his mind the words that the madman (or whatever he was) had spoken when he seized his horse's reins in the forest of Le Mans, and now he fancied that a host of enemies had come to slay him.

In this distracted frame of mind, he drew his sword and advanced on the pages, for he no longer recognized them or indeed anyone; instead, he imagined that he was surrounded by his foes in a battle. He struck out with his sword to the left and right in a way that might give one blow or several, for he did not care who or where it struck.

"Charge!" he cried, "charge on these traitors!" The pages saw that the king was enraged, and believing they had angered him by their negligence, they prudently fled to protect themselves, spurring their horses, one this way, the other that.

With drawn sword, the king approached the duke of Orléans [his brother], who was nearby, but the king could not recognize him ... because of his frenzy and weakness of heart. When the duke of Orléans saw him approach with a naked sword in hand, he grew alarmed and, prudently not wanting to wait, he rode off as hard as he could with the king after him.... The duke escaped, however, by turning this way and that, and he was aided by knights, squires, and men-at-arms who surrounded the king and allowed him to waste his strength on them, for of course the more he exerted himself, the weaker he grew.... [He is said to have killed four or five men.] At last, when he was quite worn out, with sweat running down and his horse in a lather from fatigue, a Norman knight called Sir William Martel, who was one of his chamberlains and much beloved by him, came up behind and caught him in his arms, though he had his sword still in his hand. When he was thus held, all the other lords came up and took the sword from him; he was dismounted and gently laid on the ground, so his jacket might be stripped from him to give him more air and cool him.... It was a great pity for a king of France, who is the most noble and powerful prince in the world, to be thus suddenly deprived of his senses. [He was insane intermittently for the rest of his life and hence is known as Charles the Mad.]

Jean Froissart (1337–1410), *Chronicles*[40]

The Fatal Masquerade of Six Wild Men (1393)

[After Charles VI recovered from his nervous breakdown, the French court celebrated the marriage of two members of the royal household.] Great crowds of lords attended, among whom were the dukes of Orléans, Berry, Burgundy, and their duchesses. The wedding day was passed in dancing and joy ... and everyone exerted himself to add to the gaiety because the king was enjoying himself so much.

There was in the king's household a Norman squire ... who thought of the following piece of pleasantry to amuse the king and the ladies.... For the ball that night, he had six cloth coats made and then had them covered with flax that looked like hair in shape and color. He dressed the king in one, [four young nobles in others], ... and the sixth one he wore himself. When they were all dressed up by having the coats sewed around them, they appeared to be wild men (*hommes sauvages*), for they were covered with fur from head to foot. This masquerade pleased the king greatly, and he expressed his pleasure to his squire. It was so secretly contrived that no one knew anything about it but the servants who attended on them.

Sir Evan de Foix [one of the masqueraders] ... said to the king: "Sire, I advise you to give strict orders that no one come near us with torches, for if but a spark falls on the coats we are disguised in, the flaxen fur will catch fire, and we will burn up before anyone can do anything about it." "In God's name," the king said, "you speak wisely and well, and it shall be done." ... Then he sent for one of the sergeants at arms who was on duty at the door and told him: "Go to the ballroom and in the king's name command that all the torches be placed on the far side of the room and that none of them come near the six wild men who are about to enter." ... [It was done, but] soon after this, the duke of Orléans entered, attended by four knights and six torches. He knew nothing of the king's orders or the six wild men who were about to make their appearance. First he watched the dancing and the women, then he began dancing vigorously himself....

At this point the king of France made his appearance with the five others, all dressed like wild men and covered from head to foot with flaxen fur as fine as human hair. No one present could recognize them. Five of them were attached to one another and the king came in first and led the others into the dance. When they entered the hall, every-one was so intent on watching them that the order about torches was forgotten. Fortunately the king left his companions and, impelled by his youth, went to show himself off to the ladies; passing first in front of the queen, he went along next to the duchess of Berry, who was his aunt and younger than he was. For fun the duchess took hold of him and wanted to know who he was, but the king stood there and would not give his name. "You won't ever escape me," the duchess said, "unless I know your name first."

Just then the other five wild men met a great accident caused by the duke of Orléans ... who was too eager to know who they were. As the five were dancing, he lowered the torch that one of his servants held in front of him, bringing it so close that the flame ignited the flax. And flax, as you know, cannot be put out once it is afire. Moreover, the flames heated the pitch with which the flax was attached to the cloth. The costumes themselves soon burst into flame, for they were covered with pitch and flax, were dry and delicate, and were all yoked together.

Those who wore them were in agony and began to cry out horribly. The situation was so dangerous that no one dared to get near them, although several knights did come up and try to strip the burning costumes off them, but the pitch burned their hands and disabled them for days thereafter. One of the five, Nantouillet, figured that the bar must be nearby, so he broke away and threw himself into a washtub full of water for rinsing out cups and plates. This saved him; otherwise he would have been burned to death like the others, and he still was badly injured. When the queen of France [Isabelle] heard these horrible cries made by the burning men, she feared for her husband because he had told her he would be one of the six; she was so alarmed that she fainted, and knights and ladies hastened forward to aid and comfort her. There was so much affliction, sorrow, and shouting in the hall that many were confused and distracted.

The duchess of Berry saved the king from danger, for she thrust him under her gown *elle le bouta dessoubs sa gonne* and covered him so he would escape the fire. When he tried to get away by force, she said: "Where do you want to go? You can hear that your companions are burning. Who are you? It's time to give me your name." "I am the king," he said. "Ah, my lord! Go quickly now and change your clothes. Then at least let the queen see you, for she's worried to death about you." At these words the king left the hall, went to his room, undressed as fast as he could, put on his own clothes, and came back to the queen ... who trembled for joy when she saw him.

Jean Froissart (1337–1410), *Chronicles*[41]

The Fifteenth Century

Why Henry IV Wanted To Teach French (1406)

At the same time the earl of Northumberland and Lord Bardolf, who fled into Scotland, suspected that the Scots wished to hand them over to the king of England in exchange for certain persons who were held as prisoners in England, for they were warned by the lord David Flemyng, who told them of the Scottish plot, and so they fled into Wales. Because of this, David was killed by the Scots. This murder led to dissension in Scotland, when all were moved against each other; in so much that, weakened by their feuds, they were compelled to seek annual truces [with England], which the king [Henry IV] granted to them. When these had been arranged and confirmed for the land, the Scots sent by sea the [Scots] king's son and heir [James I] so that he might be brought up in France and learn there wit and the French tongue. In the midst of a tempest the men of Cleye, daring the sea, bravely captured him, a certain bishop, and the earl of Orkney, to whom James had been entrusted by his father, and they led them to England, and handed them to the king. The King [Henry IV], dissolving into jocularity, said: "Certainly, if gratitude had flourished among the Scots, they would have sent the youth to me to be taught and brought up, for I know the French language also." The young man and the earl of Orkney were placed in the Tower; the bishop had slipped away.

The Annals of Henry IV (ca. 1406)[1]

Healing the Great Schism (ca. 1410)

Gregory XII, before he was made pope [in 1406], during the conclave [at Rome], and even after, promised to do many things for the schism that in those times was rending the Church. For some time he kept his promises and even went so far as to say that, rather than fail in his efforts, he would relinquish the papacy. But when he came to the sweets of power, he forgot his vows and promises and did nothing of what he had sworn he would do. [In 1409 he refused to resign and was deposed without effect by the council of Pisa.] The cardinal-bishop of Bordeaux [Francesco Uguccione, 1389–1412], a man of great experience and wisdom, ill supported this state of affairs, and one day he spoke to me in this fashion: "He has acted," he said, "like that quack did with the people of Bologna when he promised that he would fly from a certain tower." I begged him to tell me the story.

"A little while ago," he related, "there was in Bologna a quack who announced to the public that he would fly from a certain tower that is near the bridge of Saint Raphael for the distance of a mile from the city. On the day fixed for the performance, all the people were gathered together, and the quack made fools of them, leaving them all day waiting in the sun without food until almost evening. All eyes were turned towards the tower, waiting for the man to begin his flight. And when he showed himself on the tower and flapped his wings as if about to fly and it seemed that he was about to cast himself into the air, a great applause rose from the throng that stood watching him with open mouths. And at dusk the quack, just to do something, turned his back on the people and showed them his behind. So all the disappointed people, tired out with hunger and waiting, went off home. In the same way," he concluded, "the pope, after so many promises, contents himself with exhibiting to us his posterior rotundities."

Poggio Bracciolini (1380–1459), *Facetiae*[2]

Henry V Before the Battle of Agincourt (1415)

[On 25 October 1415, an invading English army of about 5000 faced a French army perhaps five or six times its size. The day of the battle, Henry V] our king, very calmly and quite heedless of danger, gave encouragement to his army, and he drew them up in "battles" and wings as if they were to go immediately into action.... And amongst other things which I noted as said at that time, a certain knight, Sir Walter Hungerford, expressed a desire to the king's face that he might have had, added to the little company he already had with him, ten thousand of the best archers in England, who would have been only too glad to be there. "That is a foolish way to talk," the king said to him, "because, by the God in Heaven upon whose grace I have relied and in whom is my firm hope of victory, I would not, even if I could, have a single man more than I do. For these I have here with me are God's people, whom He deigns to let me have at this time. Do you not believe," he asked, "that the Almighty, with these His humble few, is able to overcome the opposing arrogance of the French, who boast of their great number and their own strength?"

The Deeds of Henry the Fifth (ca. 1417)[3]

Ecclesiastical Liberties at the Council of Constance (1415)

In order to illustrate the type of freedom that was being demanded by many of the members of the council of Constance [1414–1418], a prominent British bishop, at a grand conclave of prelates, related the following incident:

There lived in Constance a citizen whose unmarried sister was gotten with child. When the former discovered the telltale enlargement of her loins, he snatched up a sword and, making as if to pierce her through, demanded to know what it meant and how she had come by her shame. Utterly dismayed, the maiden cried: "It was the work of the council! The council of Constance got me with child!" When the brother heard this, partly from fear of the council and partly from awe, he desisted from punishing his sister. While many at Constance were striving for freedom in other things, the seducer placed at the very head of his list freedom of sexual intercourse.

Poggio Bracciolini (1380–1459), *Facetiae*[4]

Monastic Sign Language (after 1420)

A table of signs used during the hours of silence by the sisters and brethren in the monastery of Syon [near London].

Aged. Draw down your right hand straight over your hair and over your right eye.

Ale. Make the sign of drink and draw your hand displayed before your ear downward.

Bed. Make the sign of a house, put your right hand under your cheek, and close your eyes.

Book. Wag and move your right hand in the way you turn the leaves of a book.

Bread. Make a round compass with your two thumbs and two forefingers. And if you want to have white bread, make the sign for white; if brown, touch the sleeve of your cowl.

Candle. Make the sign for butter with the sign for day.

Cheese. Hold your right hand flat in the palm of your left.

Church. Make the sign of a house and then make a benediction.

Chiming. Make a sign as if you smote with a hammer.

Cloister. Make a round circle with your right forefinger toward the earth.

Clothe. Rub up and down the ends of all your right fingers upon your left.

Cold. Make the sign of water trembling with your hand, or blow on your forefinger.

Drink. Bow your right forefinger and put it on your lower lip.

Eggs. Make a token with your right forefinger upon your left thumb to and fro as though you were peeling eggs.

Eating. Put your right thumb with two forefingers joined to your mouth.

Enough. Close your fist together and hold up your thumb; this may also serve for "I know it well."

Fish. Wag your hand displayed sideways like a fish tail.

Girdle. Draw the forefingers of either around your middle.

Glass. Make the sign of a cup with the sign of red wine.

Hot. Hold the side of your right forefinger fast in your closed mouth.

I don't know. Move the fingers of your right hand easily, flatwise, and away from you; also can be used for "no."

Incense. Put two fingers into your two nostrils.

Keeping. Put your right hand under your left armhole.

King. Put all your fingertips closed together on your forehead.

Man. Put your beard in your right hand and hold it.

Mass. Make the sign of a blessing.

Mustard. Hold your nose in the upper part of your right fist and rub it.

Red color. Put your forefinger to the red place of your cheek.

Ringing. Make a token with your fist up and down as if you were ringing a bell.

Salt. Fillip with the right thumb and forefinger over the left thumb.

Saucer. Make a round circle on your left palm with your right little finger.

Silence. Put your forefinger sidewise into your mouth and draw it up and down.

Sleeping. Put your right hand under your cheek and then close your eyes.

Washing. Rub your right hand flatwise upon the back of your left hand.

Water. Join the fingers of your right hand and move them downward droppingly.

Syon Monastery Customal (after 1420)[5]

The Spice of War (1421)

At Paris the king of England [Henry V] received great complaints against those [English troops] at Meaux [which they besieged from October 1421 to May 1422]. He was told that his men were waging war to the death [by starving Meaux into submission] and that they were ravaging the countryside with fire. To this he replied that he had given the fortress of Meaux a chance to surrender but had been forced to besiege it, and he was determined to take it at all costs. As to the complaint that his men were setting afire open fields in the countryside, he replied that this was nothing more than the custom of warfare, and that war without fire was worthless; it was no better than sausages without mustard.

Jean Juvenal des Ursins (d. 1473), *History of Charles VI*[6]

Joan of Arc Convinces the Dauphin (1429)

And the witness [Simon Charles, a royal official testifying in the proceedings to rehabilitate Joan] knows that while Joan was in the vicinity of the castle of Chinon [where the Dauphin Charles and his court were], the prince deliberated with his councel whether or not he should give her an audience. First of all they inquired why she had come and what she wanted. Although she did not wish to tell anyone except the Dauphin, she was finally forced to tell his representatives what her mission was, and she said that she had two commands from the King of

301

Heaven: one was to raise the siege of Orleans and the other was to lead the Dauphin to Rheims for his coronation and consecration. When the council heard this, some counsellors said that the Dauphin ought not to believe Joan at all, while others said that since she said she was sent from God and that she had some message for the Dauphin, he at least ought to hear her. But first the Dauphin wanted her to be examined by scholars and churchmen, which was accordingly done. Finally it was decided, although with difficulty, that the Dauphin would hear her.

And when she entered the castle of Chinon to come before the Dauphin ... and when the Dauphin heard she had arrived, he withdrew from the circle of his courtiers and stood apart from them, but Joan knew well who he was and did reverence to him, and she spoke with him [privately] for a long time. And as he heard her, the Dauphin seemed to be rejoicing.

Next, because the Dauphin refused to act in this matter without the counsel of churchmen, he sent her again to the city of Poitiers so she might be examined there by the scholars of the university of Poitiers. And after the Dauphin knew she had been examined and it had been reported to him that she had been found to be nothing but good, the Dauphin had arms made for her and gave her men, so she was equipped for warfare.

Rehabilitation Proceedings (1455)[7]

Roland and the Long-Lost Roman Empire (ca. 1430)

Ciriaco d'Ancona, a talkative and wordy fellow, one day when we [papal secretaries] were together, began deploring the fall and destruction of the Roman empire, and seemed to be greatly afflicted thereat. Then Antonio Lusco, a most learned man who was present, laughing at the foolish sorrow of the other, said: "You remind me of that man from Milan who one holiday, hearing in the public square one of those singers and travelling bards who tell the stories of the old heroes to the people, listened to his narration of the death of Roland, who had been dead seven hundred years. The man began to weep hot tears at the storyteller's words; and when he went home, his wife, who saw him all depressed and afflicted with grief, asked him what the matter was. 'Alas, my dear, I am a dead man.' 'My friend,' said the wife, 'whatever is the matter with you? What has happened? Come, cheer up and take your supper!' But he continued to weep and refused his food. Finally he gave way to the entreaties of his wife and told her the reason of his woe. 'Don't you know?' he said; 'haven't you heard?' 'What?' asked the woman. 'Roland is dead, Roland the only man who defended the Christians.' The wife consoled the foolish fellow and persuaded him to take his supper."

Poggio Bracciolini (1380–1459), *Facetiae*[8]

A Short Sermon (ca. 1430)

There is a town in our mountains where many people from various locations had come for a feast day, for it was Saint Stephen's day. According to custom, a certain monk was to deliver the sermon to the people. Since the hour of the day was late and the priests were moreover hungry and worried about the length of the sermon, they one after the other urged the monk in his ear as he ascended the pulpit to speak briefly. He allowed himself to be persuaded easily and, after the usual prefatory remarks, said: "My brethren, when I spoke in your presence last year in this place about the holiness, the life, and the miracles of this our saint, I omitted nothing of what I heard about him or what is found in holy scripture, all of which I believe you remember. But since I have learned he has done nothing new, cross yourselves, therefore, and say the *Confiteor* and the prayers that follow." And so he went away.

Poggio Bracciolini (1380–1459), *Facetiae*[9]

Joan of Arc: An Inquisitor's View (1431)

There was lately in France, within the last ten years, a maid ... named Joan, distinguished, as was thought, both for her prophetic spirit and for the power of her miracles. For she always wore man's dress, nor could all the persuasions of any doctors [of divinity] bend her to put these aside and content herself with woman's garments, especially considering that she openly professed herself a woman and a maid. "In these masculine garments," she said, "in token of future victory, I have been sent by God to preach both by word and by dress, to help Charles, the true king of France, and to set him firm upon his throne from whence

303

the king of England and the duke of Burgundy are striving to chase him." For at that time those two were allied together and oppressed France most grievously with battle and slaughter.

Joan, therefore, rode constantly like a knight with her lord, predicted many successes to come, was present at some victories in the field, and did other like wonders, whereat not only France marvelled, but every realm in Christendom.... But, after she had given great help to King Charles and had confirmed him for some years upon his throne, then at last—by God's will, as it is believed—she was taken in arms by the English and cast into prison. A great multitude were then summoned, of masters both in canon and in civil law, and she was examined for many days. And, as I have heard from Master Nicolas Midi, licentiate of theology, who was ambassador for the university of Paris, she at length confessed that she had a familiar angel from God, which, by many conjectures and proofs, and by the opinion of the most learned men, was judged to be an evil spirit; so that this spirit rendered her a sorceress; wherefore they permitted her to be burned at the stake by the common hangman.

Johann Nider (d. 1438), *The Anthill*[10]

An Unauthorised Proposition (ca. 1435)

The talk turned one day on the stupidity of some ambassadors who were sent with missions to high rulers. After some instances had been recounted, Antonio Lusco related the story of a certain ambassador who was sent by the people of Florence to Queen Joanna [II] of Naples [1414-1435]. He was called Francesco and was a doctor of law, although quite uncultured. After he had accomplished his mission, he received a request to return to the court on the following day. Meanwhile he had learned that the queen was not averse to the company of men whose appearance was pleasing to her. Thus, when he stood before her on the morrow, he spoke vaguely about this and that and finally let it be known that there were some secret matters he desired to present. The queen, under the impression that he had a message which could not be revealed in public, thereupon gave him an audience in her private chamber. Here the idiot, having an exalted opinion of his appearance, requested that he be permitted to lie with her. The queen did not move an eyelash but, looking steadily at the fellow, she asked: "Is this request a part of the commission you received from your republic?" As the poor wretch flushed and was silent, the queen added without a sign of anger: "Go back, then, and first secure the authority of Florence for your request."

Poggio Bracciolini (1380–1459), *Facetiae*[11]

A German Joan of Arc (ca. 1437)

We have in our days the distinguished professor of divinity, brother Heinrich Kaltyseren, inquisitor of heretical depravity. Last year, while he was exercising his inquisitorial office in the city of Cologne, as he himself told me, he found in the neighbourhood a certain maiden who always went about in man's dress, bore arms, and wore dissolute garments [i.e. doublet and hose] like a noble's retainer. She danced in dances with men and was so given to feasting and drink that she seemed altogether to overpass the bounds of her sex, which she did not conceal.

And because at that time (as, alas! even today) the see of Trier was sorely troubled by two rivals contending for the archbishopric, she boasted that she could and would set one party upon the throne, even as Maid Joan ... had done shortly before with King Charles of France by confirming him in his kingdom. Indeed, this woman claimed to be that same Joan resurrected by God.

One day, therefore, when she had come into Cologne with the young count of Württemberg, who protected and favoured her, and there in the sight of the nobles had performed wonders which seemed due to magic art, she was at last diligently scrutinised and publicly cited by the aforesaid inquisitor in order that she might be examined. For she was said to have cut a napkin in pieces and suddenly to have restored it whole in the sight of the people, to have thrown a glass against the wall and broken it and then to have repaired it in a moment, and to have shown many such idle devices.

But the wretched woman would not obey the commands of the Church; the count protected her from arrest and brought her secretly out of Cologne; thus she did indeed escape from the inquisitor's hands but not from the sentence of excommunication. Thus bound under curse, she quitted Germany for France, where she married a certain knight to protect herself against ecclesiastical interdict and the sword. Then a certain priest, or rather pimp, seduced this witch with talk of love, so that she stole away with him at length and went to Metz, where she lived as his concubine and showed all men openly by what spirit she was led.

Johann Nider (d. 1438), *The Anthill*[12]

Fernando the Boy Wonder (1445)

In the year 1445 there came to the Collège de Navarre [at Paris] a certain youth [Fernando of Cordova] of twenty summers who was past master of all good arts, as the most skilled masters of the university [of Paris] testified with one accord. He sang beautifully to the flute; he surpassed all in numbers, voice, modes, and symphony. He was a painter and laid colours on images best of all. In military matters he was most expert: he swung a sword with both hands so well and mightily that none dared fight with him. No sooner did he espy his foe than he would leap at him with one spring from a distance of twenty or twenty-four feet.

He was a master in arts, in medicine, in both laws [Roman and canon], and in theology. With us in the school of Navarre he engaged in disputation although we numbered more than fifty of the most perfect masters. I omit three thousand others and more who attended the bout. So shrewdly and cumulatively did he reply to all the questions which were proposed that he surpassed the belief, if not of those present, certainly of those absent. Latin, Greek, Hebrew, Arabic, and many more tongues he spoke in a most polished manner.

He was a very skillful horseman.

Nay more, if any man should live to be a hundred and pass days and sleepless nights without food and drink, he would never acquire the knowledge which that lad's mind embraced. And indeed he filled us with deep awe, for he knew more than human nature can bear. He argued four doctors of the Church out of countenance; no one seemed comparable to him in wisdom; he was taken for antichrist.

Anonymous eyewitness account[13]

The Visconti Dukes of Milan, 1385–1447

There was a certain duke [Filippo Maria, 1412-1447] so hated in Milan for his intolerable cruelties that day and night everyone prayed that ill-fortune should come upon him. A decrepit old woman, however, was in the habit of entering the church every evening at sundown and praying to God to give the tyrant health and long life. The duke, hearing of this and knowing that he did not merit any such intercession, had the old woman brought before him, and he asked her the reason of her praying to God for him. "It is true," she said, "that I have done this thing with regularity up till now, and this is the reason. When I was a girl, the Milanese had a lord who was very cruel [Gian Galeazzo, 1385–1402], so that I desired his ruin and death; but no sooner had he died than there succeeded to him a man who was in no way better [Giovanni Maria, 1402–1412], so that I thought it would be a very good thing were he to be killed too. Now we have you, our third lord, much worse and more cruel than the other two. So fearing that after your death there may come another worse yet than you, I never cease to pray to God that He may let you live for a very long time." Ashamed of himself, the tyrant had the woman killed for her rash wit.

Lodovico Domenichi, Facetiae (1562)[14]

The Turks Take Constantinople (1453)

The call to battle sounded at sunset, and the sultan [Mehmet II] was on his horse already on Monday evening [28 May], and his assembled force was very great. Now he started to fight in front of the fallen walls with his faithful, young, and powerful slaves. Ten thousand of them were engaged in fighting there like lions, and behind them and on the flanks were more than a hundred thousand battleworthy cavalry, and in the districts below to the harbour of the Golden Gate another hundred thousand and more, and from where their commander stood to the edge of the palace there were another fifty thousand, and to the boats and the bridge there were numberless men.

Those in the city were distributed about, too. The emperor [Constantine XI Palaeologus] with Giovanni Giustiniani [of Genoa] at the fallen walls outside the camp in the fortification had about three thousand Latins and Romans. The grand duke [Lucas Notaras] at the Imperial Gate had about five hundred; those at the sea walls and the ramparts from the Wooden Gate to the Beautiful Gate, crossbowmen and longbowmen, were more than five hundred. From the Beautiful

Gate around the whole circuit to the Golden Gate on each bastion was one longbowman, crossbowman, or artilleryman, continuing without sleep all night, not resting at all.

The Turks, however, with their leader hastened to approach the walls carrying numerous ladders made ready beforehand. The sultan behind the emplacement with an iron rod drove the archers to the walls, here coaxing them, there threatening. Still, the people in the city fought as bravely as they could. But Giovanni stood resisting with his men, along with the emperor in armour, too.

However, as the powerful intervention of fortune was about to change matters for the Turks, God removed from the Roman ranks their giant general and mighty, warlike man [Giovanni Giustiniani], for he was struck by a bullet in the arm back of the shoulder while it was still dark. It pierced his breastplate ... so that he could have no relief because of the wound. And he said to the emperor, "Stand bravely while I go to the ship, and when I have been treated, I shall return quickly." ... When the emperor saw Giovanni had retired, he grew afraid, as did those around him, but they still fought back as best they could.

[When the enemy had entered through a gate behind the Byzantine line], the Romans with the emperor did not see what had happened because the Turks' entry had occurred at a distance, and all the Romans' attention was on the opponents facing them. Now the Turks fighting them were good warriors, better in fact than the Romans, and outnumbered them twenty to one. The Romans' attention and concern was fixed on those Turks. Then suddenly they saw missiles coming down from above and killing them. When they looked up, they saw Turks....

The emperor accordingly was despondent, and standing with sword and shield he spoke pitifully: "Is there no one of the Christians to take my head from me." He was utterly alone. Then one of the Turks gave him a blow in the face, and he gave the Turk one in return. But another Turk gave him a fatal blow from behind, and he fell to the earth, for they did not know that he was the emperor, but those who had killed him left him lying like a common soldier....

[The sultan] asked if the emperor had escaped with the ships, and the [grand] duke answered that he did not know, for he had been at the Imperial Gate when the Turks approached and came in at Charisius' Gate. But two young men drew out of the crowd, and one said to the sultan: "My lord, I killed him. But I had to go in and plunder with my companions, so I left him dead." The other said: "I struck him first." Then the sultan sent the two and told them to bring his head. They ran quickly and finding him, cut off his head which they brought to their leader. The sultan said to the grand duke: "Tell me truly if this is the head of your emperor." After examining it the duke said: "It is his, my lord." Moreover, others saw it, too, and recognized it. Then they nailed it to the column in the Augoustaîon, where it stayed till evening. Then he had it flayed and the skin stuffed with straw. He sent it all around to show as a sign of victory to the governors of the Persians and of the Arabs and to the other Turks.

Ducas (d. 1461), *Turcobyzantine History*[15]

The Last Battle of the Hundred Years War (1453)

[The French, using their new artillery, had taken one city after another from the English, who finally sent an old veteran, Sir John Talbot, to raise the siege of Châtillon in Périgord. On arriving, he decided almost immediately to attack the French artillery park, a fortified camp outside the town.] The French disposed their artillery straight in the vanguard on that side whereon they saw my lord Talbot come with his company, which advanced in excellent fair array with many trumpets and clarions sounding. Then these English uttered a horrible and terrible cry, shouting with all their voices: "Talbot, Talbot, Saint George!"...

Then the English, by reason of the great number of artillery which the French had within their park and which played upon them with all their might, began to fall into disorder; for at the entrance there ... some five or six hundred English were slain, which caused them great fear and rout; seeing which the French opened the gate of their park and sallied forth, not only there but by the other gates and over the ditches. Then they came valiantly to fight the English hand to hand, where marvellous deeds of arms were done on either side. In this sally the aforesaid lord Talbot ... was slain by a dagger thrust in the throat, for he had already received a stroke across his face and was sore wounded with arrows through the thighs and the legs; and I have been assured ... that in that fight four thousand men or more were slain with Talbot.... The rest, seeing this defeat, withdrew; some within the town of Châtillon, and others fleeing through the woods and through the river, wherein great numbers were drowned. Moreover a good two hundred were taken prisoners....

Matthew d'Escouchy (ca. 1425—ca. 1480), *Chronicle*[16]

The Passive Resistance
of a Corrupt Convent of Nuns (1455)

When we first attempted to reform the convent of nuns at Wennigsen in the diocese of Minden, of the order of Canons Regular, we found the bishop of Minden and the great men of the country against us everywhere in the towns, but Duke William the Elder of Brunswick was on our side, together with the authority of the pope and the council of Basle.

This Duke William entered into the nuns' choir together with his chief counsellor Ludolph von Barum, Prior Roger of Wittenberg, and myself. Here the lord duke, removing his hat, said to the nuns assembled in our presence with their prioress: "My lady prioress and all you sisters! It is my will that you accept the reform and observe your rule." They, standing with hands folded on their breasts, made answer with one voice: "We have all alike determined and sworn together that we will not reform ourselves nor observe our rule. We beg you not to compel us to perjure ourselves." Then the duke said: "That is a bad answer; reconsider it."

Then the nuns left the choir but returned hastily, fell at his feet with arms folded, and made the same answer: "We have sworn together that we will not keep the reform. We beg you not to make us perjured." ... Then I said to the duke: "What profit have we from standing here and wrangling with the nuns? Let us leave the choir and take counsel what we should do next." So we left the choir and went into the dormitory.

At this the nuns with one accord immediately lay down flat upon the choir pavement, with arms and legs outstretched in the form of a cross, and at the top of their voices they chanted from beginning to end the antiphon *Media vita*—"In the midst of life we are in death" [from the funeral service, to curse the intruders with an evil death]....

I said to the duke: "... We are few here, for there are but four of us, and the nuns are many. If they assaulted us with their distaffs and with stones bound up in their long sleeves, what could we do? Let more be called to hear them with us."

Then the duke went alone into their choir and said: "You sing this upon your own bodies and souls!" And to his servants, who stood with the nuns in the choir, he said: "Come in here with us"; so they hurried out at once to join us. Then the nuns, who had ended their anthem, followed those servants to us, for they believed that we meant to break open their chests and boxes and to carry the [illegal] contents off with us. When they were therefore all assembled before us, the duke said: "How dare you sing that anthem *Media vita* over me? Here I stretch out my fingers to God's holy gospels and swear that you must reform yourselves or I will no longer permit you to live in my dominions."

[After many delays and another lie-in, the nuns finally agreed to reform.]

Johann Busch (1399–1480), *Autobiography of a Reformer*[17]

Sigismondo Malatesta: "The Infamy of our Times" (1459)

Sigismondo [1417-1468, lord of Rimini], of the noble family of the Malatesta but illegitimate, was very vigorous in body and mind, eloquent, and gifted with great military ability. He had a thorough knowledge of history and no slight acquaintance with philosophy. Whatever he attempted he seemed born for, but the evil part of his character had the upper hand.

He was such a slave to avarice that he was ready not only to plunder but to steal. His lust was so unbridled that he violated his daughters and his sons-in-law. When he was a lad he often played the bride and after taking the woman's part debauched men. No marriage was sacred to him. He ravished nuns and outraged Jewesses; boys and girls who would not submit to him he had murdered or savagely beaten. He committed adultery with many women to whose children he had been godfather and murdered their husbands.

He outdid all barbarians in cruelty. His bloody hand inflicted terrible punishments on innocent and guilty alike. He oppressed the poor, plundered the rich, spared neither widows nor orphans. No one felt safe under his rule. Wealth or a beautiful wife or handsome children were enough to cause a man to be accused of crime.

He hated priests and despised religion. He had no belief in another world and thought the soul died with the body. Nevertheless he built at Rimini a splendid church [designed by Alberti] dedicated to Saint Francis, though he filled it so full of pagan works of art that it seemed less a Christian sanctuary than a temple of heathen devil worshippers. In it he erected for his mistress a tomb of magnificent marble and exquisite worksmanship with an inscription in pagan style as follows, "Sacred to the deified Isotta."

The two wives he had married before he took Isotta for his mistress he killed one after the other with the sword or poison. The third, whom he married before these, he divorced before he had intercourse with her but kept her dowry. Meeting not far from Verona a noble lady who was going from Germany to Rome in the jubilee year [1450], he assaulted her (for she was very beautiful), and when she struggled, he left her wounded and covered with blood....

When his subjects once begged him to retire at last to a peaceful life and spare his country, which had so often been exposed to pillage on his account, he replied, "Go and be of good courage; never while I live shall you have peace."

Such was Sigismondo, intolerant of peace, a devotee of pleasure, able to endure any hardship, and greedy for war. Of all men who have ever lived or ever will live he was the worst scoundrel, the disgrace of Italy, and the infamy of our times.

Pope Pius II (1458-1464), *Commentaries*[18]

The Ballad Bequeathed to Fat Margot (ca. 1462)

Because I love and serve a whore sans glose,
Think not therefore or knave or fool am I:
She hath in her such goods as no man knows.
For love of her, buckler and blade I ply:
When clients come, I fetch a pot nearby
And get me gone for wine, without word said:
Before them water, fruit, bread, cheese, I spread.
If they pay well, I bid them "Well, God aid!
Come here again, when you by lust are led,
In this the brothel where we ply our trade."

But surely before long an ill wind blows
When, coinless, Margot comes by me to lie.
I hate the sight of her, catch up her hose,
Her gown, her surcoat and her girdle-tie,
Swearing to pawn them, meat and drink to buy.
She grips me by the throat and cuffs my head,
Cries "Antichrist!" and swears by Jesus dead,
It shall not be: till I, to quell the jade,
A potsherd seize and score her nose with red,
In this the brothel where we ply our trade.

Then she, peace made, to show we're no more foes,
A hugeous crack of wind at me lets fly
And laughing sets her fist against my nose,
Bids me "Go to" and claps me on the thigh;
Then, drunk, like logs we sleep till, by and by,
Awaking, when her womb is hungered,
To spare the child beneath her girdlestead
She mounts on me, flat as a pancake laid.
With wantoning she wears me to the thread
In this the brothel where we ply our trade.

Envoi

Hail, rain, freeze, ready baked I hold my bread:
Well worth a lecher with a wanton wed!
Which one's the worse? They differ not a shred.
Ill cat to ill rat; each for each was made.
We flee from honor; it from us hath fled:
Lewdness we love, that stands us well in stead,
In this the brothel where we ply our trade.

François Villon (died after 1463), *The Testament 1468*[19]

Some Good Years (1462–1463)

In the year 1462 nothing material or worth recording happened, and therefore I have passed over it in silence. Similarly, nothing happened worth taking notice of in the year 1463, unless it was the shortness of the winter and the length of the summer, which was extremely pleasant and very favorable to the vines, so that we had plenty of good wine that year, but a great scarcity of all other fruits of the earth.

Jean de Roye, *The Scandalous Chronicle* (1460–1483)[20]

Musetta, The Pope's Bitch (1463)

Here I shall insert a very trifling matter but one not wholly without its use, since through referring to small things it may serve to furnish counsel for great ones. [Pope] Pius had a little bitch not yet eleven months old named Musetta. It was not extraordinarily handsome but pretty and charming, and it knew how to win its way and make itself liked. While the pope was sitting in the garden hearing embassies, the dog, who was sniffing about hunting for something to eat, jumped up on the edge of a cistern and fell into the water. No one saw it fall, and when it was tired out with swimming it was on the point of drowning. It barked for help but no one came; they thought it was just barking as usual. The pope, hearing the dog's repeated cries and thinking something had happened to it, told his servants to hurry and see what it was. The dog was found at its last gasp no longer able to keep itself up and was rescued and taken to the pope to whom it continued to whimper for a long time as if it wanted to tell about its danger and stir the pope's pity.

The next day when the pope was dining in the same garden, a large monkey that had happened to get loose set upon the dog and bit it. The servants who were standing by rescued it with difficulty from the beast's jaws. Almost dead with fright the dog again seemed to be lamenting and moaning to the pope. The pope thought these were signs that the dog could not survive, since within a few days it had twice narrowly escaped death. And he was right.

A fortnight passed. The dog, as it often did, climbed up on the sill of a very high window overlooking the vineyard. Suddenly there arose a violent and terrifying whirlwind which seized the dog, hurled it outside, and dashed it dead on the rocks. When the pontiff heard this he said: "It was decreed that the puppy should die a violent death. This was predicted by its two escapes from danger: it could not escape a third. We find in animals examples from which men may learn. If anyone escapes two dangers, let him beware of a third. After two warnings he should know that the third is peremptory. Let him correct his way of life before he is summoned by a third. A dog who has no conscience to reproach it awaits death unafraid."

Pope Pius II (1458-1464), *Commentaries*[21]

The Dangers of Summitry: The Péronne Interview (1468)

[Burgundy and France were at war. To arrange a peace] it was concluded that the king [of France, Louis XI] should proceed to Péronne (which was the place he had recommended); and for his better security the duke [Charles the Bold of Burgundy] wrote a safe conduct for the king with his own hand.... The king came there without any guard other than the duke of Burgundy's safe conduct and word of honor.... Very few of the king's own retinue came along with him; however his majesty was attended by several persons of high rank.... When the king approached Péronne, the duke went out (very well attended) to meet him, conducted him into the town, and lodged him at the tax collector's, who had a fine house not far from the castle; for the lodgings in the castle were small and inconvenient....

The duke of Burgundy had sent for his army [which had many enemies of the king among the officers].... By the duke's orders, it encamped in the fields.... The king presently heard that all these persons
were at Péronne in the service of Burgundy, and he was greatly upset so
he sent to the duke asking that he might be lodged in the castle, for he
knew those gentlemen were his mortal enemies. The duke was extremely glad to hear it, assigned him his own lodgings, and assured him
by messenger that he had nothing to fear....

The two princes deputed some of their counsellors to meet and negotiate their affairs as amicably as possible. But when the negotiations
were well underway, and three or four days had already been spent in
bringing the treaty to a conclusion, news arrived of a strange turn of affairs at Liége.... The king at his coming to Péronne had quite forgotten
that he had sent two agents to Liége to stir up a rebellion against the
duke [and now news arrived that they had been most successful]....

All this [including the names of the king's agents] was reported to
the duke, and he believed it immediately. Becoming violently angry at
the king, he claimed that the meeting at Péronne was a ruse. He ordered
the gates both of the town and castle to be shut up immediately, and as
an excuse he announced that this was done to recover a lost casket which
contained money and jewels of great value.

When the king saw himself shut up in the castle and guards posted
at the gates, and especially when he found himself lodged near a certain
tower in which a count of Vermandois had caused an earlier king of
France [Charles the Simple] to be put to death [in 929], he was in great
apprehension.

I was at that time waiting upon the duke of Burgundy in the capacity of chamberlain, and (when I pleased) I slept in his chamber, as was
the custom of that family. When the duke saw the gates were shut, he
ordered the room to be cleared and told those of us who remained that
the king had come to Péronne to put him off his guard; that he himself
had never approved of the interview but had agreed only to please the
king. Then he told us what had happened at Liége.... He was much in-
censed and threatened his majesty exceedingly; and I am of the opinion
that if he had then had such persons about him as would have stirred up
his anger and encouraged him to any violence upon the king's person,
he would certainly have done it, or at least have committed him to the

tower. None were present at the speaking of these words but myself and two grooms of his chamber.... We did not exacerbate but smoothed his temper as much as we possibly could.

Some time later he expressed himself similarly to other people, and the news being carried about the town, it came at last to the king's ear, and he was terrified; and indeed everybody else was anxious, foreseeing a great deal of trouble and reflecting on how many things would have to be worked out if these two powerful princes were to be reconciled....

The king thought himself to be a prisoner in the castle of Péronne, as he had good reason to do, for all the gates were shut and guarded, and they continued so for two or three days. During that time the duke of Burgundy did not see the king and would allow just a few of his majesty's servants to be admitted into the castle and only by the wicket; but none of them were removed from his presence. Also, none of the duke's men were permitted to speak with the king or come into his chamber, at least none who had any authority with their master.

The first day there was great murmuring and anxiety all over the town. The second, the duke's anger began to cool a little, and a councel was called that sat the greater part of that day and night too. [Finally the councel advised that the peace treaty should be concluded if the king would stop supporting the rebels in Liége.] ...

The third night after this had happened, the duke of Burgundy did not take off his clothes but only lay on his bed two or three times, then got up again, and walked about, as was his habit when upset. That night I lay in his chamber and walked around with him several times. The next morning he was angrier than ever, was full of threats, and seemed ready to commit some outrageous act; but at last he collected himself, and it came to this conclusion: that if the king would swear to the peace, accompany him to Liége, and assist him to revenge the injuries which the rebels had done him and the bishop of Liége, his kinsman, he would be contented.

Having resolved on this, he went immediately to the king's chamber to confront him with his resolutions. When the duke came into the royal presence, his voice trembled with emotion, so prone was he to be angry again. However, he made a low bow with his body, although his gestures and words were sharp. [Louis readily agreed to everything, the peace was signed] and all the bells in the town were rung.

Philip de Commynes (d. 1511), *Memoirs*[22]

Wine and a Humanist of the Italian Renaissance
(1475)

A supper or a lunch without drink is considered not only disagreeable but indeed unwholesome, for a draught for a thirsty man is more pleasing than food for a hungry man, and more delightful. It is necessary to moisten food and to cool the lungs, so that what we consume is better worked and digested. Androchides, writing to Alexander, restraining his intemperance, called wine the blood of the earth which, when taken internally, has the virtue of warming and moistening, and when applied externally, of cooling and drying.

Now its virtue is warm and moist, so Homer called it *aithôpa oinon* ["fiery wine"] because it has the element of warmth. Thus it is that nothing succours weary bodies more readily if taken in moderation; nothing, however, is more harmful if there is no restraint. For because of drunkenness, men become trembling, weighed down, pallid, foul with impurities, forgetful, blear-eyed, sterile, slow to beget, gray-haired, bald, and old before their time. Therefore there must be some limit, according to the age and season of the year....

As to the system of preparing wines, let it be asked of the country folk found in the different regions. Let us be content to enumerate briefly the wines that are highly valued. I urge my readers beforehand, though, not to think that on account of this I am very greedy for wine, for by custom and by nature no one drinks more sparingly than I. The ancients used to praise the wines of their times.... And we shall praise without controversy or restraint the Ligurian wines, and especially those which originate on the shores of Genoa. For they are mild and of a most pleasant flavor, and there is nothing to prevent my calling it nectar.... Nor will I deny that wines from Picenum or Campania or all the other regions of Italy are worthy of their fame, but enough mention has been made of these, lest it might be said of our age, with no apology, that it produced better wines than men.

Bartolomeo Platina, *Respectable Pleasures* (1475)[23]

"Who Errs and Mends" (1483)

[The strong Scots nobility insisted that the king was bound by law. Some of the nobles held hereditary charters from the crown that empowered them to execute justice within their jurisdictions "absolutely," i.e. without appeal to the king. An English writer exemplified this situation with the story of] the earl of Morton's charter, which James III [king of Scotland, 1460–1488] tore openly, being offended with the absoluteness thereof, especially with this part of no appellation to the prince … but before he removed from the place where he tore it, he was forced by the nobility to sit down, and sew it up again with his own hand; and for that cause it is called yet the sewed charter.

The General State of the Scottish Commonwealth (ca. 1580)[24]

Louis the Spider and his Astrologer (1483)

An astrologer once cleverly extricated himself from a trap set for him by Louis XI, king of France [1461-1483]. This astrologer had predicted that a woman whom the king loved would die within eight days. When this happened, the king summoned the astrologer and commanded his guards to be ready to seize the man and throw him out the window if the king gave them a signal. When the astrologer arrived, the king said to him, "Can you, who claim to be such a clever man and who know so precisely the fate of others, tell me right now what your own fate shall be and how much longer you have to live?" Either the astrologer had been secretly warned of the king's plan or he guessed it. "Sire," he replied with no sign of fright, "I shall die three days before your majesty." After this response, the king was careful not to give any sort of signal to have him thrown out the window; instead, he saw to it that the man had everything he needed to live a long life.

Edme Boursault (1638–1701), *Letters*[25]

The King Who Became a Scullion (1487)

[The claim of Henry VII Tudor to the crown of England was disputed by one Lambert Simnel, a young boy who pretended to be the earl of Warwick, the Yorkist heir to the throne. He was crowned in Dublin but defeated at Stoke when he came to England.] There were taken prisoners amongst others the counterfeit Plantagenet, now Lambert Symnell again, and the crafty priest his tutor. For Lambert, the king would not take his life, both out of magnanimity, taking him but as an image of wax that others had tempered and moulded; and likewise out of wisdom, thinking that if he suffered death he would be forgotten too soon; but being kept alive he would be a continual spectacle and a kind of remedy against the enchantments of people in time to come. For which cause he was taken into service in his court to a base office in his kitchen; so that (in a kind of *mattacina* [dance] of human fortune) he turned a broach [spit] that had worn a crown. Whereas fortune commonly doth not bring in a comedy or farce after a tragedy. And afterwards he was preferred to be one of the king's falconers. As to the priest, he was committed close prisoner and heard of no more, the king loving to seal up his own dangers [i.e. keep them secret].

Francis Bacon, *The History of King Henry the Seventh* (1622)[26]

Savonarola's Last Chance (1498)

[In 1498, as Savonarola was about to be burned at the stake, he was excommunicated by the bishop] one Fra Benedetto Paganotti of the Dominicans, who had once been a friar of Saint Mark's [which was Savonarola's convent in Florence] and who had been one of Savonarola's admirers. While fulfilling his office, the bishop said, because he was so distraught: "I separate you from the Church Militant and from the Church Triumphant." The friar [Savonarola] respectfully corrected him in his usual tranquil voice: "Only from the Church Militant; the other doesn't depend on you." The good bishop laughed off his error.

Bartolomeo Cerretani, *Florentine History* (1512–1514)[27]

The Sixteenth Century

A Stag Story (1499–1514)

[King Louis XII of France (1498–1515) married Anne of Brittany, who had been the wife of his predecessor.] As she became more. experienced, her power grew under Louis XII until it reached the point that she even interfered in the most important affairs of state. The king, perhaps to make her seem less presumptuous, explained that he let her interfere "because one must bear much from a wife when she loves her honour and her husband."

But on several occasions he did not give her what she wanted because that would not have been in the best interest of the state.... Once she kept on pestering her husband incessantly until he grew tired of putting her off with promises and finally had to shut her up with this fable: "I must inform you, dear wife, that when God created the world, he gave horns to the does as well as to the stags, but when the females saw their heads were so well endowed, they took it upon themselves to lay down the law. Such behaviour made God so indignant that he took away this ornament to punish their arrogance."

François de Mézeray, *History of France* (1646)[1]

How a Friar was Inspired to Bear Arms (ca. 1500)

With great vehemence of words, fra Roberto da Lecce stirred up the princes and the people against the Turks and other enemies of the Christian faith. He became much affected by his own discourse and at the height of his eloquence began to weep because no one was offering himself for the holy cause. Thereupon he said: "If needs must be, here am I, who am not afraid of removing my habit and offering myself as a soldier." So saying, he divested himself of his habit and showed himself all armed in gleaming white armour with a sword at his side. And, thus arrayed as a captain of soldiery, he preached for half an hour. Asked by some cardinals with whom he was familiar what new idea was this, he replied that he had done it to please his ladylove, who had confided in him that the only thing she did not like in him was his friar's habit. And when he had asked her how she wished him dressed, she had said as a warrior and begged him to preach armed.

Lodovico Domenichi, *Facetie* (1562)[2]

The Roman Hierarchy (ca. 1500)

The worst men in the world live in Rome, and worse than the others are the priests, and the worst of the priests they make cardinals, and the worst of all the cardinals is made pope.

Lodovico Domenichi, *Facetie* (1562)[3]

Scholastic Complaints Against Humanism: A Satire (1517)

Magister Konrad Unckebunck sends to Magister Ortwin Gratius [at Cologne] abundant greetings [from Rome]....

I have learnt that you have of pupils but a few and complain that Buschius and Caesarius [two humanists] lure the students from you—notwithstanding that they lack your skill to expound the poets allegorically and to cite ccriptural parallels. The devil, I do believe, is in those poets. They are the bane of the universities.

An old magister of Leipzig, who has been master for these thirty years, told me that when he was a lad, then did the university greatly prosper: those were the days when there was not a poet within twenty miles. He told me, too, how the students then diligently attended lectures—whether public or bursarial; it was deemed a great scandal that the student should walk in the street without having Peter of Spain or the *Parva Logicalia* under his arm; or, if they were grammarians, then they would carry with them Alexander's *Doctrinale*.... Then were there zealous students in the schools, who held the masters of arts in honour, and if they spied a magister they fell to trembling as if they had seen a devil. He told me that in those days there were four promotions of bachelors each year, and many a time fifty or sixty graduated at once.

In those days the university was in full bloom; and when a student had resided for a year and a half, he was made bachelor, and after three years, or two and a half years in all, a magister. Thus it came to pass that his parents were well pleased and freely sent him money when they saw that their son had attained a place of honor. But nowadays all the students must needs attend lectures on Virgil and Pliny and the rest of the newfangled authors—what is more they may listen to them for five years and yet get no degree: and so, when they return home, their parents ask them, saying, "What are you?" And they reply that they are nothing but that they have been reading poetry! And then the parents are perplexed—but they see that their sons are not grammarians, and therefore they are disgruntled at the university and begrudge sorely the money they have spent. Then they say to others, "Send not your sons to the university—they'll learn nothing but go traipsing in the streets anights; money given for such a bringing-up is but thrown away."

The old magister furthermore told me that in his time there were full two thousand students at Leipzig and a like number at Erfurt; four thousand at Vienna and as many at Cologne—and so on with the rest. Nowadays there are not as many students at all the universities put together as there were then in one or two. The magisters at Leipzig bitterly lament the scarcity of scholars. It is the poets that do them this hurt. Even when students are sent by their parents to hostels and colleges they will not stay there but are off to the poets to learn stuff and nonsense. He told me that at Leipzig he used to have two score pupils, and when he went to the church or to the market, or to stroll in the Rose Garden, they would all follow after him.

In those days it was a grave offence to study poetry. If a penitent admitted in the confessional that he had privily listened to a bachelor lecturing upon Virgil, the priest would impose upon him a thumping penance—to wit, to fast every Friday, or to rehearse daily the seven penitential Psalms. He swore to me on his conscience that he saw a candidate rejected because he had once been detected by one of the examiners reading Terence on a holiday.

Would that it were thus in the universities now; then I should not have to drudge here at the curia. For what work is there for us at the universities? We cannot make a living. Students no longer will dwell in hostels under magisters. Among twenty students you will scarce find one with a mind to graduate. Yet all of them are eager to study the humanities. When a magister lectures he finds no audience; but, as for the poets, when they discourse it is a marvel to behold the crowd of listeners.

And thus the universities throughout all Germany are diminished and brought low. Let us pray God, then, that all the poets may perish, for "it is expedient that one man should die" [John 11:50]—i.e. that the poets, of whom there are but a handful in any one university, should die—rather than so many universities should perish....

The Letters of Obscure Men (1517)[4]

Notes

1 "Je n'aime de l'histoire que les anecdotes": Prosper Mérimée, quoted as titlepage motto by E. Guérard, *Dictionnaire encyclopédique d'anecdotes modernes, anciennes, françaises et étrangères*, 2nd ed. (Paris, 1872).

2 Petrus Alfonsi, *Disciplina clericalis*, ed. A. Hilka and W. Söderhjelm, Sammlung mittellateinisher Texte no. 1 (Heidelberg, 1911); trans. Joseph Ramon Jones and John Esten Keller, *The Scholar's Guide: A Translation of the Twelfth-Century Disciplina clericalis of Pedro Alfonso* (Toronto: Pontifical Institute of Mediaeval Studies, 1969), p. 34.

3 Francesco Petrarca, *Secretum meum* 3, ed. E. Carrara in Francesco Petrarca *Prose*, ed. G. Martellotti et al., La Letteratura italiana: Storia e testi, vol. 7 (Milan-Naples, 1955), pp. 190, 192; trans. William H. Draper, *Petrarch's Secret, or, The Soul's Conflict with Passion; Three Dialogues between himself and S. Augustine* (London, 1911), pp. 168-169.

Notes to pages 11–19

1 Anonymous, *Epitome de Caesaribus* 39.5-6 in Sextus Aurelius Victor, *Liber de Caesaribus*, ed. Fr. Pichlmayr, rev. R. Gruendel (Leipzig: B. G. Teubner, 1970), pp. 163-164; trans. «Oliver Phillips».

2 Eusebius of Pamphylia (260-340), bishop of Caesarea, *De vita beatissimi imperatoris Constantini* 1.27-32, ed. J. P. Migne, *Patrologia Graeca* 20:942-947; trans. Ernest C. Richardson, *The Life of Constantine the Great* in *Select Library of Nicene and Post-Nicene Fathers of the Christian Church*, 2d ser., vol. 1 (New York, 1890), pp. 489-491, rev. R. Kay.

3 *Constitutum Constantini* 6-7, 17-18, ed. K. Mirbt, *Quellen zur Geschichte des Papsttums* (Freiburg, 1895), no. 228, pp. 107-112; trans. E. F. Henderson, *Select Historical Documents of the Middle Ages*, Bohn's Antiquarian Library (London, 1892), pp. 322, 328.

4 Athanasius, patriarch of Alexandria, as quoted by Theodoret, *Historia ecclesiastica* 1.13 (14), ed. J. P. Migne, *Patrologia Graeca* 82:949-950; trans. [anon.], *A History of the Church ... by Theodoret ... and Evagrius*, Bohn's Ecclesiastical Library (London, 1854), pp. 50-51, rev. R. Kay.

5 Theodoretus, bishop of Cyrrhus in Syria (ca. 393--ca. 458), *Historia ecclesiastica* 3.20 (25), ed. J. P. Migne, *Patrologia Graeca* 82:1117-20; trans. [anon.] *A History of the Church ... by Theodoret ... and Evagrius*, Bohn's Ecclesiastical Library (London, 1854), pp. 150-151.

6   Aurelius Augustinus, *Confessiones* 2.4, ed. P. Knöll, Bibliotheca Teubneriana (Leipzig, 1909); trans. R. Kay.

7   Jerome, *Epistolae* 22.30 (= Epistola ad Eustochium), ed. F. A. Wright, *Select Letters of St. Jerome*, Loeb Classical Library (London, 1933), pp. 124-128; trans. W. H. Fremantle et al., *The Principal Works of St. Jerome*, in *Select Library of Nicene and Post-Nicene Fathers of the Christian Church*, 2d ser., vol. 6 (New York, 1893), p. 35, rev. R. Kay.

8   *Legenda Aurea*, Dec. 7; trans. Granger Ryan and Helmut Ripperger (London: Longmans, Green & Co., 1941; reprinted by the Arno Press, New York, 1969), pp. 25-26, rev. R. Kay «Lynn Nelson».

9   Jordanes, *Getica* 24.121-122, ed. T. Mommsen, *Monumenta Germaniae Historica*, Auctores Antiquissimi, 5.l (Berlin, 1882), p. 89; trans. C. C. Mierow, *The Gothic History of Jordanes* (Princeton, 1915), p. 85.

10 Paulinus Mediolanensis, *Vita Sancti Ambrosii* 7.24, ed. and trans. M. S. Kaniecka, Patristic Studies, vol. l6 (Washington, 1928), pp. 64-67 «John Lomax».

Notes to pages 20–33

1   Bede, *Historia ecclesiastica gentis Anglorum* 1.11-12, ed. R. A. B. Mynors, Oxford Medieval Texts (Oxford, 1969); *The Ecclesiastical History of the English Nation by the Venerable Bede*, trans. John Stevens, rev. J. A. Giles, Everyman's Library (New York, 1910), pp. 16-17, rev. R. Kay. Bede copied the first paragraph from Orosius, *Adversum paganos* 7.40.

2   Zosimus, *Historia nova* 5.40, ed. L. Mendelssohn (Leipzig, 1887); trans. James J. Buchanan and Harold T. Davis, *Zosimus: Historia Nova; The Decline of Rome* (San Antonio, Texas: Trinity University Press, 1967), pp. 237-238, rev. R. Kay «Cynthia Shively».

3   Jordanes, *Getica* 30.157-158, ed. T. Mommsen, *Monumenta Germaniae historica*, Auctores antiquissimi, 5.1 (Berlin, 1882), p. 99; trans. C. C. Mierow, *The Origin and Deeds of the Goths* (Princeton, 1908), p. 49, rev. R. Kay «Robin S. Hackett».

4   Jordanes, *Getica* 31.159-160, 32.164-165, ed. T. Mommsen, *Monumenta Germaniae historica*, Auctores antiquissimi, 5.1 (Berlin, 1882), pp. 99-101; trans. C. C. Mierow, *The Origin and Deeds of the Goths* (Princeton, 1908), pp. 49-51 «Robin S. Hackett».

5   Bede, *Historia ecclesiastica gentis Anglorum* 1.5, ed. R. A. B. Mynors, Oxford Medieval Texts (Oxford, 1969), pp. 5l-53; trans. John Stevens, rev. J. A. Giles, *The Ecclesiastical History of the English Nation by the Venerable Bede*, Everyman's Library (New York, 1910), pp. 22-23, rev. R. Kay.

6   Joannes Antiochenus, *Chronicon,* fragment 199, and Priscus Panites, *Historia Byzantina,* fragments 15-16, ed. C. Müller, *Fragmenta historicorum Graecorum,* vol. 4 (Paris, 1868), pp. 98, 99, 613-614; trans. C. D. Gordon *The Age of Attila: Fifth-century Byzantium and the Barbarians* (Ann Arbor: University of Michigan Press, 1960), pp. 104-106, rev. R. Kay. The first two paragraphs are by John.

7   Gregory of Tours, *Historiae* 2.5-6 (6-7), ed. B. Krusch and W. Levison in *Opera = Monumenta Germaniae historica,* Scriptores rerum Merovingicarum, 1:1, 2nd edn. (Hanover, 1951), pp. 47-50; trans. O. M. Dalton, *The History of the Franks* (Oxford, 1927), 2:46-47.

8   Joannes Antiochenus, *Chronicon,* fragments 200-201, ed. C. Müller, *Fragmenta historicorum Graecorum,* vol. 4 (Paris, 1868), pp. 614-615; trans. C. D. Gordon, *The Age of Attila: Fifth-Century Byzantium and the Barbarians* (Ann Arbor: The University of Michigan Press, 1960), pp. 51-52, rev. R. Kay.

9   Jordanes, *Getica* 49.254, ed. T. Mommsen, *Monumenta Germaniae Historica,* Auctores Antiquissimi, 5.l (Berlin, 1882), pp. 123-124; trans. C. C. Mierow, *The Gothic History of Jordanes* (Princeton, 1915), p. 123, rev. R. Kay. The story is taken from the Byzantine historian Priscus (fl. 449-472); the epigraph is also from Priscus «Dudley Stutz».

10   Eugippus, *Vita sancti Severini* 6-7, 32, ed. H. Sauppe in *Monumenta Germaniae historica,* Auctores antiquissimi, 1:2 (Berlin, 1877), pp. 11, 24; trans. George W. Robinson, *The Life of Saint Severinus,* Harvard Translations (Cambridge, 1914), pp. 45-46, 86-87, rev. R. Kay «John T. Brothers».

11   Jordanes, *Getica* 45.241-46.243, ed. T. Mommsen, *Monumenta Germaniae Historica,* Auctores Antiquissimi, 5.l (Berlin, 1882), p. 120; trans. C. C. Mierow, *The Gothic History of Jordanes* (Princeton, 1915), p. 119.

12   Gregory of Tours, *Historia Francorum* 2.27, ed. B. Krusch and W. Levison in *Opera = Monumenta Germaniae historica,* Scriptores rerum Merovingicarum, 1:1, 2nd edn. (Hanover, 1951), pp. 72-73; trans. Ernest Brehaut, *History of the Franks,* Records of Civilization no. 2 (New York, 1916), pp. 37-38, rev. R. Kay.

13   Jordanes, *Getica* 57.290-292, ed. T. Mommsen, *Monumenta Germaniae Historica,* Auctores Antiquissimi, 5.l (Berlin, 1882), p. 133; trans. C. C. Mierow, *The Gothic History of Jordanes* (Princeton, 1915), pp. 135-136. The epigraph echos Horace Greeley.

14   Gregory of Tours, *Historiae* 2.42, ed. B. Krusch and W. Levison in *Opera = Monumenta Germaniae historica,* Scriptores rerum Merovingicarum, 1:1, 2nd edn. (Hanover, 1951), pp. 92-93; trans. O. M. Dalton, *The History of the Franks* (Oxford, 1927), 2:80-81, rev. R. Kay.

15 Nennius, *Historia Britonum* 96, ed. E. Faral, *La Légende arthurienne: Études et documents*, pt. 1: *Les Plus anciens textes*, vol. 3, Bibliothèque de l'École des hautes études 257 (Paris, 1929), pp. 38-39; trans. R. Kay. This is the earliest surviving mention of Arthur by name. Nennius, a Welshman, seems to have reworked an earlier compilation that included the Arthurian material. The Welsh tradition that lies behind this Latin work probably had Arthur bearing the Virgin's image on his shield (*ysgwydd*) rather than on his shoulders (*ysgwyd*). Arthur's date is based on Bede, *Historia ecclesiastica* 1:16

16 Joannes Antiochenus, *Chronicon*, fragment 214a, ed. C. Müller, *Fragmenta historicorum Graecorum*, vol. 5 (Paris, 1870), p. 29; trans. C. D. Gordon, *The Age of Attila: Fifth-century Byzantium and the Barbarians* (Ann Arbor: The University of Michigan Press, 1960), pp. 182-183.

17 Gregory the Great, *Dialogi* 2.prol.l, ed. A. de Vogüé, *Dialogues*, vol. 2, Sources chrétiennes, no. 260 (Paris, 1979), pp. 126-127; trans. M. L. Uhlfelder, *The Dialogues of Gregory the Great, Book Two: Saint Benedict*, Library of Liberal Arts, no. 216 (Indianapolis: Bobbs-Merrill, 1967), p. 3.

18 Gregory the Great, *Dialogi* 2.2.1-3, ed. A. de Vogüé, *Dialogues*, vol. 2, Sources chrétiennes 260 (Paris, 1979), pp. 136-139; trans. M. L. Uhlfelder, *The Dialogues of Gregory the Great, Book Two: Saint Benedict*, Library of Liberal Arts 216 (Indianapolis: Bobbs-Merrill, 1967), p. 6-7.

19 Gregory of Tours, *Historiae* 2.30-31, ed. B. Krusch and W. Levison in *Opera = Monumenta Germaniae historica*, Scriptores rerum Merovingicarum, 1:1, 2nd edn. (Hanover, 1951), pp. 75-77; trans. O. M. Dalton, *The History of the Franks* (Oxford, 1927), 2:68-70, rev. R. Kay.

Notes to pages 34–58

1 Gregory of Tours, *Historiae* 2.37, ed. B. Krusch and W. Levison in *Opera = Monumenta Germaniae historica*, Scriptores rerum Merovingicarum, 1:1, 2nd edn. (Hanover, 1951), pp. 85-88; trans. O. M. Dalton, *The History of the Franks* (Oxford, 1927), 2:75-77, rev. R. Kay.

2 Gregory the Great, *Dialogi* 2.6, ed. A. de Vogüé, *Dialogues*, vol. 2, Sources chrétiennes 260 (Paris, 1979), pp. 154-157; trans. M. L. Uhlfelder, *The Dialogues of Gregory the Great, Book Two: Saint Benedict*, Library of Liberal Arts 216 (Indianapolis: Bobbs-Merrill, 1967), pp. 13-14.

3   Gregory the Great, *Dialogi* 2.7.1-3, ed. A. de Vogüé, *Dialogues*, vol. 2, Sources chrétiennes 260 (Paris, 1979), pp. 157-160; trans. M. L. Uhlfelder, *The Dialogues of Gregory the Great, Book Two: Saint Benedict*, Library of Liberal Arts 216 (Indianapolis: Bobbs-Merrill, 1967), pp. 14-15 «John Lomax». Benedict had his monks vow to obey their abbot without question: see his *Rule* 58.17 and 5.1.

4   Procopius, *Anecdota*, ch. 9 (9-10), ed. J. Haury, *Procopii Caesariensis Opera omnia*, Bibliotheca Teubneriana, vol. 3, rev. edn. (Leipzig, 1963), pp. 57-65; trans. Richard Atwater, *The Secret History of Procopius* (Chicago, 1927; rpt. Ann Arbor, 1963), pp. 46-52.

5   Procopius, *De bellis* 1.24.32-38, ed. and trans. H. B. Dewing, in *Works*, Loeb Classical Library (New York, 1914), 1:231-232.

6   Gregory the Great, *Dialogi* 2.14-15, ed. A. de Vogüé, *Dialogues*, vol. 2, Sources chrétiennes 260 (Paris, 1979), pp. 180-185; trans. M. L. Uhlfelder, *The Dialogues of Gregory the Great, Book Two: Saint Benedict*, Library of Liberal Arts 216 (Indianapolis: Bobbs-Merrill, 1967), pp. 22-24. Dated 546 by A. Mundó, *Revue bénédictine* 59 (1949), 203-206.

7   Procopius, *Anecdota* (= *Historia arcana*), chs. 8 and 13, ed. J. Haury, *Procopii Caesariensis Opera omnia*, Bibliotheca Teubneriana, vol. 3, rev. edn. (Leipzig, 1963), pp. 52-56, 88-89; trans. Richard Atwater, *The Secret History of Procopius* (Chicago, 1927; rpt. Ann Arbor, 1963), pp. 41-44, 70.

8   Gregory of Tours, *Historiae* 4.20-21, ed. B. Krusch and W. Levison in *Opera* = *Monumenta Germaniae historica,* Scriptores rerum Merovingicarum, 1:1, 2nd edn. (Hanover, 1951), pp. 153-154; trans. E. Brehaut, *History of the Franks*, Records of Civilization no. 2 (New York, 1916), pp. 85-86, rev. R. Kay.

9   Manus O'Donnell, chief of Tyrconnell, *Betha Colaim Chille* [Life of Columcille] 168; trans. A. Kelleher, *Zeitschrift für celtische Philologie* 9 (1909): 258-259, rev. R. Kay «James Ludwig». H. J. Lawlor argues for the substantial accuracy of this traditional account and identifies the transcript with the manuscript Psalter known as "The *Cathach* [= weapon] of St. Columba," now preserved in Dublin: *Proceedings of the Royal Irish Academy* 33, sec. C (1916-17): 241-436. Finnian's book seems to have been the Psalter in Jerome's Vulgate Latin translation, whereas the Irish up to then had known only the Old Latin version.

10 *Liber pontificalis* 63: *Vita papae Joannis III*, ed. L. Duchesne, *Le "Liber pontificalis"*, Bibliothèque des Écoles françaises d'Athènes et de Rome, ser. 2, no. 3, vol. 1 (Paris, 1886), p. 305; trans. Thomas Hodgkin, *Italy and Her Invaders*, vol. 5 (London, 1895), pp. 60-61, rev. R. Kay.

11 Paulus Diaconus, *Historia Langobardorum* 2.5, ed. G. Waitz, *Monumenta Germaniae historica*, Scriptores rerum Langobardicarum (Hanover, 1878), p. 75; trans. Thomas Hodgkin, *Italy and Her Invaders*, vol. 5 (London, 1895), pp. 61-62, rev. R. Kay. I hope to have clarified Narses' reply, which Hodgkin renders: "he would spin her such a hank (*talem se eidem telam orditurum*) that she should not be able to lay it down so long as she lived." For the technical senses of *tela* and *ordior*, see *The Oxford Latin Dictionary*. Although Narses most likely did not incite the Lombard invasion, the story that he did so is nonetheless contemporary.

12 Gregory of Tours, *De virtutibus sancti Martini episcopi* l.pr., ed. B. Krusch in *Gregorii episcopi Turonensis miracula et opera minora = Monumenta Germaniae historica*, Scriptores rerum Merovingicarum, vol. l, pt. 2, 2nd ed. (Hanover, 1969), pp. 135-136; trans. W. C. McDermott (1944), reprinted in *Monks, Bishops and Pagans: Christian Culture in Gaul and Italy, 500-700*, ed. Edward Peters (Philadelphia: University of Pennsylvania Press, 1975), pp. 133-134. What Gregory does here may be more sophisticated than he leads us to expect: e.g. the vision of his mother has a classical precedent in the dream of the Elder Pliny, in which he was urged by the Elder Drusus to write his biography (Pliny, *Epistolae* 3.5.4).

13 Gregory of Tours, *Historiae* 5.3, ed. B. Krusch and W. Levison in *Opera = Monumenta Germaniae historica*, Scriptores rerum Merovingicarum, 1:1, 2nd edn. (Hanover, 1951), pp. 196-198; trans. E. Brehaut, *History of the Franks*, Records of Civilization 2 (New York, 1916), pp. 106-108, rev. R. Kay.

14 Gregory of Tours, *Historiae* 5.5, ed. B. Krusch and W. Levison in *Opera = Monumenta Germaniae historica*, Scriptores rerum Merovingicarum, 1:1, 2nd edn. (Hanover, 1951), p. 200; trans. O. M. Dalton, *The History of the Franks* (Oxford, 1927), 2:172, rev. R. Kay.

15 William of Malmesbury, *De gestis regum Anglorum* l.45, ed. W. Stubbs, Rolls Series, no. 90, vol. l (London, 1887), pp. 45-46; trans. J. Sharpe (1815), rev. J. A. Giles, *William of Malmesbury's Chronicle of the Kings of England from the Earliest Period to the Reign of King Stephen*, Bohn's Antiquarian Library (London, 1847), p. 42 «Dudley Stutz». A longer and better known, but less circumstantial, version is given by Bede, *Ecclesiastical History* 2.l.

16 Gregory of Tours, *Historiae* 5.14, ed. B. Krusch and W. Levison in *Opera = Monumenta Germaniae historica*, Scriptores rerum Merovingicarum, 1:1, 2nd edn. (Hanover, 1951), pp. 211-212; trans. O. M. Dalton, *The History of the Franks* (Oxford, 1927), 2:182, rev. R. Kay.

17 Gregory of Tours, *Historiae* 6.4, ed. B. Krusch and W. Levison in *Opera = Monumenta Germaniae historica*, Scriptores rerum Merovingicarum, 1:1, 2nd edn. (Hanover, 1951), pp. 267-268; trans. O. M. Dalton, *The History of the Franks* (Oxford, 1927), 2:234, rev. R. Kay.

18 Gregory of Tours, *Historiae* 6.45, ed. B. Krusch and W. Levison in *Opera* = *Monumenta Germaniae historica*, Scriptores rerum Merovingicarum, 1:1, 2nd edn. (Hanover, 1951), pp. 317-318; trans. O. M. Dalton, *The History of the Franks* (Oxford, 1927), 2:276-277, rev. R. Kay.

19 Gregory of Tours, *Historiae* 5.17, 44, 6.46, ed. B. Krusch and W. Levison in *Opera* = *Monumenta Germaniae historica*, Scriptores rerum Merovingicarum, 1:1, 2nd edn. (Hanover, 1951), pp. 216, 252-255, 319-321; trans. O. M. Dalton, *The History of the Franks* (Oxford, 1927), 2:186, 217-218, 278-279, rev. R. Kay.

20 Gregory of Tours, *Historiae* 8.15, ed. B. Krusch and W. Levison in *Opera* = *Monumenta Germaniae historica*, Scriptores rerum Merovingicarum, 1:1, 2nd. edn. (Hanover, 1951), pp. 381-383; trans. E. Brehaut, *History of the Franks*, Records of Civilization 2 (New York, 1916), pp. 195-196, rev. R. Kay.

21 Adamnan, *Vita sancti Columbae abbatis* 2.41, ed. and trans. A. O. and M. O. Anderson, *Adomnan's Life of Columba* (London: Thomas Nelson and Sons, 1961), pp. 438-441, rev. R. Kay. For the date, see *ed. cit.*, p. 88.

22 Gregory of Tours, *Historiae* 8.20, ed. B. Krusch and W. Levison in *Opera* = *Monumenta Germaniae historica*, Scriptores rerum Merovingicarum, 1:1. 2nd edn. (Hanover, 1951), pp. 386-387; trans. O. M. Dalton, *The History of the Franks* (Oxford, 1927), 2:345, rev. R. Kay.

23 Gregory of Tours, *Historiae* 5.21, 8.34, ed. B. Krusch and W. Levison in *Opera* = *Monumenta Germaniae historica*, Scriptores rerum Merovingicarum, 1:1. 2nd edn. (Hanover, 1951), pp. 229, 403; trans. O. M. Dalton, *The History of the Franks* (Oxford, 1927), 2:197, 358-359.

24 Gregory of Tours, *Historiae* 9.15, ed. B. Krusch and W. Levison in *Opera* = *Monumenta Germaniae historica*, Scriptores rerum Merovingicarum, 1:1, 2nd edn. (Hanover, 1951), pp. 429-430; trans. O. M. Dalton, *The History of the Franks* (Oxford, 1927), 2:383-384, rev. R. Kay.

25 Gregory of Tours, *Historiae* 9.5, ed. B. Krusch and W. Levison in *Opera* = *Monumenta Germaniae historica*, Scriptores rerum Merovingicarum, 1:1, 2nd ed. (Hanover, 1951), p. 416; trans. O. M. Dalton, *The History of the Franks* (Oxford, 1927), 2:372.

26 Gregory of Tours, *Historiae* 9.33, ed. B. Krusch and W. Levison in *Opera* = *Monumenta Germaniae historica*, Scriptores rerum Merovingicarum, 1:1, 2nd edn. (Hanover, 1951), pp. 451-454; trans. O. M. Dalton, *The History of the Franks* (Oxford, 1927),2:403-404.

27 Gregory of Tours, *Historiae* 9.34, ed. B. Krusch and W. Levison in *Opera =
Monumenta Germaniae historica,* Scriptores rerum Merovingicarum, 1:1, 2nd edn.
(Hanover, 1951), pp. 454-455; trans. O. M. Dalton, *The History of the Franks* (Ox-
ford, 1927), 2:405-406, rev. R. Kay.

28 Adamnan, *Vita sancti Columbae abbatis* 1.23, 3.23, ed. and trans. A. O. and M. O.
Anderson, *Adomnan's Life of Columba* (London: Thomas Nelson and Sons, 1961),
pp. 256-257, 524-527.

29 "Fredegar," *Chronica* 4.20, ed. and trans. J. M. Wallace-Hadrill, *The Fourth Book
of the Chronicle of Fredegar with its Continuations*, Medieval Classics (London:
Thomas Nelson and Sons, 1960), pp. 12-13.

Notes to pages 59–82

1 Kai Kâ'ûs ibn Iskandar, prince of Gurgân, *Qâbûs-nâma* chs. 6-7; ed. and trans. from
the Persian by Reuben Levy, *A Mirror for Princes* (London: E. P. Dutton, 1951),
pp. 32-33, 39-40, rev. R. Kay «Lynn Nelson». Chosroës II reigned 589-628; I place
the incident during the period of his cordial relations with Byzantium, 591-602.

2 Gregory the Great, *Registrum epistolarum* 11.54, ed. J. P. Migne, *Patrologia latina,*
77:1171-1172; trans. J. Barmby in *A Select Library of Nicene and Post-Nicene Fathers
of the Christian Church*, 2nd ser., ed. P. Schaff and H. Wace, vol. 13 (New York,
1898), pp. 69-70, rev. R. Kay «Dudley Stutz. This letter became part of canon law:
Gratian, *Decretum*, Dist. 86, c.5.

3 *The Golden Legend or Lives of the Saints as Englished by William Caxton*, Temple
Classics, vol. 3 (London, 1900), p. 201, rev. R. Kay.

4 "Fredegar," *Chronica* 4.27, ed. and trans. J. M. Wallace-Hadrill, *The Fourth Book
of the Chronicle of Fredegar with its Continuations*, Medieval Classics (London:
Thomas Nelson and Sons, 1960), pp. 18-19.

5 Paulus Diaconus, *Historia Langobardorum* 4.37, ed. G. Waitz, *Monumenta Germaniae historica*, Scriptores rerum Langobardicarum (Hanover, 1878), pp. 128-
130; trans. William Dudley Foulke, *The History of the Langobards* by Paul the
Deacon, University of Pennsylvania Translations and Reprints, ser. 2, no. 3
(Philadelphia, 1907), pp. 179-184, rev. R. Kay.

6 "Fredegar," *Chronica* 4.42, ed. and trans. J. M. Wallace-Hadrill, *The Fourth Book
of the Chronicle of Fredegar with its Continuations*, Medieval Classics (London:
Thomas Nelson and Sons, 1960), pp. 34-35.

7 "Fredegar," *Chronica* 4.48, ed. and trans. J. M. Wallace-Hadrill, *The Fourth Book of the Chronicle of Fredegar with its Continuations*, Medieval Classics (London: Thomas Nelson and Sons, 1960), pp. 39-40.

8 "Fredegar," *Chronica* 4.51, ed. and trans. J. M. Wallace-Hadrill, *The Fourth Book of the Chronicle of Fredegar with its Continuations*, Medieval Classics (London: Thomas Nelson and Sons, 1960), pp. 41-43.

9 Bede, *Historia ecclesiastica gentis Anglorum* 2.12-13, ed. R. A. B. Mynors, Oxford Medieval Texts (Oxford, 1969); *The Ecclesiastical History of the English Nation by the Venerable Bede*, trans. John Stevens, rev. J. A. Giles, Everyman's Library (New York, 1910), pp. 89-92, rev. R. Kay.

10 "Fredegar," *Chronica* 4.59-60, ed. and trans. J. M. Wallace-Hadrill, *The Fourth Book of the Chronicle of Fredegar with its Continuations*, Medieval Classics (London: Thomas Nelson and Sons, 1960), p. 50.

11 Bede, *Historia ecclesiastica gentis Anglorum* 2.20, ed. R. A. B. Mynors, Oxford Medieval Texts (Oxford, 1969); *The Ecclesiastical History of the English Nation by the Venerable Bede*, trans. John Stevens, rev. J. A. Giles, Everyman's Library (New York, 1910), pp. 101-102, rev. R. Kay. This brief passage is the crux of Agnus Wilson's novel *Anglo-Saxon Attitudes*.

12 Isidore, *Etymologiae* 12.8.1-3, ed. W. M. Lindsay, *Isidori Hispalensis episcopi Etymologiarum sive originum libri XX* (Oxford, 1911), vol. 2; trans. «Oliver Phillips.

13 Bede, *Historia ecclesiastica gentis Anglorum* 3.9-10, ed. R. A. B. Mynors, Oxford Medieval Texts (Oxford, 1969); *The Ecclesiastical History of the English Nation by the Venerable Bede*, trans. John Stevens, rev. J. A. Giles, Everyman's Library (New York, 1910), pp. 117-118, rev. R. Kay.

14 'Ali ibn al-Kifti, *Ta'rikh al-Hukama*, ed. Julius Lippert (Leipzig, 1903), pp. 354-356; trans. Hussein Monés, in Edward Alexander Parsons, *The Alexandrian Library* (Amsterdam: Elsevier Press, 1952), pp. 390-392. The story is usually cited from Gregory, Abû'l Faraj, bar Hebraeus (1226-86), who however condensed it from the earlier account given here. Parsons quotes all the Arab sources *in extenso*, weighs the evidence, and, in opposition to most modern scholars, accepts the account as true, and assigns it to the year 642 «Oliver Phillips.

15 Virgilius Maro grammaticus, *Epistolae ad Julium Germanum diaconum* 2, ed. J. Huemer in his *Opera*, Bibliotheca Teubneriana (Leipzig, 1886), p. 123; trans. R. Kay «Twila Jukes». The author probably wrote in Toulouse in the seventh century; his "fan-

tastic" work must have been "a skit or parody on grammatical treatises": M. L. W. Laistner, *Thought and Letters in Western Europe A.D. 500 to 900*, 2nd ed. (London, 1957), pp. 176-177.

16   Bede, *Historia ecclesiastica gentis Anglorum* 3.17, ed. R. A. B. Mynors, Oxford Medieval Texts (Oxford, 1969); *The Ecclesiastical History of the English Nation by the Venerable Bede*, trans. John Stevens, rev. J. A. Giles, Everyman's Library (New York, 1910), p. 130, rev. R. Kay.

17   Bede, *Historia ecclesiastica gentis Anglorum* 3.18, ed. R. A. B. Mynors, Oxford Medieval Texts (Oxford, 1969); *The Ecclesiastical History of the English Nation by the Venerable Bede*, trans. John Stevens, rev. J. A. Giles, Everyman's Library (New York, 1910), pp. 131-132, rev. R. Kay. The date of the battle is uncertain, but Bede inserts this obituary between two others dated 651 and 653 (c.17 and c.20).

18   "Fredegar," *Chronica* 4.81, ed. and trans. J. M. Wallace-Hadrill, *The Fourth Book of the Chronicle of Fredegar with its Continuations*, Medieval Classics (London: Thomas Nelson and Sons, 1960), pp. 68-69.

19   Bede, *Historia ecclesiastica gentis Anglorum* 3.25, ed. R. A. B. Mynors, Oxford Medieval Texts (Oxford, 1969); *The Ecclesiastical History of the English Nation by the Venerable Bede*, trans. John Stevens, rev. J. A. Giles, Everyman's Library (New York, 1910), pp. 146-152, rev. R. Kay.

20   Bede, *Historia ecclesiastica gentis Anglorum* 4.19, ed. R. A. B. Mynors, Oxford Medieval Texts (Oxford, 1969); *The Ecclesiastical History of the English Nation by the Venerable Bede*, trans. John Stevens, rev. J. A. Giles, Everyman's Library (New York, 1910), p. 194, rev. R. Kay.

21   Continuator of the *Chronica* of "Fredegar," c.2 [written ca. 736], ed. and trans. J. M. Wallace-Hadrill, *The Fourth Book of the Chronicle of Fredegar with its Continuations*, Medieval Classics (London: Thomas Nelson and Sons, 1960), p. 81.

22   Bede, *Historia ecclesiastica gentis Anglorum* 4.13, ed. R. A. B. Mynors, Oxford Medieval Texts (Oxford, 1969); *The Ecclesiastical History of the English Nation by the Venerable Bede*, trans. John Stevens, rev. J. A. Giles, Everyman's Library (New York, 1910), pp. 184-185 [much altered by RLK].

23   Continuator of the *Chronica* of "Fredegar," c. 3 [written ca. 736] ed. and trans. J. M. Wallace-Hadrill, *The Fourth Book of the Chronicle of Fredegar with its Continuations*, Medieval Classics (London: Thomas Nelson and Sons, 1960), p. 83.

24 Bede, *Historia ecclesiastica gentis Anglorum* 4.24, ed. R. A. B. Mynors, Oxford Medieval Texts (Oxford, 1969); *The Ecclesiastical History of the English Nation by the Venerable Bede*, trans. John Stevens, rev. J. A. Giles, Everyman's Library (New York, 1910), pp. 205-207, rev. R. Kay. Although Old English poems on biblical themes do survive, only the original of the passages Bede translates here can be attributed to Caedmon with any certainty.

25 Continuator of the *Chronica* of "Fredegar," c. 5 [written ca. 736], ed. and trans. J. M. Wallace-Hadrill, *The Fourth Book of the Chronicle of Fredegar with its Continuations*, Medieval Classics (London: Thomas Nelson and Sons, 1960), p. 85.

26 Bede, *Historia ecclesiastica gentis Anglorum* 5.2, ed. R. A. B. Mynors, Oxford Medieval Texts (Oxford, 1969); *The Ecclesiastical History of the English Nation by the Venerable Bede*, trans. John Stevens, rev. J. A. Giles, Everyman's Library (New York, 1910), pp. 225-226, rev. R. Kay.

27 Bede, *Historia ecclesiastica gentis Anglorum* 5.9-11, ed. R. A. B. Mynors, Oxford Medieval Texts (Oxford, 1969); *The Ecclesiastical History of the English Nation by the Venerable Bede*, trans. John Stevens, rev. J. A. Giles, Everyman's Library (New York, 1910), pp. 235-241, rev. R. Kay.

Notes to pages 83–95

1 *Lex Alamannorum*, promulgated by Duke Lantfrid (712-730), Laws 50, 53, 56, 75, ed. K. Lehmann, *Leges Alamannorum = Monumenta Germaniae historica*, Legum sectio I [in quarto], vol. 5, pt. I, 2nd ed. by K. A. Eckhart (Hannover, 1966), trans. Theodore John Rivers, *Laws of the Alamans and Bavarians* (Philadelphia: University of Pennsylvania Press, 1977), pp. 83-85, 94. The first fine in no. 56 is given as 6 s. in the oldest MS, but the value must be 3 s., as in a later MS, if the steps of the scale are proportioned to the gravity of the offenses.

2 Paulus Diaconus, *Historia Langobardorum* 6.35, ed. G. Waitz, *Monumenta Germaniae historica*, Scriptores rerum Langobardicarum (Hanover, 1878), p. 176; trans. William Dudley Foulke, *The History of the Langobards by Paul the Deacon*, University of Pennsylvania Translations and Reprints, ser. 2, no. 3 (Philadelphia, 1907), p. 278, rev. R. Kay.

3 Pedro Marilio, *Crónica de San Juan de la Peña*, ed. Antonio Ubieto Arteta, Textos Medievales, 4 (Valencia, 1961), pp. 23-24; trans. R. Kay «Clay Stall».

4   *Vita Bonifatii auctore Willibaldo*, ed. W. Levison in *Vitae sancti Bonifatii archiepis-copi Moguntini = Monumenta Germaniae historica*, Scriptores rerum Germanicarum, 57 (Hanover-Leipzig, 1905), pp. 30-32; trans. George W. Robinson, *The Life of Saint Boniface by Willibald*, Harvard Translations (Cambridge, 1916), pp. 62-64, rev. R. Kay «Twila Jukes».

5   William of Malmesbury, *De gestis regum Anglorum* 1.36, ed. W. Stubbs, Rolls Series, no. 90, vol. 1 (London, 1887), pp. 35-36; trans. J. Sharpe (1815), rev. J. A. Giles, *William of Malmesbury's Chronicle of the Kings of England from the Earliest Period to the Reign of King Stephen*, Bohn's Antiquarian Library (London, 1847), pp. 36-37, rev. R. Kay «Dudley Stutz».

6   Continuator of the *Chronica* of "Fredegar," c. 13 [written ca. 736], ed. and trans. J. M. Wallace-Hadrill, *The Fourth Book of the Chronicle of Fredegar with its Continuations*, Medieval Classics (London: Thomas Nelson and Sons, 1960), pp. 90-91. The battle is often placed, with less likelihood, at Tours.

7   Cuthbert of Durham, abbot of Wearmouth and Jarrow, letter preserved in *Venerabilis Bedae Vita auctore et collectores Turgoto, priore Dunelmensi* 3, ed. J. P. Migne, *Patrologia Latina* 90:63-65; trans. Leo Sherley-Price in the introduction to his translation of Bede's *History of the English Church and People*, Penguin Classics (Baltimore: Penguin Books, 1955), pp. 18-20. Bede himself described the death of saints as their "heavenly birthday."

8   *Chronicon Laurissense breve* ad an. 750, ed. G. H. Pertz, *Monumenta Germaniae historica*, Scriptores, vol. 1 (Hanover, 1826), pp. 112-123; trans. Thomas Hodgkin, *Italy and Her Invaders*, vol. 7 (London, 1899), pp. 127-128, rev. R. Kay.

9   Einhard, *Vita Caroli* 1, ed. L. Halphen, *Vie de Charlemagne*, Les Classiques de l'histoire de France au Moyen âge (Paris, 1923), pp. 8-10; trans. Richard R. Ring.

10   *Vita Bonifatii auctore Willibaldo*, ed. W. Levison in *Vitae sancti Bonifatii archiepis-copi Moguntini = Monumenta Germaniae historica*, Scriptores rerum Germanicarum, 57 (Hanover-Leipzig, 1905), pp. 48-50; trans. George W. Robinson, *The Life of Saint Boniface by Willibald*, Harvard Translations (Cambridge, 1916), pp. 81-84, rev. R. Kay «Twila Jukes».

11   *Chronicon Novaliciense* 2.11, ed. L. C. Bethmann in *Monumenta Germaniae historica*, Scriptores, 7 (Hanover, 1846), p. 94; trans. G. G. Coulton, *A Medieval Garner* (London, 1910), pp. 13-14, rev. R. Kay. The chronicler associated the legendary hero Waltharius with his monastery, probably because of local traditions about a militant monk named Walther who had "dwelt in this monastery in early days," i.e. in the time of Abbot Asinarius, fl. 765.

12   Einhard, *Vita Caroli* 9, ed. L. Halphen, *Vie de Charlemagne*, Les Classiques de l'histoire de France au Moyen âge (Paris, 1923), pp. 28-30; trans. Richard R. Ring

13 *Annales regni Francorum 741-829 qui dicuntur Annales Laurissenses maiores et Einhardi* ad an. 782, ed. F. Kurze in *Monumenta Germaniae historica*, Scriptores rerum Germanicarum 6 (Hanover, 1895), pp. 59-65; trans. Berhard W. Scholz with B. Rogers, *Carolingian Chronicles* (Ann Arbor: University of Michigan Press, 1970), pp. 59-61, rev. R. Kay. This revision is often attributed to Einhard.

14 Monachus Sangallensis *de Carolo Magno* 1.9, ed. P. Jaffé in his *Bibliotheca rerum Germanicarum*, vol. 4: *Monumenta Carolina* (Berlin, 1867), pp. 638-639; trans. A. J. Grant, *Early Lives of Charlemagne by Eginhard and the Monk of St. Gall*, King's Classics (Boston, 1907) «Larry Watkins». I place the incident at the end of Alcuin's stay at the royal court.

15 Alcuin, *Epistola* 93, ed. E. Dümmler, *Epistolae Karolini aevi*, vol. 2, in *Monumenta Germaniae historica*, Epistolae, 4 (Berlin, 1895), pp. 137-138; trans. S. Z. Ehler and J. B. Morrall, *Church and State through the Centuries* (London: Burns & Oates, 1954), p. 12, rev. R. Kay.

Notes to pages 96–111

1 Einhard, *Vita Caroli* 27-28, ed. L. Halphen, *Vie de Charlemagne*, Les Classiques de l'histoire de France au Moyen âge (Paris, 1923), p. 80; trans. Richard R. Ring.

2 *Le "Liber pontificalis"*, ed. L. Duchesne, Bibliothèque des Ecoles françaises d'Athènes et de Rome, 2nd ser., no. 3, vol. 2 (Paris, 1892), p. 7; trans. R. Kay.

3 *Annales regni Francorum 741-829 qui dicuntur Annales Laurissenses maiores et Einhardi* ad an. 807, ed. F. Kurze in *Monumenta Germaniae historica*, Scriptores rerum Germanicarum 6 (Hanover, 1895), pp. 123-124; trans. Berhard W. Scholz with B. Rogers, *Carolingian Chronicles* (Ann Arbor: University of Michigan Press, 1970), p. 87, rev. R. Kay.

4 Einhard, *Vita Caroli* 22-25, ed. L. Halphen, *Vie de Charlemagne*, Les Classiques de l'histoire de France au Moyen âge (Paris, 1923), pp. 66-76; trans. Richard R. Ring.

5 Monachus Sangallensis *de Carolo Magno* 2.14, ed. P. Jaffé in his *Bibliotheca rerum Germanicarum*, vol. 4: *Monumenta Carolina* (Berlin, 1867), pp. 687-688; trans. A. J. Grant, *Early Lives of Charlemagne by Eginhard and the Monk of St. Gall*, King's Classics (London, 1905), rev. R. Kay «Larry Watkins». Following Notker, I place this improbable incident towards the end of Charlemagne's life.

6 *Annales regni Francorum 741-829 qui dicuntur Annales Laurissenses maiores et Einhardi* ad ann. 824-826, ed. F. Kurze in *Monumenta Germaniae historica*, Scriptores rerum Germanicarum 6 (Hanover, 1895), pp. 157, 166-168; trans. Berhard W. Scholz with B. Rogers, *Carolingian Chronicles* (Ann Arbor: University of Michigan Press, 1970), pp. 110, 117-118, rev. R. Kay.

7   Mohammed ibn Ish'âq al-Nadîm, *Firist-el-U'lûm* 9.2, ed. with German trans. by D. Chwolsohn [= Khvol'son], *Die Ssabier und der Ssabismus*, vol. 2 (St. Petersburg, 1856), pp. 14-17; trans. R. Kay. The original Sabians were a Judeo-Christian Gnostic sect, which still survives in lower Mesopotamia; they are usually called Mandaeans. The pseudo-Sabians of Harran, however, worshipped the stars and were adepts in astrology. Although they adopted a new name, they retained their old religion and met the Islamic requirements for a "people of the book" by claiming that their traditional astrology books were sacred texts revealed by Hermes and Orpheus, whom they said were their prophets. See *The Encyclopaedia of Islam*, 1st ed., vol. 4 (Leiden, 1934), pp. 21-22, s.v. "al-Sâb'ia."

8   Monachus Sangallensis *de Carolo Magno* 2.19, ed. P. Jaffé in his *Bibliotheca rerum Germanicarum*, vol. 4: *Monumenta Carolina* (Berlin, 1867), pp. 697-698; trans. A. J. Grant, *Early Lives of Charlemagne by Eginhard and the Monk of St. Gall*, King's Classics (Boston, 1907) rev. R. Kay «Larry Watkins». Taking Notker's story at face value, I have dated it in the 20th year of Louis's reign.

9   Nithard, *Historiae* 3.5, ed. P. Lauer, *Histoire des fils de Louis le Pieux* (Paris, 1926), pp. 101-109; trans. R. Kay «Cynthia Shively».

10   Tammam ibn-'Alqamah, quoted by ibn-Dihyah (d. 1235) in a work on Hispano-Arabic poetry, ed. Alexander Seippel, *Rerum Normannicarum fontes Arabici* (Oslo, 1896-1928), pp. 13-20; trans. A. I. Samarrai, *Medieval Islam and Europe: Implacable Enmity or Pragmatic Coexistence?* (St. Cloud, Minn.: privately published, 1971), pp. 20-21, rev. R. Kay.

11   Tammam ibn-'Alqamah, quoted by ibn-Dihyah (d. 1235) in a work on Hispano-Arabic poetry, ed. Alexander Seippel, *Rerum Normannicarum fontes Arabici* (Oslo, 1896-1928), pp. 13-20; trans. A. I. Samarrai, *Medieval Islam and Europe: Implacable Enmity or Pragmatic Coexistence?* (St. Cloud, Minn.: privately published, 1971), pp. 21-23, rev. R. Kay. For more about this affair, see W. E. D. Allen, *The Poet and the Spae-Wife* (Dublin, 1960).

12   Bartolomeo Platina, *Liber de vita Christi ac omnium pontificum* (1479), ed. W. Benham (London, 1888); trans. P. Rycaut, *The Lives of the Popes*, 2nd ed. (London, 1688), p. 165, rev. by R. Kay «Robin S. Hackett». Platina, a Renaissance humanist, was the first prefect of the Vatican Library; his source was the chronicle of the Dominican Martin of Troppau (d. 1278), ed. *Monumenta Germaniae Historica*, Scriptores, 22:428. Although in fact there has never been a female pope, in the later Middle Ages the papacy of Joan was generally believed to be authentic.

13   William of Malmesbury (d. 1143?), *De gestis pontificum Anglorum* 5.240, ed. N. E. S. A. Hamilton, Rolls Series, no. 52 (London, 1870), p. 392; trans. R. Kay «R.S. Hackett».

14 William of Malmesbury, *De gestis regum Anglorum* 2.122, ed. W. Stubbs, Rolls Series, no. 90, vol. 1 (London, 1887), pp. 131-132; trans. J. Sharpe (1815), rev. J. A. Giles, *William of Malmesbury's Chronicle of the Kings of England from the Earliest Period to the Reign of King Stephen*, Bohn's Antiquarian Library (London, 1847), p. 119, rev. R. Kay «Dudley Stutz». John actually died without incident in France shortly after 870. This unusual form of martyrdom is first mentioned by the poet Prudentius (died after 405), *Peristephanon* 9.

15 Pseudo-Asser, *Chronicon fani sancti Neoti*, an. 878, ed. William Henry Stevenson, *Asser's Life of King Alfred, together with the Annals of Saint Neots erroneously ascribed to Asser*, 2nd ed. (Oxford, 1959), p. 136; trans. R. Kay. « R.S. Hackett».

16 William of Malmesbury, *De gestis regum Anglorum* 2.121, ed. W. Stubbs, Rolls Series, no. 90, vol. 1 (London, 1887), pp. 126; trans. J. Sharpe (1815), rev. J. A. Giles, *William of Malmesbury's Chronicle of the Kings of England from the Earliest Period to the Reign of King Stephen*, Bohn's Antiquarian Library (London, 1847), p. 114, rev. R. Kay «Dudley Stutz».

17 Abbo, *De bello parisiaco* 2.163-165, 315-318, 330-334, 338-340, 442-448; ed. Georg Pertz in *Monumenta Germaniae Historica*, Scriptores rerum germanicarum, 1 (Hannover, 1871), pp. 32, 36-37, 40-41; trans. «Oliver Phillips». Abbo, a Neustrian and a monk of Saint-Germain-des-Prés, witnessed the siege.

18 Richer, *Historiae* 1.9-11, ed. and trans. Robert Latouche, *Histoire de France (888-995)*, Les Classiques de l'histoire de France au Moyen âge 12, vol. 1 (Paris, 1930), pp. 25-31. Latouche thought that Richer may have heard this tale, which is corroborated by no other source, when he was in the vicinity of Blois.

19 Paris, Bibliothèque nationale, MS. lat. 17,436, fol. 24; ed. L. Delisle, "Prière pour obtenir la grace d'être délivré des invasions normandes (vers 900)," no. 50 in his *Instructions adressées par le Comité des travaux historiques et scientifiques aux correspondants du Ministère de l'instruction publique et des beaux-arts: Littérature latine et histoire du moyen âge* (Paris, 1890), p. 17«John Maple». The often-quoted suffrage from a litany—*A furore Normannorum, libera nos Domine*, "From the fury of the Northmen, O Lord deliver us"—seems to be apocryphal, since it has no identifiable source: see Albert d'Haenens, *Les Invasions normandes en Belgique au IXe siècle*, Université de Louvain, Recueil de travaux d'histoire et de philologie, ser. 4, fasc. 38 (Louvain, 1967), pp. 196-197.

Notes to pages 112–139

1 Anonymous, *Vita S. Hugonis monachi Aeduensis* 2.13, ed. *Acta sanctorum quotquot toto orbe coluntur*, Aprilis, vol. 2 (1675; rpt. Paris-Rome, 1866), p. 764; trans. «John T. Maple».

2　Dudo of Saint-Quentin (fl. ca. 1000), *Historia Normannorum*, lib. 2, ed. J. P. Migne, *Patrologia latina*, 141:650-651; trans. R. Kay «Dudley Stutz».

3　Ekkehard IV, monk of Saint Gall, *Libri de casibus monasterii sancti Galli* 14, ed. D. I. von Arx in *Monumenta Germaniae historica*, Scriptores, 2 (Hanover, 1829), pp. 84-85; trans. R. Kay «Bradford L. Eden». Conrad did not, as E. K. Chambers thought, "bade his train roll [*antesterni!*] apples along the aisle": *The Medieval Stage* (Oxford, 1903), 2:338.

4　Liudprand, bishop of Cremona (961-972), *Antapodosis* 3.25-26, ed. J. Becker, *Liudprandi Opera; Die Werke Liudprands von Cremona* in *Monumenta Germaniae historica*, Scriptores rerum Germanicarum 41, 3rd ed. (Hanover-Leipzig, 1915), pp. 83-87; trans. F. A. Wright, *The Works of Liudprand of Cremona*, Broadway Medieval Library (London: George Routledge & Sons, 1930), pp. 119, 121-122, rev. R. Kay. Proud of his knowledge of Greek, then a rare accomplishment for Latin intellectuals, Liutprand flaunted it by interspersing his work, apparently at random, with Greek words and phrases, always condesendingly transliterated and translated into Latin. The translator has reproduced this tiresome mannerism by substituting French for Greek.

5　Liudprand, bishop of Cremona (961-972), *Antapodosis* 2.44, 51-54, ed. J. Becker, *Liudprandi Opera; Die Werke Liudprands von Cremona* in *Monumenta Germaniae historica*, Scriptores rerum Germanicarum 41, 3rd ed. (Hanover-Leipzig, 1915), pp. 57, 61-62; trans. F. A. Wright, *The Works of Liudprand of Cremona*, Broadway Medieval Library (New York, 1930), pp. 90-91, 94-95, rev. R. Kay.

6　Anonymous (fl. 1270-90), *Primera crónica general* 709, 720, ed. Ramón Menéndez Pidal, Nueva biblioteca de autores españoles (Madrid, 1906), 1:409-410, 422; trans. «Clay Stalls». Several anachronisms in this account show that it is more folklore than history: Fernán Gonzáles received Castile from King Ramiro II (930-951), not from his successor, King Sancho I (died 956); the count himself died in 970, so he could not have won the horse from Almanzor, who came to power in 976.

7　Liudprand, bishop of Cremona (961-972), *Antapodosis* 4.9-10, ed. J. Becker, *Liudprandi Opera; Die Werke Liudprands von Cremona* in *Monumenta Germaniae historica*, Scriptores rerum Germanicarum 41, 3rd ed. (Hanover-Leipzig, 1915), pp. 108-109; trans. F. A. Wright, *The Works of Liudprand of Cremona*, Broadway Medieval Library (New York, 1930), pp. 148-149, rev. R. Kay. The campaign took place at some time between 929 and 934.

8　*Povest Vremennykh Let* [Tale of Bygone Years], ed. Archeographical Commission (St. Petersburg, 1872) p. 44; trans. Samuel H. Cross, *The Russian Primary Chronicle*, Harvard Studies and Notes in Philology and Literature 12 (Cambridge, Mass.: Harvard University Press, 1930), pp. 157-158 «Jay Alexander, Tim Sistrunk». Reprinted by permission of the publishers. A Byzantine version of the episode is given by Liudprand of Cremona (*Antapodosis* 5.15), from which it appears that the Russes' boats were small and of shallow draft, but only numbered a thousand or so.

9   Liudprand, bishop of Cremona (961-972), *Antapodosis* 6.5, ed. J. Becker, *Liudprandi Opera; Die Werke Liudprands von Cremona* in *Monumenta Germaniae historica*, Scriptores rerum Germanicarum 41, 3rd ed. (Hanover-Leipzig, 1915), pp. 154-155; trans. F. A. Wright, *The Works of Liudprand of Cremona*, Broadway Medieval Library (New York, 1930), pp. 207-208, rev. R. Kay. The epigraph is from William Butler Yeats' poem, "Sailing to Byzantium."

10   Walter Map, *De nugis curialium* 2.23, ed. M. R. James, Anecdota Oxoniensia, Mediaeval and Modern Series, pt. 14 (Oxford, 1914), p. 95-96; trans. M. R. James, Cymmrodorion Record Series, no. 9 (London, 1923), pp. 105-106 «John Maple».

11   Constantinus VII Porphyrogenitus (905-959), *De administrando imperio* 13, Greek text ed. G. Moravcsik with English translation by R. J. H. Jenkins, 2nd ed., Corpus fontium historiae Byzantinae, 1 = Dumbarton Oaks Texts, 1 (Washington, D.C.: Dumbarton Oaks Center for Byzantine Studies, 1967), pp. 67-71 «Tim Sistrunk». Used with the kind permission of the publisher.

12   Hrotsvitha, *Gesta Ottonis*, lines 467-601, 608-665, in *Hrotsvithae opera*, ed. H. Homeyer (Munich, 1970), pp. 424-431; trans. «Oliver Phillips». The story has been been treated with epical *afflatus*; hence the tedious verbosity.

13   William of Malmesbury, *De gestis regum Anglorum* 2.147, ed. W. Stubbs, Rolls Series, no. 90, vol. l (London, 1887), p. 167; trans. J. Sharpe (1815), rev. J. A. Giles, *William of Malmesbury's Chronicle of the Kings of England from the Earliest Period to the Reign of King Stephen*, Bohn's Antiquarian Library (London, 1847), pp. 145-146, rev. R. Kay «Dudley Stutz».

14   *Povest Vremennykh Let* [Tale of Bygone Years], ed. Archeographical Commission (St. Petersburg, 1872) pp. 60-61; trans. Samuel H. Cross, *The Russian Primary Chronicle*, Harvard Studies and Notes in Philology and Literature 12 (Cambridge, Mass.: Harvard University Press, 1930), pp. 168-169 «Jay Alexander, Tim Sistrunk». Reprinted by permission of the publishers.

15   Liudprand, bishop of Cremona (961-972), *Historia Ottonis* 4, 10, 15, 20, ed. J. Becker, *Liutprandi Opera; Die Werke Liudprands von Cremona* in *Monumenta Germaniae historica*, Scriptores rerum Germanicarum 41, 3rd ed. (Hanover-Leipzig, 1915), pp. 161-162, 167, 171, 173-174; trans. F. A. Wright, *The Works of Liudprand of Cremona*, Broadway Medieval Library (New York, 1930), pp. 217-218, 223, 228, 231, rev. R. Kay.

16 Richer, *Historiae* 3.43-45, ed. and trans. Robert Latouche, *Histoire de France (888-995)*, Les Classiques de l'histoire de France au Moyen âge 17, vol. 2 (Paris, 1937), pp. 51-55, trans. R. Kay.

17 William of Malmesbury, *De gestis regum Anglorum* 2.164, ed. W. Stubbs, Rolls Series, no. 90, vol. 1 (London, 1887), pp. 185; trans. J. Sharpe (1815), rev. J. A. Giles, *William of Malmesbury's Chronicle of the Kings of England from the Earliest Period to the Reign of King Stephen*, Bohn's Antiquarian Library (London, 1847), pp. 165-166, rev. R. Kay «C. Warren Hollister».

18 Odilo, *De vita beati Maioli abbatis* 56-57, ed. J. P. Migne, *Patrologia Latina*, 142:959-960; trans. «Clay Stalls», rev. R. Kay. From 972 to 975, Count William of Provence conducted successful military campaigns against Saracen strongholds in the Alps, including the main base at Fraxinetum (Fréjus): see J. E. Tyler, *The Alpine Passes* (Oxford, 1930), p. 55.

19 Thietmar of Merseburg, *Chronicon* 3.12, ed. J. M. Lappenberg in *Monumenta Germaniae Historica*, Scriptores, 3 (Hanover, 1839), pp. 765-766; trans. Boyd H. Hill, *Medieval Monarchy in Action*, Historical Problems: Studies and Documents 15 (New York: Barnes and Noble, 1972), pp. 169-170. Permission granted by Barnes & Noble Books, Totowa, New Jersey.

20 *Povest Vremennykh Let* [Tale of Bygone Years], ed. Archeographical Commission (St. Petersburg, 1872) pp. 84-85; trans. Samuel H. Cross, *The Russian Primary Chronicle*, Harvard Studies and Notes in Philology and Literature 12 (Cambridge, Mass.: Harvard University Press, 1930), pp. 183-184 «Jay Alexander, Tim Sistrunk». Reprinted by permission of the publishers.

21 *Povest Vremennykh Let* [Tale of Bygone Years], ed. Archeographical Commission (St. Petersburg, 1872) p.108 ; trans. Samuel H. Cross, *The Russian Primary Chronicle*, Harvard Studies and Notes in Philology and Literature 12 (Cambridge, Mass.: Harvard University Press, 1930), p.199 «Jay Alexander». Reprinted by permission of the publishers.

22 Richer, *Historiae* 4.50, ed. and trans. Robert Latouche, *Histoire de France (888-995)*, Les Classiques de l'histoire de France au Moyen âge 17, vol. 2 (Paris, 1937), pp. 224-231

23 Snorri Sturluson, *Ólafs saga Tryggvasonar* 32, ed. Bjarni Aðalbjarnarson in *Heimskringla*, Íslenzk Fornrit 26-27 (1941-51); trans. Samuel Laing, *King Olaf Trygvesson's Saga*, in *Heimskringla*, Everyman's Library (New York, 1914), 1:29-30, rev. R. Kay «John Lomax».

Notes to pages 140–173

1 Raoul Glaber, *Historiae sui temporis* 3.4, ed. J. P. Migne, *Patrologia Latina* 142:651.

2 Anglo-Saxon Herbal, ed. and transl. Oswold Cockayne, *Leachdoms, Wortcunning and Starcraft of Early England*, vol. 1, Rolls Series, no. 35 (London, 1864), p. 132, rev. R. Kay «Martha S. Weil».

3 *Vita [S. Alphagii] auctore Osberno, ecclesiae Cantuariensis monacho* 6.30-7.39, ed. *Acta sanctorum quotquot toto orbe coluntur*, Aprilis, vol. 2 (Paris-Rome, 1865), pp. 637-639; trans. *The Golden Legend, or Lives of the Saints as Englished by William Caxton*, Temple Classics, vol. 3 (London, 1900), pp. 123-124, rev. R. Kay. This *vita* does not appear in the original *Legenda aurea* compiled by Jacobus de Voragine.

4 Walter Map, *De nugis curialium* 5.4, ed. M. R. James, Anecdota Oxoniensia, Mediaeval and Modern Series, pt. 14 (Oxford, 1914), pp.210-212; trans. M. R. James, Cymmrodorion Record Series, no. 9 (London, 1923), pp. 232-233, rev. R. Kay «John Maple».

5 Walter Map, *De nugis curialium* 5.4, ed. M. R. James, Anecdota Oxoniensia, Mediaeval and Modern Series, pt. 14 (Oxford, 1914), pp. 213-216; trans. M. R. James, Cymmrodorion Record Series, no. 9 (London, 1923), pp. 235-237, rev. R. Kay «John Maple».

6 Helgaldus, monk of Fleury, *Epitoma vitae regis Rotberti Pii* 26, ed. R. H. Bautier, *Vie de Robert le Pieux*, Sources d'histoire médiéval l (Paris, 1965), pp. 122-124; trans. R. Kay «Larry Watkins».

7 Ademar of Chabannes, *Epistola de apostolatu Martialis*, ed. J. P. Migne, *Patrologia latina* 141:107-108; trans. Helen Waddell, *The Wandering Scholars* (Boston, 1927), p. 83, rev. R. Kay.

8 Helgaldus monk of Fleury, *Epitoma vitae regis Rotberti Pii* 5, 9, ed. R. H. Bautier, *Vie de Robert le Pieux*, Sources d'histoire médiéval 1 (Paris, 1965), pp. 62-64, 70-72; trans. R. Kay.

9 Anonymous, *Crònica Najerense* 3.10, ed. Antonio Ubieto Arteta, Textos medievales, no. 15 (Valencia, 1966), p. 92; trans. Clay Stalls «Lynn Nelson».

10 Henry of Huntington, *Historia Anglorum* 6.17, sub anno 1035, ed. T. Arnold, Rolls Series, no. 74 (London, 1879), p. 189; trans. T. Forester, *The Chronicle of Henry of Huntington*, Bohn's Antiquarian Library (London, 1853), p. 199, rev. R. Kay «Robin S. Hackett».

11 *Flores historiarum*, sub anno 1057, ed. H. R. Luard, Rolls Series, no. 95, vol. l (London, 1890), p. 576; trans. J. A. Giles, *Roger of Wendover's Flowers of History*, Bohn's Antiquarian Library, vol. l (London, 1849), pp. 314-315 «Robin S. Hackett». This is the earliest form of Godiva's story, which developed somewhat as it was retold: see *Dictionary of National Biography*, s.v. "Godiva." Although Roger Wendover is

often given as the author of this chronicle, he wrote only the annals for 1220-34; the earlier portions were written anonymously after 1202 at his monastery, St. Alban's, near London.

12   William of Malmesbury, *De gestis regum Anglorum* 2.190, ed. W. Stubbs, Rolls Series, no. 90, vol. 1 (London, 1887), pp. 231-232; trans. J. Sharpe (1815), rev. J. A. Giles, *William of Malmesbury's Chronicle of the Kings of England from the Earliest Period to the Reign of King Stephen*, Bohn's Antiquarian Library (London, 1847), pp. 209-210, rev. R. Kay «Dudley Stutz». The same story is told of Charlemagne, with Einhart as the cleric.

13   Walter Map, *De nugis curialium* 5.3, ed. M. R. James, Anecdota Oxoniensia, Mediaeval and Modern Series, pt. 14 (Oxford, 1914), pp. 209-210; trans. M. R. James, Cymmrodorion Record Series, no. 9 (London, 1923), pp. 230-231, rev. R. Kay «John Maple».

14   Walter Map, *De nugis curialium* 2.22, ed. M. R. James, Anecdota Oxoniensia, Mediaeval and Modern Series, pt. 14 (Oxford, 1914), pp. 91-92; trans. M. R. James, Cymmrodorion Record Series, no. 9 (London, 1923), pp. 101-102, rev. R. Kay «John Maple».

15   William of Malmesbury, *De gestis regum Anglorum* 2.197, ed. W. Stubbs, Rolls Series, no. 90, vol. 1 (London, 1887), p. 240; trans. J. Sharpe (1815), rev. J. A. Giles, *William of Malmesbury's Chronicle of the Kings of England from the Earliest Period to the Reign of King Stephen*, Bohn's Antiquarian Library (London, 1847), pp. 217, rev. R. Kay «R. Dean Ware, John Lomax».

16   Walter Map, *De nugis curialium* 2.23, ed. M. R. James, Anecdota Oxoniensia, Mediaeval and Modern Series, pt. 14 (Oxford, 1914), pp. 94-95, rev. R. Kay; trans. M. R. James, Cymmrodorion Record Series, no. 9 (London, 1923), pp. 104-5 «John Maple».

17   Ordericus Vitalis, *Historia ecclesiastica*, book 3, ed. Marjorie Chibnall, *The Ecclesiastical History of Orderic Vitalis*, Oxford Medieval Texts, vol. 2 (Oxford, 1969), pp. 28, 76, 104; trans. Thomas Forester, *The Ecclesiastical History of England and Normandy by Ordericus Vitalis*, Bohn's Antiquarian Library, vol. 1 (London, 1853), pp. 394, 423-424, 440, rev. R. Kay.

18   Ordericus Vitalis, *Historia ecclesiastica*, book 3, ed. Marjorie Chibnall, *The Ecclesiastical History of Orderic Vitalis*, Oxford Medieval Texts, vol. 2 (Oxford, 1969), pp. 46-47, 122-124; trans. Thomas Forester, *The Ecclesiastical History of England and Normandy by Ordericus Vitalis*, Bohn's Antiquarian Library, vol. 1 (London, 1853), pp. 405-406, 451-452, rev. R. Kay. See the year 1077 for Mabel's own death.

19 William of Poitiers, *Gesta Willelmi ducis Normannorum et regis Anglorum,* ed. J. P. Migne, *Patrologia Latina,* 149:1236-37; trans. David C. Douglas and George W. Greenaway, *English Historical Documents, 1042-1149,* 2nd ed. (New York: Oxford University Press, 1981), pp. 231-232, rev. R. Kay «John Maple».

20 Joannes Zonaras, *Epitome historiarum* 18.14.2-26, ed. Theodor Büttner-Wobst in *Corpus scriptorum historiae Byzantinae* (Bonn, 1897), pp. 699-703; trans. «Oliver Phillips».

21 Guibert of Nogent (1064?—ca. 1125), *De vita sua sive Monodiae* 1.6, ed. J. P. Migne, *Patrologia Latina,* 156:847; trans. C. C. Swinton Bland, *The Autobiography of Guibert, Abbot of Nogent-sous-Coucy,* Broadway Translations (London, 1925), pp. 23-24, rev. R. Kay.

22 Ordericus Vitalis, *Historia ecclesiastica* book 5, ed. Marjorie Chibnall, *The Ecclesiastical History of Orderic Vitalis,* Oxford Medieval Texts, vol. 3 (Oxford, 1972), pp. 134-136; trans. Thomas Forester, *The Ecclesiastical History of England and Normandy by Ordericus Vitalis,* Bohn's Antiquarian Library, vol. 2 (London, 1854), pp. 193-194, rev. R. Kay.

23 Gregory VII, *Registrum* 4.12, ed. P. Jaffé, in his *Bibliotheca rerum Germanicarum,* vol. 2: *Monumenta Gregoriana* (Berlin, 1865), pp. 256-258; trans. Ernest F. Henderson, *Select Historical Documents of the Middle Ages,* Bohn's Antiquarian Library (London, 1892), pp. 385-387, rev. R. Kay «James J. Ludwig».

24 Anselm of Bec, archbishop of Canterbury, *Proslogion* pr., ed. J. P. Migne, *Patrologia Latina* 158:223-225; trans. S. N. Deane (La Salle, Ill., 1903), pp. 1-3, rev. R. Kay.

25 Eadmer, *Vita sancti Anselmi archiepiscopi Cantuariensis,* ed. and trans. R. W. Southern, *The Life of St Anselm, Archbishop of Canterbury,* Oxford Medieval Texts (Oxford: Clarendon Press, 1972), pp. 27-31, rev. R. Kay.

26 *Vita Bennonis II Episcopi Osnabrugensis, auctore Nortberto abbate Iburgensi,* ed. H. Bresslau, in *Monumenta Germaniae Historica,* Scriptores rerum Germanicarum 56 (Hanover, 1902), pp. 24-25; trans. R. Kay «Tim Sistrunk».

27 William of Malmesbury, *De gestis regum Anglorum* 5.390, ed. W. Stubbs, Rolls Series, no. 90, vol. 2 (London, 1889), p. 467; trans. J. Sharpe (1815), rev. J. A. Giles, *William of Malmesbury's Chronicle of the Kings of England,* Bohn's Antiquarian Library (London, 1847), p. 425, rev. R. Kay «Dudley Stutz».

28 Anna Comnena, *Alexiad* 4.7, ed. J. P. Migne, *Patrologia Graeca,* 131:368-369; trans. Elizabeth A. S. Dawes, *The Alexiad of the Princess Anna Comnena, Being the History of the Reign of Her Father, Alexius I, Emperor of the Romans, 1081-1118 A.D.* (London, 1928; Kegan Paul, Trench, Trubner & Co. 1967), pp. 111-113, rev. R. Kay.

29 Kai Kâ'ûs ibn Iskandar, prince of Gurgân, *Qâbûs-nâma* chs. 15, 23, 24, 26, 28, 35, 39; ed. and trans. from the Persian by Reuben Levy, *A Mirror for Princes* (London: E. P. Dutton, 1951), pp. 77-78, 107, 110, 117, 127, 182, 109-210, rev. R. Kay «Lynn Nelson».

30 William of Malmesbury, *De gestis regum Anglorum* 4.306, ed. W. Stubbs, Rolls Series, no. 90, vol. 2 (London, 1889), p. 361; trans. J. Sharpe (1815), rev. J. A. Giles, *The History of the Kings of England*, Bohn 's Antiquarian Library (London, 1847), p. 119, and rev. R. Kay «Dudley Stutz».

31 Paul Bernried, *Vita Gregorii VII* 110, ed. J. M. Watterich, *Pontificium Romanorum vitae* (Leipzig, 1862), 1:539-540; trans. «John T. Brothers», rev. R. Kay. Gregory summarised his career by ironically altering Ps. 44:8—"Thou hast loved justice, and hated iniquity: therefore God, thy God, hath anointed thee with the oil of gladness above thy fellows" (Vulgate).

32 Giovanni Villani, *Croniche fiorentine* 4.19; trans. R. E. Selfe, *Villani's Chronicle*, 2nd ed. (New York, 1904), pp. 88-89, rev. R. Kay. Similar tales are told of many medieval notables, e.g. Edward I.

33 William of Malmesbury, *De gestis regum Anglorum* 4.313, ed. W. Stubbs, Rolls Series, no. 90, vol. 2 (London, 1889), p. 368; trans. J. Sharpe (1815), rev. J. A. Giles, *The History of the Kings of England*, Bohn's Antiquarian Library (London, 1847), p. 335, and rev. R. Kay «Dudley Stutz».

34 Robert the Monk, *Historia Hierosolymitana* 1.1-2, ed. *Recueil des historiens des croisades, Historiens occidentaux*, vol. 3 (Paris, 1866), pp. 727-729; trans. Dana C. Munro, *Urban and the Crusaders,* Translations and Reprints from the Original Sources of European History, vol. l, no. 2, 2nd ed. (Philadelphia, 1895), pp. 5-8, rev. R. Kay «Dudley Stutz».

35 Fulcher of Chartres, *Historia Hierosolymitana* l.7, ed. J. P. Migne, *Patrologia Latina* 155:839; trans. Martha E. McGinty in *The First Crusade*, ed. Edward M. Peters (Philadelphia: The University of Pennsylvania Press, 1971), p. 38 «Dudley Stutz».

36 Ivo of Chartres, *Epistolae* 67, ed. J. P. Migne, *Patrologia Latina,* 162:84-85; trans. R. Kay «Cynthia Shively»

37 Ibn al-Athir, *Kamil at-Tawarikh*, ed. C. J. Tornberg, vol. l0 (Leiden, 1853), pp. 185-186; trans. Francesco Gabrieli and E. J. Costello, *Arab Historians of the Crusades* (London: Routledge and Kegan Paul, 1969), pp. 4-5 «Dudley Stutz». The episode is pure fiction, since the First Crusade always had the Holy Land as its destination; at the time, Roger was still busy conquering Sicily.

38 Ibn al-Athir, *Kamil at-Tawarikh*, ed. C. J. Tornberg, vol. 10 (Leiden, 1853), pp. 188-190; trans. Francesco Gabrieli and E. J. Costello, *Arab Historians of the Crusades* (London: Routledge and Kegan Paul, 1969), pp. 7-8 «Dudley Stutz».

39 Ordericus Vitalis, *Historia ecclesiastica 3.5*, ed. Marjorie Chibnall, *The Ecclesiastical History of Orderic Vitalis*, Oxford Medieval Texts, vol. 2 (Oxford, 1969), pp. 84-86; trans. Thomas Forester, *The Ecclesiastical History of England and Normandy by Ordericus Vitalis*, Bohn's Antiquarian Library, vol. 1 (London, 1853), pp. 428-429, rev. R. Kay.

Notes to pages 174–221

1 William of Malmesbury, *De gestis regum Anglorum* 4.333, ed. W. Stubbs, Rolls Series, no. 90, vol. 2 (London, 1889), pp. 377-379, trans. J. Sharpe (1815), rev. J. A. Giles, *William of Malmesbury's Chronicle of the Kings of England*, Bohn 's Antiquarian Library (London, 1847), pp. 344-346, rev. R. Kay «Dudley Stutz». Some doubt that the death was an accident; Tirel always denied that he had done it. See C. Warren Hollister, "The Strange Death of William Rufus," *Speculum* 48 (1973), 637-653, and D. Grinnell-Milne, *The Killing of William Rufus* (Newton Abbot, 1968) «John T. Maple».

2 Guibert of Nogent (1064?–ca. 1125), *De vita sua sive Monodiae* 3.11, 14, ed. J. P. Migne, *Patrologia Latina*, 156:933-934, 944; trans. C. C. Swinton Bland, *The Autobiography of Guibert, Abbot of Nogent-sous-Coucy*, Broadway Translations (New York, 1925), pp. 173-174, 192-193, rev. R. Kay. Guibert's description of the last atrocity is unclear and perhaps garbled: see John Benton, *Self and Society in Medieval France* (New York, 1970), p. 201.

3 Guibert of Nogent (1064?–ca. 1125), *De vita sua sive Monodiae* 1.12, ed. J. P. Migne, *Patrologia Latina*, 156:857-858, trans. C. C. Swinton Bland, *The Autobiography of Guibert, Abbot of Nogent-sous-Coucy*, Broadway Translations (New York, 1925), pp. 41-43, rev. R. Kay.

4 William of Malmesbury, *De gestis regum Anglorum* 5.439, ed. W. Stubbs, Rolls Series, no. 90, vol. 2 (London, 1889), pp. 510-511, trans. J. Sharpe (1815), rev. J. A. Giles, *William of Malmesbury's Chronicle of the Kings of England*, Bohn 's Antiquarian Library (London, 1847), pp. 469-470, rev. R. Kay «C. Warren Hollister, Dudley Stutz».

5 Duke William IX of Aquitaine, "Farai un vers, pos mi somelh," stanzas 3-11 (lines 7-84), ed. and trans. Frederick Golden, *Lyrics of the Troubadours and Trouvères* (Garden City, NY: Anchor Press/Doubleday, 1973), pp. 28-33. Copyright (c) 1973 by Frederick Golden. Reprinted by permission of Doubleday, a division of Bantam, Doubleday, Dell Publishing Group, Inc.

6   Peter Abelard, *Historia calamitatum* 6, ed. J. T. Muckle, "Abelard's Letter of Consolation to a Friend (Historia Calamitatum)," *Mediaeval Studies*, 12 (1950), pp.182-183; trans. C. K. Scott Moncrieff, *The Letters of Abelard and Heloise* (New York, 1926), pp. 11-13, rev. R. Kay.

7   Peter Abelard, *Historia calamitatum* 6-7, ed. J. T. Muckle, "Abelard's Letter of Consolation to a Friend (Historia Calamitatum)," *Mediaeval Studies*, 12 (1950), pp. 183-190; trans. C. K. Scott Moncrieff, *The Letters of Abelard and Heloise* (New York, 1926), pp. 13-20, rev. R. Kay.

8   Ordericus Vitalis, *Historia ecclesiastica* 12.24, ed. Marjorie Chibnall, *The Ecclesiastical History of Orderic Vitalis*, Oxford Medieval Texts, vol. 6 (Oxford, 1978), pp. 291-295; trans. Thomas Forester, *The Ecclesiastical History of England and Normandy by Ordericus Vitalis*, vol. 4, Bohn's Antiquarian Library (London, 1856), pp. 29-31, rev. R. Kay «John Maple».

9   Ordericus Vitalis, *Historia ecclesiastica* 12.26, ed. Marjorie Chibnall, *The Ecclesiastical History of Orderic Vitalis*, Oxford Medieval Texts, vol. 6 (Oxford, 1978), pp. 195-303; trans. Thomas Forester, *The Ecclesiastical History of England and Normandy by Ordericus Vitalis*, Bohn's Antiquarian Library, vol. 4 (London, 1856), pp. 33-38, rev. R. Kay.

10   Based on Josèphe Chartrou, *L'Anjou de 1109 à 1151* (Paris, 1928), pp. 83-84 «Twila Jukes». The text quoted reads: "Precepta Gaufridi formosi consulis Andegavorum miricem plantantis." Another of the same provenance: "Mathildis quae fuit soror Goffridi ... miricem plantantis." Geoffrey was also surnamed "the Fair" (*Formosus = le Bel*).

11   William of Malmesbury, *Historia novella* 1.453, ed. W. Stubbs, Rolls Series, no. 90, vol. 2 (London, 1889), pp. 530-531; trans. J. Sharpe (1815), rev. J. A. Giles, *William of Malmesbury's Chronicle of the Kings of England*, Bohn's Antiquarian Library (London, 1847), pp. 483-484 «Dudley Stutz».

12   Pedro Marfilo, *Cronica de San Juan de la Peña*, ed. Antonio Ubieto Arteta, Textos Medievales, 4 (Valencia, 1961), pp. 88-89; trans. «Clay Stalls John Lomax».

13   Walter Map, *De nugis curialium* 5.5, ed. M. R. James, Anecdota Oxoniensia, Mediaeval and Modern Series, pt. 14 (Oxford, 1914), p. 220; trans. M. R. James, Cymmrodorion Record Series, no. 9 (London, 1923), pp. 242-243, rev. R. Kay «John Maple».

14   Caesarius of Heisterbach, *Dialogus miraculorum* 12.2, ed. J. Strange (Cologne, 1851), 2:316; trans. H. von E. Scott and C. C. Swinton Bland, *The Dialogue on Miracles,* Broadway Classics (New York: 1929), 2:290-291, rev. R. Kay «Robin S. Hackett».

15 Walter Map, *De nugis curialium* 5.4, ed. M. R. James, Anecdota Oxoniensia, Mediaeval and Modern Series, pt. 14 (Oxford, 1914), pp. 213-214; trans. M. R. James, Cymmrodorion Record Series, no. 9 (London, 1923), p. 235, rev. R. Kay «John Maple».

16 Usâmah ibn Murshid, *Kitâb al-I'tibâr*, ed. H. Derenbourg as vol. 2 of his *Ousâma ibn Mounkidh*, Publications de l'Ecole des langues orientales (Paris, 1893); trans. from the original MS. by Philip K. Hitti, *An Arab-Syrian Gentleman and Warrior in the Period of the Crusades; Memoirs of Usâmah ibn-Munqidh (Kitâb al-I'tibâr)*, Records of Civilization 10 (New York: Columbia University Press, 1929), pp. 164-165, rev. R. Kay.

17 Walter Map, *De nugis curialium* 1.24, ed. M. R. James, Anecdota Oxoniensia, Mediaeval and Modern Series, pt. 14 (Oxford, 1914), pp. 38-39; trans. M. R. James, Cymmrodorion Record Series, no. 9 (London, 1923), pp. 42-43, rev. R. Kay «John Maple».

18 Giovanni Villani, *Croniche fiorentine* 5.39; trans. R. E. Selfe, *Villani's Chronicle*, 2nd ed. (New York, 1907), p. 123. A later German legend, first mentioned in 1425, dates the use of these warcries to the siege of Weinsberg in 1140: *The Cambridge Medieval History*, ed. J. B. Bury et al., vol. 5 (London, 1926), p. 394, n.1. Villani reports their use in Italy under the year 1215.

19 John of Salisbury, *Historia pontificalis* 40, ed. and trans. Marjorie Chibnall, Medieval Texts (London: Thomas Nelson and Sons, 1956), pp. 77-80, rev. R. Kay «Tim Sistrunk».

20 *Legenda aurea*, Aug. 20; trans. Granger Ryan and Helmut Ripperger (London: Longmans, Green & Co., 1941; New York, 1969), pp. 471-472.

21 Stephanus de Borbone, O.P., *Tractatus de diversis materiis praedicabilibus* 490, ed. A. Lecoy de la Marche, *Anecdotes historiques, légendes et apologues tirés du recueil inédit d'Étienne de Bourbon, Dominicain du XIIIe siècle*, Société de l'histoire de France 185 (Paris, 1877), p. 422; trans. G. G. Coulton, *A Medieval Garner* (London, 1910), p. 60, rev. R. Kay. One of Stephen's informants was Bernard's grand-nephew, Lord Calon de Fontaines.

22 Walter Map, *De nugis curialium* 5.5, ed. M. R. James, Anecdota Oxoniensia, Mediaeval and Modern Series, pt. 14 (Oxford, 1914), pp. 223-224; trans. M. R. James, Cymmrodorion Record Series, no. 9 (London, 1923), pp. 245-247, rev. and verse trans. R. Kay «John Maple». Dated by the provost, who flourished in 1154.

23 Helmold of Bosau, *Chronica Slavorum* 1.81, ed. B. Schmeidler, in *Monumenta Germaniae historica*, Scriptores rerum Germanicarum 32, 3rd ed. (Hanover, 1937), pp. 152-154; trans. R. Kay «Twila Jukes».

24 Helmold of Bosau, *Chronica Slavorum* 1.84, ed. B. Schmeidler, rev. H. Stoob, Ausgewählte Quellen zur deutschen Geschichte des Mittelalters 19 (Berlin, 1963), p. 292; trans. F. J. Tschan, *The Chronicle of the Slavs*, Records of Civilization, no. 21 (New York: Columbia University Press, 1935), p. 221 «James Ludwig».

25 Otto of Freising incorporated this text in his *Gesta Friderici I imperatoris* 3.11, ed. G. Waitz and B. de Simson in *Monumenta Germaniae historica*, Scriptores rerum Germanicarum 46, 3rd ed. (Hanover, 1912), pp. 178-179; trans. Ernest F. Henderson, *Select Historical Documents of the Middle Ages*, Bohn's Antiquarian Library (London, 1892), pp. 412-413, rev. R. Kay «Twila Jukes».

26 Otto Morena, *Historia Frederici I*, ed. Ferdinand Güterbock, *Monumenta Germaniae Historica*, Scriptores rerum Germanicarum, n.s., 7 (Berlin, 1930), p. 59; trans. R. Kay. A variant appears in *Il Novellino*, no. 24. Güterbock argues that the exchange really took place in 1194 between Barbarossa's son, Henry VI, and the lawyers Lotharius and Azo.

27 Caesarius of Heisterbach, *Dialogus miraculorum* 6.15, ed. J. Strange (Cologne, 1851), 1:368-369; trans. H. von E. Scott and C. C. Swinton Bland, *The Dialogue on Miracles*, Broadway Classics (New York: 1929), 1:425-426, rev. R. Kay «Robin S. Hackett».

28 William Fitzstephen, *Vita Sancti Thomae Cantuariensis archiepiscopi et martyris* 22, ed. J. C. Robertson in *Materials for the History of Thomas Becket*, Rolls Series, no. 67, vol. 3 (London, 1877), pp. 33-34; trans. «Clay Stalls.»

29 Walter Map, *De nugis curialium* 5.5, ed. M. R. James, Anecdota Oxoniensia, Mediaeval and Modern Series, pt. 14 (Oxford, 1914), p. 213; trans. M. R. James, Cymmrodorion Record Series, no. 9 (London, 1923), p. 249, rev. R. Kay «John Maple».

30 Ricobaldo of Ferrara, *Istoria imperiale*, Italian translation by Matteo Maria Bojardo, ed. L. Muratori, *Rerum Italicarum scriptores*, 9 (Milan, 1726), pp. 371-372; trans. «Oliver Phillips». Ricobaldo's account of the circumstances is so garbled that modern historians have felt free to relocate the story after Barbarossa's defeat at Legnano in 1176. In fact, Barbarossa did cross over into Asia and soon died there.

31 Herbert of Bosham, *Vita sancti Thomae archiepiscopi et martyris* 11, ed. J. C. Robertson, *Materials for the History of Thomas Becket, Archbishop of Canterbury*, Rolls Series 67, vol. 3 (London, 1877), p. 487; trans. R. Kay «Tim Sistrunk».

32 *Exordium magnum ordinis Cisterciensis*, Dist. 5, c. 11, ed. J. P. Migne, *Patrologia Latina*, 185:1144-45; trans. G. G. Coulton, *A Medieval Garner* (London, 1910), pp. 77-79, rev. R. Kay. Coulton remarks that "this is perhaps the earliest version of the now famous legend" on which R. H. Barham based his poem "The Jackdaw of Rheims" in *The Ingoldsby Legends* (1840-47).

33 Stephanus de Borbone, O.P. (d. 1261), *De diversis materiis praedicabilibus*, ed. A. Lecoy de la Marche,*Anecdotes historiques, légendes et apologues d'Étienne de Bourbon, Dominicain du XIIIe siècle*, Société de l'histoire de France 185 (Paris, 1877), p. 249; trans. Henry Osborn Taylor, *The Medieval Mind*, 4th ed. (New York, 1925), 1:488, rev. R. Kay «John Brothers». During the pontificate of Eugenius III (1145-53), the bishopric of Tournai was vacant only in 1149.

34 Walter Map, *De nugis curialium* 1.22, ed. M. R. James, Anecdota Oxoniensia, Mediaeval and Modern Series, pt. 14 (Oxford, 1914), p. 33; trans. M. R. James, Cymmrodorion Record Series, no. 9 (London, 1923), p. 37, rev. R. Kay «John Maple».

35 Gervase of Canterbury, *Chronica*, pt. 1, ad an. 1176, ed. William Stubbs, *The Historical Works of Gervase of Canterbury*, Rolls Series 73, vol. 1 (London, 1879), p. 258; trans. G. G. Coulton,*A Medieval Garner* (London, 1910), p. 127, rev. R. Kay.

36 Ranulphus Higden, *Polychronicon* 7.22, ed. J. R. Lumby, Rolls Series 41, vol. 8 (1882), pp. 52-55; trans. John Trevisa (1367), *ibidem*, rev. R. Kay. On the history and legend of Rosamund Clifford, see V. B. Helzel, *Fair Rosamund* (Evanston, Ill., 1947).

37 Bonincontrus de Bovis, *Hystoria de discordia et persecutione quam habuit Ecclesia cum imperatore Federico Barba-rossa*, ed. G. Monticolo with *Le Vite dei dogi de Marin Sanudo* in *Rerum Italicarum Scriptores*, 2nd ed., vol. 22, pt. 4 (Città di Castello, 1900), p. 403; trans. R. Kay «John Maple». In a earlier version (G. Villani, *Croniche fiorentine* 5.3), the pope's reply is less elegant: "I am Peter's vicar (*Ego sum vicarius Petri*)."

38 Walter Map, *De nugis curialium* 5.5, ed. M. R. James, Anecdota Oxoniensia, Mediaeval and Modern Series, pt. 14 (Oxford, 1914), p. 225; trans. M. R. James, Cymmrodorion Record Series, no. 9 (London, 1923), p. 248, rev. R. Kay «John Maple».

39 *Gesta Fulconis filii Warini; The Legend of Fulk Fitz-Warin*, ed. and trans. Joseph Stevenson, Rolls Series, no. 66 (London, 1875), pp. 324-325, rev. R. Kay «Dudley Stutz».

40 Walter Map, *De nugis curialium* 1.30, ed. M. R. James, Anecdota Oxoniensia, Mediaeval and Modern Series, pt. 14 (Oxford, 1914), p. 57; trans. M. R. James, Cymmrodorion Record Series, no. 9 (London, 1923), pp. 62-63, rev. R. Kay «John Maple».

41 Gerald of Wales (Giraldus Cambrensis), *Itinerarium Kambriae* 1.4, ed. J. F. Dimock in *Opera*, Rolls Series, no. 21, vol. 6 (London, 1868), p. 54; trans. Sir Richard Colt Hoare (1806), reprinted in *The Itinerary through Wales and the Description of Wales*, Everyman's Library (London, 1908), p. 50, rev. R. Kay «Cynthia Shively».

42   Walter Map, *De nugis curialium* 4.1, ed. M. R. James, Anecdota Oxoniensia, Mediaeval and Modern Series, pt. 14 (Oxford, 1914), p. 139; trans. M. R. James, Cymmrodorion Record Series, no. 9 (London, 1923), pp. 156-157, rev. R. Kay «John Maple».

43   Giovanni Boccaccio, "De Constantia Romanorum imperatrice," *De claris mulieribus*, ed. Eberatus Rumlang (Bern: Mathias Apiarius, 1539), fol. lxxvi; trans. «Oliver Phillips». The tale has been much improved at the expense of accuracy: Constance was the daughter of Roger II, not William II, who was was her nephew; she was 31 at the time of her marriage and 40 when Frederick was born to her, not in Palermo, but in Iesi. That she had been a nun was a Guelf libel, immortalized by Dante (*Paradiso* 4.109-120).

44   Ansbert, *Historia de expeditione Friderici imperatoris*, ed. A. Chroust, *Quellen zur Geschichte des Kreuzzuges Kaiser Friedrichs I* in *Monumenta Germaniae historica*, Scriptores rerum Germanicarum, n.s., vol. 5 (Berlin, 1928), p. 91; trans. R. Kay «Twila Jukes».

45   Albert, abbot of Stade, *Annales Stadenses*, ed. I. M. Lappenberg in *Monumenta Germaniae historica*, Scriptores, vol. 16 (Hanover, 1859), p. 351; trans. R. Kay «Twila Jukes».

46   Ludwig Bechstein, *Die Sagen des Kyffhäusers* (1835), collected in his *Deutschen Sagenbuch* (1853) and reprinted in his *Deutsche Märchen und Sagen* (Berlin, 1960), pp. 417-418; trans. R. Kay. A collector of Thuringian legends, Bechstein, like J. Grimm and many others, believed the emperor in the mountain to be Frederick Barbarossa; Peter Munz, however, argues instead for Frederick II: *Frederick Barbarossa: A Study in Medieval Politics* (Ithaca, N.Y., 1969), pp. 3-22.

47   *Le Novelle antiche* 25, ed. S. Lo Nigro, *Novellino e conti del duecento* (Turin, 1963), p. 102; trans. Edward Storer, *Il Novellino; The Hundred Old Tales,* Broadway Translations (New York, 1925), no. 25, pp. 86-87, rev. R. Kay.

48   'Imad ad-Din, *Conquête de la Syrie et de la Palestine par Salâh ed-dîn*, ed. Carlo Landberg, vol. 1 (Leiden, 1888), pp. 228-229; trans. Francesco Gabrieli and E. J. Costello, *Arab Historians of the Crusades* (London: Routledge and Kegan Paul, 1969), pp. 204-206. «Dudly Stutz». The author, a rhetorician who was Saladin's chancellor, based his histories on facts but would elaborate them to display his stylistic skill.

49   A minstrel from Rheims, *Récits* 12.77-83, ed. N. de Wailly, *Récits d'un ménestrel de Reims au treizième siècle*, Société de l'histoire de France (Paris, 1876), pp. 41-44; trans. R. Kay «Dudley Stutz, Norris Lacy». The minstrel has his basic facts wrong: Richard was captured near Vienna on 21 Dec.

50 *Del Tumbeor Nostre-Dame*, ed. Wilhelm Foerster, *Romania* 2 (1873), 315-325; trans. Alice Kemp-Welch, *Of the Tumbler of Our Lady and Other Miracles* (New York, 1908), rev. R. Kay. The original is in rhymed, 8-syllable verses; the language places it near Paris and dates it as well (the only extant copy was made in 1268). Anatole France retold the story in his *L'Etui de nacre* (1892) and Jules Massenet turned it into an opera.

51 "A Tale of Robin Hood, or, Robin Hood and the Monk," stanzas 9b-17, ed. John Mathew Gutch, *A Lytell Geste of Robin Hode with Other Ancient & Modern Ballads and Songs Relating to This Celebrated Yeoman* (London, 1847), 2:8-9; trans. R. Kay «Cynthia Shively».

52 *Chronica magistri Rogeri de Houedene*, ed. W. Stubbs, Rolls Series 51, vol. 4 (London, 1871), pp. 82-84; trans. H. T. Riley, *The Annals of Roger de Hoveden*, Bohn's Antiquarian Library (London, 1853), 2:452-454, rev. R. Kay «Tim Sistrunk». The Winchester chronicler says that Gurdun was turned over to the king's sister, Joanna, who tore out his eyes and had him tortured until he died.

53 *Vita sancti Wilhelmi abbatis Roschildensis* 6.58, ed. *Acta sanctorum quotquot toto orbe coluntur*, Aprilis, vol. 1 (Paris, 1865), p. 633-634; trans. G. G. Coulton, *A Medieval Garner* (London, 1910), p. 114, rev. R. Kay. The *Vita* pretends to be contemporary but is in fact much later and of doubtful authenticity.

Notes to pages 222–262

1 *Carmina Burana* 44 (21), ed. K. Langosch, *Vagantes Dichtung*, Sammlung Dietrich 316 (Bremen-Leipzig, 1968), pp. 280-283; trans. Ephraim Emerton, *Mediaeval Europe* (Boston, 1894), p. 475, rev. R. Kay. I have placed this prose satire between the 12th and 13th centuries because it could belong to either. Over 30 passages from the Bible are echoed in this parody.

2 Caesarius of Heisterbach, *Dialogus miraculorum*, ed. J. Strange (Cologne, 1851), 1:167; trans. G. G. Coulton, *A Medieval Garner* (London, 1910), pp. 219-220, rev. R. Kay.

3 Caesarius of Heisterbach, *Dialogus miraculorum* 2.24, ed. J. Strange (Cologne, 1851), 1:94-95; trans. H. von E. Scott and C. C. Swinton Bland, *The Dialogue on Miracles* (New York: 1929), 1:104-106, rev. R. Kay.

4 *L'Histoire de Guillaume le Maréchal* 12675-12704; ed. Paul Meyer, Société de l'histoire de France (Paris, 1894), 2:92-93; trans. R. Kay «Dudley Stutz». This biographical poem forms the basis for Sidney Painter's *William Marshall: Knight-errant, Baron and Regent of England* (Baltimore, 1933).

5   Thomas of Celano, *Prima vita sancti Francisci* 1.7.16-17, ed. E. d'Alençon (Rome, 1906); trans. A. G. F. Howell, *The Lives of S. Francis of Assisi by Brother Thomas of Celano* (London, 1908), pp. 17-18, rev. R. Kay.

6   Letter from Thomas de Merleberge to Evesham Abbey (1206), incorporated in *Chronicon abbatiae de Evesham* ad an. 1205-1206, ed. W. D. Macray, Rolls Series, no. 29 (London, 1863), pp. 153, 189; trans. R. Kay «Cynthia Shively».

7   *Annales de Waverleia* (an. 1208) in *Annales monastici*, ed. H. R. Luard, Rolls Series, no. 36, vol. 2 (London, 1865), p. 261; trans. R. Kay «Larry Watkins».

8   Caesarius of Heisterbach, *Dialogus miraculorum* 5.21, ed. J. Strange (Cologne, 1851), 1:301-302; trans. H. von E. Scott and C. C. Swinton Bland, *The Dialogue on Miracles* (New York: 1:345-346, rev. R. Kay «Robin S. Hackett». The massacre of Béziers actually took place in July 1209; Arnaud-Amaury was the pope's legate.

9   Thomas of Celano, *Prima vita sancti Francisci* 1.16.42-43, ed. E. d'Alençon (Rome, 1906); trans. A. G. F. Howell, *The Lives of S. Francis of Assisi by Brother Thomas of Celano* (New York, 1908), pp. 42-43, rev. R. Kay.

10   Thomas of Celano, *Prima vita sancti Francisci* 1.21.58, ed. E. d'Alençon (Rome, 1906); trans. A. G. F. Howell, *The Lives of S. Francis of Assisi by Brother Thomas of Celano* (New York, 1908), pp. 57-59, rev. R. Kay.

11   Matthew Paris, *Chronica majora*, ed. H. R. Luard, Rolls Series, no. 57, vol. 2 (London, 1874), pp. 558-559; trans. R. Kay «John T. Brothers». In his earlier *Historia Anglorum*, Matthew had John make the last remark at the death of Hubert Walter (Rolls Series, no. 44, 2:104).

12   Giovanni Villani, *Croniche fiorentine* 5.24-25; trans. R. E. Selfe, *Villani's Chronicle*, 2nd ed. (New York, 1907), p. 114-115, rev. R. Kay.

13   Giovanni Villani, *Croniche fiorentine* 5.38; trans. R. E. Selfe, *Villani's Chronicle*, 2nd ed. (New York, 1907), p. 121-123, rev. R. Kay.

14   Thomas of Celano, *Prima vita sancti Francisci* 1.21.57, ed. E. d'Alençon (Rome, 1906); trans. A. G. F. Howell, *The Lives of S. Francis of Assisi by Brother Thomas of Celano* (New York, 1907), pp. 56-57, rev. R. Kay.

15   Jordan of Giano, *Chronica fratris Jordani* ad an. 1219, ed. H. Boehmer (Paris, 1908); trans. G. G. Coulton, *Social Life in Britain from the Conquest to the Reformation* (Cambridge, Eng., 1918), pp. 239-240. Jordan took part in the second Franciscan mission to Germany in 1221.

16 Thomas of Celano, *Secunda vita sancti Francisci* 2.110.150, ed. E. d'Alençon (Rome, 1906); trans. A. G. F. Howell, *The Lives of S. Francis of Assisi by Brother Thomas of Celano* (New York, 1908), pp. 280-281, rev. R. Kay.

17 British Library, MS. Add. 8167, fol. 104, ed. and trans. Charles Homer Haskins, "The Life of Medieval Students as Illustrated by Their Letters," *American Historical Review* 3 (1898), 203-229, at p. 210; rev. R. Kay. The classical allusion is to Terence, *Eunuchus* 4.5.6.

18 *Carmina Burana* 75, ed. K. Langosch, *Vagantes Dichtung*, Sammlung Dietrich 316 (Bremen-Leipzig, 1968), p. 68; trans. R. Kay.

19 *I Fioretti* 3; trans. Thomas Okey, *The Little Flowers*..., Everyman's Library (London, 1910), pp. 5-6, rev. R. Kay «Larry Watkins».

20 Sibt ibn al-Jauzî, *Mir'ât az-zamân*, ed. J. R. Jewett (Chicago, 1907), pp. 432-434; trans. Francesco Gabrieli and E. J. Costello, *Arab Historians of the Crusades* (London: Routledge and Kegan Paul, 1969), pp. 273-275, rev. R. Kay «Dudley Stutz». No one has been able to explain what the "pieces of paper" were; another version of the story, by Ibn Wasil, says the man was carrying a copy of the New Testament into the shrine. Amari turned Frederick's witticism about the sparrows *(asafîr)* into a pun by emending *jabbarîn* ("giants/magnates") to *khanazîr* ("pigs"). Though Frederick was capable of punning in Arabic, the emendation would seem to be gratuitous.

21 Aubry (Albericus) des Troisfontaines, *Chronicon*, ed. *Monumenta Germaniae Historica*, Scriptores, vol. 23 (1874), p. 943; trans. R. Kay «Gregory G. Guzman».

22 Jacques de Vitry, cardinal 1228--ca. 1240, *Exempla ex sermonibus vulgaribus* 218, ed. Thomas Frederick Crane, *The Exempla, or Illustrative Stories from the Sermones Vulgares of Jacques de Vitry*, Publications of the Folk-Lore Society 26 (London, 1890), p. 91; trans. R. Kay «Karl F. Morrison».

23 *Chronica fratris Salimbene de Adam ordinis minorum*, ed. O. Holder-Egger, *Monumenta Germaniae historica*, Scriptores, vol. 32 (Hanover-Leipzig, 1905-1913), pp. 71-72; trans. G. G. Coulton, *From St. Francis to Dante*, 2nd ed. (London, 1907), p. 22, rev. R. Kay.

24 Giovanni Villani, *Croniche fiorentine* 6.23; trans. R. E. Selfe, *Villani's Chronicle*, 2nd ed. (New York, 1906), p. 134, rev. R. Kay.

25 William of Tocco, O.P., *Hystoria beati Thomae* c.2, ed. *Acta sanctorum quotquot toto orbe coluntur*, Martius, vol. 1 (1668; rpt. Paris-Rome, 1865), p. 659; trans. R. Kay «Ronald Steckling, Dudley Stutz».

26   Giovanni Villani, *Croniche fiorentine* 6.24; trans. R. E. Selfe, *Villani's Chronicle* 2nd ed. (New York, 1907), pp. 135-137, rev. R. Kay.

27   Stephanus de Borbone, O.P., *Tractatus de diversis materiis praedicabilibus* 319, ed. A. Lecoy de la Marche, *Anecdotes historiques, légendes et apologues tirés du recueil inédit d'Étienne de Bourbon, Dominicain du XIIIe siècle*, Société de l'histoire de France 185 (Paris, 1877), pp. 268-269; trans. G. G. Coulton, *A Medieval Garner* (London, 1910), p. 305, rev. R. Kay. I have assigned this incident to 1246, the year in which Bishop Peter III of Grenoble passed a dress code for his cathedral chapter: *Gallia Christiana*, vol. 16 (Paris, 1865), col. 246.

28   Lucas Tudensis, *De altera vita fideique controversiis adversus Albigensium errores libri III* 2.9 (Ingolstadt, 1612), p. 93; trans. G. G. Coulton, *Social Life in Britain From the Conquest to the Reformation* (Cambridge, Eng., 1918), p. 474, rev. R. Kay. Luke, a provincial Spanish bishop, was reacting to Gothic realism; the representation he describes, which is the familiar one today, was introduced in the 13th century. Coulton not only prints a picture of the older form but also the 1306 case of an artist whose crucifix was banned from London for its novelty in 1306.

29   Giovanni Villani, *Croniche fiorentine* 6.1; trans. R. E. Selfe, *Villani's Chronicle*, 2nd ed. (New York, 1907), pp. 127-128.

30   Giovanni Boccaccio, *Decameron*, day 1, novella 2, ed. Vittore Branca, in his *Tutte le opere di Giovanni Boccaccio*, vol. 4 (Milan, 1976), pp. 48-53; trans. J. M. Rigg, *The Decameron* (London, 1903), rev. R. Kay. I date the story circa 1250 because it was first written down then by Etienne de Bourbon, who attributed it to Emperor Frederick II.

31   Jamâl ad-Din Ibn Wasil, *Mufarrij al-Kurûb fi akhbâr Bani Ayyûb* [The Dissipator of Anxieties Concerning the History of the Ayyubids], MS. Paris, Arsenal 1702, fols. 372v-373v; trans. Francesco Gabrieli and E. J. Costello, *Arab Historians of the Crusades* (London: Routledge and Kegan Paul, 1969), p. 299, rev. R. Kay «Dudley Stutz».

32   Giovanni Villani, *Croniche fiorentine* 6.53; trans. R. E. Selfe, *Villani's Chronicle*, 2nd ed. (New York, 1907), pp. 161-162, rev. R. Kay.

33   Robert Grosseteste, O.S.F., bishop of Lincoln (1235-53), *Epistolae* 128, ed. H. R. Luard, Rolls Series, no. 25 (London, 1861), pp. 436-437; trans. F. S. Stevenson, *Robert Grosseteste, Bishop of Lincoln* (New York, 1899), pp. 310-311 «James Ludwig». As a result, Pope Innocent IV countermanded the offensive order.

34   Jean, sire de Joinville (1224?--1317), *Histoire de Saint Louis* 1.4.29; trans. Frank T. Marzials, *Memoirs of the Crusades by Villehardouin & De Joinville*, Everyman's Library (London, 1908), p. 141.

35 Jean, sire de Joinville (1224?--1317), *Histoire de Saint Louis* 1.8.45; trans. Frank T. Marzials, *Memoirs of the Crusades by Villehardouin & De Joinville*, Everyman's Library (London, 1908), p. 146.

36 Jean, sire de Joinville (1224?--1317), *Histoire de Saint Louis* 1.12.55, 57-60; trans. Frank T. Marzials, *Memoirs of the Crusades by Villehardouin & De Joinville*, Everyman's Library (London, 1908), p. 149-150, rev. R. Kay.

37 Jean, sire de Joinville (1224?--1317), *Histoire de Saint Louis* 1.10.51-53, trans. Frank T. Marzials, *Memoirs of the Crusades by Villehardouin & De Joinville*, Everyman's Library (London, 1908), p. 148, rev. R. Kay.

38 Matthew Paris, *Chronica majora*, ed. H. R. Luard, Rolls Series, no. 57, vol. 5 (London, 1880), p. 706; trans. W. H. Hutton, *Simon de Montfort and His Cause, 1251-1266* (New York, 1888), pp. 93-94, rev. R. Kay «John Maple».

39 Giovanni Villani, *Croniche fiorentine* 7.9; trans. R. E. Selfe, *Villani's Chronicle*, 2nd ed. (New York, 1907), pp. 214-217, rev. R. Kay. Dante was one who believed in the disinterment: *Purg.* 3.118-135.

40 Bernardus Guidonis, *Vita s. Thomae Aquinatis* 25, ed. D. Prümmer, in *Fontes vitae s. Thomae Aquinatis*, Documents inédits publiés par la *Revue Thomiste* (Saint-Maximin, 1937), pp. 191-192; trans. R. Kay

41 William Camden, *Remaines concerning Britain* (London, 1657), p. 260; spelling and punctuation modernized «Tim Sistrunk». Camden attributes the story of Eleanor's leechcraft to Rodericus Sanctius, but it is already found in Ptolemy of Lucca, *Historia ecclesiastica* (1312), ed. L. A. Muratori, *Rerum Italicarum scriptores,* vol. 11 (Milan, 1727), p. 1168.

42 Testimony of Bartholomew of Capua, chancellor of the kingdom of Sicily, on 8 August 1319, *Processus inquisitionis factae super vita, conversatione et miraculis recol. memor. fr. Thomae de Aquino O.P.* 79, in *Acta sanctorum quotquot toto orbe coluntur...*, 3rd ed., Martius, vol. 1 (Paris-Rome, 1865), p. 711; trans. Kenelm Foster, *The Life of Saint Thomas Aquinas: Biographical Documents* (Baltimore: Helicon Press, 1959), pp. 109-110, rev. R. Kay «Twila Jukes».

43 *Chronicon de Lanercost* s.a. 1272, ed. Joseph Stevenson, Maitland and Bannatyne Clubs (Glasgow, 1839); trans. Herbert Maxwell, "Chronicle of Lanercost," *Scottish Historical Review* 6 (1909): 16, rev. R. Kay.

44 *Chronicon de Lanercost* s.a. 1282, ed. Joseph Stevenson, Maitland and Bannatyne Clubs (Glasgow, 1839); trans. Herbert Maxwell, "Chronicle of Lanercost," *Scottish Historical Review* 6 (1909): 177, rev. R. Kay.

45 Giovanni Villani, *Croniche fiorentine* 7.61; trans. R. E. Selfe, *Villani's Chronicle*, 2nd ed. (New York, 1907), pp. 267-268, rev. R. Kay.

46 Don Ramón Muntaner, *Crònica* [written in Catalan], ch. 124, ed. J. F. Vidal-Jové, Biblioteca selecta 468 (Barcelona, 1973), pp. 263-264; trans. G. G. Coulton, *A Medieval Garner* (London, 1910), pp. 438-439, rev. R. Kay.

47 John Stow, *Annales, or a Generale Chronicle of England from Brute to the Present Year of Christ 1580* (London, 1580), pp. 309-310 (orthography modernized). Stow slightly abridged an unidentified account that was printed more fully a few years later in *The Historie of Cambria, now called Wales... by* H. Lhoyd [*sic* for Lloyd] and ed. by David Powel (1584; reprinted, London, 1811), pp. 275-276 «Cynthia Shively».

48 Dino Compagni, *Cronica* 1.10, ed. I. Del Lungo, *La Cronica di Dino Compagni delle cose occurrenti ne' tempi suoi*, in L. A. Muratori, *Rerum Italicarum scriptores*, 2nd ed., vol. 9, pt. 2 (Città di Castello, 1907-1916), pp. 25-27; trans. Else C. M. Benecke and A. G. Ferrers Howell, *The Chronicle of Dino Compagni*, Temple Classics (London, J.M.Dent & Co., 1906), pp. 23-24, rev. R. Kay. Dante seems to have been an eyewitness and presumably a participant (*Inferno* 22.1-5).

49 *Memorials of London and London Life*, ed. H. T. Riley (London, 1868), p. 27; trans. G. G. Coulton, *Social Life in Britain From the Conquest to the Reformation* (Cambridge, Eng., 1918), pp. 317-318, rev. R. Kay. *The Oxford English Dictionary* simply defines the objectionable word as "an expression of contempt" (s.v. "Tprot"). Louis VI the Fat, king of France 1108-1137, defied an arrogant German embassy with the words: "Tpwrut Aleman!" (Walter Map, *De nugis curialium* 5.5, ed. James, p. 229).

50 Giovanni Villani, *Croniche fiorentine* 8.5; trans. R. E. Selfe, *Villani's Chronicle*, 2nd ed. (New York, 1907), pp. 304-305, rev. R. Kay.

51 Ferreto de' Ferreti, *Historia rerum in Italia gestarum ab a. 1250 usque ad a. 1318* 2.25, ed. Carlo Cipolla in *Le Opere di Ferreto de' Ferreti vicentino*, vol. 1, Fonti per la storia d'Italia 42 (Rome, 1908), p. 64; trans. R. Kay «Tim Sistrunk». The device was already a century old in folklore: see Caesarius of Heisterbach's tale of the clerk who fooled the Jews, given above at the year 1200.

52 *Le Novelle antiche* 35, ed. S. Lo Nigro, *Novellino e conti del duecento* (Turin, 1963), pp. 115-116; trans. Edward Storer, *Il Novellino; The Hundred Old Tales*, Broadway Translations (New York, 1925), no. 35, pp. 101-102, rev. R. Kay.

53 Walter of Guisborough (*alias* of Hemingford or Heminburgh), *Chronicle*, ed. H. Rothwell in Camden Third Series, vol. 89 (London: Royal Historical Society, 1957), pp. 289-290; trans. R. Kay «Clay Stalls, Cynthia Shively».

Notes to pages 263–296

1 Continuation of Rishanger's *Chronica*, ed. H. T. Riley, *Chronica monasterii s. Albani*, Rolls Series 28, vol. 2 (London, 1865), pp. 197-198; trans. R. Kay.

2 Franco Sacchetti, *Le Novelle*, no. 114, ed. O. Gigli, *Le Novelle di Franco Sacchetti*, 2nd ed. (Florence, 1888), 1:274-275; trans. Paget Toynbee, *Dante Alighieri: His Life and Works*, 4th ed. (London, 1910), pp. 147-148, rev. R. Kay.

3 Jacques de Meyer, *Commentarii, sive Annales rerum Flandriacum* (Antwerp, 1561), fols. 88v-89r; trans. «Clay Stalls».

4 Robertus de Graystanes, *Chronicon,* ed. J. Raine in *Historiae Dunelmensis scriptores tres*, Surtees Society 9 (London-Edinburgh, 1839), p. 64; trans. G. G. Coulton, *A Medieval Garner* (London, 1910), pp. 484-485, rev. R. Kay.

5 Dino Compagni, *Cronica* 2.25, ed. I. Del Lungo, *La Cronica di Dino Compagni delle cose occurrenti ne' tempi suoi*, in L. A. Muratori, *Rerum Italicarum scriptores*, 2nd ed., vol. 9, pt. 2 (Città di Castello, 1907-1916), pp. 135-142; trans. Else C. M. Benecke and A. G. Ferrers Howell, *The Chronicle of Dino Compagni*, Temple Classics (London, J.M.Dent & Co.,1906), pp. 134-136, rev. R. Kay. In the end, Charles made a personal profit of over 100,000 florins out of his confiscations as the pope's peacemaker.

6 Giovanni Villani, *Croniche fiorentine* 8.63; trans. R. E. Selfe, *Villani's Chronicle*, 2nd ed. (New York, 1907), pp. 346-349, rev. R. Kay.

7 Sir Walter Scott, *Tales of a Grandfather*, I: *History of Scotland* (1828), ch. 8, in *The Miscellaneous Works of Sir Walter Scott*, vol. 22 (Edinburgh, 1870), pp. 108-110 «Cynthia Shively».

8 Giovanni Villani, *Croniche fiorentine* 8.92; trans. R. E. Selfe, *Villani's Chronicle*, 2nd ed. (New York, 1907), pp. 377-379, rev. R. Kay.

9 Das Weisse Buch über die Befreiung der Waldstätte (anonymous MS written between 1467 and 1474), ed. Anton Gisler, *Die Tellfrage: Versuch ihrer Geschichte und Lösung* (Bern, 1895), pp. 207-208; trans. W. D. McCrackan, *The Rise of the Swiss Republic*, 2nd ed. (New York, 1901), pp. 96-97, rev. R. Kay «John Lomax». A slightly earlier, much briefer version exists in ballad form, but subsequent retellings have been based on the White Book. Dates ranging from 1260 to 1334 have been proposed for the fictitious event, but since the 18th century the preferred one has been 18 November 1307.

10 Jean Froissart, *Les Chroniques* 1.1.59, ed. J. A. C. Buchon (Paris, 1835), 1:53-54; trans. Thomas Johnes, *Chronicles of England, France, Spain and the Adjoining Countries* (New York, 1855), p. 29, rev. R. Kay.

11 *Annales Paulini* (i.e. St. Paul's, London), ed. W. Stubbs in *Chronicles of the Reigns of Edward I and Edward II*, Rolls Series, no. 76, vol. 1 (London, 1882), p. 265; trans. «James J. Ludwig». Presumably Bruce's jibe gave rise to Froissart's tale.

12 Giovanni Villani, *Croniche fiorentine* 8.92; trans. R. E. Selfe, *Villani's Chronicle*, 2nd ed. (New York, 1907), pp. 379-381, rev. R. Kay.

13 Giovanni Villani, *Croniche fiorentine* 9.47; trans. R. E. Selfe, *Villani's Chronicle*, 2nd ed. (New York, 1907), pp. 416, 419, rev. R. Kay «Herbert Oerter». The second paragraph is an anonymous addition to the original chronicle.

14 Poggio Bracciolini, *Facetiae* 197, ed. in his *Opera* (Strasbourg: J. Knobluch, 1513), fol. 177r; trans. anon., *Facetia* [sic] *Erotica of Poggio Fiorentino* (New York: Valhalla Books, 1964), p. 93. The *Clementines* is a collection of canon law, named after Pope Clement V, who issued it in 1313; the *Novels* of Justinian contains the new laws he made between 535 and 556 and forms the last part of his *Corpus juris civilis*.

15 Giovanni Villani, *Croniche fiorentine* 9.66; trans. R. E. Selfe, *Villani's Chronicle*, 2nd ed. (New York, 1907), pp. 428-429, rev. R. Kay.

16 Francesco Petrarca, *Rerum memorandum libri*, book 2, ed. G. Billanovich, Edizione nazionale delle opere di Francesco Petrarca, vol. 14 (Florence, 1945); trans. Paget Toynbee, *Dante Alighieri: His Life and Works*, 4th ed. (London, 1910), pp. 144-145, rev. R. Kay

17 Charles Homer Haskins, *The Renaissance of the Twelfth Century* (Cambridge, Mass., 1927; rpt. New York, 1957), p. 9.

18 Robertus de Graystanes, *Chronicon*, ed. J. Raine in *Historiae Dunelmensis scriptores tres*, Surtees Society 9 (London-Edinburgh, 1839), p. 118; trans. G. G. Coulton, *A Medieval Garner* (London, 1910), pp. 486-487, rev. R. Kay. Graystanes was known for his learning; he was subprior of Durham and very nearly succeeded de Beaumont as bishop in 1333.

19 Sir Thomas de la More (Moor, -e), *Vita et mors Edwardi secundi regis Angliae*, ed. William Stubbs, in *Chronicles of the Reigns of Edward I and Edward II*, Rolls Series 76, vol. 2 (London, 1883), pp. 318-319; trans. R. Kay «Dudley Stutz». The biography that goes under Sir Thomas' name is an extract from the chronicle of Geoffrey Baker, who learned details of the murder from one of the participants.

20 Giorgio Vasari, *Delle Vite de' più eccellenti pittori, scultori, ed architettori*, in *Le Opere di Giorgio Vasari*, ed. G. Milanesi (Florence, 1906), *The Lives of the Painters, Sculptors and Architects*, Everyman's Library (New York, 1927), p. 76 «Larry Watkins».

21 Giorgio Vasari, *Delle Vite de' più eccellenti pittori, scultori, ed architettori*, in *Le Opere di Giorgio Vasari*, ed. G. Milanesi (Florence, 1906), 1:390-391; trans. R. Kay.

22 Giovanni Boccaccio, *Decameron*, day 6, novella 5, ed. Vittore Branca, in his *Tutte le opere di Giovanni Boccaccio*, vol. 4 (Milan, 1976), pp. 550-552; trans. J. M. Rigg, *The Decameron* (London, 1903), rev. R. Kay «Larry Watkins».

23 Jean Froissart, *Chroniques* 1.256, ed. Siméon Luce et al., Société de l'histoire de France, vol. 3 (Paris, 1872), p. 133; trans. John Bourchier, Lord Berners (1523), ed. G. C. Macaulay, *The Chronicles of Froissart* (London, 1904), p. 94, rev. R. Kay «Dudley Stutz».

24 Jean Froissart, *Chroniques* 1.165-167, ed. Siméon Luce et al., Société de l'histoire de France, vol. 2 (Paris, 1870), pp. 142-146, trans. Thomas Johnes, *Chronicles of England, France, Spain and Adjoining Countries* ... (New York, 1855), 1:56-57, rev. R. Kay «Twila Jukes». The countess was Joan of Flanders.

25 Thomas Walsingham, monk of St. Alban's, *Historia Anglicana* ad an. 1343, ed. H. T. Riley, in *Chronica monasterii s. Albani*, Rolls Series, no. 28, vol. 1 (London, 1863), pp. 261-262; trans. G. G. Coulton, *A Medieval Garner* (London, 1910), pp. 523-524, rev. R. Kay. The epigraph is the title of J. D. Salinger's novel (1951), which does not refer to this account.

26 *Mémoires historiques de la Société des antiquaires de la Morinie*, vol. 6, pt. 2 (1838), pp. XL ff.; trans. G. G. Coulton, *A Medieval Garner* (London, 1910), pp. 494-495, rev. R. Kay.

27 *Epistolario di Cola di Rienzo* 24, ed. Annibale Gabrielli, Fonti per la storia d'Italia 6 (Rome, 1890), 6:67-71; trans. F. Duncalf and A. C. Krey, *Parallel Source Problems in Medieval History* (New York, 1912), pp. 222-226, rev. R. Kay «John Brothers». Cola writes as one who was by profession a notary.

28 Poggio Bracciolini, *Facetiae* 221, ed. in his *Opera* (Strasbourg: J. Knobluch, 1513), fol. 178v; trans. anon., *Facetia* [sic] *Erotica of Poggio Fiorentino* (New York: Valhalla Books, 1964), p. 102, rev. R. Kay. The lawyer, better known as Johannes Andreae, taught both Roman and Canon Law; he died in 1348.

29 Henry Knighton, *Chronicon* ad an. 1348, ed. J. R. Lumby, *Chronicon Henrici Knighton vel Cnitthon, monachi Leycestrensis*, Rolls Series, no. 92, vol. 2 (London, 1895), p. 57-58; trans. G. G. Coulton, *A Medieval Garner* (London, 1910), pp. 495-496, rev. R. Kay.

30 Henry Knighton, *Chronicon* ad ann. 1348-49, ed. J. R. Lumby, *Chronicon Henrici Knighton vel Cnitthon, monachi Leycestrensis*, Rolls Series, no. 92, vol. 2 (London, 1895), pp. 58-64; trans. M. M. McLaughlin in *The Portable Medieval Reader*, ed. J. B. Ross and M. M. McLaughlin (New York: The Viking Press, 1949), pp. 216-221.

31   Giovanni Boccaccio, *Decameron*, day 6, novella 10, ed. Vittore Branca, in his *Tutte le opere di Giovanni Boccaccio*, vol. 4 (Milan, 1976), pp. 565-574; trans. J. M. Rigg, *The Decameron* (London, 1903), rev. R. Kay.

32   Anonynmous, *Historiae Romanae fragmenta* 4.7, ed. L. A. Muratori, in his *Antiquitates Italicae Medii Aevi*, vol. 3 (Milan, 1740), col. 500; trans. R. Kay «John T. Brothers». Since 1647 excerpts from this chronicle have been better known as *La Vita di Cola di Rienzo*, ed. A. M. Ghisalberti (Rome, 1928); trans. John Wright, *The Life of Cola di Rienzo* (Toronto, 1975); see book 3, ch. 4, for the passage given here. The quotation in the title occurs in the next chapter.

33   Poggio Bracciolini, *Facetiae* 124, ed. in his *Opera* (Strasbourg: J. Knobluch, 1513), fol. 169v; trans. Edward Storer, *The Facetiae of Poggio and Other Medieval Storytellers*, Broadway Translations (New York, 1928), no. 48, pp. 75-76, rev. R. Kay.

34   Franco Sacchetti, *Le Novelle*, no. 228, ed. O. Gigli, *Le Novelle di Franco Sacchetti*, 2nd ed. (Florence, 1888), 2:275-277; trans. Mary G. Steegmann, *Tales from Sacchetti* (London, 1908), no. 83 (CCXXVII), pp. 296-298, rev. R. Kay. If the tale has any basis in fact, it probably represents the fiscal system instituted in 1366 by Duke Philip the Bold.

35   Jean Froissart, *Chroniques*, ed. Siméon Luce et al., Société de l'histoire de France, vol. 7 (Paris, 1878), pp. 62-64; trans. Thomas Johnes, *Chronicles of England, France, Spain and Adjoining Countries* ... (New York, 1855), 1:170-171, rev. R. Kay «Timothy G. Sistrunk».

36   Guerriero da Gubbio, *Cronaca*, sub an. 1360, ed. G. Mazzatinti, in *Rerum Italicarum scriptores*, 2nd ed., vol. 21, pt. 4 (Città di Castello, 1902), p. 16; trans. Ephraim Emerton, *Humanism and Tyranny: Studies in the Italian Trecento* (Cambridge, Mass., 1925), pp. 208-209, rev. R. Kay «Clay Stalls».

37   *The History of Sir Richard Whittington by T. H.* [first printed 1656], ed. H. B. Wheatley, Chap-Books and Folk-Lore Tracts, 1st ser., no. 5 (London, 1885), pp. 9, 11-12, rev. R. Kay «John T. Maple». This familiar tale is pure fantasy, since the real Richard Whittington came from a well-to-do family. He was born ca. 1356 and died in 1423; when about 13, in 1379, he made a small loan to the city. The story of how he made a fortune from the sale of his cat is a widespread folktale. Both stories came to be connected with him about a century after his death; this is the earliest prose version.

38   *Anonimalle Chronicle*, written in French at St. Mary's, York, ad an. 1381, ed. V. H. Galbraith (Manchester, 1927), pp. 146-149; trans. Charles Oman, *The Great Revolt of 1381* (Oxford, 1906), pp. 200-203, rev. R. Kay.

39 Franco Sacchetti, *Le Novelle*, no. 181, ed. O. Gigli, *Le Novelle di Franco Sacchetti*, 2nd ed. (Florence, 1888), 2:114-115; trans. Mary G. Steegmann *Tales from Sacchetti* (London, J.M.Dent &Co., 1908), no. 58 (CLXXXI), p. 207, rev. R. Kay. Hawkwood acquired the castle of Montecchio in 1384 and still held it at his death in 1394: *Dictionary of National Biography*, 9:339.

40 Jean Froissart, *Chroniques* 4.44, ed. Kervyn de Lettenhove, *Oeuvres de Froissart*, vol. 15 (Brussels, 1871), pp. 36-43; trans. Thomas Johnes, *Chronicles of England, France, Spain and Adjoining Countries* ... (London, 1839), 2:532-534, rev. R. Kay. The casualties are reported by other sources.

41 Jean Froissart, *Chroniques* 4.53, ed. Kervyn de Lettenhove, *Oeuvres de Froissart*, vol. 15 (Brussels, 1871), pp. 84-89; trans. Thomas Johnes, *Chronicles of England, France, Spain and Adjoining Countries* ... (London, 1839), 2:532-534, rev. R. Kay.

Notes to pages 297196320

1 Anonymous, *Annales Henrici Quarti*, ed. Henry Thomas Riley, in *Chronica Monasterii S. Albani*, Rolls Series, no. 28, vol. 3 (London, 1866), pp. 418-419; trans. A. R. Myers, *English Historical Documents, 1327-1485* (New York: Oxford University Press, 1969), p. 199 «John Maple».

2 Poggio Bracciolini, *Facetiae* 49, ed. in *Opera* (Strasbourg: J. Knobluch, 1513), fol. 162v; trans. Edward Storer, *The Facetiae of Poggio and Other Medieval Story-tellers*, Broadway Translations (New York, 1928), no. 66, pp. 92-94, rev. R. Kay. Pope Gregory finally resigned at the Council of Constance in 1415.

3 Anonymous, *Gesta Henrici Quinti*, ed. and trans. Frank Taylor and J. S. Roskell, *The Deeds of Henry the Fifth*, Oxford Medieval Texts (Oxford: Clarendon, 1975), pp. 78-79 «Dudley Stutz».

4 Poggio Bracciolini, *Facetiae* 27, ed. in his *Opera* (Strasbourg: J. Knobluch, 1513), fol. 160v; trans. anon., *Facetia* [sic] *Erotica of Poggio Fiorentino* (New York: Valhalla Books, 1964), pp. 126-127, rev. R. Kay.

5 *Syon Monastery Customal*, ed. G. J. Aungier in his *History and Antiquities of Syon Monastery* (London, 1840), pp. 405 ff.; reprinted by G. G. Coulton, *Life in the Middle Ages* (Cambridge, Eng., 1928), 4:322-324, rev. R. Kay. These have been selected from a list of over a hundred signs.

6 Jean Juvenal des Ursins, archbishop of Rheims 1449-73, *Histoire de Charles VI, roy de France*, ed. J. F. Michaud and J. J. F. Poujoulat in their *Nouvelle Collection des mémoires pour servir à l'histoire de France depuis le XIIIe jusqu'à la fin du XVIIIe*, vol. 2 (Paris, 1836), p. 561; trans. R. Kay «Cynthia Shively».

7   *Procès de condamnation et de réhabilitation de Jeanne d'Arc dite la Pucelle,* ed. Jules Quicherat, vol. 3 (Paris, 1845), pp. 115-116; trans. R. Kay «James J. Ludwig». The witness respectfully refers to Charles VII as "the king," his title at the time of the deposition, an anachronisim which I have altered to "the Dauphin."

8   Poggio Bracciolini, *Facetiae* 81, ed. in his *Opera* (Strasbourg: J. Knobluch, 1513), fol. 165r; trans. Edward Storer, *The Facetiae of Poggio and Other Medieval Story-tellers,* Broadway Translations (New York, 1928), no. 57, pp. 83-84, rev. R. Kay.

9   Poggio Bracciolini, *Facetiae* 37, ed. in his *Opera* (Strasbourg: J. Knobluch, 1513), fol. 161v; trans. «Oliver Phillips».

10 Johann Nider, O.P., *Formicarius* 5.8 (Augsburg: Anton Sorg, [ca. 1484]), fol. 172r-172v; trans. G. G. Coulton, *Life in the Middle Ages* (Cambridge, Eng., 1928), 1:212-213, rev. R. Kay.

11 Poggio Bracciolini, *Facetiae* 104, ed. in his *Opera* (Strasbourg: J. Knobluch, 1513), fol. 167v; trans. anon., *Facetia* [sic] *Erotica of Poggio Fiorentino* (New York: Valhalla Books, 1964), pp. 49-50.

12 Johann Nider, O.P. *Formicarius* 5.8 (Augsburg: Anton Sorg, [ca. 1484]), fol. 171v-172r; trans. G. G. Coulton, *Life in the Middle Ages* (Cambridge, Eng., 1928), 1:211, rev. R. Kay.

13 The anonymous eyewitness wrote a history, from the manuscript of which this extract was published by Etienne Paschal (1588-1651) in his *Disquisitions* 5.23, which in turn was quoted by Jean de Launoy, *Regii Navarrae gymnasii Parisiensis historia,* vol. 1 (Paris, 1667), pp. 157-158; trans. Lynn Thorndike, *University Records and Life in the Middle Ages* (New York: Columbia University Press, 1944), pp. 341-342, rev. R. Kay. Fernando's accomplishments were already known to John Trithemius (1461-1516), whose independent account is also given by Thorndike.

14 Lodovico Domenichi, *Facetie, motti, et burle...* (Florence, 1562); trans. Edward Storer, *The Facetiae of Poggio and Other Medieval Story-tellers,* Broadway Translations (New York, l928), no. 7, pp. 38-39, rev. R. Kay.

15 Ducas, *Historia Turcobyzantina* 39.7-14, 40.3, ed. Vasile Grecu in *Scriptores Byzantini,* vol. l (Bucharest, 1958), pp. 355-361; trans. «Oliver Phillips».

16 Mathieu d'Escouchy (Coussy, Coucy), *Chronique,,* ch. 92, ed. G. DuFresne de Beaufort, Société de l'histoire de France 120, vol. 2 (Paris, 1863), pp. 36-41; trans. G. G. Coulton, *A Medieval Garner* (London, 1910), pp. 623-624, rev. R. Kay.

17   *Liber de reformatione monasteriorum* 2.1, ed. K. Grube, *Des Augustinerpropstes Ioannes Busch Chronicon Windeshemense und Liber de reformatione monasteriorum*, Geschichtesquellen der Provinz Sachsen und angrenzender Gebiete 19 (Halle, 1886), p. 555; trans. G. G. Coulton, *A Medieval Garner* (London, 1910), pp. 650-652, rev. R. Kay.

18   Pope Pius II, *Commentarii* 2, ad an. 1459 (Vatican MS. Reg. lat. 1995); trans. Leona C. Gabel, *The Commentaries of Pius II*, Smith College Studies in History 25 (Northampton, Mass.: Department of History, Smith College, 1940), pp. 167-168.

19   François Villon (1431 — after 1463), "Ballade de la grosse Margot" in *Le Testament*, ed. J. Dufournet and A. Mary, *Oeuvres*, 2nd ed. (Paris, 1972), pp. 98-99; trans. John Payne (1878, rev. 1881), included in *The Testaments of François Villon*, trans. J. H. Lepper (New York, 1926), pp. 252-253, rev. R. Kay. An acrostic in the *envoi* spells out VILLON with the first letter of each line.

20   *Journal de Jean de Roye, connu sous le nom de "Chronique scandaleuse," 1460-1483*, ed. B. de Mandrot, Société de l'histoire de France, vol. 1 (Paris, 1894), pp. 33-34; trans. A. S. Scoble, *History of Louis XI ... Otherwise Called the Scandalous Chronicle, Written by a Clerk in the Hotel de Ville of Paris*, appended to Scoble's edition of *The Memoirs of Philip de Commines*, Bohn's Standard Library (London, 1856; rpt. 1879), p. 309. The author's name is sometimes given as Jean de Troyes.

21   Pope Pius II, *Commentarii* 11, ad an. 1463 (Vatican MS. Reg. lat. 1995); trans. Leona C. Gabel, *The Commentaries of Pius II*, Smith College Studies in History 43 (Northampton, Mass.: Department of History, Smith College, 1957), p. 767.

22   Philippe de Commynes, *Mémoires* 2.6-7, 9 (5-6), ed. J. Calmette and G. Durville, Les Classiques de l'histoire de France au Moyen Age 3, vol. 1 (Paris, 1924), p. 125-128, 131-134, 142; trans. A. R. Scoble, *The Memoirs of Philip de Commines*, Bohn's Standard Library, vol. 1 (London, 1855; rpt. 1880), pp. 112-129, rev. R. Kay.

23   Bartolomeo Platina, *De honesta voluptate* (Venice, 1475), fol. 91v-92v; trans. with facsimile of the first edition by Elizabeth Buermann Andrews, *De honesta voluptate; The First Dated Cookery Book*, Mallinckrodt Collection of Food Classics, no. 5 (St. Louis: Mallinckrodt Chemical Works, 1967) «Jerry Stannard». Platina was the first prefect of the Vatican Library.

24   British Library, MS. Add. 35,844, fol. 194v: "The General State of the Scottish Commonwealth with the Cause of Their Often Mutinies and Other Disorders" (late l6th century), quoted by Norman Macdougall, *James III: A Political Study* (Edinburgh: John Donald, [1982]), p. 286 «Cynthia Shively». The epigraph is from Thomas Shelton's translation of Cervantes, *Don Quixote* (1615); the couplet concludes: "To God himself commends."

25 Edme Boursault, *Lettres;* as given by E. Guérard, *Dictionnaire d'anecdotes,* 2nd ed. (Paris, 1872), 1:90; trans. R. Kay.

26 Francis Bacon, *The History of King Henry the Seventh,* ed. F. J. Levy (Indianapolis, 1971), p. 95. Bacon's source was Polydore Vergil, *Anglica historia* 24.254, ed. Denys Hay, Camden Series 74 (London, 1950), p. 70 «Cynthia Shively».

27 Bartolomeo Cerretani, *Storia fiorentina,* ed. J. Schnitzer, *Quellen und Forschungen zur Geschichte Savonarolas,* vol. 3, Veröffentlichungen aus dem kirchenhistorischen Seminar München, ed. A. Knöfler, ser. 2, no. 5; trans. «James J. Ludwig».

Notes to pages 321–324

1 François de Mézeray, *Histoire de France,* vol. 2 (Paris, 1646), pp. 374-375; trans. R. Kay «Twila Jukes». They were married in 1499; Anne died in 1514.

2 Lodovico Domenichi, *Facetie, motti, et burli...* (Florence, 1562); trans. Edward Storer, *The Facetiae of Poggio and Other Medieval Story-tellers,* Broadway Translations (London, 1928), no. 32, pp. 59-60.

3 Lodovico Domenichi, *Facetie, motti, et burli...* (Florence, 1562); trans. Edward Storer, *The Facetiae of Poggio and Other Medieval Story-tellers,* Broadway Translations (New York, 1928), no. 7, p. 37.

4 *Epistolae obscurorum virorum* 2.46, ed. and trans. Francis Griffin Stokes (New York, 1909), pp. 227-230 and 484-486, rev. R. Kay. This satirical series of letters, which appeared in 1515-1517, was purportedly written to Ortwin Gratius, a professor at Cologne who had attacked Humanism; actually it ridiculed the Scholastic establishment and its medieval learning. The authors, who masqueraded as a variety of fictitious correspondents, were most probably Johann Jäger (Crotus Rubianus) and Ulrich von Hutten; Stokes attributes the present letter to the latter.

Acknowledgments

(Roman numerals refer to centuries, arabic numerals to note numbers)

Barnes & Noble Books, Totowa, New Jersey: X.19; Bobbs-Merrill Co., Inc.: V.17, 18, VI.2, 3, 6; Burns & Oates, Ltd.: VIII.15; University of California Press: XI.37, 38, XII.48, XIII.20, 31; Cambridge University Press: XIII.15, 28, 49, XV.5, 10, 12; Constable & Co.: VIII.11, XII.21, 32, 35, 53, XIII.2, 27, 46, XIV.4, 18, 25, 26, 29, XV.16, 17; Columbia University Press: XII.16, 24, XV.13; J. M. Dent & Co.: XIII.48, XIV.5, 39; John Donald Publishers, Edinburgh: XV.24; Doubleday, A Division of Bantam, Doubleday, Dell Publishing Group, Inc.: XII.5; Dumbarton Oaks: X.11; E. P. Dutton: VII.1, XI.29; Eyre & Spottiswoode (Publishers) Ltd.: XI.19, XV.1; Harvard University Press: X.8, 14, 20, 21; Helicon Press, Baltimore: XIII.42; Kegan Paul, Trench, Trübner & Co.: XI.28; David McKay Co., Inc.: IV.8, XII.20; Mallinkrodt, Inc.: XV.23; The University of Michigan Press: V.6, 8, 16, VIII.13, IX.3, 6; Oxford University Press: V.7, 14, 19, VI.1, 14, 16-19, 21-29, VII.4, 6-8, 10, 18, 21, 23, 25, VIII.6, XI.25, XII.19, XIV.38, XV.3; Estate of Edward Alexander Parsons: VII.14; University of Pennsylvania Press: VI.12, VIII.1, XI.35; Penguin Books, Ltd.: VIII.7; Pontifical Institute of Mediaeval Studies, Toronto: Epigraph n.2; Richard R. Ring: VIII.9, 12, IX.1, 4; Routledge & Kegan Paul: XI.37, 38, XII.48, XIII.20, 31; A. I Samarrai: IX.10, 11; Department of History, Smith College: XV.18, 21; Trinity University Press: V.2; Viking Penguin Inc.: XIV.30; World Wide Book Service: XIV.14, 28, XV.2, 11.